BK 828.3 R163S
SELECTED WRITINGS
1984 21.00
3000 678911 30018
St. Louis Community College
W9-DHG-946

WITHDRAWN
St. Louis Community College

Sir Walter Ralegh
Selected Writings

For Patsy

Sir Walter Ralegh

SELECTED WRITINGS

edited by Gerald Hammond

FYFIELD BOOKS
CARCANET

First published in Great Britain in 1984
by the Carcanet Press
208–212 Corn Exchange Building
Manchester M4 3BQ

Ralegh, *Sir* Walter, *1552?–1618*
Selected writings.—(Fyfield books)
I. Title II. Hammond, Gerald, *1945–*
III. Series
942.05'5'0924 PR2334

ISBN 0-85635-440-6

The publisher acknowledges the financial assistance of the Arts Council of Great Britain

Typesetting by Paragon Photoset, Aylesbury
Printed in England by Short Run Press, Exeter

Contents

Prose

Introduction

Sir Walter Ralegh was a bad walker and did not know Hebrew.[1] These two readily admitted deficiencies apart, it is difficult to think of any other large limitations to his achievement or ambition. He was soldier, scholar, horseman, and much else: father of the idea of the British Empire; chemist and alchemist; patron of poets, and yet a fine enough poet himself to rival any he patronized; prize courtier of England's greatest monarch, but a hero of the republican generation after his death; introducer of the potato to Ireland and tobacco to England; a founder of modern historical writing; explorer; ship-designer; naval and military strategist; quack doctor; notorious atheist, but the last great asserter of God's providential pattern of history; the most hated man in England after Essex's downfall, but the most loved after his own. The list could go on and on, and any selection from his writings can hardly fail to lay open to us the extraordinary energy of the man.

Yet the prevailing tone of virtually everything Ralegh wrote is of disappointment and defeat. His favourite line of his own poetry seems to have been 'Of all which past, the sorrow only stays'; and his favourite image, of life as a play acted out on a stage, is usually tragic, and if comic, only sardonically so. In the Preface to his *History of the World* he describes men as 'Comedians in religion', but God as 'the author of all our tragedies', setting his plays on the 'great Theatre' where 'the change of fortune . . . is but as the change of garments on the less'.

Here is the clue to what makes Ralegh's writing, whether verse or prose, so enthralling: the collision of an energetic and strenuous mind with a nature which gravitated towards resignation and endurance, as if the entire combustible world burnt on and on in the one small room, rather than flaring up for a brief instant of time. This is true of even the two most vigorous pieces of prose reproduced here, the narrative of the last fight of the *Revenge* and Ralegh's account of his voyage to Guiana. Both are, in their ways, propaganda pieces: the one to turn a defeat into a kind of victory, the other to persuade the Queen and the gentlemen of England to sink their money into a colonial adventure. But both emerge as tales of endurance. The time scales are different, the *Revenge* spanning only hours, while *Guiana* takes up months, but for both Grenville and

Ralegh the test is ultimately the same — the need to continue, whatever the opposition of men or elements. The terms I use here are almost Miltonic, and rightly so, for Ralegh's influence on Milton should not be underestimated; but still Ralegh avoids the heroic fortitude which Milton gives Samson or Adam. Grenville emerges from the *Revenge* narrative as a bungler, not really the heroic figure which Tennyson fashioned out of Ralegh's account. A brave bungler, perhaps, but the cause of the worst loss the English navy had experienced. In *Guiana* likewise, we do not have to read too far between the lines to perceive Ralegh's own failure in the expedition, and the sense that it gradually delivers up of a failed enterprise which never will generate support from the monarch or the merchants.

Still, it is Ralegh the poet I ought to consider first, for there have been, both in his day, and in this century, strong claims for Ralegh's achievement in verse. Among his contemporaries George Puttenham[2] found the vein of Ralegh's 'dittie and amorous Ode' to be 'most loftie, insolent, and passionate', and for Edmund Spenser[3] he was 'the sommers Nightingale' whose verse ravished with 'melting sweetness'. The twentieth-century view of Ralegh is that while he may be too limited to be considered a great poet, his achievement is too substantial for him not to be thought a major one. To cite two poet-critics, Yvor Winters[4] described him as 'a far more serious poet than Sidney and Spenser', and Donald Davie[5] 'a greatly endowed and greatly scrupulous poet'.

To begin, though, I ought to emphasize that any claims for Ralegh's poetic stature are inevitably based on shaky foundations. We simply cannot be sure that half of the poems commonly attributed to him are actually his; and strong and frequent attempts are made to deny him some of his best known poems, such as 'The passionate man's pilgrimage' or 'The nymph's reply to the shepherd'. Ralegh the poet is, in effect, a composite figure. At the centre are a few poems which are undoubtedly his. Then come layers of accretions, perhaps attracted to him because they fit his tone or circumstances, or perhaps really his. And there is too the chance, in a poet who shunned the 'stigma of print', that some of his best work has disappeared. Not the least, it is possible, if unlikely, that twenty books of 'The Ocean to Cynthia' have been lost.

Nonetheless, from those poems which are certainly his we can gather a strong impression of Ralegh's fascinatingly grim poetic personality. Peter Ure, in a brief but fine survey of Ralegh's poetry,[6] drew attention to one of the sonnets which he wrote to herald Spenser's *Faerie Queene* (p. 30), where instead of a poem of welcome and praise, we find 'all the force of feeling gathering into the sestet', in a vision of tears, regret, and oblivion. Equally distinctive is another dedicatory sonnet which Ralegh wrote nearly a quarter of a century later. It is 'To the Translator of Lucan', prefixed to Sir Arthur Gorge's translation of Lucan's *Pharsalia* (p. 55). If Milton recalled the opening line of the *Faerie Queene* sonnet when he wrote his most personal sonnet, 'Methought I saw My Late Espoused Saint', it is not inconceivable that this sonnet praising Gorges' translation should have pointed the way towards the sterner tone of Milton's republican sonnets. This is fitting, for Lucan was the poet of *libertas* and *res publica*, and had earlier been translated in part by Marlowe, a radical spirit often linked with Ralegh. Now Ralegh's sonnet stamps Gorges' translation with the prophecy that Lucan's fate — execution by being forced to commit suicide — may well be Gorges' own; but the parallel to Ralegh himself, the prisoner in the Tower, is, of course, much the closer. In Miltonic fashion the sonnet's lines are brought to the point of buckling by the strenuous syntax they are required to carry:

> For this thou hast been bruised: but yet those scars
> Do beautify no less than those wounds do
> Received in just and in religious wars,
> Though thou hast bled by both, and bear'st them too.
> Change not. To change thy fortune 'tis too late . . .

And given the strength of these two sonnets, we might reasonably find support for Ralegh's authorship of the sonnet 'To his Son', a poem which appears only in manuscript versions (p. 53). Its opening picks up the tone of the riddles in the Book of Proverbs: 'Three things there be that prosper up apace/And flourish. . .' recalling 'There be three things that order well their going: yea, four are comely in going' (Prov. 30:29, Geneva version); but the poem develops into a grim account of the coming together of the wood, the weed, and the wag. 'Grim', incidentally, is Agnes Latham's[7] word for this sonnet, although she opposes its being read tragically, as if it were a 'painful poem'. Still, behind this sonnet lies the poet's grasp of the mystery of riddles: that to fail to solve them means death. Ralegh gives the solution to this one in two lines of characteristically epigrammatic force, at the close of the third quatrain:

> But when they meet, it makes the timber rot,
> It frets the halter, and it chokes the child.

Describing Ralegh as characteristically epigrammatic may seem strange, however, when one considers the long, sprawling poem (or fragment) in Ralegh's own hand, 'The Ocean to Cynthia' (p. 37). Here endurance is stretched to the limits of mental agony, in a poem so undisciplined that it mocks the attempts of commentators to explicate it. The image which is most often used to describe it is of tides of passion. In this sense only does it fulfil the promise of its title, for there is little in its imagery or theme to explain the ocean-moon (Cynthia) reference. But possibly much of its oddness lies in its being, in all its length, the stuff of epigrams, for frequently the wave of passion breaks on an epigrammatic line:

> Joys under dust that never live again (4)
>
> The broken monuments of my great desires (14)
>
> Woes without date, discomforts without end (20)
>
> Whom love defends, what fortune overthrows? (52)
>
> And worlds of thoughts described by one last sithing (96)
>
> Of all which past, the sorrow only stays (123)

Not single lines only, but whole passages are hammered out in the concise, pithy manner of the epigram, as in the remarkable lines towards the end, which follow the sudden appearance of Hero and Leander (487–96):

> On Sestos' shore, Leander's late resort,
> Hero hath left no lamp to guide her love —
> Thou lookest for light in vain, and storms arise:
> She sleeps thy death, that erst thy danger sithed.
> Strive then no more, bow down thy weary eyes —
> Eyes which to all these woes thy heart have guided.
> She is gone, she is lost, she is found, she is ever fair:
> Sorrow draws weakly, where love draws not too.
> Woe's cries sound nothing but only in love's ear:
> Do then by dying what life cannot do.

The result is curious, as if every word were loaded with passion and meaningful reference, but with little or no sense of continuity, or even progression — only the constant drive toward the epigram.

In his finished poems Ralegh uses this drive toward the epigram to create some of his most powerful effects. It appears first in the 'Epitaph' upon Sir Philip Sidney (p. 25), where the stately dignity of the poem's first half gives way to a greater intensity of expression, as if the lines were now being asked to contain double the meaning:

Tears to the soldiers, the proud Castilian's shame,
Virtue expressed, and honour truly taught. (39–40)

The aim of poems changes too, so that 'Nature, that washed her hands in milk' (p. 34) moves from being a conceited love poem to a plain meditation on time and death. And Ralegh's Shakespearean readiness to employ such great generalizations makes his answer to Marlowe's 'Passionate shepherd' poem so much more moving than any of its rivals (p. 31). It opens in parody, but suddenly gains emotional depth at the beginning of the second stanza, on the lines 'Time drives the flocks from field to fold,/When rivers rage, and rocks grow cold', where the images expand through night, winter, and death, to the death of the whole planet.

Another source of the power of Ralegh's poetry comes from his being the one major late Elizabethan poet who had absorbed and retained the style of earlier poets like Wyatt and Gascoigne. 'Plain' was the word which came to be used to describe this style, but it now seems too vague to describe usefully the curious rhythms of Wyatt and the heavily literal language of Gascoigne. Again, it is Peter Ure who makes this point most tellingly: that what we might fancy to be Ralegh's precocious anticipation of Jacobean cynicism is, more truly, a distinctive belatedness, a real inheritance from those earlier poets and Tottel's *Miscellany*. Indeed, the first poem in this selection, a tribute to Gascoigne, reads very much like something out of the *Miscellany*; and one would not need to be too uncharitable to describe it as a poor poem, halting and inflexible, if not actually clumsy. But in retrospect it deserves the pride of place it has, as a young poet's (Ralegh was twenty-three when he wrote it) declaration that one cannot please all, and ought therefore to aim to please the worthiest audience only. The poem opens with great emphasis, and develops towards a Wyatt-like image of the slippery slope of achievement:

Sweet were the sauce would please each kind of taste;
The life likewise were pure that never swerved;
. . .
For whoso reaps renown above the rest
With heaps of hate shall surely be oppressed. (1–2, 11–12).

One can see how this young poet will later write a poem as vehement as 'The lie'. While Gascoigne was praised for having had the nerve to censure abuses which range 'from prince to poor, from high estate to low', 'The lie' (p. 51) not only censures all, but challenges them too, with the certain knowledge that to speak such truth 'deserves no less than stabbing'. In this poem Ralegh finds the ideal fusion of inflexible form and starkly literal content: the rhythms are jagged, pretence of grammatical logic dissolves, all imagery is discarded, and even words are finally dismissed by the brutal acknowledgement that the only truthful human intercourse is with a dagger (67–78):

> Tell faith it's fled the City,
> Tell how the country erreth,
> Tell manhood shakes off pity,
> Tell virtue least preferreth;
> And if they do reply,
> Spare not to give the lie.
>
> So when thou hast, as I
> Commanded thee, done blabbing,
> Although to give the lie
> Deserves no less than stabbing,
> Stab at thee he that will,
> No stab thy soul can kill.

Again, giving the lie is a matter not of heroism, but of fortitude — similar in kind to the pilgrimages of the two poems of resolution, 'The passionate man's pilgrimage' and 'As you came from the holy land' (pp. 53 and 35).

Whatever our qualifications about the authorship of Ralegh's poems, we need have none about his prose. There used to be some doubt, based on a remark of Ben Jonson's,[8] about the degree to which he might have had help in writing the *History of the World*, but it is generally accepted now that the work is almost entirely Ralegh's own. And to clear away any doubts one might have about Ralegh as a prose stylist, there are already the splendid examples of *A Report of the Truth of the Fight About the Isles of Azores . . . Betwixt the Revenge . . . and an Armada of the King of Spain* (1591) and *The Discovery of the Large, Rich and Beautiful Empire of Guiana* (1596).

Despite its being his first piece of published prose, the *Revenge* shows Ralegh's total control over his material. The centre of the narrative, the battle itself, is made memorable by the economy with which he describes the hopelessness of the *Revenge*'s situation:

> . . . Unto ours there remained no comfort at all, no hope, no supply either of ships, men, or weapons; the masts all beaten overboard, all her tackle cut asunder, her upper work altogether razed, and in effect evened she was with the water, but the very

> foundation or bottom of a ship, nothing being left over head either for flight or defence.

But Ralegh does not allow the action to overwhelm his account, and for all its heroism and adventure, the sense it leaves with us is of the coolness, even percipience, of its narrator. There are key sentences, early on, where he makes it clear that not even the most well-disposed judge can excuse Grenville for his foolhardiness:

> But Sir *Richard* utterly refused to turn from the enemy, alleging that he would rather choose to die, than to dishonour himself, his country, and her Majesty's ship, persuading his company that he would pass through the two Squadrons, in despite of them: and enforce those of *Seville* to give him way. Which he performed upon diverse of the foremost, who as the Mariners term it, sprang their luff, and fell under the lee of the *Revenge*. But the other course had been the better, and might right well have been answered in so great an impossibility of prevailing. Notwithstanding out of the greatness of his mind, he could not be persuaded.

This idea, that outstanding bravery most often leads to disaster becomes a common theme of the *History of the World*. Here it should already make the reader question the positive quality which he might normally attribute to 'greatness of mind'. The final part of the *Revenge* is written very much in the detached, judging tone of the *History*, too, as Ralegh carefully analyses the inevitable consequences for any Englishman who could be persuaded to betray himself to the Spaniards. Just as Grenville stands for all the great-hearted fools of history, so is Maurice of Desmond, the seducer towards Spain, who contrived in three years to lose all that his family had spent three centuries building up, the model for all traitors. The lesson is one of *realpolitik*: 'But what man can be so blockishly ignorant ever to expect place or honour from a foreign king, having no other argument or persuasion than his own disloyalty?'

In the *Discovery of Guiana* Ralegh is no longer merely a narrator, but the chief participant too. The result is one of the finest pieces of Elizabethan prose, for it has all the narrative control of the *Revenge*, but with the advantage that one is, all the time, inside the head of the ever inquisitive Ralegh, seeing the land through his eyes. There are some marvellous perceptions too — not least of natural phenomena, like the oysters on trees, or the sudden unexpected paradise which they encounter after hours of arduous travel

> . . . here we beheld plains of twenty mile in length, the grasses short and green, and in divers parts groves of trees by themselves,

> as if they had been by all the art and labour in the world so made of purpose: and still as we rowed, the Deer came down feeding by the water's side, as if they had been used to a keeper's call.

Most interesting of all are the people who inhabit the country: the canny Berrio, Spanish Butcher, but elegant gentleman too; an old Indian guide who comes as close to an execution as he could possibly get, as he spins out excuses as to why the settlement he promised has not yet been reached; a beautiful native woman who reminds Ralegh of a certain lady back in England; and his own men also, not individualized, but suffering along with him heat, hunger, torrential rain, near shipwreck — but not one of whom, Ralegh rightly boasts, failed to return safe and sound. And at the edge of the narrative there are figures reported to Ralegh, but which he can only imagine: the Amazons, and the Ewaipanoma who have their eyes in their shoulders and their mouths in the middle of their breasts. Imagined places haunt the narrative as well: most of all, El Dorado and the gold mines which fed it, and which Ralegh's imagination never lost grip of, even as he mouldered in the Tower.

It may well be that the *Discovery* was too well written — so evocative that the hard-headed Elizabethans preferred to treat it as a good yarn rather than as a map of England's colonial future. Richard Hakluyt,[9] for instance, included it in his *Voyages*, but it also seems probable that he was instrumental in advising men like Robert Cecil against any further involvement. Its influence was literary, not economic. No Contractation house was set up in London, but some of the exotic lists of places in *Paradise Lost* drew their inspiration from it (and perhaps Othello's anthropophagi too). Its main target, Elizabeth herself, remained unimpressed. Ralegh had lost her favour after his affair and marriage with Elizabeth Throckmorton, and not even the engaging reference to her as *Ezrabeta Cassipuna Acarewana* (p. 83), a true Amazonian queen, could win her round. No investment was made in Guiana, and English explorations there gradually petered out.

Ezrabeta Cassipuna Acarewana is only one in a long list of descriptions which Ralegh made of Elizabeth. Most of them occur in the poetry — Cynthia, Diana, the Queen whose memory was 'more strong than were ten thousand ships of war' — and there is the remarkable letter where he pictures her as 'hunting like Diana, walking like Venus' (p. 273). But Ralegh's most poignant description came soon after her death, while on trial for his life: 'and instead of a Lady whom Time had surprised. . .'. Instead of that lady there was now 'an active King', whose activity centred most on the removal of

Ralegh. The trial was a moral defeat for James; so much so that it saved Ralegh from execution, but condemned him, instead, to thirteen years in the Tower. One consequence of this imprisonment was the desperate attempt to salvage all on a final voyage to Guiana (see the letter describing this débâcle, p. 277); another was the *History of the World*.

In many senses Ralegh had been preparing to write the *History* all his life, not least in the omnivorous reading which he engaged in, even while at sea. At odd points in the poetry, also, one comes across the embryo of an historical imagination, as in the 'Ocean to Cynthia':

> We should begin by such a parting light
> To write the story of all ages past,
> And end the same before th' approaching night.
> Such is again the labour of my mind,
> Whose shroud, by sorrow woven now to end,
> Hath seen that ever-shining sun declined
> So many years that so could not descend . . . (101–7)

There is, too, the cool analysis of power in 'The lie'. Then, towards the end of the *Revenge*, Ralegh shows his early readiness to see the workings of Providence in the rise and fall of nations, as he comments on God's judgment of the Spanish abuse of power: 'Thus it hath pleased God to fight for us, and to defend the justice of our cause, against the ambitious and bloody pretences of the Spaniards, who seeking to devour all nations, are themselves devoured'. Most of all, Ralegh had experience of power and the people who wield it. He had seen, and possibly aided, Essex's overthrow, and had himself been the victim of the arbitrary abuse of power by both Elizabeth and James. So although the *History* takes care to emphasize a providential pattern to history, the 'first cause' of things, it spends most of its strength delineating the arbitrariness of second causes, usually rulers and their flatterers.

There are heroic figures in the *History*, but they come few and far between. One, perhaps, is Hannibal, but his heroism derives in part from his not having total power. Ralegh makes a powerful case for the causes of Hannibal's failure lying with the Carthaginian power-brokers who would not let him have the money and materials he needed. The one indisputable hero is Epaminondas,[10] eulogized by Ralegh in the only unqualified paean of praise in the *History*. This, by implication, is what all other princes have fallen short of:

> So died *Epaminondas*, the worthiest man that ever was bred in

> that Nation of *Greece*, and hardly to be matched in any Age or Country: for he equalled all others in the several virtues, which in each of them were singular. His Justice, and Sincerity, his Temperance, Wisdom, and high Magnanimity, were no way inferior to his Military virtue; in every part whereof he so excelled, that he could not properly be called a Wary, a Valiant, a Politic, a Bountiful, or an Industrious, and a Provident Captain; all these Titles, and many other, being due unto him, which with his notable Discipline, and good Conduct, made a perfect composition of an Heroic General. Neither was his private Conversation unanswerable to those high parts, which gave him praise abroad. For he was Grave, and yet very Affable and Courteous; resolute in public business, but in his own particular easy, and of much mildness; a lover of his People, bearing with men's infirmities, witty and pleasant in speech, far from insolence, Master of his own affections, and furnished with all qualities that might win and keep love. To these Graces were added great ability of body, much Eloquence, and very deep knowledge in all parts of Philosophy and Learning, wherewith his mind being enlightened, rested not in the sweetness of Contemplation, but brake forth into such effects as gave unto *Thebes*, which had evermore been an underling, a dreadful reputation among all people adjoining, and the highest command in *Greece*.

The magisterial style of this passage is typical of the whole *History*, but it is more often used for scorn and contempt than for praise. A succession of princes strut through the pages, only to be brought dramatically low: Jezebel eaten by the dogs; Nebuchadnezzar eating grass; Xerxes forced to flee back to Asia leaving a shattered army of millions; Darius reduced to a chained captive in a cart; and Perseus 'beholding to the courtesy of his enemies for a wretched life'.

But the *History* is no mere *Mirror for Magistrates*. Ralegh's aim is less to educate men in the way the wheel of fortune turns than to show the invariably terrible effects of power. Under its pressure men always choose to do the wrong thing. In the hands of a succession of English and European monarchs, as the Preface shows, it led to ambition for more power, miscalculation, and retribution. Apart from Epaminondas, and a few like him, the actual *History* itself presents an unremitting analysis of the tyranny of rulers. No wonder that James I condemned it for being 'too saucy in censuring princes', and no wonder either that it became a prime text for the regicides of the next generation; Oliver Cromwell,[11] for instance, recommended it to his son to 'recreate' himself with 'Sir Walter Ralegh's

History: it's a body of History, and will add much more to your understanding than fragments of story'.

Another regicide who read it carefully was John Milton. The *History's* influence has been traced through *Paradise Lost*, but there are signs, too, that for the young Milton it was a formative work. At twenty-one he included in his 'Nativity Ode' the image of the silencing of the pagan deities at Christ's coming

> The oracles are dumb,
> No voice or hideous hum
>   Runs through the archèd roof in words deceiving.
> Apollo from his shrine
> Can no more divine,
>   With hollow shriek the steep of Delphos leaving.
> No nightly trance, or breathèd spell,
> Inspires the pale-eyed priest from the prophetic cell.

The idea is a commonplace, but one which Ralegh repeatedly turns to in the opening book of the *History*, and often in terms which seem very close to Milton's

> . . . There are none now in *Phoenicia*, that lament the death of *Adonis*; nor any in *Libya*, *Creta*, *Thessalia*, or elsewhere, that can ask counsel or help from *Jupiter*. The great god *Pan* hath broken his pipes, *Apollo's* Priests are become speechless . . . (p. 159).

It is worth emphasizing that Milton was probably most interested in those parts of the *History* which are the least attractive to a modern taste. It is a massive work, and to choose extracts from it as I have done is certainly to misrepresent it. Ralegh's developing, cumulative picture of man's history is lost in reducing it to a series of purple passages. Also, in a selection such as this, the choice of extracts is governed more by a literary than an historical bias. In the first two books Ralegh uses the Bible as his yardstick, both for chronology and for the recounting of what happened. Whole sections are given over to his attempts to make biblical chronology consistent and to fit it into what was known of the rest of the world's history during that period. Such speculations seem arid now, and they were the kind of thing which drew down Matthew Arnold's[12] scorn on the whole enterprise — but they helped set a pattern of parallelism between the biblical and the pagan, which probably had a greater influence upon *Paradise Lost*[13] than any of the specific passages to which commentators have drawn our attention.

In this selection the emphasis falls on two other elements of the *History*: Ralegh's digressions and his narrative skill. The two are really elements of the same thing, as Ralegh explains in the defence of his digressionary style which he gives in the Preface, in a striking anticipation of modern narrative theory:

> For seeing we digress in all the ways of our lives: yea seeing the life of man is nothing else but digression; I may the better be excused in writing their lives and actions. I am not altogether ignorant in the Laws of *History*, and of the *Kinds*. (p. 148).

This principle of digression runs through the entire *History*. Sometimes whole sections explore such matters as whether the Roman or the English soldier were the better, or the strategy of defending 'hard passages' (see pp. 209 and 189). Then there are digressions at the lower levels of paragraph and sentence, where we see the love of the sententious and epigrammatic which marks the poetry, as in this passage from Book V, where Ralegh sums up the character of Dionysius. It moves outward, from discussion of the specific man, to generalized comment on all flatterers:

> When he had reigned eight and thirty years, he died: some say, in his bed, peaceably; which is the most likely, though others report it otherwise. A cruel man he was, and a faithless; a great Poet, but a foolish one. He entertained *Plato* a while, but afterward, for speaking against his tyranny, he gave order to have him slain, or sold for a slave. For he could endure no man, that flattered him not beyond measure. His Parasites therefore styled his cruelty, *The hate of evil men*; and his lawless slaughters, *The ornaments and effects of his justice*. True it is, that flatterers are a kind of vermin, which poison all the Princes of the World; and yet they prosper better, than the worthiest and valiantest men do: And I wonder not at it; for it is a world; and as our *Saviour Christ* hath told us, *The world will love her own*. (chap. 1:4)

Flattery brings out the best in Ralegh's prose. Too 'damnable proud', in Aubrey's words, to consider himself ever to have been a flatterer, he must have looked mordantly upon the hangers-on at the Stuart court. Such types pop up again and again in the *History* — as in the description of Darius as one 'who had been accustomed to nothing so much as to his own praises, and to nothing so little as to hear truth' (p. 198), or the sardonic generalizations in the opening chapter of Book I:

> For whosoever shall tell any great man or Magistrate, that he is not just, the General of an Army, that he is not valiant, and great Ladies that they are not fair, shall never be made a Counsellor, a Captain, or a Courtier. (p. 151).

Another idea which Ralegh returns to eloquently is the unpredictability of history, the complete uncertainty we must have for the perpetuation of any state of affairs, prosperous or otherwise. In a telling phrase from the Preface he describes the fortunate and the wretched, the two extreme states of human existence, as both being 'so tied by God to the very instant, and both so subject to interchange'. This becomes a dominant theme of the *History*: part of the reciprocal process whereby the children of an oppressor become the victims of the children of their father's victims. And in one fine digression the uncertainty of things is tied firmly to Ralegh's disgust at flattery:

> All, or the most, have a vain desire of ability to do evil without control: which is a dangerous temptation unto the performance. God, who best can judge what is expedient, hath granted such power to very few: among whom also, very few there are, that use it not to their own hurt. For who sees not, that a Prince, by racking his Sovereign authority to the utmost extent, enableth (besides the danger of his own person) some one of his own sons or nephews to root up all his progeny? Shall not many excellent Princes, notwithstanding their brotherhood, or other nearness in blood, be driven to flatter the Wife, the Minion, or perhaps the Harlot, that governs one, the most unworthy of his whole house, yet reigning over all? (p. 269)

As these extracts show, it is possible to praise Ralegh's style at the level of single sentences, even phrases. He writes, for example, of the greatest men who, 'to be made greater, could lose the sense of other men's sorrow and subjection' (p. 187). He defines peace 'between ambitious Princes, and States' as 'a kind of breathing' (p. 232); and pithily traces the workings of Providence in the epigram that 'where God hath a purpose to destroy, wise men grow short lived' (p. 194). Sometimes, as befits his prophetic role, he moves from the historian's register to the biblical prophet's 'The vanities of men beguile their vain contrivers, and the prosperity of the wicked, is the way leading to their destruction . . .' (p. 172). Other times he introduces eloquent images into his prose, as in the ambiguous rats (hostile readers or literal rats in the Tower?) who gnaw his papers in the Preface; or, from elsewhere in the Preface, time as a 'consuming disease'; Opinion travelling the world 'without a passport'; Ralegh himself being 'on the ground already' and therefore having 'not far to fall'; or the prospect for the writer of modern histories, that by following truth 'too near the heels, it may happily strike out his teeth'. Flattery also gets an idiomatic image, when Ralegh denies that he is one of those who 'flatter the world between the bed and the grave'. Occasionally the literal sense of what he says is so disturbing that one flinches from it and gives it the distance of an image, as in the digressionary paragraph where he describes the degeneration of mankind (p. 217, my italics):

> . . . we have now greater Giants, for vice and injustice, than the World had in those days, for bodily strength; for cottages, and houses of clay and timber, we have raised Palaces of stone; we carve them, we paint them, and adorn them with gold; insomuch as men are rather known by their houses, than their houses by them; we are fallen from two dishes, to two hundred; from water, to wine and drunkenness; from the covering of our bodies with the skins of beasts, not only to silk and gold, but *to the very skins of men*.

These, however, are the individual felicities of Ralegh's style. Most of the extracts here, especially from Books III–V, show his skill in telling sustained narratives — in particular, of battles, and of the fall of tyrants. Greater matters are narrated too, but at a length too great to be demonstrated in any selection: the rise and fall of whole nations, for instance. The pattern is, in its particulars, cyclical. Rome starts and ends with a shepherd's crook (although the *History* itself only gets as far as 168 BC); Macedon begins and ends in obscurity. Great rulers, like Caesar and Alexander, are reduced to 'troublers of the world', agents of decline rather than progress:

> *Caesar*, and *Alexander*, have unmade and slain, each of them, more than a million of men: but they made none, nor left none behind them. Such is the error of Man's judgment, in valuing things according to common opinion. (p. 226).

But the *History* as a whole, in its general view, is apocalyptic; summed up in a theatrical image which Ralegh uses early in Book I, when he writes of 'the long day of mankind drawing fast towards an evening, and the world's Tragedy and time near at an end' (p. 160). Over the whole lies the shadow of death, both Prince Henry's, and Ralegh's own. Seldom can a great work have come into the world with a preface which begins so bleakly, with Ralegh picturing himself as one wounded by fortune and time, disabled, defective, aching, uncured, and tried by the fire of adversity. Through the five books he expands this vision to cover the whole of mankind, whose history is one long tale of endurance, ending with the phrase 'here lies'. The *History of the World* deserves to be set near *King Lear* as one of the English Renaissance's powerfully negative visions of the state of man on 'this stage-play world'[14].

The text and notes

All who work on Ralegh's poems owe their greatest debt to Agnes Latham's two editions of the poetry. I have kept largely to the order of poems as given in her *Muses Library* edition (1951), with some change of punctuation, and occasional preferred readings from other sources than the one Miss Latham chose to print (signalled in the notes). Poems which Miss Latham includes, but which are not found here, on grounds of doubtful authorship or quality, are (keyed to the poem numbers in her edition):

II 'Sweet are the thoughts, where Hope Persuadeth Hap'
III 'A poem put into my Lady Laiton's pocket'
VI–VII fragments from 'The Arte of English Poesie'
XIV Ralegh's second sonnet on *The Faerie Queene*
XVIII 'Wrong not dear empress of my heart', which Miss Latham prints as a continuation of 'Sir Walter Ralegh to the Queen'
XIX 'To his love when he had obtained her'
XXVII 'The word of denial and the letter of fifty'
XXVIII 'On the cards, and dice'
XXXII 'A song made by Sir Walter Ralegh'
XXXIV 'Virtue the best monument'
XXXVI I have included only a few of the metrical translations from the *History of the World*
XXXIX 'Conjectural fragments of another petition to Queen Anne'
XLI 'On the snuff of a candle the night before he died'

(Poem XXXIII, 'Epitaph on the Earl of Salisbury', is described in the notes, p. 287). I have not included any of the poems she lists as doubtful. My major change is to have modernized the spelling, but I have retained some forms which are close to modern versions, but which embody a noticeable difference in punctuation or meaning (e.g. *vade*, *sithe*).

Details of the texts of the prose extracts can be found in the notes. I have kept the annotation generally to the minimum necessary. With the *History*, for example, a thorough annotation, giving details of Ralegh's sources and references, is very desirable, but belongs to a Collected rather than Selected Works. I have thought it best to give as much space as possible to Ralegh's writings.

One final point worth mention here is that Ralegh's prose gains most from being read aloud: this is especially so with the *History of the World*, and to that end I have retained the original punctuation, which is as much rhetorical as it is grammatical.

Poetry

Walter Ralegh of the Middle Temple, in commendation of 'The Steel Glass'

Sweet were the sauce would please each kind of taste;
The life likewise were pure that never swerved;
For spiteful tongues in cankered stomachs placed
Deem worst of things which best, percase, deserved.
But what for what? This medicine may suffice
To scorn the rest, and seek to please the wise.

Though sundry minds in sundry sort do deem,
Yet worthiest wights yield praise for every pain;
But envious brains do nought, or light, esteem
Such stately steps as they cannot attain. 10
For whoso reaps renown above the rest
With heaps of hate shall surely be oppressed.

Wherefore to write my censure of this book:
This Glass of Steel unpartially doth show
Abuses all, to such as in it look,
From prince to poor, from high estate to low;
As for the verse, who list like trade to try,
I fear me much, shall hardly reach so high.

An epitaph upon the Honourable Sir Philip Sidney Knight: Lord Governor of Flushing

To praise thy life or wail thy worthy death
And want thy wit — thy wit high, pure, divine —
Is far beyond the power of mortal line,
Nor any one hath worth that draweth breath;

Yet rich in zeal, though poor in learning's lore,
And friendly care obscured in secret breast,
And love that envy in thy life suppressed,
Thy dear life done, and death hath doubled more;

And I, that in thy time and living state
Did only praise thy virtues in my thought, 10
As one that, seeled, the rising sun hath sought,
With words and tears now wail thy timeless fate.

Drawn was thy race aright from princely line,
Nor less than such — by gifts that nature gave,
The common mother that all creatures have —
Doth virtue show, and princely lineage shine.

A king gave thee thy name. A kingly mind,
That God thee gave, who found it now too dear
For this base world, and hath resumed it near,
To sit in skies and sort with powers divine. 20

Kent thy birth-days, and Oxford held thy youth;
The heavens made haste and stayed nor years nor time:
The fruits of age grew ripe in thy first prime,
Thy will, thy words; thy words, the seals of truth.

Great gifts and wisdom rare employed thee thence,
To treat from kings with those more great than kings,
Such hope men had to lay the highest things
On thy wise youth, to be transported hence.

Whence to sharp wars sweet honour did thee call,
Thy country's love, religion, and thy friends — 30
Of worthy men the marks, the lives, and ends —
And her defence, for whom we labour all.

There didst thou vanquish shame and tedious age,
Grief, sorrow, sickness, and base fortune's might:
Thy rising day saw never woeful night,
But passed with praise from off this worldly stage.

Back to the camp, by thee that day was brought,
First thine own death, and, after, thy long fame,
Tears to the soldiers, the proud Castilian's shame,
Virtue expressed, and honour truly taught. 40

What hath he lost that such great grace hath won?
Young years for endless years, and hope unsure

Of fortune's gifts for wealth that still shall dure —
Oh happy race, with so great praises run!

England doth hold thy limbs, that bred the same;
Flanders thy valour, where it last was tried;
The camp thy sorrow, where thy body died;
Thy friends, thy want; the world, thy virtue's fame;

Nations, thy wit; our minds lay up thy love;
Letters, thy learning; thy loss, years long to come; 50
In worthy hearts sorrow hath made thy tomb;
Thy soul and spright enrich the heavens above.

Thy liberal heart embalmed in grateful tears,
Young sighs, sweet sighs, sage sighs, bewail thy fall;
Envy, her sting, and spite hath left her gall;
Malice herself a mourning garment wears.

That day their Hannibal died, our Scipio fell —
Scipio, Cicero, and Petrarch of our time —
Whose virtues, wounded by my worthless rhyme,
Let angels speak, and heaven thy praises tell.

A farewell to false Love

Farewell false Love, the oracle of lies,
A mortal foe and enemy to rest:
An envious boy, from whom all cares arise,
A bastard vile, a beast with rage possessed,
A way of error, a temple full of treason,
In all effects contrary unto reason:

A poisoned serpent covered all with flowers,
Mother of sighs and murderer of repose,
A sea of sorrows from whence are drawn such showers
As moisture lends to every grief that grows, 10
A school of guile, a net of deep deceit,
A gilded hook that holds a poisoned bait;

A fortress foiled, which reason did defend,
A Siren song, a fever of the mind,

A maze wherein affection finds no end,
A ranging cloud that runs before the wind,
A substance like the shadow of the sun,
A goal of grief for which the wisest run;

A quenchless fire, a nurse of trembling fear,
A path that leads to peril and mishap, 20
A true retreat of sorrow and despair,
An idle boy that sleeps in pleasure's lap,
A deep mistrust of that which certain seems,
A hope of that which reason doubtful deems.

Sith, then, thy trains my younger years betrayed,
And for my faith ingratitude I find,
And sith repentance hath my wrongs bewrayed,
Whose course was ever contrary to kind,
False Love, Desire, and Beauty frail, adieu —
Dead is the root whence all these fancies grew. 30

The excuse

Calling to mind mine eye long went about
T' entice my heart to seek to leave my breast,
All in a rage I thought to pull it out,
By whose device I lived in such unrest.
What could it say to purchase so my grace?
Forsooth, that it had seen my mistress' face.

Another time I likewise call to mind
My heart was he that all my woe had wrought,
For he my breast, the fort of love, resigned,
When of such wars my fancy never thought. 10
What could it say, when I would him have slain,
But he was yours and had forgot me clean?

At length, when I perceived both eye and heart
Excused themselves as guiltless of mine ill,
I found my self was cause of all my smart,
And told my self, 'My self now slay I will'.
But when I found my self to you was true,
I loved my self, because my self loved you.

Praised be Diana's fair and harmless light

Praised be Diana's fair and harmless light,
Praised be the dews wherewith she moists the ground;
Praised be her beams, the glory of the night,
Praised be her power, by which all powers abound.

Praised be her nymphs, with whom she decks the woods,
Praised be her knights, in whom true honour lives,
Praised be that force by which she moves the floods,
Let that Diana shine, which all these gives.

In Heaven Queen she is among the spheres,
In aye she mistress-like makes all things pure; 10
Eternity in her oft change she bears,
She beauty is, by her the fair endure.

Time wears her not, she doth his chariot guide;
Mortality below her orb is placed;
By her the virtue of the stars down slide,
In her is virtue's perfect image cast.

A knowledge pure it is her worth to know;
With Circes let them dwell that think not so.

Like to a hermit poor

Like to a hermit poor in place obscure
I mean to spend my days of endless doubt,
To wail such woes as time cannot recure,
Where none but Love shall ever find me out.

My food shall be of care and sorrow made,
My drink nought else but tears fallen from mine eyes,
And for my light in such obscured shade
The flames shall serve which from my heart arise.

A gown of grey my body shall attire,
My staff of broken hope whereon I'll stay, 10

Of late repentance linked with long desire
The couch is framed whereon my limbs I'll lay,

And at my gate despair shall linger still,
To let in death when Love and Fortune will.

Farewell to the Court

Like truthless dreams, so are my joys expired,
And past return are all my dandled days:
My love misled, and fancy quite retired,
Of all which past, the sorrow only stays.

My lost delights, now clean from sight of land,
Have left me all alone in unknown ways;
My mind to woe, my life in Fortune's hand,
Of all which past, the sorrow only stays.

As in a country strange without companion,
I only wail the wrong of death's delays, 10
Whose sweet spring spent, whose summer well nigh done,
Of all which past, the sorrow only stays;

Whom care forewarns, ere age and winter cold,
To haste me hence, to find my fortune's fold.

A vision upon this conceit of 'The Faerie Queene'

Methought I saw the grave where Laura lay,
Within that Temple, where the vestal flame
Was wont to burn, and passing by that way,
To see that buried dust of living fame,
Whose tomb fair love, and fairer virtue kept,
All suddenly I saw the Faery Queen:
At whose approach the soul of Petrarch wept,
And from thenceforth those graces were not seen.
For they this Queen attended, in whose stead
Oblivion laid him down on Laura's hearse: 10

Hereat the hardest stones were seen to bleed,
And groans of buried ghosts the heavens did pierce.
    Where Homer's spright did tremble all for grief,
    And cursed th' access of that celestial thief.

The advice

Many desire, but few or none deserve
To win the fort of thy most constant will:
Therefore take heed, let fancy never swerve
But unto him that will defend thee still.
    For this be sure, the fort of fame once won,
    Farewell the rest, thy happy days are done.

Many desire, but few or none deserve
To pluck the flowers and let the leaves to fall:
Therefore take heed, let fancy never swerve,
But unto him that will take leaves and all. 10
    For this be sure, the flower once plucked away,
    Farewell the rest, thy happy days decay.

Many desire, but few or none deserve
To cut the corn, not subject to the sickle:
Therefore take heed, let fancy never swerve,
But constant stand, for mowers' minds are fickle.
    For this be sure, the crop being once obtained,
    Farewell the rest, the soil will be disdained.

The nymph's reply to the shepherd

If all the world and love were young,
And truth in every shepherd's tongue,
These pretty pleasures might me move,
To live with thee and be thy love.

Time drives the flocks from field to fold,
When rivers rage, and rocks grow cold,
And Philomel becometh dumb,
The rest complains of cares to come.

The flowers do fade, and wanton fields,
To wayward winter reckoning yields, 10
A honey tongue, a heart of gall,
Is fancy's spring, but sorrow's fall.

Thy gowns, thy shoes, thy beds of roses,
Thy cap, thy kirtle, and thy poesies,
Soon break, soon wither, soon forgotten,
In folly ripe, in reason rotten.

The belt of straw and ivy buds,
Thy coral clasps and amber studs,
All these in me no means can move,
To come to thee, and be thy love. 20

But could youth last, and love still breed,
Had joys no date, nor age no need,
Then these delights my mind might move,
To live with thee, and be thy love.

A poesy to prove affection is not love

Conceit, begotten by the eyes,
Is quickly born and quickly dies,
For while it seeks our hearts to have,
Meanwhile there Reason makes his grave:
For many things the eyes approve,
Which yet the heart doth seldom love.

For as the seeds in springtime sown
Die in the ground ere they be grown,
Such is conceit, whose rooting fails,
As child that in the cradle quails, 10
Or else within the mother's womb
Hath his beginning and his tomb.

Affection follows Fortune's wheels
And soon is shaken from her heels,
For following beauty or estate
Her liking still is turned to hate:
For all affections have their change,
And fancy only loves to range.

Desire himself runs out of breath
And getting, doth but gain his death; 20
Desire nor reason hath nor rest,
And, blind, doth seldom choose the best:
Desire attained is not desire,
But as the cinders of the fire.

As ships in port desired are drowned,
As fruit once ripe then falls to ground,
As flies that seek for flames are brought
To cinders by the flames they sought:
So fond desire, when it attains,
The life expires, the woe remains. 30

And yet some poets fain would prove
Affection to be perfect love,
And that desire is of that kind,
No less a passion of the mind,
As if wild beasts and men did seek
To like, to love, to choose alike.

Sir Walter Ralegh to Queen Elizabeth

Our passions are most like to floods and streams,
The shallow murmur, but the deep are dumb.
So, when affections yield discourse, it seems
The bottom is but shallow whence they come.
    They that are rich in words must needs discover
    That they are poor in that which makes a lover.

Nature, that washed her hands in milk

Nature, that washed her hands in milk
And had forgot to dry them,
Instead of earth took snow and silk
At Love's request to try them,
If she a mistress could compose
To please Love's fancy out of those.

Her eyes he would should be of light,
A violet breath and lips of jelly,
Her hair not black, nor over-bright,
And of the softest down her belly; 10
As for her inside, he'ld have it
Only of wantonness and wit.

At Love's entreaty such a one
Nature made, but with her beauty
She hath framed a heart of stone,
So as Love by ill destiny
Must die for her whom Nature gave him
Because her darling would not save him.

But Time, which Nature doth despise,
And rudely gives her love the lie, 20
Makes hope a fool and sorrow wise,
His hands do neither wash, nor dry,
But being made of steel and rust,
Turns snow and silk and milk to dust.

The light, the belly, lips, and breath
He dims, discovers, and destroys;
With those he feeds, but fills not, Death,
Which sometimes were the food of joys;
Yea, Time doth dull each lively wit,
And dries all wantonness with it. 30

Oh cruel Time, which takes in trust
Our youth, our joys, and all we have,
And pays us but with age and dust;
Who in the dark and silent grave,
When we have wandered all our ways,
Shuts up the story of our days.

As you came from the holy land

As you came from the holy land
        Of Walsingham,
Met you not with my true love
        By the way as you came?

How shall I know your true love
        That have met many one,
As I went to the holy land
        That have come, that have gone?

She is neither white nor brown
        But as the heavens fair,   10
There is none hath a form so divine
        In the earth or the air.

Such an one did I meet, good sir,
        Such an angelic face,
Who like a queen, like a nymph, did appear
        By her gait, by her grace.

She hath left me here all alone,
        All alone as unknown,
Who sometimes did me lead with herself,
        And me loved as her own.   20

What's the cause that she leaves you alone
        And a new way doth take,
Who loved you once as her own
        And her joy did you make?

I have loved her all my youth,
        But now old, as you see;
Love likes not the falling fruit
        From the withered tree.

Know that love is a careless child
        And forgets promise past,   30
He is blind, he is deaf when he list,
        And in faith never fast.

His desire is a dureless content
And a trustless joy,
He is won with a world of despair
And is lost with a toy.

Of women kind such indeed is the love,
Or the word Love abused,
Under which many childish desires
And conceits are excused. 40

But true love is a durable fire,
In the mind ever burning,
Never sick, never old, never dead,
From itself never turning.

If Cynthia be a Queen

If Cynthia be a Queen, a princess, and supreme,
Keep these among the rest, or say it was a dream,
For those that like, expound, and those that loathe, express
Meanings according as their minds are moved more or less.
For writing what thou art, or showing what thou were,
Adds to the one disdain, to th' other but despair.
Thy mind of neither needs, in both seeing it exceeds.

My body in the walls captived

My body in the walls captived
Feels not the wounds of spiteful envy,
But my thralled mind, of liberty deprived,
Fast fettered in her ancient memory,
Doth naught behold but sorrow's dying face.
Such prison erst was so delightful
As it desired no other dwelling place,
But time's effects, and destinies despiteful,
Have changed both my keeper and my fare.
Love's fire and beauty's light I then had store, 10
But now close kept, as captives wonted are,
That food, that heat, that light I find no more.
Despair bolts up my doors, and I alone
Speak to dead walls, but those hear not my moan.

The 21st (and last) Book of the Ocean to Cynthia

Sufficeth it to you, my joys interred,
In simple words that I my woes complain,
You that then died when first my fancy erred,
Joys under dust that never live again.
If to the living were my muse addressed,
Or did my mind her own spirit still inhold,
Were not my living passion so repressed,
As to the dead, the dead did these unfold,
Some sweeter words, some more becoming verse,
Should witness my mishap in higher kind; 10
But my love's wounds, my fancy in the hearse,
The Idea but resting of a wasted mind,
The blossoms fallen, the sap gone from the tree,
The broken monuments of my great desires,
From these so lost what may th' affections be,
What heat in cinders of extinguished fires?
Lost in the mud of those high-flowing streams
Which through more fairer fields their courses bend,
Slain with self-thoughts, amazed in fearful dreams
Woes without date, discomforts without end, 20
From fruitful trees I gather withered leaves,
And glean the broken ears with miser's hands,
Who sometime did enjoy the weighty sheaves;
I seek fair flowers and the brinish sand.
All in the shade, even in the fair sun days,
Under those healthless trees I sit alone,
Where joyful birds sing neither lovely lays
Nor Philomen recounts her direful moan.
No feeding flocks, no shepherd's company,
That might renew my dolorous conceit, 30
While happy then, while love and fantasy
Confined my thoughts on that fair flock to wait;
No pleasing streams fast to the ocean wending,
The messengers sometimes of my great woe,
But all on earth as from the cold storms bending
Shrink from my thoughts in high heavens and below.
Oh hopeful love, my object and invention!
Oh true desire, the spur of my conceit!
Oh worthiest spirit, my mind's impulsion!
Oh eyes transpersant, my affection's bait! 40

Oh princely form, my fancy's adamant,
Divine conceit, my pain's acceptance,
Oh all in one, oh heaven on earth transparent,
The seat of joys and love's abundance!
Out of that mass of miracles my Muse
Gathered those flowers, to her pure senses pleasing;
Out of her eyes — the store of joys — did choose
Equal delights, my sorrows counterpoising.
Her regal looks my rigorous sithes suppressed,
Small drops of joys sweetened great worlds of woes, 50
One gladsome day a thousand cares redressed:
Whom love defends, what fortune overthrows?
When she did well, what did there else amiss?
When she did ill, what empires could have pleased?
No other power effecting woe or bliss,
She gave, she took, she wounded, she appeased.

The honour of her love, love still devising,
Wounding my mind with contrary conceit,
Transferred itself sometime to her aspiring,
Sometime the trumpet of her thought's retreat; 60
To seek new worlds, for gold, for praise, for glory,
To try desire, to try love severed far,
When I was gone she sent her memory
More strong than were ten thousand ships of war
To call me back, to leave great honour's thought,
To leave my friends, my fortune, my attempt,
To leave the purpose I so long had sought
And hold both cares and comforts in contempt.
Such heat in ice, such fire in frost remained,
Such trust in doubt, such comfort in despair, 70
Much like the gentle lamb, though lately weaned,
Plays with the dug though finds no comfort there.
But as a body violently slain
Retaineth warmth although the spirit be gone,
And by a power.in nature moves again
Till it be laid beneath the fatal stone;
Or as the earth, even in cold winter days,
Left for a time by her life-giving sun,
Doth by the power remaining of his rays
Produce some green, though not as it hath done; 80
Or as a wheel forced by the falling stream,
Although the course be turned some other way,

Doth for a time go round upon the beam
Till, wanting strength to move, it stands at stay;
So my forsaken heart, my withered mind,
Widow of all the joys it once possessed,
My hopes clean out of sight, with forced wind
To kingdoms strange, to lands far-off addressed,
Alone, forsaken, friendless on the shore,
With many wounds, with death's cold pangs embraced, 90
Writes in the dust, as one that could no more,
Whom love and time and fortune had defaced,
Of things so great, so long, so manifold,
With means so weak, the soul even then departing,
The weal, the woe, the passages of old,
And worlds of thoughts described by one last sithing;
As if, when after Phoebus is descended
And leaves a light much like the past day's dawning,
And, every toil and labour wholly ended,
Each living creature draweth to his resting, 100
We should begin by such a parting light
To write the story of all ages past,
And end the same before th' approaching night.
Such is again the labour of my mind,
Whose shroud, by sorrow woven now to end,
Hath seen that ever-shining sun declined
So many years that so could not descend,
But that the eyes of my mind held her beams
In every part transferred by love's swift thought:
Far off or near, in waking or in dreams, 110
Imagination strong their lustre brought.
Such force her angelic appearance had
To master distance, time, or cruelty,
Such art to grieve, and after to make glad,
Such fear in love, such love in majesty.
My weary limbs her memory embalmed,
My darkest ways her eyes make clear as day:
What storms so great but Cynthia's beams appeased?
What rage so fierce that love could not allay?

Twelve years entire I wasted in this war, 120
Twelve years of my most happy younger days,
But I in them, and they now wasted are,
Of all which past, the sorrow only stays.
So wrote I once and my mishap foretold,

My mind still feeling sorrowful success,
Even as before a storm the marble cold
Doth by moist tears tempestuous times express.
So felt my heavy mind my harms at hand,
Which my vain thought in vain sought to recure;
At middle day my sun seemed under land 130
When any little cloud did it obscure.
And as the icicles in a winter's day,
Whenas the sun shines with unwonted warm,
So did my joys melt into secret tears,
So did my heart dissolve in wasting drops;
And as the season of the year outwears,
And heaps of snow from off the mountain tops
With sudden streams the valleys overflow,
So did the time draw on my more despair;
Then floods of sorrow and whole seas of woe 140
The banks of all my hope did overbear
And drowned my mind in depths of misery.
Sometime I died, sometime I was distract,
My soul the stage of fancy's tragedy,
Then furious madness, where true reason lacked,
Wrote what it would, and scourged mine own conceit.
Oh heavy heart, who can thee witness bear?
What tongue, what pen, could thy tormenting treat,
But thine own mourning-thoughts which present were?
What stranger mind believe the meanest part, 150
What altered sense conceive the weakest woe
That tore, that rent, that pierced thy sad heart?
And as a man distract, with treble might
Bound in strong chains, doth strive and rage in vain,
Till, tired and breathless, he is forced to rest,
Finds by contention but increase of pain
And fiery heat inflamed in swollen breast,
So did my mind in change of passion
From woe to wrath, from wrath return to woe,
Struggling in vain from love's subjection. 160
Therefore all lifeless, and all helpless bound,
My fainting spirits sunk, and heart appalled,
My joys and hopes lay bleeding on the ground,
That not long since the highest heaven scaled.
I hated life and cursed destiny:
The thoughts of passed times like flames of hell
Kindled afresh within my memory

The many dear achievements that befell
In those prime years and infancy of love,
Which to describe were but to die in writing. 170
Ah, those I sought, but vainly, to remove,
And vainly shall, by which I perish living.
And though strong reason hold before mine eyes
The images and forms of worlds past,
Teaching the cause why all those flames that rise
From forms external can no longer last
Than that those seeming beauties hold in prime,
Love's ground, his essence, and his empery,
All slaves to age and vassals unto time,
Of which repentance writes the tragedy. 180
But this my heart's desire could not conceive,
Whose love outflew the fastest flying time;
A beauty that can easily deceive
Th' arrest of years, and creeping age outclimb,
A spring of beauties which time ripeth not —
Time that but works on frail mortality—
A sweetness which woe's wrongs outwipeth not,
Whom love hath chose for his divinity;
A vestal fire that burns but never wasteth,
That loseth naught by giving light to all, 190
That endless shines eachwhere, and endless lasteth,
Blossoms of pride that can nor vade nor fall.
These were those marvellous perfections,
The parents of my sorrow and my envy,
Most deathful and most violent infections;
These be the tyrants that in fetters tie
Their wounded vassals, yet nor kill nor cure,
But glory in their lasting misery,
That as her beauties would our woes should dure,
These be th' effects of powerful empery. 200

Yet have these wounders want, which want compassion,
Yet hath her mind some marks of human race,
Yet will she be a woman for a fashion,
So doth she please her virtues to deface.
And like as that immortal power doth seat
An element of waters to allay
The fiery sunbeams that on earth do beat,
And temper by cold night the heat of day,
So hath perfection, which begat her mind,

Added thereto a change of fantasy 210
And left her the affections of her kind,
Yet free from every evil but cruelty.

But leave her praise, speak thou of naught but woe,
Write on the tale that sorrow bids thee tell,
Strive to forget, and care no more to know,
Thy cares are known, by knowing those too well.
Describe her now as she appears to thee,
Not as she did appear in days foredone;
In love those things that were no more may be,
For fancy seldom ends where it begun. 220

And as a stream by strong hand bounded in
From nature's course, where it did sometime run,
By some small rent or loose part doth begin
To find escape, till it a way hath won,
Doth then all unawares in sunder tear
The forced bounds, and raging run at large
In th' ancient channels, as they wonted were,
Such is of women's love the careful charge
Held and maintained with multitude of woes;
Of long erections such the sudden fall: 230
One hour diverts, one instant overthrows,
For which our lives, for which our fortunes' thrall
So many years those joys have dearly bought,
Of which when our fond hopes do most assure,
All is dissolved, our labours come to nought,
Nor any mark thereof there doth endure,
No more than when small drops of rain do fall
Upon the parched ground, by heat updried
No cooling moisture is perceived at all,
Nor any show or sign of wet doth bide. 240
But as the fields, clothed with leaves and flowers,
The banks of roses smelling precious sweet,
Have but their beauty's date and timely hours,
And then defaced by winter's cold and sleet,
So far as neither fruit nor form of flower
Stays for a witness what such branches bare,
But as time gave, time did again devour,
And changed our rising joy to falling care,
So of affection which our youth presented,
When she that from the sun reaves power and light, 250

Did but decline her beams as discontented,
Converting sweetest days to saddest night;
All droops, all dies, all trodden under dust,
The person, place, and passages forgotten,
The hardest steel eaten with softest rust,
The firm and solid tree both rent and rotten.
Those thoughts so full of pleasure and content,
That in our absence were affection's food,
Are razed out and from the fancy rent,
In highest grace and heart's dear care that stood, 260
Are cast for prey to hatred, and to scorn
Our dearest treasures and our heart's true joys,
The tokens hung on breast and kindly worn
Are now elsewhere disposed or held for toys,
And those which then our jealousy removed,
And others for our sakes then valued dear,
The one forgot, the rest are dear beloved,
When all of ours doth strange or vile appear.
Those streams seem standing puddles which before
We saw our beauties in, so were they clear; 270
Belphoebe's course is now observed no more:
That fair resemblance weareth out of date.
Our ocean seas are but tempestuous waves,
And all things base that blessed were of late.
And as a field wherein the stubble stands
Of harvest past, the ploughman's eye offends,
He tills again, or tears them up with hands,
And throws to fire as foiled and fruitless ends,
And takes delight another seed to sow,
So doth the mind root up all wonted thought 280
And scorns the care of our remaining woe.
The sorrows which themselves for us have wrought
Are burnt to cinders by new-kindled fires,
The ashes are dispersed into the air,
The sighs, the groans of all our past desires
Are clean outworn, as things that never were.

With youth is dead the hope of love's return,
Who looks not back to hear our after cries.
Where he is not, he laughs at those that mourn,
Whence he is gone, he scorns the mind that dies, 290
When he is absent he believes no words,
When reason speaks he careless stops his ears,

Whom he hath left he never grace affords,
But bathes his wings in our lamenting tears.

Unlasting passion, soon outworn conceit
Whereon I built, and on so dureless trust:
My mind had wounds — I dare not say deceit —
Were I resolved her promise was not just.
Sorrow was my revenge, and woe my hate;
I powerless was to alter my desire. 300
My love is not of time or bound to date;
My heart's internal heat and living fire
Would not, nor could be quenched with sudden showers.
My bound respect was not confined to days,
My vowed faith not set to ended hours.
I love the bearing and not-bearing sprays
Which now to others do their sweetness send,
Th' incarnate, snow-driven white, and purest azure,
Who from high heaven doth on their fields descend,
Filling their barns with grain, and towers with treasure. 310
Erring or never erring, such is Love,
As while it lasteth scorns the account of those
Seeking but self contentment to improve,
And hides, if any be, his inward woes,
And will not know, while he knows his own passion,
The often and unjust perseverance
In deeds of love, and state, and every action
From that first day and year of their joy's entrance.

But I unblessed, and ill-born creature,
That did embrace the dust her body bearing, 320
That loved her both by fancy and by nature,
That drew even with the milk in my first sucking
Affection from the parent's breast that bare me,
Have found her as a stranger so severe,
Improving my mishap in each degree.
But love was gone: so would I my life were!
A Queen she was to me, no more Belphoebe,
A lion then, no more a milk-white dove.
A prisoner in her breast I could not be:
She did untie the gentle chains of love. 330
Love was no more the love of hiding
All trespass and mischance for her own glory:
It had been such — it was still for th' elect —

But I must be th' example in love's story:
This was of all forepast the sad effect.
But thou, my weary soul and heavy thought,
Made by her love a burden to my being,
Dost know my error never was forethought,
Or ever could proceed from sense of loving.
Of other cause if then it had proceeding 340
I leave th' excuse, sith judgment hath been given:
The limbs divided, sundered and a-bleeding,
Cannot complain the sentence was uneven.
This did that Nature's wonder, Virtue's choice,
The only paragon of Time's begetting,
Divine in words, angelical in voice,
That spring of joys, that flower of Love's own setting,
Th' Idea remaining of those golden ages,
That beauty braving heavens, and earth embalming,
Which after worthless worlds but play on stages, 350
Such didst thou her long since describe, yet sithing
That thy unable spirit could not find aught
In heaven's beauties or in earth's delight
For likeness, fit to satisfy thy thought.
But what hath it availed thee so to write?
She cares not for thy praise who knows not theirs;
It's now an idle labour and a tale
Told out of time, that dulls the hearer's ears,
A merchandise whereof there is no sale.
Leave them, or lay them up with thy despairs: 360
She hath resolved, and judged thee long ago;
Thy lines are now a murmuring to her ears,
Like to a falling stream which passing slow
Is wont to nourish sleep and quietness.
So shall thy painful labours be perused
And draw on rest, which sometime had regard;
But those her cares thy errors have excused,
Thy days fordone have had their day's reward.
So her hard heart, so her estranged mind,
In which above the heavens I once reposed, 370
So to thy error have her ears inclined,
And have forgotten all thy past deserving,
Holding in mind but only thine offence,
And only now affecteth thy depraving,
And thinks all vain that pleadeth thy defence.
Yet greater fancy beauty never bred,

A more desire the heart blood never nourished,
Her sweetness an affection never fed
Which more in any age hath ever flourished.
The mind and virtue never have begotten 380
A firmer love since love on earth had power,
A love obscured, but cannot be forgotten,
Too great and strong for Time's jaws to devour;
Containing such a faith as ages wound not,
Care, wakeful ever of her good estate,
Fear, dreading loss, which sithes and joys not,
A memory of the joys her grace begat,
A lasting gratefulness for those comforts past,
Of which the cordial sweetness cannot die.
These thoughts, knit up by faith, shall ever last, 390
These Time assays, but never can untie;
Whose life once lived in her pearl-like breast,
Whose joys were drawn but from her happiness,
Whose heart's high pleasure and whose mind's true rest
Proceeded from her fortune's blessedness,
Who was intentive, wakeful, and dismayed,
In fears, in dreams, in feverous jealousy,
Who long in silence served and obeyed
With secret heart and hidden loyalty;
Which never change to sad adversity, 400
Which never age, or nature's overthrow,
Which never sickness, or deformity,
Which never wasting care, or wearing woe —
If subject unto these she could have been —

Which never words, or wits malicious,
Which never honour's bait, or world's fame,
Achieved by attempts adventurous,
Or aught beneath the sun, or heaven's frame,
Can so dissolve, dissever, or destroy,
The essential love, of no frail parts compounded, 410
Though of the same now buried be the joy,
The hope, the comfort, and the sweetness ended,
But that the thoughts and memories of these
Work a relapse of passion, and remain
Of my sad heart the sorrow-sucking bees.
The wrongs received, the scorns, persuade in vain,
And though these medicines work desire to end,
And are in others the true cure of liking,

The salves that heal love's wounds and do amend
Consuming woe, and slake our hearty sithing, 420
They work not so in thy mind's long disease:
External fancy time alone recureth,
All whose effects do wear away with ease.
Love of delight while such delight endureth
Stays by the pleasure, but no longer stays;
But in my mind so is her love enclosed,
And is therefore not only the best part,
But into it the essence is disposed.
Oh love — the more my woe — to it thou art
Even as the moisture in each plant that grows, 430
Even as the sun unto the frozen ground,
Even as the sweetness to th' incarnate rose,
Even as the centre in each perfect round,
As water to the fish, to men as air,
As heat to fire, as light unto the sun —
Oh Love, it is but vain to say thou were,
Ages and times cannot thy power outrun.
Thou art the soul of that unhappy mind
Which, being by nature made an idle thought,
Began even then to take immortal kind 440
When first her virtues in thy spirits wrought.
From thee therefore that mover cannot move,
Because it is become thy cause of being:
Whatever error may obscure that love,
Whatever frail effect of mortal living,
Whatever passion from distempered heart,
What absence, time, or injuries effect,
What faithless friends, or deep dissembled art
Present, to feed her most unkind suspect.
Yet as the air in deep caves under ground 450
Is strongly drawn when violent heat hath rent
Great clefts therein, till moisture do abound,
And then the same, imprisoned and up-pent,
Breaks out in earthquakes, tearing all asunder,
So in the centre of my cloven heart —
My heart, to whom her beauties were such a wonder —
Lies the sharp poisoned head of that love's dart,
Which, till all break and all dissolve to dust,
Thence drawn it cannot be, or therein known.
There, mixed with my heart blood, the fretting rust 460
The better part hath eaten and outgrown.

But what of those, or these, or what of aught
Of that which was, or that which is, to treat?
What I possess is but the same I sought:
My love was false, my labours were deceit.
Nor less than such they are esteemed to be,
A fraud bought at the price of many woes,
A guile whereof the profits unto me:
Could it be thought premeditate for those?
Witness those withered leaves left on the tree, 470
The sorrow-worren face, the pensive mind:
The external shows what may th' internal be;
Cold care hath bitten both the root and rind.

But stay, my thoughts, make end; give fortune way;
Harsh is the voice of woe and sorrow's sound;
Complaints cure not, and tears do but allay
Griefs for a time, which after more abound.
To seek for moisture in th' Arabian sand
Is but a loss of labour and of rest.
The links which time did break of hearty bands 480
Words cannot knit, or wailings make anew.
Seek not the sun in clouds when it is set:
On highest mountains where those cedars grew,
Against whose banks the troubled ocean beat,
And were the marks to find thy hoped port,
Into a soil far off themselves remove —
On Sestos' shore, Leander's late resort,
Hero hath left no lamp to guide her love —
Thou lookest for light in vain, and storms arise:
She sleeps thy death, that erst thy danger sithed. 490
Strive then no more, bow down thy weary eyes —
Eyes which to all these woes thy heart have guided.
She is gone, she is lost, she is found, she is ever fair:
Sorrow draws weakly, where love draws not too.
Woe's cries sound nothing but only in love's ear:
Do then by dying what life cannot do.
Unfold thy flocks and leave them to the fields
To feed on hills or dales, where likes them best,
Of what the summer or the springtime yields,
For love and time hath given thee leave to rest. 500
Thy heart, which was their fold, now in decay,
By often storms and winter's many blasts
All torn and rent, become misfortune's prey;

False hope, my shepherd's staff, now age hath brast.
My pipe, which love's own hand gave my desire
To sing her praises and my woe upon,
Despair hath often threatened to the fire,
As vain to keep now all the rest are gone.
Thus home I draw as death's long night draws on;
Yet, every foot, old thoughts turn back mine eyes; 510
Constraint me guides, as old age draws a stone
Against the hill, which over-weighty lies
For feeble arms or wasted strength to move.
My steps are backward, gazing on my loss,
My mind's affection and my soul's sole love,
Not mixed with fancy's chaff or fortune's dross.
To God I leave it, who first gave it me,
And I her gave, and she returned again,
As it was hers. So let His mercies be
Of my last comforts the essential mean. 520
But be it so, or not, th' effects are past.
Her love hath end: my woe must ever last.

The beginning of the 22nd Book of the Ocean to Cynthia, entreating of sorrow

My day's delights, my springtime joys fordone,
Which in the dawn and rising sun of youth
Had their creation and were first begun,
Do in the evening and the winter sad
Present my mind, which takes my time's account,
The grief remaining of the joy it had.
My times that then ran o'er themselves in these,
And now run out in others' happiness,
Bring unto those new joys, and new-born days.
So could she not, if she were not the sun, 10
Which sees the birth and burial of all else,
And holds that power with which she first begun,
Leaving each withered body to be torn
By fortune, and by times tempestuous,
Which by her virtue once fair fruit have borne;
Knowing she can renew, and can create
Green from the ground, and flowers even out of stone,
By virtue lasting over time and date,

Leaving us only woe, which, like the moss,
Having compassion of unburied bones, 20
Cleaves to mischance and unrepaired loss,
For tender stalks —

Now we have present made

Now we have present made
To Cynthia, Phoebe, Flora,
Diana and Aurora,
Beauty that cannot vade.

A flower of love's own planting,
A pattern kept by nature
For beauty, form, and stature,
When she would frame a darling.

She as the valley of Peru,
Whose summer ever lasteth, 10
Time conquering all she mastereth
By being always new,

As elemental fire,
Whose food and flame consumes not,
Or as the passion ends not
Of virtue's true desire,

So her celestial frame
And quintessential mind,
Which heavens together bind,
Shall ever be the same. 20

Then to her servants leave her,
Love, nature, and perfection,
Princes of world's affection,
Or praises but deceive her.

If love could find a quill
Drawn from an angel's wing,
Or did the muses sing
That pretty wanton's will,

Perchance he could indite
To please all other sense, 30
But love's and woe's expense
Sorrow can only write.

The lie

Go, soul, the body's guest,
Upon a thankless errand,
Fear not to touch the best,
The truth shall be thy warrant:
Go, since I needs must die,
And give the world the lie.

Say to the Court it glows
And shines, like rotten wood;
Say to the Church it shows
What's good, and doth no good; 10
If Church and Court reply,
Then give them both the lie.

Tell Potentates they live
Acting but others' action,
Not loved unless they give,
Not strong but by a faction;
If Potentates reply,
Give Potentates the lie.

Tell men of high condition,
That manage the estate, 20
Their purpose is ambition,
Their practice only hate;
And if they once reply,
Then give them all the lie.

Tell them that brave it most,
They beg for more by spending,
Who in their greatest cost
Like nothing but commending;
And if they make reply,
Then give them all the lie. 30

Tell zeal it wants devotion,
  Tell love it is but lust,
Tell time it metes but motion,
  Tell flesh it is but dust;
And wish them not reply,
  For thou must give the lie.

Tell age it daily wasteth,
  Tell honour how it alters,
Tell beauty how she blasteth,
  Tell favour how it falters; 40
And as they shall reply,
  Give every one the lie.

Tell wit how much it wrangles
  In tickle points of niceness,
Tell wisdom she entangles
  Herself in over-wiseness;
And when they do reply,
  Straight give them both the lie.

Tell Physic of her boldness,
  Tell skill it is prevention, 50
Tell charity of coldness,
  Tell law it is contention;
And as they do reply
  So give them still the lie.

Tell fortune of her blindness,
  Tell nature of decay,
Tell friendship of unkindness,
  Tell justice of delay;
And if they will reply,
  Then give them all the lie. 60

Tell Arts they have no soundness,
  But vary by esteeming;
Tell schools they want profoundness
  And stand too much on seeming;
If Arts and schools reply,
  Give Arts and schools the lie.

Tell faith it's fled the City,
  Tell how the country erreth,
Tell manhood shakes off pity,

Tell virtue least preferreth; 70
And if they do reply,
Spare not to give the lie.

So when thou hast, as I
Commanded thee, done blabbing,
Although to give the lie
Deserves no less than stabbing,
Stab at thee he that will,
No stab thy soul can kill.

Sir Walter Ralegh to his son

Three things there be that prosper up apace
And flourish, whilst they grow asunder far,
But on a day they meet all in one place,
And when they meet they one another mar;
And they be these — the wood, the weed, the wag.
The wood is that which makes the gallow tree,
The weed is that which strings the hangman's bag,
The wag, my pretty knave, betokeneth thee.
Mark well, dear boy: whilst these assemble not,
Green springs the tree, hemp grows, the wag is wild; 10
But when they meet, it makes the timber rot,
It frets the halter, and it chokes the child.
Then bless thee, and beware, and let us pray
We part not with thee at this meeting day.

The passionate man's pilgrimage

Give me my scallop-shell of quiet,
My staff of Faith to walk upon,
My scrip of joy, immortal diet,
My bottle of salvation,
My gown of glory, hope's true gage,
And thus I'll take my pilgrimage.

Blood must be my body's balmer,
No other balm will there be given
Whilst my soul, like a white palmer,

Travels to the land of heaven, 10
Over the silver mountains,
Where spring the nectar fountains;
And there I'll kiss
The bowl of bliss,
And drink my eternal fill
On every milken hill.
My soul will be a-dry before,
But after it will ne'er thirst more.

And by the happy blissful way
More peaceful pilgrims I shall see, 20
That have shook off their gowns of clay,
And go apparelled fresh like me.
I'll bring them first
To slake their thirst,
And then to taste those nectar suckets,
At the clear wells
Where sweetness dwells,
Drawn up by saints in crystal buckets.

And when our bottles and all we
Are filled with immortality, 30
Then the holy paths we'll travel
Strewed with rubies thick as gravel,
Ceilings of diamonds, sapphire floors,
High walls of coral, and pearl bowers.

From thence to heaven's bribeless hall,
Where no corrupted voices brawl,
No conscience molten into gold,
Nor forged accusers bought and sold,
No cause deferred, nor vain-spent journey,
For there Christ is the king's attorney, 40
Who pleads for all without degrees,
And he hath angels, but no fees.

When the grand twelve million jury
Of our sins and sinful fury,
'Gainst our souls black verdicts give,
Christ pleads his death, and then we live.
Be thou my speaker, taintless pleader,
Unblotted lawyer, true proceeder;

Thou movest salvation even for alms,
Not with a bribed lawyer's palms. 50

And this is my eternal plea
To him that made heaven, earth, and sea:
Seeing my flesh must die so soon,
And want a head to dine next noon,
Just at the stroke, when my veins start and spread,
Set on my soul an everlasting head.
Then am I ready, like a palmer fit,
To tread those blest paths which before I writ.

On the life of man

What is our life? A play of passion;
Our mirth, the music of division;
Our mothers' wombs the tiring houses be,
When we are dressed for this short comedy.
Heaven the judicious sharp spectator is,
That sits and marks still who doth act amiss;
Our graves that hide us from the searching sun
Are like drawn curtains when the play is done.
Thus march we playing to our latest rest —
Only we die in earnest, that's no jest.

To the translator of Lucan

Had Lucan hid the truth to please the time,
He had been too unworthy of thy pen,
Who never sought nor ever cared to climb
By flattery, or seeking worthless men.
For this thou hast been bruised; but yet those scars
Do beautify no less than those wounds do
Received in just and in religious wars,
Though thou hast bled by both, and bear'st them too.
Change not. To change thy fortune 'tis too late:
Who with a manly faith resolves to die 10

May promise to himself a lasting state,
Though not so great, yet free from infamy.
    Such was thy Lucan, whom so to translate,
    Nature thy muse, like Lucan's, did create.

Metrical translations from the 'History of the World'

Virgil: *Aeneid*, vi. 724–7

The heaven, the earth, and all the liquid main,
The Moon's bright Globe, and Stars Titanian,
A Spirit within maintains: and their whole Mass,
A Mind, which through each part infused doth pass,
Fashions, and works, and wholly doth transpierce
All this great body of the Universe.

Sedulius: 1. 226–31

Ah wretched they that worship vanities,
And consecrate dumb Idols in their heart,
Who their own Maker (God on high) despise,
And fear the work of their own hands and art.
What fury? what great madness doth beguile
Men's minds? that man should ugly shapes adore,
Of Birds, or Bulls, or Dragons, or the vile
Half-dog half-man on knees for aid implore.

Ovid: *Metamorphoses*, i. 322–3

No man was better, nor more just than he:
Nor any Woman godlier than she.

Horace: Satire I. i. 68–70

The thirsting Tantalus doth catch at streams that from him flee.
Why laughest thou? the name but changed, the tale is told of thee.

Horace: *Odes*, III. xvi. 1–11

The brasen Tower with doors close barred,
And watchful bandogs frightful guard,
  Kept safe the Maidenhead
Of Danae from secret love:
Till smiling Venus, and wise Jove
  Beguiled her Father's dread.
For changed into a golden shower,
The God into her lap did pour
  Himself, and took his pleasure.
Through guards and stony walls to break, 10
The thunder-bolt is far more weak,
  Than is a golden treasure.

Lucretius: v. 325–8

If all this world had no original,
But things have ever been as now they are:
Before the siege of Thebes or Troy's last fall,
Why did no Poet sing some elder war?

Virgil: *Aeneid*, iii. 104–12

In the main Sea the Isle of Crete doth lie:
Where Jove was born, thence is our progeny.
There is mount Ida: there in fruitful Land
An hundred great and goodly Cities stand.
Thence (if I follow not mistaken fame)
Teucer the eldest of our grandsires came
To the Rhaetean shores: and reigned there
Ere yet fair Ilion was built, and ere
The Towers of Troy: their dwelling place they sought
In lowest vale. Hence Cybel's rites were brought: 10
Hence Corybantian Cymbales did remove:
And hence the name of our Idaean grove.

Horace: *Odes*, IV. ix. 25–8

Many by valour have deserved renown
  Ere Agamemnon: yet lie all oppressed
Under long night unwept for and unknown:
  For with no sacred Poet were they blest.

Ausonius: *Epigrammata*, cxviii

I am that Dido which thou here dost see,
Cunningly framed in beauteous Imagery.
Like this I was, but had not such a soul,
As Maro feigned, incestuous and foul.
Aeneas never with his Trojan host
Beheld my face, or landed on this coast.
But flying proud Iarbas' villainy,
Not moved by furious love or jealousy;
I did with weapon chaste, to save my fame,
Make way for death untimely, ere it came. 10
This was my end; but first I built a Town,
Revenged my husband's death, lived with renown.
Why did'st thou stir up Virgil, envious Muse,
Falsely my name and honour to abuse?
Readers, believe Historians; not those
Which to the world Jove's thefts and vice expose.
Poets are liars, and for verse's sake
Will make the Gods of human crimes partake.

Horace: *Odes*, III. ii. 31–2

Seldom the villain, though much haste he make
Lame-footed Vengeance fails to overtake.

First draft? of the petition to Queen Anne

My day's delight, my springtime joys foredone,
Which in the dawn and rising sun of youth
Had their creation and were first begun,

Do in the evening and the winter sad
Present my mind, which takes my time's account,
The grief remaining of the joy it had.

For as no fortune stands, so no man's love
Stays by the wretched and disconsolate;
All old affections from new sorrows move.

Moss to unburied bones, ivy to walls, 10
Whom life and people have abandoned,
Till th' one be rotten, stays, till th' other falls;

But friendships, kindred, and love's memory
Dies sole, extinguished hearing or beholding
The voice of woe or face of misery;

Who, being in all like those winter showers,
Do come uncalled, but then forbear to fall,
When parching heat hath burnt both leaves and flowers,

And what we sometime were we seem no more —
Fortune hath changed our shapes, and destiny 20
Defaced our very form we had before.

For did in cinders any heat remain
Of those clear fires of love and friendliness,
I could not call for right and call in vain;

Or had truth power the guiltless could not fall,
Malice, vainglory, and revenge triumph;
But truth alone cannot encounter all.

All love and all desert of former times
Malice hath covered from my sovereign's eyes
And largely laid abroad supposed crimes, 30

Burying the former with their memory,
Teaching offence to speak before it go,
Disguising private hate with public duty.

But mercy is fled to God that mercy made,
Compassion dead, faith turned to policy,
Which knows not those which sit in sorrow's shade.

Cold walls, to you I speak, but you are senseless;
Celestial powers, you heard, but have determined
And shall determine to the greatest happiness.

To whom then shall I cry, to whom shall wrong
Cast down her tears or hold up folded hands?
To her to whom remorse doth most belong,

To her that is the first and may alone
Be called Empress of the Britons.
Who should have mercy if a queen have none?

Who should resist strong hate, fierce injury,
Or who relieve th' oppressed state of truth,
Who is companion else to powerful majesty

But you, great, godliest, powerful princess,
Who have brought glory and posterity 50
Unto this widow land and people hopeless?

Sir Walter Ralegh's petition to the Queen, 1618

Oh had truth power the guiltless could not fall,
Malice win glory, or revenge triumph;
But truth alone cannot encounter all.

Mercy is fled to God which mercy made,
Compassion dead, faith turned to policy,
Friends know not those who sit in sorrow's shade.

For what we sometime were we are no more —
Fortune hath changed our shape, and destiny
Defaced the very form we had before.

All love and all desert of former times 10
Malice hath covered from my sovereign's eyes,
And largely laid abroad supposed crimes.

But kings call not to mind what vassals were,
But know them now, as envy hath descrived them;
So can I look on no side from despair.

Cold walls to you I speak, but you are senseless;
Celestial powers, you hear, but have determined,
And shall determine, to the greatest happiness.

Then unto whom shall I unfold my wrong,
Cast down my tears, or hold up folded hands? 20
To her to whom remorse doth most belong:

To her who is the first and may alone
Be justly called the Empress of the Britons.
Who should have mercy if a queen have none?

Save those that would have died for your defence;
Save him whose thoughts no treason ever tainted;
For, lo, destruction is no recompense.

If I have sold my duty, sold my faith
To strangers, which was only due to one,
Nothing I should esteem so dear as death. 30

But if both God and time shall make you know
That I your humblest vassal am oppressed,
Then cast your eyes on undeserved woe,

That I and mine may never mourn the miss
Of her we had, but praise our living Queen,
Who brings us equal, if not greater bliss.

Even such is Time

Even such is Time, which takes in trust
Our youth, our joys, and all we have,
And pays us but with age and dust;
Who in the dark and silent grave,
When we have wandered all our ways,
Shuts up the story of our days.
But from which earth and grave and dust
The Lord shall raise me up, I trust.

Prose

A report of the truth of the fight about the Isles of Azores, this last summer, betwixt the Revenge, one of her Majesty's Ships, and an Armada of the king of Spain

Because the rumours are diversely spread, as well in England as in the low countries and elsewhere, of this late encounter between her majesty's ships and the Armada of *Spain*; and that the Spaniards according to their usual manner, fill the world with their vain glorious vaunts, making great appearance of victories: when on the contrary, themselves are most commonly and shamefully beaten and dishonoured; thereby hoping to possess the ignorant multitude by anticipating and forerunning false reports: It is agreeable with all good reason, for manifestation of the truth to overcome falsehood and untruth; that the beginning, continuance and success of this late honourable encounter of *Sir Richard Grenville*, and other her majesty's Captains, with the Armada of *Spain*; should be truly set down: and published without partiality or false imaginations. And it is no marvel that the Spaniard should seek by false and slanderous Pamphlets, advisoes and Letters, to cover their own loss, and to derogate from others their due honours, especially in this fight being performed far off: seeing they were not ashamed in the year 1588 when they purposed the invasion of this land, to publish in sundry languages in print, great victories in words, which they pleaded to have obtained against this Realm; and spread the same in a most false sort over all parts of *France*, *Italy*, and elsewhere. When shortly after it was happily manifested in very deed to all Nations, how their Navy which they termed invincible, consisting of 240 sail of ships, not only of their own kingdom, but strengthened with the greatest Argosies, *Portugal* Carracks, Florentines and huge Hulks of other countries: were by thirty of her Majesty's own ships of war, and a few of our own Merchants, by the wise, valiant, and most advantageous conduction of the Lord *Charles Howard*, high Admiral of England, beaten and shuffled together; even from the Lizard in *Cornwall*: first to *Portland*, where they shamefully left *Don Pedro de Valdes*, with his mighty ship: from *Portland* to *Calais*, where they lost *Hugo de Moncado*, with the Galliass of which he was Captain, and from *Calais*, driven with squibs from their anchors: were chased out of the sight of England, round about *Scotland* and *Ireland*. Where for the sympathy of their barbarous religion, hoping to find succour and assistance: a great part of them were crushed against the rocks, and those other that landed, being very many in number, were notwithstanding broken, slain, and taken, and so sent from village to village coupled in halters to be shipped into England. Where her Majesty of her Princely and invincible disposition, disdaining to put them to death, and scorning either to retain or entertain them: were all sent back again to their countries, to witness and recount the worthy achievements of their invincible and dreadful Navy. Of which the number of soldiers, the fearful burden of their ships, the commanders' names of every squadron, with all other their magazines of provisions, were put in print, as an Army and Navy unresistible, and disdaining prevention. With all which so great and terrible an ostentation, they did not in all their sailing round about England, so much as sink or take one ship, Bark, Pinnace, or Cockboat of ours: or ever burnt so much as one sheepcote of this land. Whenas on the contrary, Sir *Francis Drake*, with only 800 soldiers not long before, landed in their Indies, and forced *Santiago, Santo Domingo, Cartagena*, and the Forts of *Florida*.

And after that, Sir *John Norris* marched from *Peniche* in *Portugal* with a handful of soldiers, to the gates of *Lisbon*, being above 40 English miles. Where the Earl of *Essex* himself and other valiant Gentlemen, braved the City of *Lisbon*, encamped at the very gates; from whence after many days' abode, finding neither promised party, nor provision to batter: made retreat by land, in despite of all their Garrisons, both of Horse and foot. In this sort I have a little digressed from my first purpose, only by the necessary comparison of theirs and our actions: the one covetous of honour without vaunt or ostentation; the other so greedy to purchase the opinion of their own affairs, and by false rumours to resist the blast of their own dishonours, as they will not only blush to spread all manner of untruths: but even for the least advantage, be it but for the taking of one poor adventurer of the English, will celebrate the victory with bonfires in every town, always spending more in faggots, than the purchase was worth they obtained. Whenas we never yet thought it worth the consumption of two billets, when we have taken eight or ten of their Indian ships at one time, and twenty of the Brasil fleet. Such is the difference between true valour, and ostentation: and between honourable actions, and frivolous vainglorious vaunts. But now to return to my first purpose.

The Lord *Thomas Howard*, with six of her Majesty's ships, six victuallers of London, the bark Ralegh, and two or three Pinnaces riding at anchor near unto Flores, one of the Westerly Islands of the Azores, the last of August in the after noon, had intelligence by one

Captain *Middleton*, of the approach of the Spanish Armada. Which *Middleton* being in a very good Sailer, had kept them company three days before, of good purpose, both to discover their forces the more, as also to give advice to my Lord *Thomas* of their approach. He had no sooner delivered the news but the Fleet was in sight: many of our ships' companies were on shore in the Island; some providing ballast for their ships; others filling of water and refreshing themselves from the land with such things as they could either for money, or by force recover. By reason whereof our ships being all pestered and rummaging every thing out of order, very light for want of ballast. And that which was most to our disadvantage, the one half part of the men of every ship sick, and utterly unserviceable. For in the *Revenge* there were ninety diseased: in the *Bonaventure*, not so many in health as could handle her mainsail. For had not twenty men been taken out of a Bark of Sir *George Carey's*, his being commanded to be sunk, and those appointed to her, she had hardly ever recovered England. The rest for the most part, were in little better state. The names of her Majesty's ships were these as followeth: the *Defiance*, which was Admiral, the *Revenge* Vice-Admiral, the *Bonaventure* commanded by Captain *Cross*, the *Lion* by *George Fenner*, the *Foresight* by Master *Thomas Vavasour*, and the *Crane* by *Duffield*. The *Foresight* and the *Crane* being but small ships; only the other were of the middle size; the rest besides the Bark *Ralegh*, commanded by Captain *Thin*, were victuallers, and of small force or none. The Spanish fleet having shrouded their approach by reason of the Island; were now so soon at hand, as our ships had scarce time to weigh their anchors, but some of them were driven to let slip their Cables and set sail. Sir *Richard Grenville* was the last weighed, to recover the men that were upon the Island, which otherwise had been lost. The Lord *Thomas* with the rest very hardly recovered the wind, which Sir *Richard Grenville* not being able to do, was persuaded by the master and others to cut his mainsail, and cast about, and to trust to the sailing of the ship: for the squadron of Seville were on his weather bow. But Sir *Richard* utterly refused to turn from the enemy, alleging that he would rather choose to die, than to dishonour himself, his country, and her Majesty's ship, persuading his company that he would pass through the two Squadrons, in despite of them: and enforce those of *Seville* to give him way. Which he performed upon divers of the foremost, who as the Mariners term it, sprang their luff, and fell under the lee of the *Revenge*. But the other course had been the better, and might right well have been answered in so great an impossibility of prevailing. Notwithstanding out of the greatness of his mind, he could not be persuaded. In the meanwhile as he attended those which were nearest him, the great *San Philip* being in the wind of him, and coming towards him, becalmed his sails in such sort, as the ship could neither make way nor feel the helm: so huge and high carged was the Spanish ship, being of a thousand and five hundred tons. Who after laid the *Revenge* aboard. When he was thus bereft of his sails, the ships that were under his lee luffing up, also laid him aboard: of which the next was the Admiral of the Biscayans, a very mighty and puissant ship commanded by *Bertendona*. The said *Philip* carried three tier of ordnance on a side, and eleven pieces in every tier. She shot eight forthright out of her chase, besides those of her Stern ports.

After the *Revenge* was entangled with this *Philip*, four other boarded her; two on her larboard, and two on her starboard. The fight thus beginning at three of the clock in the afternoon, continued very terrible all that evening. But the great *San Philip* having received the lower tier of the *Revenge*, discharged with crossbarshot, shifted herself with all diligence from her sides, utterly misliking her first entertainment. Some say that the ship foundered, but we cannot report it for truth, unless we were assured. The Spanish ships were filled with companies of soldiers, in some two hundred besides the Mariners; in some five, in others eight hundred. In ours there were none at all, beside the Mariners, but the servants of the commanders and some few voluntary Gentlemen only. After many interchanged volleys of great ordnance and small shot, the Spaniards deliberated to enter the *Revenge* and made divers attempts, hoping to force her by the multitudes of their armed soldiers and Musketeers, but were still repulsed again and again, and at all times beaten back, into their own ships, or into the seas. In the beginning of the fight, the *George Noble* of *London*, having received some shot through her by the Armadas, fell under the Lee of the *Revenge*, and asked Sir *Richard* what he would command him, being but one of the victuallers and of small force: Sir *Richard* bid him save himself, and leave him to his fortune. After the fight had thus without intermission, continued while the day lasted and some hours of the night, many of our men were slain and hurt, and one of the great Galleons of the Armada, and the Admiral of the Hulks both sunk, and in many other of the Spanish ships great slaughter was made. Some write that Sir *Richard* was very dangerously hurt almost in the beginning of the fight, and lay speechless for a time ere he recovered. But two of the *Revenge's* own company, brought home in a ship of Lyme from the Islands, examined by some of the Lords, and others: affirmed that he was never so wounded as that he forsook the upper deck, till an hour before midnight; and then being shot into the body with a Musket as he was a dressing, was again shot into the head, and withal his Surgeon wounded to death. This agreeth also with an examination taken by Sir *Frances Godolphin*, of 4 other Mariners of the same ship being returned, which examination, the said Sir *Francis* sent unto master *William Killigrew*, of her Majesty's privy Chamber.

But to return to the fight, the Spanish ships which attempted to board the *Revenge*, as they were wounded and beaten off, so always others came in their places, she having never less than two mighty Galleons by her sides, and aboard her. So that ere the morning, from three of the clock of the day before, there had fifteen several Armados assailed her; and all so ill approved their entertainment, as they were by the break of day, far more willing to hearken to a composition, than hastily to make any more assaults or entries. But as the day increased, so our men decreased: and as the light grew more and more, by so much more grew our discomforts. For none appeared in sight but enemies, saving one small ship called the *Pilgrim*, commanded by *Jacob Whiddon*, who hovered all night to see the success: but in the morning bearing with the *Revenge*, was hunted like a hare amongst many ravenous hounds, but escaped.

All the powder of the *Revenge* to the last barrel was now spent, all her pikes broken, forty of her best men slain, and the most part of the rest hurt. In the beginning of the fight she had but one hundred free from sickness, and fourscore and ten sick, laid in hold upon the Ballast. A small troop to man such a ship, and a weak Garrison to resist so mighty an Army. By those hundred all was sustained, the volleys, boarding, and enterings of fifteen ships of war, besides those which beat her at large. On the contrary, the Spanish were always supplied with soldiers brought from every squadron: all manner of Arms and powder at will. Unto ours there remained no comfort at all, no hope, no supply either of ships, men, or weapons; the masts all beaten overboard, all her tackle cut asunder, her upper work altogether razed, and in effect evened she was with the water, but the very foundation or bottom of a ship, nothing being left over head either for flight or defence. Sir *Richard* finding himself in this distress, and unable any longer to make resistance, having endured in this fifteen hours fight, the assault of fifteen several Armados, all by turns aboard him, and by estimation eight hundred shot of great artillery, besides many assaults and entries. And that himself and the ship must needs be possessed by the enemy, who were now all cast in a ring about him; The *Revenge* not able to move one way or other, but as she was moved with the waves and billow of the sea: commanded the master Gunner, whom he knew to be a most resolute man, to split and sink the ship; that thereby nothing might remain of glory or victory to the Spaniards: seeing in so many hours fight, and with so great a Navy they were not able to take her, having had fifteen hours time, fifteen thousand men, and fifty and three sail of men of war to perform it withal. And persuaded the company, or as many as he could induce, to yield themselves unto God, and to the mercy of none else; but as they had like valiant resolute men, repulsed so many enemies, they should not now shorten the honour of their nation, by prolonging their own lives for a few hours, or a few days. The master Gunner readily condescended and divers others; but the Captain and the Master were of another opinion, and besought Sir *Richard* to have care of them: alleging that the Spaniard would be as ready to entertain a composition as they were willing to offer the same: and that there being divers sufficient and valiant men yet living, and whose wounds were not mortal, they might do their prince acceptable service hereafter. And (that where Sir *Richard* had alleged that the Spaniards should never glory to have taken one ship of her Majesty's, seeing that they had so long and so notably defended themselves) they answered, that the ship had six foot water in hold, three shot under water which were so weakly stopped, as with the first working of the sea, she must needs sink, and was besides so crushed and bruised, as she could never be removed out of the place.

And as the matter was thus in dispute, and Sir *Richard* refusing to hearken to any of those reasons; the master of the *Revenge* (while the Captain won unto him the greater party) was convoyed aboard the General *Don Alfonso Bassan*. Who finding none over hasty to enter the *Revenge* again, doubting lest Sir *Richard* would have blown them up and himself, and perceiving by the report of the master of the *Revenge* his dangerous disposition: yielded that all their lives should be saved, the company sent for England, and the better sort to pay such reasonable ransom as their estate would bear, and in the mean season to be free from Galley or imprisonment. To this he so much the rather condescended as well as I have said, for fear of further loss and mischief to themselves, as also for the desire he had to recover Sir *Richard Grenville*; whom for his notable valour he seemed greatly to honour and admire.

When this answer was returned, and that safety of life was promised, the common sort being now at the end of their peril, the most drew back from Sir *Richard* and the master Gunner, being no hard matter to dissuade men from death to life. The master Gunner finding himself and Sir *Richard* thus prevented and mastered by the greater number, would have slain himself with a sword, had he not been by force withheld and locked into his Cabin. Then the

General sent many boats aboard the *Revenge*, and divers of our men fearing Sir *Richard's* disposition, stole away aboard the General and other ships. Sir *Richard* thus overmatched, was sent unto by *Alfonso Bassan* to remove out of the *Revenge*, the ship being marvellous unsavoury, filled with blood and bodies of the dead, and wounded men like a slaughter house. Sir *Richard* answered that he might do with his body what he list, for he esteemed it not, and as he was carried out of the ship he swounded, and reviving again desired the company to pray for him. The General used Sir *Richard* with all humanity, and left nothing unattempted that tended to his recovery, highly commending his valour and worthiness, and greatly bewailed the danger wherein he was, being unto them a rare spectacle, and a resolution seldom approved, to see one ship turn toward so many enemies, to endure the charge and boarding of so many huge Armados, and to resist and repel the assaults and entries of so many soldiers. All which and more, is confirmed by a Spanish Captain of the same Armada, and a present actor in the fight, who being severed from the rest in a storm, was by the *Lion* of London a small ship taken, and is now prisoner in London.

The general commander of the Armada, was *Don Alfonso Bassan*, brother to the Marquess of *Santa Cruz*. The Admiral of the Biscayan squadron, was *Bertendona*. Of the squadron of *Seville*, Marquess of *Arumburch*. The Hulks and Flyboats were commanded by *Luis Cutino*. There were slain and drowned in this fight, well near two thousand of the enemies, and two especial commanders *Don Luis de Saint John*, and *Don George de Prunaria de Mallaga*, as the Spanish Captain confesseth, besides divers others of special account, whereof as yet report is not made.

The Admiral of the Hulks and of the Ascension of *Seville*, were both sunk by the side of the *Revenge*; one other recovered the road of Saint *Michaels*, and sunk also there; a fourth ran herself with the shore to save her men. Sir *Richard* died as it is said, the second or third day aboard the General, and was by them greatly bewailed. What became of his body, whether it were buried in the sea or the land we know not: the comfort that remaineth to his friends is, that he hath ended his life honourably in respect of the reputation won to his nation and country, and of the same to his posterity, and that being dead, he hath not outlived his own honour.

For the rest of her Majesty's ships that entered not so far into the fight of the *Revenge*, the reasons and causes were these. There were of them but six in all, whereof two but small ships; the *Revenge* engaged past recovery: The Island of *Flores* was on the one side, 53 sail of the Spanish, divided into squadrons on the other, all as full filled with soldiers as they could contain. Almost the one half of our men sick and not able to serve: the ships grown foul, unrummaged, and scarcely able to bear any sail for want of ballast, having been six months at the sea before. If all the rest had entered, all had been lost. For the very hugeness of the Spanish fleet, if no other violence had been offered, would have crushed them between them into shivers. Of which the dishonour and loss of the Queen had been far greater than the spoil or harm that the enemy could any way have received. Notwithstanding it is very true, that the Lord *Thomas* would have entered between the squadrons, but the rest would not condescend; and the master of his own ship offered to leap into the sea, rather than to conduct that her Majesty's ship and the rest to be a prey to the enemy, where there was no hope nor possibility either of defence or victory. Which also in my opinion had ill sorted or answered the discretion and trust of a General to commit himself and his charge to an assured destruction, without hope or any likelihood of prevailing: thereby to diminish the strength of her Majesty's Navy, and to enrich the pride and glory of the enemy. The Foresight of the Queen's commanded by Master *Thomas Vavasour*, performed a very great fight, and stayed two hours as near the *Revenge* as the weather would permit him, not forsaking the fight, till he was like to be encompassed by the squadrons, and with great difficulty cleared himself. The rest gave divers vollies of shot, and entered as far as the place permitted and their own necessities, to keep the weather gauge of the enemy, until they were parted by night. A few days after the fight was ended, and the English prisoners dispersed into the Spanish and Indy ships, there arose so great storm from the West and Northwest, that all the fleet was dispersed, as well the Indian fleet which were then come unto them as the rest of the Armada that attended their arrival, of which 14 sail together with the *Revenge*, and in her 200 Spaniards, were cast away upon the Isle of *Saint Michaels*. So it pleased them to honour the burial of that renowned ship the *Revenge*, not suffering her to perish alone, for the great honour she achieved in her lifetime. On the rest of the Islands there were cast away in this storm, 15 or 16 more of the ships of war; and of a hundred and odd sail of the Indy fleet, expected this year in *Spain*, what in this tempest, and what before in the bay of *Mexico*, and about the *Bermudas* there were 70 and odd consumed and lost, with those taken by our ships of London, besides one very rich *Indian* ship, which set herself on fire, being boarded by the Pilgrim, and five other taken by Master *Watts* his ships of London, between the *Havana* and *Cape Antonio*. The 4 of this month of November, we received letters from the *Tercera*, affirming that there are 3000 bodies of men remaining in that Island, saved out of the perished ships: and that by the Spaniards' own confession, there are 10000 cast away in this storm, besides those that are perished between the Islands and the main. Thus it hath pleased God to fight for us, and to defend the justice of our cause, against the ambitious and bloody pretences of the Spaniard, who seeking to devour all nations, are themselves devoured. A manifest testimony how injust and displeasing, their attempts are in the sight of God, who hath pleased to witness by the success of their affairs, his mislike of their bloody and injurious designs, purposed and practised against all Christian Princes, over whom they seek unlawful and ungodly rule and Empery.

One day or two before this wrack happened to the spanish fleet, whenas some of our prisoners desired to be set on shore upon the Islands, hoping to be from thence transported into England, which liberty was formerly by the General promised: One *Maurice Fitz John*, son of old *John* of *Desmond* a notable traitor, cousin german to the late Earl of *Desmond*, was sent to the English from ship to ship, to persuade them to serve the King of *Spain*. The arguments he used to induce them, were these. The increase of pay which he promised to be trebled: advancement to the better sort: and the exercise of the true Catholic religion, and safety of their souls to all. For the first, even the beggarly and unnatural behaviour of those English and Irish rebels, that served the King in that present action, was sufficient to answer that first argument of rich pay. For so poor and beggarly they were, as for want of apparel they stripped their poor countrymen prisoners out of their ragged garments, worn to nothing by six months service, and spared not to despoil them even of their bloody shirts, from their wounded bodies, and the very shoes from their feet; A notable testimony of their rich entertainment and great wages. The second reason was hope of advancement if they served well, and would continue faithful to the King. But what man can be so blockishly ignorant ever to expect place or honour from a foreign king, having no other argument or persuasion than his own disloyalty; to be unnatural to his own country that bred him; to his parents that begat him, and rebellious to his true prince, to whose obedience he is bound by oath, by nature, and by religion. No, they are only assured to be employed in all desperate enterprises, to be held in scorn and disdain ever among those whom they serve. And that ever traitor was either trusted or advanced I could never yet read, neither can I at this time remember any example. And no man could have less becomed the place of an Orator for such a purpose, than this *Maurice* of *Desmond*. For the Earl his cousin being one of the greatest subjects in that kingdom of *Ireland*, having almost whole countries in his possession; so many goodly manors, Castles, and Lordships; the County Palatine of *Kerry*, five hundred gentlemen of his own name and family to follow him, besides others. All which he possessed in peace for three or four hundred years: was in less than three years after his adhering to the Spaniards and rebellion, beaten from all his holds, not so many as ten gentlemen of his name left living, himself taken and beheaded by a soldier of his own nation, and his land given by a Parliament to her Majesty, and possessed by the English. His other Cousin Sir *John* of *Desmond* taken by Master *John Zouch*, and his body hanged over the gates of his native city to be devoured by Ravens: the third brother Sir *James* hanged, drawn, and quartered in the same place. If he had withal vaunted of this success of his own house, no doubt the argument would have moved much, and wrought great effect; which because he for that present forgot, I thought it good to remember in his behalf. For matter of religion it would require a particular volume, if I should set down how irreligiously they cover their greedy and ambitious pretences, with that veil of piety. But sure I am, that there is no kingdom or commonwealth in all Europe, but if they be reformed, they then invade it for religion sake: if it be, as they term Catholic, they pretend title; as if the Kings of *Castile* were the natural heirs of all the world: and so between both, no kingdom is unsought. Where they dare not with their own forces to invade, they basely entertain the traitors and vagabonds of all nations; seeking by those and by their runagate *Jesuits* to win parts, and have by that mean ruined many Noble houses and others in this land, and have extinguished both their lives and families. What good, honour, or fortune ever man yet by them achieved, is yet unheard of, or unwritten. And if our English Papists do but look into *Portugal*, against whom they have no pretence of religion, how the Nobility are put to death, imprisoned, their rich men made a prey, and all sorts of people captived; they shall find that the obedience even of the Turk is easy and a liberty, in respect of the slavery and tyranny of *Spain*. What they have done in *Sicil*, in *Naples*, *Milan*, and in the low countries; who hath there been spared for religion at all? And it cometh to my remembrance of a certain Burgher of *Antwerp*, whose house being entered by a company of Spanish soldiers, when they first sacked the City, he besought them to spare him and his goods, being a good Catholic, and one of their own party and faction. The Spaniards answered, that they knew him to be of a good conscience for himself, but his money, plate, jewels, and goods were all heretical, and therefore good prize. So they abused and tormented the foolish Fleming, who hoped that an *Agnus Dei* had been a sufficient Target against all force of that holy and charitable nation. Neither have they at any time as they protest invaded the kingdoms of the *Indies* and *Peru*, and elsewhere, but only led thereunto, rather, to reduce the people to Christianity, than for either gold or empery. Whenas in one only Island called *Hispaniola*, they have wasted thirty hundred thousand of the natural people, besides many millions else in other places of the *Indies*: a poor and harmless people created of God, and might have been won to his knowledge, as many of them were, and almost as many as ever were persuaded thereunto. The Story whereof is at large written by a Bishop of their own nation called *Bartholome de las Casas*, and translated into English and many other languages, entitled *The Spanish cruelties*. Who would therefore repose trust in such a nation of ravenous strangers, and especially in those Spaniards which more greedily thirst after English blood, than after the lives of any other people of Europe; for the many overthrows and dishonours they have received at our hands, whose weakness we have discovered to the world, and whose forces at home, abroad, in *Europe*, in *India*, by sea and land; we have even with handfuls of men and ships, overthrown and dishonoured. Let not therefore any English man of what religion soever, have other opinion of the Spaniards, but that those whom he seeketh to win of our nation, he esteemeth base and traitorous, unworthy persons, or unconstant fools: and that he useth his pretence of religion, for no other purpose, but to bewitch us from the obedience of our natural prince; thereby hoping in time to bring us to slavery and subjection, and then none shall be unto them so odious, and disdained as the traitors themselves, who have sold their country to a stranger, and forsaken their faith and obedience contrary to nature or religion; and contrary to that human and general honour, not only of Christians, but of heathen and irreligious nations, who have always sustained what labour soever, and embraced even death itself, for their country, prince or commonwealth. To conclude, it hath ever to this day pleased God, to prosper and defend her Majesty, to break the purposes of malicious enemies, of forsworn traitors, and of injust practices and invasions. She hath ever been honoured of the worthiest Kings, served by faithful subjects, and shall by the favour of God, resist, repel, and confound all whatsoever attempts against her sacred Person or kingdom. In the meantime, let the Spaniard and traitor vaunt of their success; and we her true and obedient vassals guided by the shining light of her virtues, shall always love her, serve her, and obey her to the end of our lives.

The Discovery of the Large, Rich and Beautiful Empire of Guiana, With a relation of the Great and Golden City of Manoa (which the Spaniards call El Dorado) And the provinces of Emeria, Arromaia, Amapaia and other Countries, with their rivers, adjoining.

The Epistle Dedicatory:
To the right honourable my singular good Lord and kinsman, Charles Howard, knight of the Garter, Baron, and Councillor, and of the Admirals of England the most renowned: And to the Right Honourable Sir Robert Cecil Knight, Councillor in her Highness' privy Councils.

For your Honour's many Honourable and friendly parts, I have hitherto only returned promises, and now for answer of both your adventures, I have sent you a bundle of papers which I have divided between your Lordship and Sir Robert Cecil in these two respects chiefly: First for that it is reason, that wasteful factors, when they have consumed such stocks as they had in trust, do yield some colour for the same in their account, secondly for that I am assured, that whatsoever shall be done, or written by me, shall need a double protection and defence. The trial that I had of both your loves, when I was left of all, but of malice and revenge, makes me still presume that you will be pleased (knowing what little power I had to perform aught, and the great advantage of forewarned enemies) to answer that out of knowledge, which others shall but object out of malice. In my more happy times as I did especially honour you both, so I found that your loves sought me out in the darkest shadow of adversity, and the same affection which accompanied my better fortune, soared not away from me in my many miseries: all which though I cannot requite, yet I shall ever acknowledge: and the great debt which I have no power to pay, I can do no more for a time but confess to be due. It is true that as my errors were great, so they have yielded very grievous effects, and if aught might have been deserved in former times to have counterpoised any part of offences, the fruit thereof (as it seemeth) was long before fallen from the tree and the dead stock only remained. I did therefore even in the winter of my life, undertake these travels, fitter for bodies less blasted with misfortunes, for men of greater ability, and for minds of better encouragement, that thereby if it were possible I might recover but the moderation of excess, and the least taste of the greatest plenty formerly possessed. If I had known other way to win, if I had imagined how greater adventures might have regained, if I could conceive what farther means I might yet use, but even to appease so powerful displeasure, I would not doubt for one year more to hold fast my soul in my teeth, till it were performed. Of that little remain I had, I have wasted in effect all herein, I have undergone many constructions, I have been accompanied with many sorrows, with labour, hunger, heat, sickness, and peril: It appeareth notwithstand that I made no other bravado of going to sea, than was meant, and that I was neither hidden in Cornwall or elsewhere, as was supposed. They have grossly belied me, that forejudged that I would rather become a servant to the Spanish king, than return, and the rest were much mistaken, who would have persuaded, that I was too easeful and sensual to undertake a journey of so great travail. But, if what I have done receive the gracious construction of a painful pilgrimage, and purchase the least remission, I shall think all too little, and that there were wanting to the rest, many miseries: But if both the times past, the present, and what may be in the future, do all by one grain of gall continue in an eternal distaste, I do not then know whether I should bewail myself either for my too much travail and expence, or condemn myself for doing less than that, which can deserve nothing. From myself I have deserved no thanks, for I am returned a beggar, and withered, but that I might have bettered my poor estate, it shall appear by the following discourse, if I had not only respected her Majesty's future Honour, and riches. It became not the former fortune in which I once lived, to go journies of picorie, and it had sorted ill with the offices of Honour, which by her Majesty's grace, I hold this day in England, to run from Cape to Cape, and from place to place, for the pillage of ordinary prizes. Many years since, I had knowledge by relation, of that mighty, rich, and beautiful Empire of *Guiana*, and of that great and Golden City, which the spaniards call *El Dorado*, and the naturals *Manoa*, which City was conquered, reedified, and enlarged by a younger son of *Guainacapa* Emperor of *Peru*, at such time as *Francisco Pizarro* and others conquered the said Empire, from his two elder brethren *Huascar*, and *Atabalipa*, both then contending for the same, the one being favoured by the *Oreiones* of *Cuzco*, the other by the people of *Caximalca*. I sent my servant *Jacob Whiddon* the year before, to get knowledge of the passages, and I had some light from Captain *Parker* sometime my servant, and now attending on your Lordship that such a place there was to the southward of the great bay of *Charuas*, or *Guanipa*: but I found that it was 600 miles farther off, than they supposed, and many other impediments to them unknown and unheard. After I had displanted *Don Antonio de Berrio*, who was upon the same enterprise, leaving my ships at *Trinidado*, at the port called *Curiapan*, I wandered 400 miles, into the said country by land and river: the particulars I will leave to the following discourse. The country hath more quantity of Gold by manifold, than the best parts of the *Indies*, or *Peru*: All the most of the kings of the borders are already become her Majesty's vassals: and seem to desire nothing more than her Majesty's protection and the return of the English nation. It hath another ground and assurance of riches and glory, than the voyages of the west *Indies*, and an easier way to invade the best parts thereof, than by the common course. The king of *Spain* is not so impoverished by taking 3 or 4 port towns in *America* as we suppose, neither are the riches of *Peru*, or *Nueva Espania* so left by the sea side, as it can be easily washed away, with a great flood, or springtide, or left dry upon the sands on a low ebb. The port towns are few and poor in respect of the rest within the land, and are of little defence, and are only rich when the fleets are to receive the treasure for spain: And we might think the spaniards very simple, having so many horses and slaves, that if they could not upon two days warning, carry all the Gold they have into the land, and far enough from the reach of our footmen, especially the *Indies* being (as it is for the most part) so mountainous, so full of woods, rivers, and marshes. In the port towns of the province of *Venezuala*, as *Cumana*, *Coro*, and *Santiago* (whereof *Coro* and *Santiago* were taken by Captain *Preston* and *Cumana* and *San Joseph* by us) we found not the value of one riall of plate in either: but the Cities of *Barquisimeta*, *Valencia*, *San Sebastian*, *Corora*, *Santa Lucia*, *Alleguna*, *Maracaibo*, and *Truxillo*, are not so easily invaded: neither doth the burning of those on the coast impoverish the king of spain any one ducket, and if we sack the river of *Hache*, *Santa Marta*, and *Cartagena*, which are the ports of *Nueva reyno* and *Popayan*. There are besides within the land which are indeed rich and populous, the towns and Cities of *Merida*, *La Grita*, *San Christofero*, the great Cities of *Pamplona*, *Santa Fe de Bogota*, *Tunja* and *Muzo* where the *Emeralds* are found, the towns and Cities of *Mariquita*, *Velez*, *La Villa de Leva*, *La Palma*, *Honda*, *Angostura*, the great City of *Timana*, *Tocaima*, *Sant Aguila*, *Pasto*, *Juago*, the great city of *Popayan* itself, *Los Remedios*, and the rest. If we take the ports and villages within the bay of *Uraba* in the kingdom or rivers of *Dariena*, and *Caribana*, the cities and towns of *San Juan de Rodas*, of *Caceres*, of *Antioquia*, *Caramanta*, *Ancerma* have gold enough to pay the King part, and are not easily invaded by the way of the *Ocean*, or if *Nombre de Dios* and *Panama* be taken in the province of *Castillo de Oro*, and the villages upon the rivers of *Zinu* and *Chagres*, *Peru* hath besides those and besides the magnificent cities of *Quito* and *Lima* so many Islands, ports, Cities, and mines, as if I should name them with the rest it would seem incredible to the reader: of all which because I have written a particular treatise of the west *Indies*, I will omit their repetition at this time, seeing that in the said treatise I have anatomised the rest of the sea towns as well of *Nicaragua*, *Yucatan*, *Nueva Espania*, and the Islands, as those of the Inland, and by what means they may be best invaded, as far as any mean Judgment can comprehend. But I hope it shall appear that there is a way found to answer every man's longing, a better Indies for her majesty than the King of Spain hath any, which if it shall please her highness to undertake, I shall most willingly end the rest of my days in following the same: If it be left to the spoil and sackage of common persons, if the love and service of so many nations be despised, so great riches, and so mighty an Empire refused, I hope her Majesty will yet take my humble desire and my labour therein in gracious part, which if it had not been in respect of her highness' future honour and riches, I could have laid hands and ransomed many of the kings and *Cassiqui* of the Country, and have had a reasonable proportion of gold for their redemption: But I have chosen rather to bear the burden of poverty, than reproach, and rather to endure a second travail and the chances thereof, than to have defaced an enterprise of so great assurance, until I knew whether it pleased God to put a disposition in her princely and royal heart either to follow or foreslow the same: I will therefore leave it to his ordinance that hath only power in all things, and do humbly pray that your honours will excuse such errors, as without the defence of art, overrun in every part, the following discourse, in which I have neither studied phrase, form, nor fashion, and that you will be pleased to esteem me as your own (though over dearly bought) and I shall ever remain ready to do you all honour and service.

W.R

The Discovery of Guiana

On Thursday the 6 of February in the year 1595, we departed *England*, and the sunday following had sight of the North cape of *Spain*, the wind for the most part continuing prosperous: we passed in sight of the *Burlings*, and the rock, and so onwards for the *Canaries*, and fell with *Fuente ventura* the 17 of the same month, where we spent two or three days, and relieved our companies with some fresh meat. From thence we coasted by the *Gran Canaria*, and so to *Tenerife*, and stayed there for the Lion's whelp your Lordship's ship, and for Captain *Amyas Preston* and the rest: But when after 7 or 8 days we found them not, we departed and directed our course for *Trinidado* with mine own ship, and a small bark of Captain *Cross's* only (for we had before lost sight of a small Gallego on the coast of *Spain*, which came with us from *Plymouth*:) we arrived at *Trinidado* the 22 of March, casting anchor at Point *Curiapan*, which the Spaniards call *Punto de Gallo*, which is situate in 8 degrees or thereabouts: we abode there 4 or 5 days, and in all that time we came not to the speech of any Indian or Spaniard: on the coast we saw a fire, as we sailed from the point *Carao* towards *Curiapan*, but for fear of the Spaniards, none durst come to speak with us. I myself coasted it in my barge close aboard the shore and landed in every Cove, the better to know the island, while the ships kept the channel. From *Curiapan* after a few days we turned up Northeast to recover that place which the Spaniards call *Peurto de los Hispanioles*, and the inhabitants *Conquerabia*, and as before (revictualling my barge) I left the ships and kept by the shore, the better to come to speech with some of the inhabitants, and also to understand the rivers, watering places and ports of the island which (as it is rudely done) my purpose is to send your Lordship after a few days. From *Curiapan* I came to a port and seat of Indians called *Parico* where we found a fresh-water river, but saw no people. From thence I rowed to another port, called by the naturals *Piche*, and by the Spaniards *Tierra de Brea*: In the way between both were divers little brooks of fresh water and one salt river that had store of oysters upon the branches of the trees, and were very salt and well tasted. All their oysters grow upon those boughs and sprays, and not on the ground: the like is commonly seen in the West Indies and elsewhere. This tree is described by *Andrew Thevet* in his French *Antartique*, and the form figured in the book as a plant very strange, and by *Pliny* in his XII book of his natural history. But in this Island, as also in *Guiana*, there are very many of them.

At this point called *Tierra de Brea* or *Biche* there is that abundance of stone pitch, that all the ships of the world may be therewith loaden from thence, and we made trial of it in trimming our ships to be most excellent good, and melteth not with the sun as the pitch of *Norway*, and therefore for ships trading the south parts very profitable. From thence we went to the mountain foot called *Annaperima*, and so passing the river *Carone*, on which the Spanish City was seated, we met with our ships at *Puerto de los Hispanioles* or *Conquerabia*.

The Island of *Trinidado* hath the form of a sheep-hook, and is but narrow; the north part is very mountainous, the soil is very excellent and will bear sugar, ginger, or any other commodity that the Indies yield. It hath store of deer, wild porks, fruits, fish and fowl: It hath also for bread sufficient *Maize*, *Cassavi*, and of those roots and fruits which are common everywhere in the west *Indies*. It hath divers beasts, which the *Indies* have not: the Spaniards confessed that they found grains of gold in some of the rivers, but they having a purpose to enter *Guiana* (the *Magazine* of all rich metals) cared not to spend time in the search thereof any farther. This island is called by the people thereof *Cairi*, and in it are divers nations: those about *Parico* are called *Iaio*, those at *Punto Carao* are of the *Arwacas*, and between *Carao* and *Curiapan* they are called *Salvaios*, between *Carao* and *Punto Galera* are the *Nepoios*, and those about the Spanish City term themselves *Carinepagotos*: Of the rest of the nations, and of other ports and rivers I leave to speak here, being impertinent to my purpose, and mean to describe them as they are situate in the particular plot and description of the Island, three parts whereof I coasted with my barge, that I might the better describe it.

Meeting with the ships at *Puerto de los Hispanioles*, we found at the landing place a company of Spaniards who kept a guard at the descent, and they offering a sign of peace I sent Captain *Whiddon* to speak with them, whom afterward to my great grief I left buried in the said Island after my return from *Guiana*, being a man most honest and valiant. The Spaniards seemed to be desirous to trade with us, and to enter into terms of peace, more for doubt of their own strength than for aught else, and in the end upon pledge, some of them came aboard: the same evening there stole also aboard us in a small *Canoa* two Indians, the one of them being a *Cassique* or Lord of people called *Cantyman*, who had the year before been with Captain *Whiddon*, and was of his acquaintance. By this *Cantyman* we understood what strength the Spaniards had, how far it was to their City, and of *Don Antonio de Berrio* the governor, who was said to be slain in his second attempt of *Guiana*, but was not.

While we remained at *Puerto de los Hispanioles* some Spaniards came aboard us to buy linen of the company, and such other things as they wanted, and also to view our ships and company, all which I entertained kindly and feasted after our manner: by means whereof I learned of one and another as much of the estate of *Guiana* as I could, or as they knew, for those poor soldiers having been many years without wine, a few draughts made them merry, in which mood they vaunted of *Guiana* and of the riches thereof, and all what they knew of the ways and passages, myself seeming to purpose nothing else than the entrance or discovery thereof, but bred in them an opinion that I was bound only for the relief of those English, which I had planted in *Virginia*, whereof the bruit was come among them, which I had performed in my return if extremity of weather had not forced me from the said coast.

I found occasions of staying in this place for two causes: the one was to be revenged of *Berrio*, who the year before betrayed 8 of Captain *Whiddon's* men, and took them while he departed from them to seek the *Elizabeth Bonaventure*, which arrived at *Trinidado* the day before from the East *Indies*: in whose absence *Berrio* sent a *Canoa* aboard the pinnace only with *Indians* and dogs inviting the company to go with them into the woods to kill a deer, who like wise men in the absence of their Captain followed the *Indians*, but were no sooner one arquebus shot from the shore, but *Berrio's* soldiers lying in ambush had them all, notwithstanding that he had given his word to Captain *Whiddon* that they should take water and wood safely: the other cause of my stay was, for that by discourse with the *Spaniards* I daily learned more and more of *Guiana*, of the rivers and passages, and of the enterprise of *Berrio*, by what means or fault he failed, and how he meant to prosecute the same.

While we thus spent the time I was assured by another *Cassique* of the north side of the Island, that *Berrio* had sent to *Marguerita* and to *Cumana* for soldiers, meaning to have given me a *Cassado* at parting, if it had been possible. For although he had given order through all the Island that no *Indian* should come aboard to trade with me upon pain of hanging and quartering, (having executed two of them for the same which I afterwards found) yet every night there came some with most lamentable complaints of his cruelty, how he had divided the Island and given to every soldier a part, that he made the ancient *Cassiqui* which were Lords of the country to be their slaves, that he kept them in chains, and dropped their naked bodies with burning bacon, and such other torments, which I found afterwards to be true: for in the city after I entered the same, there were 5 of the Lords or little kings (which they call *Cassiqui* in the west Indies) in one chain almost dead of famine, and wasted with torments: these are called in their own language *Acarewana*, and now of late since English, French, and Spanish are come among them, they call themselves *Captains*, because they perceive that the chiefest of every ship is called by that name. Those five *Captains* in the chain were called *Wannawanare*, *Carroaori*, *Marquarima*, *Tarroopanama*, and *Aterima*. So as both to be revenged of the former wrong, as also considering that to enter *Guiana* by small boats, to depart 400 or 500 miles from my ships, and to leave a garrison in my back interessed in the same enterprise, who also daily expected supplies out of Spain, I should have savoured very much of the Ass: and therefore taking a time of most advantage, I set upon the *Corp du guard* in the evening, and having put them to the sword, sent Captain *Calfield* onwards with 60 soldiers, and myself followed with 40 more and so took their new city which they called *Saint Joseph*, by break of day: they abode not any fight after a few shot, and all being dismissed but only *Berrio* and his companion, I brought them with me aboard, and at the instance of the Indians, I set their new city of *Saint Josephs* on fire.

The same day arrived Captain *George Gifford* with your Lordship's ship, and Captain *Keymis* whom I lost on the coast of Spain, with the *Gallego*, and in them divers Gentlemen and others, which to our little army was a great comfort and supply.

We then hastened away towards our purposed discovery, and first I called all the Captains of the island together that were enemies to the Spaniards, for there were some which *Berrio* had brought out of other countries, and planted there to eat out and waste those that were natural of the place, and by my Indian interpreter, which I carried out of England, I made them understand that I was the servant of a Queen, who was the great *Cassique* of the north, and a virgin, and had more *Cassiqui* under her than there were trees in their Island: that she was an enemy to the *Castellani* in respect of their tyranny and oppression, and that she delivered all such nations about her, as were by them oppressed, and having freed all the coast of the northern world from their servitude had sent me to free them also, and withal to defend the country of *Guiana* from their invasion and conquest. I showed them her majesty's picture which they so admired and honoured, as it had been easy to have brought them Idolatrous thereof.

The like and a more large discourse I made to the rest of the nations both in my passing to *Guiana*, and to those of the borders, so as in that part of the world her majesty is very famous and admirable, whom they now call *Ezrabeta Cassipuna Aquerewana*, which is as much as *Elizabeth*, the great princess or greatest commander. This done we left *Puerto de los Hispaniolas*, and returned to *Curiapan*, and having *Berrio* my prisoner I gathered from him as much of *Guiana* as he knew.

This *Berrio* is a gentleman well descended, and had long served the Spanish king in *Milan*, *Naples*, the low Countries and elsewhere, very valiant and liberal, and a Gentleman of great assuredness, and of a great heart: I used him according to his estate and worth in all things I could, according to the small means I had.

I sent Captain *Whiddon* the year before to get what knowledge he could of *Guiana*, and the end of my journey at this time was to discover and enter the same, but my intelligence was far from truth, for the country is situate above 600 English miles further from the sea, than I was made believe it had been, which afterward understanding to be true by *Berrio*, I kept it from the knowledge of my company, who else would never have been brought to attempt the same: of which 600 miles I passed 400 leaving my ships so far from me at anchor in the sea, which was more of desire to perform that discovery, than of reason, especially having such poor and weak vessels to transport ourselves in; for in the bottom of an old *Gallego* which I caused to be fashioned like a Galley, and in one barge, two wherries, and a ship boat of the Lion's whelp, we carried 100 persons and their victuals for a month in the same, being all driven to lie in the rain and weather, in the open air, in the burning sun, and upon the hard boards, and to dress our meat, and to carry all manner of furniture in them, wherewith they were so pestered and unsavoury, that what with victuals being most fish, with the wet clothes of so many men thrust together and the heat of the sun, I will undertake there was never any prison in England, that could be found more unsavoury and loathsome, especially to my self, who had for many years before been dieted and cared for in a sort far differing.

If Captain *Preston* had not been persuaded that he should have come too late to *Trinidado* to have found us there (for the month was expired which I promised to tarry for him there ere he could recover the coast of Spain) but that it had pleased God he might have joined with us, and that we had entered the country but some ten days sooner ere the rivers were overflown, we had adventured either to have gone to the great City of *Manoa*, or at least taken so many of the other Cities and towns nearer at hand, as would have made a royal return: but it pleased not God so much to favour me at this time: if it shall be my lot to prosecute the same, I shall willingly spend my life therein, and if any else shall be enabled thereunto, and conquer the same, I assure him thus much, he shall perform more than was ever done in *Mexico* by *Cortez*, or in *Peru* by *Pizarro*, whereof the one conquered the Empire of *Montezuma*, the other of *Huascar*, and *Atabalipa*, and whatsoever Prince shall possess it, that Prince shall be Lord of more gold, and of a more beautiful Empire, and of more Cities and people, than either the king of Spain, or the great Turk.

But because there may arise many doubts, and how this Empire of *Guiana* is become so populous, and adorned with so many great Cities, Towns, Temples, and treasures, I thought good to make it known, that the Emporer now reigning is descended from those magnificent Princes of *Peru* of whose large territories, of whose policies, conquests, edifices, and riches *Pedro de Cieza, Francisco Lopez*, and others have written large discourses: for when *Francisco Pizarro*, *Diego Almagro* and others conquered the said Empire of *Peru*, and had put to death *Atabalipa* son to *Huaynacapa*, which *Atabalipa* had formerly caused his eldest brother *Huascar* to be slain, one of the younger sons of *Huaynacapa* fled out of *Peru*, and took with him many thousands of those soldiers of the Empire called *Oreiones*, and with those and many others which followed him, he vanquished all that tract and valley of *America* which is situate between the great rivers of *Amazones* and *Baraguan*, otherwise called *Orinoco* and *Maranion*.

The Empire of *Guiana* is directly east from *Peru* towards the sea, and lieth under the Equinoctial line, and it hath more abundance of Gold than any part of *Peru*, and as many or more great Cities than ever *Peru* had when it flourished most: it is governed by the same laws, and the Emperor and people observe the same religion, and the same form and policies in government as was used in *Peru*, not differing in any part: and as I have been assured by such of the *Spaniards* as have seen *Manoa* the imperial City of *Guiana*, which the *Spaniards* call *El Dorado*, that for the greatness, for the riches, and for the excellent seat, it far exceedeth any of the world, at least of so much of the world as is known to the Spanish nation: it is founded upon a lake of salt water of 200 leagues long like unto *mare caspiun*. And if we compare it to that of *Peru*, and but read the report of *Francisco Lopez* and others, it will seem more than credible, and because we may judge of the one by the other, I thought good to insert part of the 120 chapter of *Lopez* in his general history of the *Indies*, wherein he describeth the court and magnificence of *Huaynacapa*, ancestor to the Emperor of *Guiana*, whose very words are these. . .

[*Ralegh quotes the Spanish*]

. . . That is, 'All the vessels of his home, table, kitchen were of Gold and Silver, and the meanest of silver and copper for strength and hardness of the metal. He had in his wardrobe hollow statues of gold which seemed giants, and the figures in proportion and bigness of all the beasts, birds, trees and herbs, that the earth bringeth forth: and of all the fishes that the sea or waters of his kingdom breedeth. He had also ropes, budgets, chests and troughs of gold and silver, heaps of billets of gold that seemed wood, marked out to burn. Finally there was nothing in his country, whereof he had not the counterfeit in gold: Yea and they say, The *Incas* had a garden of pleasure in an Island near *Puna*, where they went to recreate themselves, when they would take the air of the sea, which had all kind of garden herbs, flowers and trees of Gold and Silver, an invention, and magnificence till then never seen. Besides all this, he had an infinite quantity of silver and gold unwrought in *Cuzco* which was lost by the death of *Huascar*, for the Indians hid it, seeing that the Spaniards took it, and sent it into Spain.'

And in the 117 chapter *Francisco Pizarro* caused the Gold and Silver of *Atabalipa* to be weighed, after he had taken it, which Lopez setteth down in these words following. . . 'They found fifty and two thousand marks of good silver, and one million, and three hundred twenty and six thousand and five hundred pesoes of gold.'

Now although these reports may seem strange, yet if we consider the many millions which are daily brought out of *Peru* into Spain, we may easily believe the same, for we find that by the abundant treasure of that country, the Spanish King vexeth all the Princes of Europe, and is become in a few years from a poor king of *Castile* the greatest monarch of this part of the world, and likely every day to increase, if other Princes foreslow the good occasions offered, and suffer him to add this Empire to the rest, which by far exceedeth all the rest: if his gold now endanger us, he will then be unresistible. Such of the Spaniards as afterward endeavoured the conquest thereof (whereof there have been many as shall be declared hereafter) thought that this *Inca* (of whom this Emperor now living is descended) took his way by the river *Amazones*, by that branch which is called *Papamene*, for by that way followed *Orellano* (by the commandment of the Marquis *Pizarro* in the year 1542) whose name the river also beareth this day, which is also by others called *Maragnon*, although *Andrew Thevet* doth affirm that between *Maragnon* and *Amazones* there are 120 leagues: but sure it is that those rivers have one head and beginning, and that *Maragnon* which *Thevet* describeth is but a branch of *Amazones*, or *Orellana*, of which I will speak more in another place. It was also attempted by *Diego Ordaz*, but whether before *Orellana* or after I know not: but it is now little less than 70 years since that *Ordaz* a knight of the order of *Saint Iago* attempted the same: and it was in the year 1542 that *Orellana* discovered the river of *Amazones*; but the first that ever saw *Manoa* was *Johannes Martinez* master of the munition to *Ordaz*. At a port called *Morequito* in *Guiana* there lieth at this day a great anchor of *Ordaz's* ship, and this port is some 300 miles within the land, upon the great river of *Orinoco*.

I rested at this port four days: twenty days after I left the ships at *Curiapan*. The relation of this *Martinez* (who was the first that discovered *Manoa*) his success and end is to be seen in the Chancery of *Saint Juan de puerto rico*, whereof *Berrio* had a copy, which appeared to be the greatest encouragement as well to *Berrio* as to the others that formerly attempted the discovery and conquest. *Orellana* after he failed of the discovery of *Guiana*, by the said river of *Amazones*, passed into Spain, and there obtained a patent of the king for the invasion and conquest, but died by sea about the Islands, and his fleet being severed by tempest, the action for that time proceeded not. *Diego Ordaz* followed the enterprise, and departed Spain with 600 soldiers and 30 horse, who arriving at the coast of *Guiana*, was slain in a mutiny with the most part of such as favoured him, as also of the rebellious part, in so much as his ships perished, and few or none returned, neither was it certainly known what became of the said *Ordaz*, until *Berrio* found the anchor of his ship in the river Orinoco; but it was supposed, and so it is written by *Lopez*, that he perished on the seas, and of other writers diversely conceived and reported. And hereof it came that *Martinez* entered so far within the land and arrived at that city of *Inca* the Emperor, for it chanced that while *Ordaz* with his army rested at the port of *Morequito* (who was either the first or second that attempted *Guiana*), by some negligence, the whole store of powder provided for the service was set on fire, and *Martinez* having the chief charge was condemned by the general *Ordaz* to be executed forthwith: *Martinez* being much favoured by the soldiers had all the mean possible procured for his life, but it could not be obtained in other sort than this: That he should be set in a *Canoa* alone without any victual, only with his arms, and so turned loose into the great river: but it pleased God that the *Canoa* was carried down the stream, and that certain of the *Guianians* met it the same evening, and having not at any time seen any Christian, nor any man of that colour, they carried *Martinez* into the land to be wondered at, and so from town to town, until he came to the great city of *Manoa*, the seat and residence of *Inca* the Emperor. The Emperor after he had beheld him, knew him to be a Christian (for it was not long before that his brethren *Huascar* and *Atabalipa* were vanquished by the Spaniards in *Peru*) and caused him to be lodged in his palace, and well entertained: he lived 7 months in *Manoa*, but not suffered to wander into the country anywhere: he was also brought thither all the way blindfold, led by the Indians, until he came to the entrance of *Manoa* itself, and was 14 or 15 days in the passage: he avowed at his death that he entered the City at *Noon*, and then they uncovered his face, that he travelled all that day till night through the City, and the next day from sun rising to sun setting, ere he came to the palace of *Inca*. After that *Martinez* had lived 7 months in *Manoa*, and began to understand the language of the country, *Inca* asked him whether he desired to return into his own country, or would willingly abide with him: but *Martinez* not desirous to stay, obtained the favour of *Inca* to depart, with whom he sent divers *Guianians* to conduct him to the river of *Orinoco* all loaden with as much gold as they could carry, which he gave to *Martinez* at his departure: but when he was arrived near the river's side, the borderers which are called *Orenoqueponi* robbed him and his *Guianians* of all the treasure (the borderers being at that time at wars with *Inca*, and not conquered) save only of two great bottles of gourds, which were filled with beads of gold curiously wrought, which those *Orenoqueponi* thought had been no other thing than his drink or meat or grain for food with which *Martinez* had liberty to pass, and so in *Canoas* he fell down from the river of *Orinoco* to *Trinidado*, and from thence to *Marguerita*, and so to *Saint Juan de puerto rico*, where remaining a long time for passage into *Spain* he died. In the time of his extreme sickness, and when he was without hope of life, receiving the *Sacrament* at the hands of his Confessor, he delivered these things, with the relation of his travels, and also called for his *Calabaza* or gourds of the gold beads which he gave to the Church and friars to be prayed for. This *Martinez* was he that christened the city of *Manoa*, by the name of *El Dorado*, and as *Berrio* informed me upon this occasion. Those *Guianians* and also the borderers, and all other in that tract which I have seen are marvellous great drunkards, in which vice I think no nation can compare with them: and at the times of their solemn feasts when the Emperor carouseth with his Captains, tributaries, and governors, the manner is thus. All those that pledge him are first stripped naked, and their bodies anointed all over with a kind of white *Balsamum* (by them called *Curcai*) of which there is great plenty and yet very dear amongst them, and it is of all other the most precious, whereof we have had good experience: when they are anointed all over, certain servants of the Emperor having prepared gold made into fine powder blow it through hollow canes upon their naked bodies, until they be all shining from the foot to the head, and in this sort they sit drinking by twenties and hundreds and continue in drunkenness sometimes six or seven days together: the same is also confirmed by a letter written into *Spain* which was intercepted, which master *Robert Dudley* told me he had seen. Upon this sight, the Images of gold in their Temples, the plate, armours, and shields of gold which they use in the wars, he called it *El Dorado*. After *Orellana* who was employed by *Pizarro* afterwards *Marquess Pizarro* conqueror and governor of *Peru*, and the death of *Ordaz* and *Martinez*, one *Pedro de Ursua*, a knight of *Navarre* attempted *Guiana*, taking his way from *Peru*, and built his brigantines upon a river called *Oia*, which riseth to the southward of *Quito*, and is very great: this river falleth into *Amazones*, by which *Ursua* with his companies descended, and came out of that Province which is called *Mutylones*: and it seemeth to me that this Empire is reserved for her Majesty and the *English* nation, by reason of the hard success which all these and other *Spaniards* found in attempting the same . . .

[*Ralegh describes various Spanish attempts to explore Guiana; then speculates on the possibility of reaching it by way of the Amazon.*]

. . . I made enquiry amongst the most ancient and best travelled of the *Orenoqueponi*, and I had knowledge of all the rivers between *Orinoco* and *Amazones*, and was very desirous to understand the truth of those warlike women, because of some it is believed, of others not: And though I digress from my purpose, yet I will set down what hath been delivered me for truth of those women, and I spake with a *Cassique* or Lord of people that told me he had been in the river, and beyond it also. The nations of those women are on the south side of the river in the Provinces of *Topago*, and their chiefest strengths and retreats are in the Islands situate on the south side of the entrance, some 60 leagues within the mouth of the said river. The memories of the like women are very ancient as well in *Africa* as in *Asia*: In *Africa* those that had *Medusa* for *Queen*: others in *Scythia* near the rivers of *Tanais* and *Thermadon*: we find also that *Lampedo* and *Marthesia* were *Queens* of the *Amazons*: in many histories they are verified to have been, and in divers ages and Provinces: But they which are not far from *Guiana* do accompany with men but once in a year, and for the time of one month, which I gather by their relation to be in April. At that time all the Kings of the borders assemble, and the *Queens* of the *Amazons*, and after the Queens have chosen, the rest cast lots for their *Valentines*. This one month, they feast, dance, and drink of their wines in abundance, and the Moon being done, they all depart to their own Provinces. If they conceive, and be delivered of a son, they return him to the father, if of a daughter they nourish it, and retain it, and as many as have daughters send unto the begetters a Present, all being desirous to increase their own sex and kind, but that they cut off the right dug of the breast I do not find to be true. It was farther told me, that if in these wars they took any prisoners that they used to accompany with those also at what time soever, but in the end for certain they put them to death: for they are said to be very cruel and bloodthirsty, especially to such as offer to invade their territories. These *Amazons* have likewise great store of these plates of gold, which they recover by exchange chiefly for a kind of green stones, which the Spaniards call *Piedrus Hijadas*, and we use for spleen stones, and for the disease of the stone we also esteem them: of these I saw divers in *Guiana*, and commonly every king or *Cassique* hath one, which their wives for the most part wear, and they esteem them as great jewels. . .

> [*Ralegh tells the long story of Berrio's attempts to reach Guiana, culminating in a treacherous Indian ambush. Berrio, in revenge, captured and executed the Indian chief Morequito.*]

. . . Among many other trades those *Spaniards* used in *Canoas* to pass to the rivers of *Barema*, *Pawroma*, and *Dissequebe*, which are on the south side of the mouth of Orinoco, and there buy women and children from the *Cannibals*, which are of that barbarous nature, as they will for 3 or 4 hatchets sell the sons and daughters of their own brethren and sisters, and for somewhat more even their own daughters: hereof the Spaniards make great profit, for buying a maid of 12 or 13 years for three or four hatchets, they sell them again at *Marguerita* in the west Indies for 50 and 100 pesoes, which is so many crowns.

The master of my ship *John Douglas* took one of the *Canoas* which came loaden from thence with people to be sold, and the most of them escaped, yet of those he brought, there was one as well favoured, and as well shaped as ever I saw any in England, and afterward I saw many of them, which but for their tawny colour may be compared to any of *Europe*. They also trade in those rivers for bread of *Cassavi*, of which they buy an hundred pound weight for a knife, and sell it at *Marguerita* for ten pesoes. They also recover great store of cotton, brasil wood, and those beds which they call *Hamacas* or brasil beds, wherein in hot countries all the Spaniards use to lie commonly, and in no other, neither did we ourselves while we were there: By means of which trades, for ransom of divers of the *Guianians*, and for exchange of hatchets and knives, *Berrio* recovered some store of gold plates, eagles of gold, and Images of men and divers birds, and despatched his Campmaster for Spain with all that he had gathered, therewith to levy soldiers, and by the show thereof to draw others to the love of the enterprise: and having sent divers

Images as well of men as beasts, birds and fishes so curiously wrought in gold, doubted not but to persuade the king to yield to him some further help, especially for that this land hath never been sacked, the mines never wrought, and in the Indies their works were well spent, and the gold drawn out with great labour and charge: he also despatched messengers to his son in *Nuevo reyno* to levy all the forces he could, and to come down the river of *Orinoco* to *Emeria*, the province of *Carapana*, to meet him: he had also sent to *Santiago de Leon* on the coast of the *Caracas* to buy horses and mules.

After I had thus learned of his proceedings past and purposed: I told him that I had resolved to see *Guiana*, and that it was the end of my journey, and the cause of my coming to *Trinidado*, as it was indeed, (and for that purpose I sent *Jacob Whiddon* the year before to get intelligence, with whom *Berrio* himself had speech at that time, and remembered how inquisitive *Jacob Whiddon* was of his proceedings, and of the country of *Guiana*,) *Berrio* was stricken into a great melancholic sadness, and used all the arguments he could to dissuade me, and also assured the gentlemen of my company that it would be labour lost: and that they should suffer many miseries if they proceeded: And first he delivered that I could not enter any of the rivers with any bark or pinnace, nor hardly with any ship's boat, it was so low, sandy, and full of flats, and that his companies were daily grounded in their *Canoas* which drew but twelve inches water: he further said that none of the country would come to speak with us, but would all fly, and if we followed them to their dwellings, they would burn their own towns, and besides that the way was long, the winter at hand, and that the rivers beginning once to swell, it was impossible to stem the current, and that we could not in those small boats by any means carry victual for half the time, and that (which indeed most discouraged my company) the Kings and Lords of all the borders and of *Guiana* had decreed, that none of them should trade with any Christians for gold, because the same would be their own overthrow, and that for the love of gold the Christians meant to conquer and dispossess them of all together.

Many and most of these I found to be true, but yet I resolving to make trial of all whatsoever happened, directed Captain *George Gifford* my Vice-admiral to take the *Lion's whelp*, and Captain *Calfield* his bark to turn to the eastward, against the breeze what they could possible, to recover the mouth of a river called *Capuri*, whose entrance I had before sent Captain *Whiddon* and *John Douglas* the master, to discover, who found some nine foot water or better upon the flood, and five at low water, to whom I had given instructions that they should anchor at the edge of the shoal, and upon the best of the flood to thrust over, which shoal *John Douglas* buoyed and beaconed for them before: but they laboured in vain, for neither could they turn it up altogether so far to the east, neither did the flood continue so long, but the water fell ere they could have passed the sands, as we after found by a second experience: so as now we must either give over our enterprise, or leaving our ships at adventure 400 mile behind us, to run up in our ship's boats, one barge, and two wherries, but being doubtful how to carry victuals for so long a time in such baubles, or any strength of men, especially for that *Berrio* assured us that his son must be by that time come down with many soldiers, I sent away one *King* master of the *Lion's whelp* with his ship's boat to try another branch of a river in the bottom of the bay of *Guanipa*, which was called *Amana*, to prove if there were water to be found for either of the small ships to enter: But when he came to the mouth of *Amana*, he found it as the rest, but stayed not to discover it throughly, because he was assured by an Indian his guide that the *Cannibals* of *Guanipa* would assail them with many *Canoas*, and that they shot poisoned arrows, so as if he hasted not back they should all be lost.

In the mean time fearing the worst I caused all the Carpenters we had to cut down a *Gallego* boat, which we meant to cast off, and to fit her with banks to row on, and in all things to prepare her the best they could, so as she might be brought to draw but five foot, for so much we had on the bar of *Capuri* at low water. And doubting of *King's* return I sent *John Douglas* again in my long barge, as well to relieve him as also to make a perfect search in the bottom of that bay. For it hath been held for infallible that whatsoever ship or boat shall fall therein, can never disembogue again, by reason of the violent current which setteth into the said bay, as also for that the breeze and easterly wind bloweth directly into the same, of which opinion I have heard *John Hampton* of *Plymouth* one of the greatest experience of *England*, and divers others besides that have traded *Trinidado*.

I sent with *John Douglas* an old *Cassique* of *Trinidado* for a Pilot, who told us that we could not return again by the bay or gulf, but that he knew a by-branch which ran within the land to the Eastward, and that he thought by it we might fall into *Capuri*, and so return in four days: *John Douglas* searched those rivers, and found four goodly entrances, whereof the least was as big as the *Thames* at *Woolwich*, but in the bay thitherward it was shoal and but six foot water, so as we were now without hope of any ship or bark to pass over, and therefore resolved to go on with the boats, and the bottom of the *Gallego*, in which we thrust 60 men: In the *Lion's whelp's* boat and wherry we carried 20. Captain *Calfield* in his wherry carried ten more, and in my barge other ten, which made up a hundred: we had no other means but to carry victual for a month in the same, and also to lodge therein as we could, and to boil and dress our meat. Captain *Gifford* had with him Master *Edward Porter*, captain *Eynos*, and eight more in his wherry with all their victual, weapons, and provisions: Captain *Calfield* had with him my cousin *Butshead Gorges* and eight more. In the galley, of gentlemen and officers myself had captain *Thin*, my cousin *John Grenville*, my nephew *John Gilbert*, captain *Whiddon*, captain *Keymis*, *Edward Hancock*, captain *Clarke*, lieutenant Hughes, *Thomas Upton*, captain *Facy*, *Jerome Ferrar*, *Anthony Wells*, *William Connock*, and about 50 more. We could not learn of *Berrio* any other way to enter but in branches, so far to the windward as it was impossible for us to recover: for we had as much sea to cross over in our wherries as between *Dover* and *Calais*, and in a great billow, the wind and current being both very strong, so as we were driven to go in those small boats directly before the wind into the bottom of the bay of *Guanipa*, and from thence to enter the mouth of some one of those rivers, which *John Douglas* had last discovered, and had with us for Pilot an *Indian* of *Barema*, a river to the south of *Orinoco*, between that and *Amazones*, whose *Canoas* we had formerly taken as he was going from the said *Barema*, laden with *Cassavi* bread to sell at *Marguerita*: this *Arwacan* promised to bring me into the great river of *Orinoco*, but indeed of that which we entered he was utterly ignorant, for he had not seen it in twelve years before, at which time he was very young, and of no judgment, and if God had not sent us another help, we might have wandered a whole year in that labyrinth of rivers, ere we had found any way, either out or in, especially after we were past the ebbing and flowing, which was in four days: for I know all the earth doth not yield the like confluence of streams and branches, the one crossing the other so many times, and all so fair and large, and so like one to another, as no man can tell which to take: and if we went by the Sun or compass hoping thereby to go directly one way or other, yet that way we were also carried in a circle amongst multitudes of Islands, and every Island so bordered with high trees, as no man could see any further than the breadth of the river, or length of the breach: But this it chanced that entering into a river, (which because it had no name we called the river of the *Red cross*, ourselves being the first *Christians* that ever came therein:) the 22 of May as we were rowing up the same, we espied a small *Canoa* with three *Indians*, which (by the swiftness of my barge, rowing with eight oars) I overtook ere they could cross the river, the rest of the people on the banks shadowed under the thick wood gazed on with a doubtful conceit what might befall those three which we had taken: But when they perceived that we offered them no violence, neither entered their *Canoa* with any of ours, nor took out of the *Canoa* any of theirs, they then began to show themselves on the bank's side, and offered to traffic with us for such things as they had, and as we drew near they all stayed, and we came with our barge to the mouth of a little creek which came from their town into the great river.

As we abode there a while, our Indian Pilot called *Ferdinando* would needs go ashore to their village to fetch some fruits, and to drink of their artificial wines, and also to see the place, and to know the Lord of it another time, and took with him a brother of his which he had with him in the journey: when they came to the village of these people, the Lord of the Island offered to lay hands on them, purposing to have slain them both, yielding for reason that this Indian of ours had brought a strange nation into their territory to spoil and destroy them: But the Pilot being quick and of a disposed body slipped their fingers, and ran into the woods, and his brother being the better footman of the two, recovered the creek's mouth, where we stayed in our barge, crying out that his brother was slain, with that we set hands on one of them that was next us, a very old man, and brought him into the barge, assuring him that if we had not our Pilot again, we would presently cut off his head. This old man being resolved that he should pay the loss of the other, cried out to those in the woods to save *Ferdinando* our Pilot, but they followed him notwithstanding, and hunted after him upon the foot with their Deer dogs, and with so main a cry that all the woods echoed with the shout they made, but at last this poor chased Indian recovered the river side, and got upon a tree, and as we were coasting, leaped down and swam to the barge half dead with fear; but our good hap was, that we kept the other old Indian, which we handfasted to redeem our Pilot withal, for being natural of those rivers, we assured ourselves he knew the way better than any stranger could, and indeed, but for this chance I think we had never found the way either to *Guiana*, or back to our ships: for *Ferdinando* after a few days knew nothing at all, nor which way to turn, yea and many times the old man himself was in great doubt which river to take. Those people which dwell in these broken Islands and drowned lands are generally called *Tivitivas*, there are of them two sorts, the one called *Ciawani*, and the other *Waraweete*.

The great river of *Orinoco* or *Baraguan* hath nine branches which fall out on the north side of his own main mouth: on the south side it hath seven other fallings into the sea, so it disembogueth by 16 arms in all, between Islands and broken ground, but the Islands are very great, many of them as big as the Isle of *Wight* and bigger, and many less: from the first branch on the north to the last of the south it is at least 100 leagues, so as the river's mouth is no less than 300 miles wide at his entrance into the sea, which I take to be far bigger than that of *Amazones*: all those that inhabit in the mouth of this river upon the several north branches are these *Tivitivas*, of which there are two chief Lords which have continual wars one with the other: the Islands which lie on the right hand are called *Pallamos*, and the land on the left *Hororotomaka*, and the river by which *John Douglas* returned within the land from *Amana* to *Capuri*, they call *Macuri*.

These *Tivitivas* are a very much goodly people and very valiant, and have the most manly speech and most deliberate that ever I heard of what nation soever. In the summer they have houses on the ground as in other places: In the winter they dwell upon the trees, where they build very artificial towns and villages, as it is written in the Spanish story of the *West Indies*, that those people do in the low lands near the gulf of *Uraba*: for between *May* and *September* the river of *Orinoco* riseth thirty foot upright, and then are those Islands overflown twenty foot high above the level of the ground, saving some few raised grounds in the middle of them: and for this cause they are enforced to live in this manner. They never eat of any thing that is set or sown, and as at home they use neither planting nor other manurance, so when they come abroad they refuse to feed of aught, but of that which nature without labour bringeth forth. They use the tops of *Palmitos* for bread, and kill Deer, fish and porks for the rest of their sustenance, they have also many sorts of fruits that grow in the woods, and great variety of birds and fowl.

And if to speak of them were not tedious and vulgar, surely we saw in those passages of very rare colours and forms, not elsewhere to be found, for as much as I have either seen or read. Of these people those that dwell upon the branches of *Orinoco* called *Capuri* and *Macureo*, are for the most part Carpenters of *Canoas*, for they make the most and fairest houses, and sell them into *Guiana* for gold, and into *Trinidado* for *Tobacco*, in the excessive taking whereof, they exceed all nations, and notwithstanding the moistness of the air in which they live, the hardness of their diet, and the great labours they suffer to hunt, fish, and fowl for their living, in all my life either in the Indies or in Europe did I never behold a more goodly or better favoured people, or a more manly. They were wont to make war upon all nations, and especially on the *Cannibals*, so as none durst without a good strength trade by those rivers, but of late they are at peace with their neighbours, all holding the *Spaniards* for a common enemy. When their commanders die, they use great lamentation, and when they think the flesh of their bodies is putrified, and fallen from the bones, then they take up the carcass again, and hang it in the *Cassique's* house that died, and deck his skull with feathers of all colours, and hang all his gold plates about the bones of his arms, thighs, and legs. Those nations which are called *Arwacas* which dwell on the south of *Orinoco* (of which place and nation our Indian Pilot was) are dispersed in many other places, and do use to beat the bones of their Lords into powder, and their wives and friends drink it all in their several sorts of drinks.

After we departed from the port of these *Ciawani*, we passed up the river with the flood, and anchored the ebb, and in this sort we went onward. The third day that we entered the river our *Galley* came on ground, and stuck so fast, as we thought that even there our discovery had ended, and that we must have left 60 of our men to have inhabited like rooks upon trees with those nations: but the next morning, after we had cast out all her ballast, with tugging and hauling to and fro, we got her afloat, and went on: At four days' end we fell into as goodly a river as ever I beheld, which was called the great *Amana*, which ran more directly without windings and turnings than the other. But soon after the flood of the sea left us, and we enforced either by main strength to row against a violent current, or to return as wise as we went out, we had then no shift but to persuade the companies that it was but two or three days' work, and therefore desired them to take pains, every gentleman and others taking their turns to row, and to spell one the other at the hour's end. Every day we passed by goodly branches of rivers, some falling from the west, others from the east into *Amana*, but those I leave to the description in the *Chart* of discovery, where every one shall be named with his rising and descent. When three days more were overgone, our companies began to despair, the weather being extreme hot, the river bordered with very high trees that kept away the air, and the current against us every day stronger than other: But we ever more commanded our Pilots to promise an end the next day, and used it so long as we were driven to assure them from four reaches of the river to three, and so to two, and so to the next reach: but so long we laboured as many days were spent, and so driven to draw ourselves to harder allowance, our bread even at the last, and no drink at all: and our men and our selves so wearied and scorched, and doubtful withal whether we should ever perform it or no, the heat increasing as we drew towards the line; for we were now in five degrees.

The farther we went on (our victual decreasing and the air breeding great faintness) we grew weaker and weaker when we had most need of strength and ability, for hourly the river ran more violently than other against us, and the barge, wherries, and ship's boat of Captain *Gifford* and Captain *Calfield*, had spent all their provisions, so as we were brought into despair and discomfort, had we not persuaded all the company that it was but only one day's work more to attain the land where we should be relieved of all we wanted, and if we returned that we were sure to starve by the way, and that the world would also laugh us to scorn. On the banks of these rivers were divers sorts of fruits good to eat, flowers and trees of that variety as were sufficient to make ten volumes of herbals, we relieved ourselves many times with the fruits of the country, and sometimes with fowl and fish: we saw birds of all colours, some carnation, some crimson, orange, tawny, purple, green, watchet, and of all other sorts both simple and mixed, as it was unto us a great good passing of the time to behold them, besides the relief we found by killing some store of them with our fouling pieces, without which, having little or no bread and less drink, but only the thick and troubled water of the river, we had been in a very hard case.

Our old Pilot of the *Ciawani* (whom, as I said before, we took to redeem *Ferdinando*,) told us, that if we would enter a branch of the river on the right hand with our barge and wherries, and leave the *Galley* at anchor the while in the great river, he would bring us to a town of the *Arwacas* where we should find store of bread, hens, fish, and of the country wine, and persuaded us that departing from the *Galley* at noon, we might return ere night: I was very glad to hear this speech, and presently took my barge, with eight musketeers, Captain *Gifford's* wherry, with himself and four musketeers, and Captain *Calfield* with his wherry and as many, and so we entered the mouth of this river, and because we were persuaded that it was so near, we took no victual with us at all: when we had rowed three hours, we marvelled we saw no sign of any dwelling, and asked the Pilot where the town was, he told us a little farther: after three hours more the *Sun* being almost set, we began to suspect that he led us that way to betray us, for he confessed that those Spaniards which fled from *Trinidado*, and also those that remained with *Carapana* in *Emeria*, were joined together in some village upon that river. But when it grew towards night, and we demanding where the place was, he told us but four reaches more: when we had rowed four and four, we saw no sign, and our poor water-men even heart broken, and tired, were ready to give up the ghost; for we had now come from the *Galley* near forty miles.

At the last we determined to hang the Pilot, and if we had well known the way back again by night, he had surely gone, but our own necessities pleaded sufficiently for his safety: for it was as dark as pitch, and the river began so to narrow itself, and the trees to hang over from side to side, as we were driven with arming swords to cut a passage through those branches that covered the water. We were very desirous to find this town hoping of a feast, because we made but a short breakfast aboard the *Galley* in the morning, and it was now eight a clock at night, and our stomachs began to gnaw apace: but whether it was best to return or go on, we began to doubt, suspecting treason in the Pilot more and more: but the poor old Indian ever assured us that it was but a little farther, and but this one turning, and that turning, and at last about one a clock after midnight we saw a light, and rowing towards it, we heard the dogs of the village. When we landed we found few people, for the Lord of that place was gone with divers *Canoas* above 400 miles off, upon a journey towards the head of *Orinoco* to trade for gold, and to buy women of the *Cannibals*, who afterward unfortunately passed by us as we rode at an anchor in the port of *Morequito* in the dark of night, and yet came so near us, as his *Canoas* grated against our barges: he left one of his company at the port of *Morequito*, by whom we understood that he had brought thirty young women, divers plates of gold, and had great store of fine pieces of cotton cloth, and cotton beds. In his house we had good store of bread, fish, hens, and Indian drink, and so rested that night, and in the morning after we had traded with such of his people as came down, we returned towards our *Galley*, and brought with us some quantity of bread, fish, and hens.

On both sides of this river, we passed the most beautiful country that ever mine eyes beheld: and whereas all that we had seen before was nothing but woods, prickles, bushes, and thorns, here we beheld plains of twenty miles in length, the grasses short and green, and in divers parts groves of trees by themselves, as if they had been by all the art and labour in the world so made of purpose: and still as we rowed, the Deer came down feeding by the water's side, as if they had been used to a keeper's call. Upon this river there were great store of fowl, and of many sorts: we saw in it divers sorts of strange fishes, and of marvellous bigness, but for *Lagartos* it exceeded, for there were thousands of those ugly serpents, and the people call it for the abundance of them the river of *Lagartos*, in their language. I had a *Negro* a very proper young fellow, that leaping out of the *Galley* to swim in the mouth of this river, was in all our sights taken and devoured with one of those *Lagartos*. In the meanwhile our companies in the *Galley* thought we had been all lost, (for we promised to return before night) and sent the *Lion's Whelp's* ship's boat with

Captain *Whiddon* to follow us up the river, but the next day after we had rowed up and down some four score miles, we returned, and went on our way, up the great river, and when we were even at the last cast for want of victuals, Captain *Gifford* being before the *Galley* and the rest of the boats, seeking out some place to land upon the banks to make fire, espied four *Canoas* coming down the river, and with no small joy caused his men to try the uttermost of their strengths, and after a while two of the 4 gave over, and ran themselves ashore, every man betaking himself to the fastness of the woods, the two other lesser got away, while he landed to lay hold on these, and so turned into some by-creek, we knew not whither: those *Canoas* that were taken were loaden with bread, and were bound for *Marguerita* in the west Indies, while those Indians (called *Arwacas*) purposed to carry thither for exchange: But in the lesser, there were three Spaniards, who having heard of the defeat of their governor in *Trinidado*, and that we purposed to enter *Guiana*, came away in those *Canoas*: one of them was a *Cavallero*, as the Captain of the *Arwacas* after told us, another a soldier, and the third a refiner.

In the meantime, nothing on the earth could have been more welcome to us next unto gold, than the great store of very excellent bread which we found in these *Canoas*, for now our men cried, 'let us go on, we care not how far'. After that Captain *Gifford* had brought the two *Canoas* to the *Galley*, I took my barge, and went to the bank's side with a dozen shot, where the *Canoas* first ran themselves ashore, and landed there, sending out Captain *Gifford* and Captain *Thin* on one hand, and Captain *Calfield* on the other, to follow those that were fled into the woods, and as I was creeping through the bushes, I saw an Indian basket hidden, which was the refiner's basket, for I found in it, his quicksilver, saltpetre, and divers things for the trial of metals, and also the dust of such ore as he had refined, but in those *Canoas* which escaped there was a good quantity of ore and gold. I then landed more men, and offered 500 pound to what soldier soever could take one of those 3 Spaniards that we thought were landed. But our labours were in vain in that behalf, for they put themselves into one of the small *Canoas*: and so while the greater *Canoas* were in taking, they escaped: but seeking after the Spaniards, we found the *Arwacas* hidden in the woods which were pilots for the Spaniards, and rowed their *Canoas*: of which I kept the chiefest for a Pilot, and carried him with me to *Guiana*, by whom I understood, where and in what countries the Spaniards had laboured for gold, though I made not the same known to all: for when the springs began to break, and the rivers to raise themselves so suddenly as by no means we could abide the digging of any mine, especially for that the richest are defended with rocks of hard stone, which we call the *White spar*, and that it required both time, men, and instruments fit for such a work, I thought it best not to hover thereabouts, lest if the same had been perceived by the company, there would have been by this time many barks and ships set out, and perchance other nations would also have gotten of ours for Pilots, so as both ourselves might have been prevented, and all our care taken for good usage of the people been utterly lost, by those that only respect present profit, and such violence or insolence offered, as the nations which are borderers would have changed their desire of our love and defence, into hatred and violence. And for any longer stay to have brought a more quantity (which I hear hath been often objected) whosoever had seen or proved the fury of that river after it began to arise, and had been a month and odd days as we were from hearing aught from our ships, leaving them meanly manned, above 400 miles off, would perchance have turned somewhat sooner than we did, if all the mountains had been gold, or rich stones: And to say the truth all the branches and small rivers which fell into *Orinoco* were raised with such speed, as if we waded them over the shoes in the morning outward, we were covered to the shoulders homeward the very same day: and to stay to dig out gold with our nails, had been *Opus laboris*, but not *Ingenii*: such a quantity as would have served our turns we could not have had, but a discovery of the mines to our infinite disadvantage we had made, and that could have been the best profit of farther search or stay, for those mines are not easily broken, nor opened in haste, and I could have returned a good quantity of gold ready cast, if I had not shot at another mark, than present profit.

This *Arwacan* Pilot with the rest, feared that we would have eaten them, or otherwise have put them to some cruel death, for the Spaniards to the end that none of the people in the passage towards *Guiana* or in *Guiana* itself might come to speech with us, persuaded all the nations, that we were man eaters, and *Cannibals*: but when the poor men and women had seen us, and that we gave them meat, and to every one something or other, which was rare and strange to them, they began to conceive the deceit and purpose of the *Spaniards*, who indeed (as they confessed) took from them both their wives, and daughters daily, and used them for satisfying of their own lusts, especially such as they took in this manner by strength. But I protest before the majesty of the living God, that I neither know nor believe, that any of our company one or other, ever knew any of their women, and yet we saw many hundreds, and had many in our power, and of those very young, and excellently favoured which came among us without deceit, stark naked.

Nothing got us more love among them than this usage, for I suffered not any man to take from any of the nations so much as a *Pina*, or a *Potato* root, without giving them contentment, nor any man so much as to offer to touch any of their wives or daughters: which course, so contrary to the Spaniards (who tyrannise over them in all things) drew them to admire her Majesty, whose commandment I told them it was, and also wonderfully to honour our nation. But I confess it was a very impatient work to keep the meaner sort from spoil and stealing, when we came to their houses, which because in all I could not prevent, I caused my Indian interpreter at every place when we departed, to know of the loss or wrong done, and if aught were stolen or taken by violence, either the same was restored, and the party punished in their sight, or else it was paid for to their uttermost demand. They also much wondered at us, after they heard that we had slain the Spaniards at *Trinidado*, for they were before resolved, that no nation of *Christians* durst abide their presence, and they wondered more when I had made them known of the great overthrow that her Majesty's army and fleet had given them of late years in their own countries.

After we had taken in this supply of bread, with divers baskets of roots which were excellent meat, I gave one of the *Canoas* to the *Arwacas*, which belonged to the Spaniards that were escaped, and when I had dismissed all but the Captain (who by the *Spaniards* was christened *Martin*) I sent back in the same *Canoa* the old *Ciawan*, and *Ferdinando* my first Pilot, and gave them both such things as they desired, with sufficient victual to carry them back, and by them wrote a letter to the ships, which they promised to deliver, and performed it, and then I went on with my new hired Pilot *Martin* and *Arwacan*: but the next or second day after, we came aground again with our galley, and were like to cast her away, with all our victual and provision, and so lay on the sand one whole night, and were far more in despair at this time to free her than before, because we had no tide of flood to help us, and therefore feared that all our hopes would have ended in mishaps: but we fastened an anchor upon the land, and with main strength drew her off: and so the 15 day we discovered afar off the mountains of *Guiana* to our great joy, and towards the evening had a slant of a northerly wind that blew very strong, which brought us in sight of the great river of *Orinoco*, out of which this river descended wherein we were: we descried afar off three other *Canoas* as far as we could discern them, after whom we hastened with our barge and wherries, but two of them passed out of sight, and the third entered up the great river, on the right hand to the westward, and there stayed out of sight, thinking that we meant to take the way eastward towards the province of *Carapana*, for that way the Spaniards keep, not daring to go upwards to *Guiana*, the people in those parts being all their enemies, and those in the *Canoas* thought us to have been those Spaniards that were fled from *Trinidado*, and had escaped killing: and when we came so far down as the opening of that branch into which they slipped, being near them with our barge and wherries, we made after them, and ere they could land, came within call, and by our interpreter told them what we were, wherewith they came back willingly aboard us: and of such fish and *Tortuga's* eggs as they had gathered, they gave us, and promised in the morning to bring the Lord of that part with them, and to do us all other services they could.

That night we came to an anchor at the parting of three goodly rivers (the one was the river of *Amana* by which we came from the north, and ran athwart towards the south, the other two were of *Orinoco* which crossed from the west and ran to the sea towards the east) and landed upon a fair sand, where we found thousands of *Tortuga's* eggs, which are very wholesome meat, and greatly restoring, so as our men were now well filled and highly contented both with the fare, and nearness of the land of *Guiana* which appeared in sight. In the morning there came down according to promise the Lord of that border called *Toparimaca*, with some thirty or forty followers, and brought us divers sorts of fruits, and of his wine, bread, fish, and flesh, whom we also feasted as we could, at least he drank good Spanish wine (whereof we had a small quantity in bottles) which above all things they love. I conferred with this *Toparimaca* of the next way to *Guiana*, who conducted our galley and boats to his own port, and carried us from thence some mile and a half to his town, where some of our captains caroused of his wine till they were reasonable pleasant, for it is very strong with pepper, and the juice of divers herbs, and fruits digested and purged, they keep it in great earthen pots of ten or twelve gallons very clean and sweet, and are themselves at their meetings and feasts the greatest carousers and drunkards of the world: when we came to his town we found two *Cassiques*, whereof one of them was a stranger that had been up the river in trade, and his boats, people, and wife encamped at the port where we anchored, and the other was of that country a follower of *Toparimaca*: they lay each of them in a cotton *Hamaca*, which we call brasil beds, and two women attending them with six cups and a little ladle to fill them, out of an earthen pitcher of wine, and so they drank each of them three of those cups at a time, one to the other, and in this sort they drink drunk at their feasts and meetings.

That *Cassique* that was a stranger had his wife staying at the port where we anchored, and in all my life I have seldom seen a better favoured woman: She was of good stature, with black eyes, fat of body, of an excellent countenance, her hair almost as long as herself, tied up again in pretty knots, and it seemed she stood not in that awe of her husband, as the rest, for she spake and discoursed, and drank among the gentlemen and captains, and was very pleasant, knowing her own comeliness, and taking great pride therein. I have seen a Lady in England so like her, as but for the difference in colour I would have sworn might have been the same.

The seat of this town of *Toparimaca* was very pleasant, standing on a little hill, in an excellent prospect, with goodly gardens a mile compass round about it, and two very fair and large ponds of excellent fish adjoining. This town is called *Arowacai*: the people are of the nation called *Nepoios*, and are followers of *Carapana*. In that place I saw very aged people, that we might perceive all their sinews and veins without any flesh, and but even as a case covered only with skin. The Lord of this place gave me an old man for Pilot, who was of great experience and travel, and knew the river most perfectly both by day and night, and it shall be requisite for any man that passeth it to have such a Pilot, for it is four, five, and six miles over in many places, and twenty miles in other places, with wonderful eddies, and strong currents, many great Islands and divers shoals, and many dangerous rocks, and besides upon any increase of wind so great a billow, as we were sometimes in great peril of drowning in the galley, for the small boats durst not come from the shore, but when it was very fair.

The next day we hasted thence, and having an easterly wind to help us, we spared our arms from rowing: for after we entered *Orinoco*, the river lieth for the most part east and west, even from the sea unto *Quito* in *Peru*. This river is navigable with ships little less than 1000 miles, and from the place where we entered it may be sailed up in small pinnaces to many of the best parts of *Nuevo reyno de granado*, and of *Popayan*: and from no place may the cities of these parts of the Indies be so easily taken and invaded as from hence. All that day we sailed up a branch of that river, having on the left hand a great Island, which they call *Assapana*, which may contain some five and twenty miles in length, and 6 miles in breadth, the great body of the river running on the other side of this Island: Beyond that middle branch there is also another Island in the river, called *Iwana*, which is twice as big as the Isle of *Wight*, and beyond it, and between it and the main of *Guiana*, runneth a third branch of *Orinoco* called *Arraroopana*: all three are goodly branches, and all navigable for great ships. I judge the river in this place to be at least thirty miles broad, reckoning the Islands which divide the branches in it, for afterwards I sought also both the other branches.

After we reached to the head of this Island, called *Assapana*, a little to the westward on the right hand there opened a river which came from the north, called *Europa*, and fell into the great river, and beyond it, on the same side, we anchored for that night, by another Island six miles long, and two miles broad, which they call *Ocaywita*: From hence in the morning we landed two *Guianians*, which we found in the town of *Toparimaca*, that came with us, who went to give notice of our coming to the Lord of that country called *Putyma*, a follower of *Topiawari*, chief Lord of *Arromaia*, who succeeded *Morequito*, whom (as you have heard before) *Berrio* put to death, but his town being far within the land, he came not unto us that day, so as we anchored again that night near the banks of another Island, of bigness much like the other, which they call *Putapayma*, on the main land, over against which Island was a very high mountain called *Oecope*: we coveted to anchor rather by these Islands in the river, than by the main, because of the *Tortugas'* eggs, which our people found on them in great abundance, and also because the ground served better for us to cast our nets for fish, the main banks being for the most part stony and high, and the rocks of a blue metalline colour, like unto the best steel ore, which I assuredly take it to be: of the same blue stone are also divers great mountains, which border this river in many places.

The next morning towards nine of the clock, we weighed anchor, and the breeze increasing, we sailed always west up the river, and after a while opening the land on the right side, the country appeared to be champaign, and the banks showed very perfect red: I therefore sent two of the little barges with captain *Gifford*, and with him captain *Thin*, captain *Calfield*, my cousin *Grenville*, my nephew *John Gilbert*, captain *Eynos*, master *Edward Porter*, and my cousin *Butshead Gorges*, with some few soldiers, to march over the banks of that red land, and to discover what manner of country it was on the other side, who at their return found it all a plain level, as far as they went or could discern, from the highest tree they could get upon: And my old Pilot, a man of great travel brother to the *Cassique Toparimaca* told me, that those were called the plains of *Sayma*, and that the same level reached to *Cumana*, and *Caracas* in the west Indies, which are 120 leagues to the north, and that there inhabited four principal nations. The first were the *Sayma*, the next *Assawi*, the third and greatest the *Wikiri*, by whom *Pedro Hernandez de Serpa* before mentioned was overthrown, as he passed with three hundred horse from *Cumana* towards *Orinoco*, in his enterprise of *Guiana*, the fourth are called *Aroras*, and are as black as *Negros*, but have smooth hair, and these are very valiant, or rather desperate people, and have the most strong poison on their arrows, and most dangerous of all nations, of which poison I will speak somewhat being a digression not unnecessary.

There was nothing whereof I was more curious, than to find out the true remedies of these poisoned arrows, for besides the mortality of the wound they make, the party shot endureth the most insufferable torment in the world, and abideth a most ugly and lamentable death, sometimes dying stark mad, sometimes their bowels breaking out of their bellies and are presently discoloured, as black as pitch, and so unsavoury, as no man can endure to cure, or to attend them: And it is more strange to know, that in all this time there was never Spaniard, either by gift or torment that could attain to the true knowledge of the cure, although they have martyred and put to invented torture I know not how many of them. But every one of these Indians know it not, no not one among thousands, but their soothsayers and priests, who do conceal it, and only teach it but from the father to the son.

Those medicines which are vulgar, and serve for the ordinary poison, are made of the juice of a root called *Tupara*: the same also quencheth marvellously the heat of burning fevers, and healeth inward wounds, and broken veins, that bleed within the body. But I was more beholding to the *Guianians* than any other, for *Antonio de Berrio* told me that he could never attain to the knowledge thereof, and yet they taught me the best way of healing as well thereof, as of all other poisons. Some of the Spaniards have been cured in ordinary wounds, of the common poisoned arrows with the juice of garlic: but this is a general rule for all men that shall hereafter travel the Indies where poisoned arrows are used, that they must abstain from drink, for if they take any liquor into their body, as they shall be marvellously provoked thereunto by drought, I say, if they drink before the wound be dressed, or soon upon it, there is no way with them but present death.

And so I will return again to our journey which for this third day we finished, and cast anchor again near the continent, on the left hand between two mountains, the one called *Aroami*, and the other *Aio*: I made no stay here but till midnight, for I feared hourly lest any rain should fall, and then it had been impossible to have gone any further up, notwithstanding that there is every day a very strong breeze, and easterly wind. I deferred the search of the country on *Guiana* side, till my return down the river. The next day we sailed by a great Island, in the middle of the river, called *Manoripano*, and as we walked a while on the Island, while the *Galley* got ahead of us, there came after us from the main, a small *Canoa* with seven or eight *Guianians*, to invite us to anchor at their port, but I deferred it till my return; It was that *Cassique* to whom those *Nepoios* went, which came with us from the town of *Toparimaca*: and so the fifth day we reached as high up as the Province of *Arromaia* the country of *Morequito* whom *Berrio* executed, and anchored to the west of an Island called *Murrecotima*, ten miles long and five broad: and that night the *Cassique Aramiari*, (to whose town we made our long and hungry voyage out of the river of *Amana*) passed by us.

The next day we arrived at the port of *Morequito*, and anchored there, sending away one of our Pilots to seek the king of *Aromaia*, uncle to *Morequito*, slain by *Berrio* as aforesaid. The next day following, before noon he came to us on foot from his house, which was 14 English miles, (himself being 110 years old) and returned on foot the same day, and with him many of the borderers, with many women and children, that came to wonder at our nation, and to bring us down victual, which they did in great plenty, as venison, pork, hens, chickens, fowl, fish, with divers sorts of excellent fruits, and roots, and great abundance of *Pinas*, the princess of fruits, that grow under the *Sun*, especially those of *Guiana*. They brought us also store of bread, and of their wine, and a sort of *Paraquitos*, no bigger than wrens, and of all other sorts both small and great: one of them gave me a beast called by the Spaniards *Armadilla*, which they call *Cassacam*, which seemeth to be all barred over with small plates somewhat like to a *Renocero*, with a white horn growing in his hinder parts, as big as a great hunting horn, which they use to wind instead of a trumpet. *Monardus* writeth that a little of the powder of that horn put into the ear, cureth deafness.

After this old king had rested a while in a little tent, that I caused to be set up, I began by my interpreter to discourse with him on the death of *Morequito* his predecessor, and afterward of the Spaniards, and ere I went any farther I made him know the cause of my coming thither, whose servant I was, and that the Queen's pleasure was, I should undertake the voyage for their defence, and to deliver them from the tyranny of the Spaniards, dilating at large (as I had done before to those of *Trinidado*) her Majesty's greatness, her justice, her charity to all oppressed nations, with as many of the rest of her beauties and virtues, as either I could express, or they conceive, all which being with great admiration attentively heard, and marvellously admired, I began to sound the old man as touching *Guiana*, and the state thereof, what sort of commonwealth it was, how governed, of what strength and policy, how far it extended, and what nations were friends or enemies adjoining, and finally of the distance, and way to enter the same: he told me that himself and his people with all those down the river towards the sea, as far as *Emeria* the Province of *Carapana*, were of *Guiana*, but that they called themselves *Orenoqueponi*, because they bordered the great river of *Orinoco*, and that all the nations between the river and those mountains in sight called *Wacarima*, were of the same cast and appellation: and that on the other side of those mountains of *Wacarima* there was a large plain (which after I discovered in my return) called the valley of *Amariocapana*, in all that valley the people were also of the ancient *Guianians*. I asked what nations those were which inhabited on the further side of those mountains, beyond the valley of *Amariocapana*, he answered with a great sigh (as a man which had inward feeling of the loss of his country and liberty, especially for that his eldest son was slain in a battle on that side of the mountains, whom he most entirely loved,) that he remembered in his father's lifetime when he was very old, and himself a young man that there came down into that large valley of *Guiana*, a nation from so far off as the *Sun* slept, (for such were his own words,) with so great a multitude as they could not be numbered nor resisted, and that they wore large coats, and hats of crimson colour, which colour he expressed, by showing a piece of red wood, wherewith my tent was supported, and that they were called *Oreiones*, and *Epuremei*, those that had slain and rooted out so many of the ancient people as there were leaves in the wood upon all the trees, and had now made themselves Lords of all, even to that mountain foot called *Curaa*, saving only of two nations, the one called *Iwarawaqueri*, and the other *Cassipagotos*, and that in the last battle fought between the *Epuremei*, and the *Iwarawaqueri*, his eldest son was chosen to carry to the aid of the *Iwarawaqueri*, a great troop of the *Orenoqueponi*, and was there slain, with all his people and friends, and that he had now remaining but one son: and farther told me that those *Epuremei* had built a great town called *Macureguarai* at the said mountain foot, at the beginning of the great plains of *Guiana*, which have no end: and that their houses have many rooms, one over the other, and that therein the great king of the *Oreiones* and *Epuremei* kept three thousand men to defend the borders against them, and withal daily to invade and slay them: but that of late years since the Christians offered to invade his territories, and those frontiers, they were all at peace, and traded one with another, saving only the *Iwarawaqueri*, and those other nations upon the head of the river of *Caroli*, called *Cassipagotos* which we afterwards discovered, each one holding the

Spaniard for a common enemy.

After he had answered thus far, he desired leave to depart, saying that he had far to go, that he was old, and weak, and was every day called for by death, which was also his own phrase: I desired him to rest with us that night, but I could not entreat him, but he told me that at my return from the country above, he would again come to us, and in the meantime provide for us the best he could, of all that his country yielded: the same night he returned to *Orocotona* his own town, so as he went that day 28 miles, the weather being very hot, the country being situate between 4 and 5 degrees of the *Equinoctial*. This *Topiawari* is held for the proudest, and wisest of all the *Orenoqueponi*, and so he behaved himself towards me in all his answers at my return, as I marvelled to find a man of that gravity and judgment, and of so good discourse, that had no help of learning nor breed.

The next morning we also left the port and sailed westward up the river, to view the famous river called *Caroli*, as well because it was marvellous of itself, as also for that I understood it led to the strongest nations of all the frontiers, that were enemies to the *Epuremei*, which are subjects to *Inca*, Emperor of *Guiana*, and *Manoa*, and that night we anchored at another Island called *Caiama*, of some five or six miles in length, and the next day arrived at the mouth of *Caroli*, when we were short of it as low or further down as the port of *Morequito* we heard the great roar and fall of the river, but when we came to enter with our barge and wherries thinking to have gone up some forty miles to the nations of the *Cassipagotos*, we were not able with a barge of eight oars to row one stone's cast in an hour, and yet the river as broad as the Thames at Woolwich, and we tried both sides, and the middle, and every part of the river, so as we encamped upon the banks adjoining, and sent off our *Orenoqueponi* (which came with us from *Morequito*) to give knowledge to the nations upon the river of our being there, and that we desired to see the Lords of *Canuaria*, which dwelt within the province upon that river, making them know that we were enemies to the Spaniards, (for it was on this river's side that *Morequito* slew the *Friar*, and those nine Spaniards which came from *Manoa*, the City of *Inca*, and took from them 40000 pesoes of Gold) so as the next day there came down a Lord or *Cassique* called *Wanuretona* with many people with him, and brought all store of provisions to entertain us, as the rest had done. And as I had before made my coming down known to *Topiawari*, so did I acquaint this *Cassique* therewith, and how I was sent by her Majesty for the purpose aforesaid, and gathered also what I could of him touching the estate of *Guiana*, and I found that those also of

Caroli were not only enemies to the Spaniards but most of all to the *Epuremei*, which abound in Gold, and by this *Wanuretona*, I had knowledge that on the head of this river were three mighty nations, which were seated on a great lake, from whence this river descended, and were called *Cassipagotos*, *Eparagotos*, and *Arawagotos*, and that all those either against the Spaniards, or the *Epuremei* would join with us, and that if we entered the land over the mountains of *Curaa*, we should satisfy ourselves with gold and all other good things: he told us farther of a nation called *Iwarawaqueri* before spoken of, that held daily war with the *Epuremei* that inhabited *Macureguarai* the first civil town of *Guiana*, of the subjects of *Inca* the Emperor.

Upon this river one Captain *George*, that I took with *Berrio* told me there was a great silver mine, and that it was near the banks of the said river. But by this time as well *Orinoco*, *Caroli*, as all the rest of the rivers were risen four or five foot in height, so as it were not possible by the strength of any men, or with any boat whatsoever to row into the river against the stream. I therefore sent Captain *Thin*, Captain *Grenville*, my nephew *John Gilbert*, my cousin *Butshead Gorges*, Captain *Clarke*, and some 30 shot more to coast the river by land, and to go to a town some twenty miles over the valley called *Amnatapoi*, and if they found guides there, to go farther towards the mountain foot to another great town, called *Capurepana*, belonging to a *Cassique* called *Haharacoa* (that was a nephew to old *Topiawari* king of *Arromaia* our chiefest friend) because this town and province of *Capurepana* adjoined to *Macureguarai*, which was the frontier town of the Empire: and the meanwhile myself with Captain *Gifford*, Captain *Calfield*, *Edward Hancock*, and some half a dozen shot marched over land to view the strange overfalls of the river of *Caroli*, which roared so far off, and also to see the plains adjoining, and the rest of the province of *Canuri*: I sent also Captain *Whiddon*, *William Connock*, and some eight shot with them, to see if they could find any mineral stone alongst the river side. When we ran to the tops of the first hills of the plains adjoining to the river, we beheld that wonderful breach of waters, which ran down *Caroli*: and might from that mountain see the river how it ran in three parts, above twenty miles off, and there appeared some ten or twelve overfalls in sight, every one as high over the other as a Church tower, which fell with that fury, that the rebound of waters made it seem, as if it had been all covered over with a great shower of rain: and in some places we took it at the first for a smoke that had risen over some great town. For mine own part I was well persuaded from thence to have returned, being a very ill footman, but the rest were all so desirous to go near the said strange thunder of waters, as they drew me on by little and little, till we came into the next valley, where we might better discern the same. I never saw a more beautiful country, nor more lively prospects, hills so raised here and there over the valleys, the river winding into divers branches, the plains adjoining without bush or stubble, all fair green grass, the ground of hard sand easy to march on, either for horse or foot, the deer crossing in every path, the birds towards the evening singing on every tree with a thousand several tunes, cranes and herons of white, crimson, and carnation perching on the river's side, the air fresh with a gentle easterly wind, and every stone that we stooped to take up, promised either gold or silver by his complexion. Your Lordships shall see of many sorts, and I hope some of them cannot be bettered under the sun, and yet we had no means but with our daggers and fingers to tear them out here and there, the rocks being most hard of that mineral spar aforesaid, and is like a flint, and is altogether as hard or harder, and besides the veins lie a fathom or two deep in the rocks. But we wanted all things requisite save only our desires, and good will to have performed more if it had pleased God. To be short when both our companies returned, each of them brought also several sorts of stones that appeared very fair, but were such as they found loose on the ground, and were for the most part but coloured, and had not any gold fixed in them, yet such as had no judgment or experience kept all that glistered, and would not be persuaded but it was rich because of the lustre, and brought of those, and of *Marquesites* withal, from *Trinidado*, and have delivered of those stones to be tried in many places, and have thereby bred an opinion that all the rest is of the same: yet some of these stones I showed afterward to a Spaniard of the *Caracas* who told me that it was *El Madre del oro*, and that the mine was farther in the ground. But it shall be found a weak policy in me, either to betray myself, or my Country with imaginations, neither am I so far in love with that lodging, watching, care, peril, diseases, ill savours, bad fare, and many other mischiefs that accompany these voyages, as to woo myself again into any of them, were I not assured that the sun covereth not so much riches in any part of the earth. Captain *Whiddon*, and our Surgeon *Nicholas Millechap* brought me a kind of stones like *Sapphires*, what they may prove I know not, I showed them to some of the *Orenoqueponi*, and they promised to bring me to a mountain, that had of them very large pieces growing Diamond-wise: whether it be Crystal of the mountain, *Bristol Diamond*, or *Sapphire* I do not yet know, but I hope the best, sure I am that the place is as likely as those from whence all the rich stones are brought, and in the same height or very near. On the left hand of this river *Caroli* are seated those nations which are called *Iwarawakeri* before remembered, which are enemies of the *Epuremei*: and on the head of it adjoining to the great lake *Cassipa*, are situate those other nations which also resist *Inca*, and the *Epuremei*, called *Cassepagotos*, *Eparegotos*, and *Arrawagotos*. I farther understood that this lake of *Cassipa* is so large, as it is above one day's journey for one of their *Canoas* to cross, which may be some 40 miles, and that therein fall divers rivers, and that great store of grains of Gold are found in the summer time when the lake falleth by the banks, in those branches. There is also another goodly river beyond *Caroli* which is called *Arui*, which also runneth through the lake *Cassipa*, and falleth into *Orinoco* farther west, making all that land between *Caroli* and *Arui* an Island, which is likewise a most beautiful country. Next unto *Arui* there are two rivers *Atoica* and *Caora*, and on that branch which is called *Caora* are a nation of people, whose heads appear not above their shoulders, which though it may be thought a mere fable, yet for mine own part I am resolved it is true, because every child in the provinces of *Arromaia* and *Canuri* affirm the same: they are called *Ewaipanoma*: they are reported to have their eyes in their shoulders, and their mouths in the middle of their breasts, and that a long train of hair groweth backward between their shoulders. The son of *Topiawari*, which I brought with me into England told me that they are the most mighty men of all the land, and use bows, arrows, and clubs thrice as big as any of *Guiana*, or of the *Orenoqueponi*, and that one of the *Iwarawakeri* took a prisoner of them the year before our arrival there, and brought him into the borders of *Arromaia* his father's Country: And farther when I seemed to doubt of it, he told me that it was no wonder among them, but that they were as great a nation, and as common, as any other in all the provinces, and had of late years slain many hundreds of his father's people, and of other nations their neighbours, but it was not my chance to hear of them till I was come away, and if I had but spoken one word of it while I was there, I might have brought one of them with me to put the matter out of doubt. Such a nation was written of by *Mandeville*, whose reports were held for fables many years, and yet since the East *Indies* were discovered, we find his relations true of such things as heretofore were held incredible: whether it be true or no the matter is not great, neither can there be any profit in the imagination, for mine own part I saw them not, but I am resolved that so many people did not all combine, or forethink to make the report.

When I came to *Cumana* in the west *Indies* afterwards, by chance I spake with a spaniard dwelling not far from thence, a man of great travel, and after he knew that I had been in *Guiana*, and so far directly west as *Caroli*, the first question he asked me was whether I had seen any of the *Ewaipanoma*, which are those without heads: who being esteemed a most honest man of his word, and in all things else, told me that he had seen many of them: I may not name him because it may be for his disadvantage, but he is well known to *Monsieur Mucheron's* son of London, and to *Peter Mucheron* merchant of the *Flemish* ship that was there in trade, who also heard what he avowed to be true of those people. The fourth river to the west of *Caroli* is *Casnero* which falleth into *Orinoco* on this side of *Amapaia*, and that river is greater than *Danubius*, or any of *Europe*: it riseth on the south of *Guiana* from the mountains which divide *Guiana* from *Amazones*, and I think it to be navigable many hundred miles: but we had no time, means, nor season of the year, to search those rivers for the causes aforesaid, the winter being come upon us, although the winter and summer as touching cold and heat differ not, neither do the trees ever sensibly lose their leaves, but have always fruit either ripe or green, and most of them both blossoms, leaves, ripe fruit, and green at one time: But their winter only consisteth of terrible rains, and overflowings of the rivers, with many great storms and gusts, thunder, and lightnings, of which we had our fill, ere we returned. On the North side, the first river that falleth into *Orinoco* is *Cari*, beyond it on the same side is the river of *Limo*, between these two is a great nation of *Cannibals*, and their chief town beareth the name of the river and is called *Acamacari*: at this town is a continual market of women for 3 or 4 hatchets a piece, they are bought by the *Arwacas*, and by them sold into the west Indies. To the west of *Limo* is the river *Pao*, beyond it *Caturi*, beyond that *Voari* and *Capuri* which falleth out of the great river of *Meta*, by which *Berrio* descended from *Nuevo reyno de granada*. To the westward of *Capuri* is the province of *Amapaia*, where *Berrio* wintered, and had so many of his people poisoned with the tawny water of the marshes of the *Anebas*. Above *Amapaia*, towards *Nuevo reyno* fall in, *Meta*, *Pato*, and *Cassanar*: to the west of these towards the provinces of the *Ashaguas* and *Catetios* are the rivers of *Beta*, *Dawney*, and *Ubarro*, and towards the frontier of *Peru* are the provinces of *Thomebamba* and *Caximalta*: adjoining to *Quito* in the North of *Peru* are the rivers of *Guiacar* and *Goauar*: and on the other side of the said mountains the river of *Papamene* which descendeth into *Maragnon* or *Amazones* passing through the province of *Mutylones* where *Don Pedro de Osua* who was slain by the traitor *Aguirre* before rehearsed, built his *Brigandines*, when he sought *Guiana* by the way of *Amazones*. Between *Dawney* and *Beta* lieth a famous Island in *Orinoco* now called *Baraquan* (For above *Meta* it is not known by the name of *Orinoco*) which is called

Athule, beyond which, ships of burden cannot pass by reason of a most forcible overfall, and Current of waters: but in the eddy all smaller vessels may be drawn even to *Peru* itself: But to speak of more of these rivers without the description were but tedious, and therefore I will leave the rest to the desciption. This river of *Orinoco* is navigable for ships little less than 1000 miles, and for lesser vessels near 2000. By it (as aforesaid) *Peru*, *Nuevo reyno*, and *Popayan*, may be invaded: it also leadeth to that great Empire of *Inca*, and to the provinces of *Ampaia* and *Anebas* which abound in gold: his branches of *Cosnero*, *Manta*, *Caora* descend from the middle land and valley, which lieth between the eastern province of *Peru* and *Guiana*; and it falls into the sea between *Maragnon* and *Trinidado* in two degrees and a half, all which your Honours shall better perceive in the general description of *Guiana*, *Peru*, *Nuevo reyno*, the kingdom of *Popayan*, and *Roidas*, with the province of *Venezuala*, to the bay of *Uraba* behind *Cartagena*, westward: and to *Amazones* southward. While we lay at anchor on the coast of *Canuri*, and had taken knowledge of all the nations upon the head and branches of this river, and had found out so many several people, which were enemies to the *Epuremei*, and the new Conquerors: I thought it time lost to linger any longer in that place, especially for that the fury of *Orinoco* began daily to threaten us with dangers in our return, for no half day passed, but the river began to rage and overflow very fearfully, and the rains came down in terrible showers, and gusts in great abundance: and withal, our men began to cry out for want of shift, for no man had place to bestow any other apparel than that which he wore on his back, and was thoroughly washed on his body for the most part ten times in one day: and we had now been well near a month, every day passing to the westward, farther and farther from our ships. We therefore turned towards the east, and spent the rest of the time in discovering the river towards the sea, which we had not yet viewed, and which was most material. . .

[*Ralegh discusses with Topiawari, a tribal chief, the possibility of their getting to the 'golden parts of Guiana' and to the towns of the 'apparelled people of Inca'. He turns down the idea that he should leave fifty of his men there until he could return, being worried about the arrival of Spanish reinforcements. Ensured of tribal support in a future campaign, the party heads downstream.*]

. . . When it grew towards sunset, we entered a branch of a river that fell into *Orinoco* called *Winicapora*, where I was informed of the mountain of Crystal, to which in truth for the length of the way, and the evil season of the year, I was not able to march, nor abide any longer upon the journey: we saw it afar off and it appeared like a white Church tower of an exceeding height: There falleth over it a mighty river which toucheth no part of the side of the mountain, but rusheth over the top of it, and falleth to the ground with a terrible noise and clamour, as if 1000 great bells were knocked one against another. I think there is not in the world so strange an overfall, nor so wonderful to behold: *Berrio* told me that it hath Diamonds and other precious stones on it, and that they shined very far off: but what it hath I know not, neither durst he or any of his men ascend to the top of the said mountain, those people adjoining being his enemies (as they were) and the way to it so impassable.

Upon this river of *Winecapora* we rested a while, and from thence marched into the Country to a town called after the name of the river, whereof the chief was one *Timitwara* who also offered to conduct me to the top of the said mountain called *Wacarima*: But when we came in first to the house of the said *Timitwara*, being upon one of their feast days, we found them all as drunk as beggars, and the pots walking from one to another without rest: we that were weary, and hot with marching, were glad of the plenty, though a small quantity satisfied us, their drink being very strong and heady, and so rested ourselves awhile; after we had fed, we drew ourselves back to our boats, upon the river, and there came to us all the Lords of the Country, with all such kind of victual as the place yielded, and with their delicate wine of *Pinas*, and with abundance of hens, and other provisions, and of those stones which we call spleen stones. We understood by these chieftains of *Winicapora*, that their Lord *Carapana* was departed from *Emeria* which was now in sight, and that he was fled to *Cairamo*, adjoining to the mountains of *Guiana*, over the valley called *Amariocapana*, being persuaded by those ten Spaniards which lay at his house, that we would destroy him, and his country.

But after these *Cassiqui* of *Winicapora* and *Saporatona* his followers perceived our purpose, and saw that we came as enemies to the Spaniards only, and had not so much as harmed any of those nations, no though we found them to be of the Spaniards' own servants, they assured us that *Carapana* would be as ready to serve us, as any of the Lords of the provinces, which we had passed; and that he durst do no other till this day but entertain the Spaniards, his country lying so directly in their way, and next of all other to any entrance that should be made in *Guiana* on that side.

And they farther assured us, that it was not for fear of our coming that he was removed, but to be acquitted of those Spaniards or any other that should come hereafter. For the province of *Cairoma* is situate at the mountain foot, which divideth the plains of *Guiana*, from the countries of the *Orenoqueponi*: by means whereof if any should come in our absence into his towns, he would slip over the mountains into the plains of *Guiana* among the *Epuremei*, where the Spaniards durst not follow him without great force.

But in mine opinion, or rather I assure myself, that *Carapana* (being a notable wise and subtle fellow, a man of one hundred years of age, and therefore of great experience) is removed, to look on, and if he find that we return strong, he will be ours, if not, he will excuse his departure to the Spaniards, and say it was for fear of our coming.

We therefore thought it bootless to row so far down the stream, or to seek any farther for this old fox: and therefore from the river of *Waricapana* (which lieth at the entrance of *Emeria*), we turned again, and left to the Eastward those 4 rivers which fall from out of the mountains of *Emeria* and *Orinoco*, which are *Waracapari*, *Coirama*, *Akaniri*, and *Iparoma*: below these 4 are also these branches and mouths of *Orinoco*, which fall into the East sea, whereof the first is *Araturi*, the next *Amacura*, the third *Barima*, the fourth *Wana*, the fifth *Morooca*, the sixth *Paroma*, the last *Wijmi*: beyond them, there fall out of the land between *Orinoco* and *Amazones* 14 rivers which I forbear to name, inhabited by the *Arwacas* and *Cannibals*.

It is now time to return towards the North, and we found it a wearisome way back, from the borders of *Emeria*, to recover up again to the head of the river *Carerupana*, by which we descended, and where we parted from the galley, which I directed to take the next way to the Port of *Toparimaca*, by which we entered first.

All the night it was stormy and dark, and full of thunder and great showers, so as we were driven to keep close by the banks in our small boats, being all heartily afraid both of the billow, and terrible Currents of the river. By the next morning we recovered the mouth of the river of *Cumaca*, where we left Captain *Eynos* and Edward Porter to attend the coming of Captain *Keymis* over land: but when we entered the same, they had heard no news of his arrival, which bred in us a great doubt what might be become of him: I rowed up a league or two farther into the river, shooting off pieces all the way, that he might know of our being there: And the next morning we heard them answer us also with a piece: we took them aboard us, and took our leave of *Putijma* their guide, who of all others most lamented our departure, and offered to send his son with us into England, if we could have stayed till he had sent back to his town: but our hearts were cold to behold the great rage and increase of *Orinoco*, and therefore departed, and turned toward the west, till we had recovered the parting of the 3 branches aforesaid, that we might put down the stream after the Galley.

The next day we landed on the Island of *Assapana*, (which divideth the river from that branch by which we went down to *Emeria*) and there feasted ourselves with that beast which is called *Armadilla* presented unto us before at *Winicapora*, and the day following we recovered the galley at anchor at the port of *Toparimaca*, and the same evening departed with very foul weather and terrible thunder, and showers, for the winter was come on very far: the best was, we went no less than 100 miles a day, down the river: but by the way we entered, it was impossible to return, for that the river of *Amana*, being in the bottom of the bay of *Guanipa*, cannot be sailed back by any means, both the breeze and current of the sea were so forcible, and therefore we followed a branch of *Orinoco* called *Capuri*, which entered into the sea eastward of our ships, to the end we might bear with them before the wind, and it was not without need, for we had by that way as much to cross of the main sea, after we came to the river's mouth as between *Gravelin* and *Dover*, in such boats as your Honours have heard.

To speak of what passed homeward were tedious, either to describe or name any of the rivers, Islands, or villages of the *Tivitivas* which dwell on trees, we will leave all those to the general map: And to be short, when we were arrived at the sea side then grew our greatest doubt, and the bitterest of all our journey forepassed, for I protest before God, that we were in a most desperate estate: for the same night which we anchored in the mouth of the river of *Capuri*, where it falleth into the sea, there arose a mighty storm, and the river's mouth was at least a league broad, so as we ran before night close under the land with our small boats, and brought the Galley as near as we could, but she had as much ado to live as could be, and there wanted little of her sinking, and all those in her: for mine own part, I confess, I was very doubtful which way to take, either to go over in the pestered Galley, there being but six foot water over the sands, for two leagues together, and that also in the channel, and she drew five: or to adventure in so great a billow, and in so doubtful weather, to cross the seas in my barge. The longer we tarried the worse it was, and therefore I took Captain *Gifford*, Captain *Calfield*, and my cousin *Grenville*, into my barge, and after it cleared up, about midnight we put ourselves into God's keeping, and thrust out into the sea, leaving the Galley at anchor, who durst not adventure but by daylight. And so being all very sober, and melancholy, one faintly cheering another to show courage, it pleased God that the next day about nine of the clock, we descried the Island of *Trinidado*, and steering for the nearest part of it, we kept the shore till we came to

Curiapan, where we found our ships at anchor, than which, there was never to us a more joyful sight.

Now that it hath pleased God to send us safe to our ships, it is time to leave *Guiana* to the Sun, whom they worship, and steer away towards the north: I will therefore in a few words finish the discovery thereof. Of the several nations which we found upon this discovery I will once again make repetition, and how they are affected. At our first entrance into *Amana*, which is one of the outlets of *Orinoco*, we left on the right hand of us in the bottom of the bay, lying directly against *Trinidado*, a nation of inhuman *Cannibals*, which inhabit the rivers of *Guanipa* and *Berbese*; in the same bay there is also a third river which is called *Areo*, which riseth on *Paria* side towards *Cumana*, and that river is inhabited with the *Wikiri*, whose chief town upon the said river is *Sayma*; In this bay there are no more rivers, but these three before rehearsed, and the four branches of *Amana*, all which in the winter thrust so great abundance of water into the sea, as the same is taken up fresh, two or three leagues from the land. In the passages towards *Guiana*, (that is, in all those lands which the eight branches of *Orinoco* fashion into Islands) there are but one sort of people called *Tivitivas*, but of two castes as they term them, the one called *Ciawary*, the other *Waraweeti*, and those war one with the other.

On the hithermost part of *Orinoco*, as at *Toparimaca*, and *Winicapora*, those are of a nation called *Nepoios*, and are of the followers of *Carapana*, Lord of *Emeria*. Between *Winicapora* and the port of *Morequito* which standeth in *Aromaia*, and all those in the valley of *Amariocapana* are called *Orenoqueponi*, and did obey *Morequito*, and are now followers of *Topiawari*. Upon the river of *Caroli*, are the *Canuri*, which are governed by a woman (who is inheritrix of that province) who came far off to see our nation, and asked me divers questions of her Majesty, being much delighted with the discourse of her Majesty's greatness, and wondering at such reports as we truly made of her highness' many virtues. And upon the head of *Caroli*, and on the lake of *Cassipa*, are the three strong nations of the *Cassipagotos*. Right south into the land are the *Capurepani*, and *Emparepani*, and beyond these adjoining to *Macureguarai*, (the first City of *Inca*), are the *Iwarawakeri*: all these are professed enemies to the Spaniards, and to the rich *Epuremei* also. To the west of *Caroli* are divers nations of *Cannibals*, and of those *Ewaipanoma* without heads. Directly west are the *Amapaias* and *Anebas*, which are also marvellous rich in gold. The rest towards *Peru* we will omit. On the north of *Orinoco*, between it and the west Indies are the *Wikiri*, *Saymi*, and the rest before spoken of, all mortal enemies to the Spaniards. On the south side of the main mouth of *Orinoco*, are the *Arwacas*: and beyond them the *Cannibals*: and to the south of them the *Amazons*.

To make mention of the several beasts, birds, fishes, fruits, flowers, gums, sweet woods, and of their several religions and customs, would for the first require as many volumes as those of *Gesnerus*, and for the rest another bundle of *Decades*. The religion of the *Epuremei* is the same which the *Incas*, Emperors of *Peru* used, which may be read in *Cieca*, and other Spanish stories, how they believe the immortality of the Soul, worship the Sun, and bury with them alive their best beloved wives and treasure, as they likewise do in *Pegu* in the east Indies, and other places. The *Orenoqueponi* bury not their wives with them, but their Jewels, hoping to enjoy them again. The *Arwacas* dry the bones of their Lords, and their wives and friends drink them in powder. In the graves of the *Peruvians*, the Spaniards found their greatest abundance of treasure: The like also is to be found among these people in every province. They have all many wives, and the Lords fivefold to the common sort: their wives never eat with their husbands, nor among the men, but serve their husbands at meals, and afterwards feed by themselves. Those that are past their younger years, make all their bread and drink, and work their cotton beds, and do all else of service and labour, for the men do nothing but hunt, fish, play, and drink, when they are out of the wars.

I will enter no further into discourse of their manners, laws and customs: and because I have not myself seen the cities of *Inca*, I cannot avow on my credit what I have heard, although it be very likely, that the Emperor *Inca* hath built and erected as magnificent palaces in *Guiana*, as his ancestors did in *Peru*, which were for their riches and rareness most marvellous and exceeding all in *Europe*, and I think of the world, *China* excepted, which also the Spaniards (which I had) assured me to be of truth, as also the nations of the borderers, who being but *Salvaios*, to those of the Inland, do cause much treasure to be buried with them, for I was informed of one of the *Cassiqui* of the valley of *Amariocapana* which had buried with him a little before our arrival, a chair of Gold most curiously wrought, which was made either in *Macureguarai* adjoining, or in *Manoa*: But if we should have grieved them in their religion at the first, before they had been taught better, and have digged up their graves, we had lost them all: and therefore I held my first resolution, that her majesty should either accept or refuse the enterprise, ere any thing should be done that might in any sort hinder the same. And if *Peru* had so many heaps of Gold, whereof those *Incas* were Princes, and that they delighted so much therein, no doubt but this which now liveth and reigneth in *Manoa*, hath the same humour, and I am assured hath more abundance of Gold, within his territory, than all *Peru*, and the west Indies.

For the rest, which myself have seen I will promise these things that follow and know to be true. Those that are desirous to discover and to see many nations, may be satisfied within this river, which bringeth forth so many arms and branches leading to several countries, and provinces, above 2000 miles east and west, and 800 miles south and north; and of these, the most either rich in Gold, or in other merchandises. The common soldier shall here fight for gold, and pay himself instead of pence, with plates of half a foot broad, whereas he breaketh his bones in other wars for provant and penury. Those commanders and Chieftains, that shoot at honour, and abundance, shall find there more rich and beautiful cities, more temples adorned with golden Images, more sepulchres filled with treasure, than either *Cortez* found in *Mexico*, or *Pizarro* in *Peru*: and the shining glory of this conquest will eclipse all those so far extended beams of the Spanish nation. There is no country which yieldeth more pleasure to the Inhabitants, either for these common delights of hunting, hawking, fishing, fowling, and the rest, than *Guiana* doth. It hath so many plains, clear rivers, abundance of Pheasants, Partridges, Quails, Rails, Cranes, Herons, and all other fowl: Deer of all sorts, Porks, Hares, Lions, Tigers, Leopards, and divers other sorts of beasts, either for chase, or food. It hath a kind of beast called *Cama*, or *Anta*, as big as an English beef, and in great plenty.

To speak of the several sorts of every kind, I fear would be troublesome to the Reader, and therefore I will omit them, and conclude that both for health, good air, pleasure, and riches, I am resolved it cannot be equalled by any region either in the east or west. Moreover the country is so healthful, as 100 persons and more, which lay (without shift most sluttishly, and were every day almost melted with heat in rowing and marching, and suddenly wet again with great showers, and did eat of all sorts of corrupt fruits, and made meals of fresh fish without seasoning, of *Tortugas*, of *Lagartos*, and of all sorts good and bad, without either order or measure, and besides lodged in the open air every night) we lost not any one, nor had one ill disposed to my knowledge, nor found any *Callentura*, or other of those pestilent diseases which dwell in all hot regions, and so near the Equinoctial line.

Where there is store of gold, it is in effect needless to remember other commodities for trade: but it hath towards the south part of the river, great quantities of Brasil wood, and of divers berries, that dye a most perfect crimson and Carnation: And for painting, all *France*, *Italy*, or the east Indies yield none such: For the more the skin is washed, the fairer the colour appeareth, and with which, even those brown and tawny women spot themselves, and colour their cheeks. All places yield abundance of Cotton, of silk, of *Balsamum*, and of those kinds most excellent, and never known in Europe: of all sorts of gums, of *Indian* pepper: and what else the countries may afford within the land we know not, neither had we time to abide the trial, and search. The soil besides is so excellent and so full of rivers, as it will carry sugar, ginger, and all those other commodities, which the west Indies hath.

The navigation is short, for it may be sailed with an ordinary wind in six weeks, and in the like time back again, and by the way neither lee shore, Enemy's coast, rocks, nor sands, all which in the voyages to the West Indies, and all other places, we are subject unto, as the channel of *Bahama*, coming from the West Indies, cannot be passed in the Winter, and when it is at the best, it is a perilous and fearful place: The rest of the Indies for calms, and diseases very troublesome, and the *Bermudas* a hellish sea for thunder, lightning, and storms.

This very year there were seventeen sail of Spanish ships lost in the channel of *Bahama*, and the great *Philip* like to have sunk at the *Bermudas* was put back to Saint *Juan de puerto rico*. And so it falleth out in that Navigation every year for the most part, which in this voyage are not to be feared: for the time of the year to leave *England*, is best in July, and the Summer in *Guiana* is in October, November, December, January, February, and March, and then the ships may depart thence in April, and so return again into England in June, so as they shall never be subject to Winter weather, either coming, going, or staying there, which for my part, I take to be one of the greatest comforts and encouragements that can be thought on, having (as I have done) tasted in this voyage by the west Indies so many Calms, so much heat, such outrageous gusts, foul weather, and contrary winds.

To conclude, *Guiana* is a Country that hath yet her Maidenhead, never sacked, turned, nor wrought, the face of the earth hath not been torn, nor the virtue and salt of the soil spent by manurance, the graves have not been opened for gold, the mines not broken with sledges, nor their Images pulled down out of their temples. It hath never been entered by any army of strength, and never conquered or possessed by any Christian Prince. It is besides so defensible, that if two forts be builded in one of the Provinces which I have seen, the flood setteth so near the bank, where the channel also lieth, that no ship can pass up, but within a Pike's length of the Artillery, first of the one, and afterwards of the other: Which two Forts will be a sufficient Guard both to the Empire of *Inca*, and to an hundred other several kingdoms, lying within the said River, even to the city of *Quito* in *Peru*.

There is therefore great difference between the easiness of the conquest of *Guiana*, and the defence of it being conquered, and the West or East Indies: *Guiana* hath but one entrance by the sea (if it have that) for any vessels of burden, so as whosoever shall first possess it, it shall be found unaccessible for any Enemy, except he come in Wherries, Barges, or *Canoas*, or else in flat bottomed boats, and if he do offer to enter it in that manner, the woods are so thick 200 miles together upon the rivers of such entrance, as a mouse cannot sit in a boat unhit from the bank. By land it is more impossible to approach, for it hath the strongest situation of any region under the Sun, and is so environed with impassable mountains on every side, as it is impossible to victual any company in the passage, which hath been well proved by the Spanish nation, who since the conquest of *Peru* have never left five years free from attempting this Empire, or discovering some way into it, and yet of 23 several gentlemen, knights, and noble men, there was never any that knew which way to lead an army by land, or to conduct ships by sea, anything near the said country. *Orellana*, of which the river of *Amazones* taketh name was the first, and *Don Antonio de Berrio* (whom we displanted) the last: and I doubt much, whether he himself or any of his, yet know the best way into the said Empire. It can therefore hardly be regained, if any strength be formerly set down, but in one or two places, and but two or three crumsters or galleys built, and furnished upon the river within: The west Indies hath many ports, watering places, and landings, and nearer than 300 miles to *Guiana*, no man can harbour a ship, except he know one only place, which is not learned in haste, and which I will undertake there is not any one of my companies that knoweth, whosoever hearkened most after it.

Besides by keeping one good fort, or building one town of strength the whole Empire is guarded, and whatsoever companies shall be afterwards planted within the land, although in twenty several provinces, those shall be able all to reunite themselves upon any occasion either by the way of one river, or be able to march by land without either wood, bog, or mountain: whereas in the west Indies there are few towns, or provinces that can succour or relieve one the other, either by land or sea: By land the countries are either desert, mountains, or strong Enemies: By sea, if any man invade to the Eastward, those to the west cannot in many months turn against the breeze and easterwind, besides the Spaniards are therein so dispersed, as they are nowhere strong, but in *Nueva Hispania* only: the sharp mountains, the thorns, and poisoned prickles, the sandy and deep ways in the valleys, the smothering heat and air, and want of water in other places, are their only and best defence, which (because those nations that invade them are not victualled or provided to stay, neither have any place to friend adjoining) do serve them instead of good arms and great multitudes.

The west Indies were first offered her Majesty's Grandfather by *Columbus* a stranger, in whom there might be doubt of deceit, and besides it was then thought incredible that there were such and so many lands and regions never written of before. This Empire is made known to her Majesty by her own vassal, and by him that oweth to her more duty than an ordinary subject, so that it shall ill sort with the many graces and benefits which I have received to abuse her highness, either with fables or imaginations. The country is already discovered, many nations won to her Majesty's love and obedience, and those Spaniards which have latest and longest laboured about the conquest, beaten out, discouraged and disgraced, which among these nations were thought invincible. Her majesty may in this enterprise employ all those soldiers and gentlemen that are younger brethren, and all captains and Chieftains that want employment, and the charge will be only the first setting out in victualling and arming them: for after the first or second year I doubt not but to see in London a Contractation house of more receipt for *Guiana*, than there is now in Seville for the West indies.

And I am resolved that if there were but a small army afoot in *Guiana*, marching towards *Manoa* the chief City of Inca, he would yield her Majesty by composition so many hundred thousand pounds yearly, as should both defend all enemies abroad, and defray all expenses at home, and that he would besides pay a garrison of 3000 or 4000 soldiers very royally to defend him against other nations: For he cannot but know, how his predecessors, yea how his own great uncles *Huascar* and *Atabalipa* sons to *Huanacapa* Emperor of *Peru*, were (while they contended for the Empire) beaten out by the Spaniards, and that both of late years, and ever since the said conquest, the Spaniards have sought the passages and entry of his country: and of their cruelties used to the borderers he cannot be ignorant. In which respects no doubt but he will be brought to tribute with great gladness, if not, he hath neither shot nor Iron weapon in all his Empire, and therefore may easily be conquered.

And I farther remember that *Berrio* confessed to me and others (which I protest before her Majesty of God to be true) that there was found among prophecies in *Peru* (at such time as the Empire was reduced to the Spanish obedience) in their chiefest temples, amongst divers others which foreshowed the loss of the said Empire, that from *Inglatierra* those *Incas* should be again in time to come restored, and delivered from the servitude of the said Conquerors. And I hope, as we with these few hands have displanted the first garrison, and driven them out of the said country, so her Majesty will give order for the rest, and either defend it, and hold it as tributary, or conquer and keep it as Empress of the same. For whatsoever Prince shall possess it, shall be greatest, and if the king of Spain enjoy it, he will become unresistible. Her Majesty hereby shall confirm and strengthen the opinions of all nations, as touching her great and princely actions. And where the south border of *Guiana* reacheth to the Dominion and Empire of the *Amazons*, those women shall hereby hear the name of a virgin, which is not only able to defend her own territories and her neighbours, but also to invade and conquer so great Empires and so far removed.

To speak more at this time, I fear would be but troublesome: I trust in God, this being true, will suffice, and that he which is king of all kings and Lord of Lords, will put it into her heart which is Lady of Ladies to possess it, if not, I will judge those men worthy to be kings thereof, that by her grace and leave will undertake it of themselves.

The History of the World

The Preface

How unfit and how unworthy a choice I have made of myself, to undertake a work of this mixture; mine own reason, though exceeding weak, hath sufficiently resolved me. For had it been begotten then with my first dawn of day, when the light of common knowledge began to open itself to my younger years: and before any wound received, either from Fortune or Time: I might yet well have doubted, that the darkness of Age and Death would have covered over both It and Me, long before the performance. For, beginning with the Creation: I have proceeded with the History of the World; and lastly purposed (some few sallies excepted) to confine my discourse, within this our renowned Island of Great Britain. I confess that it had better sorted with my disability, the better part of whose times are run out in other travails; to have set together (as I could) the unjointed and scattered frame of our English Affairs, than of the universal: in whom had there been no other defect (who am all defect) than the time of the day, it were enough; the day of a tempestuous life, drawn on to the very evening ere I began. But those inmost, and soul-piercing wounds, which are ever aching while uncured: with the desire to satisfy those few friends, which I have tried by the fire of adversity; the former enforcing, the latter persuading; have caused me to make my thoughts legible, and myself the Subject of every opinion wise or weak.

To the world I present them, to which I am nothing indebted: neither have others that were, (Fortune changing) sped much better in any age. For, Prosperity and Adversity have evermore tied and untied vulgar affections. And as we see it in experience, that dogs do always bark at those they know not; and that it is in their nature to accompany one another in those clamours; so is it with the inconsiderate multitude. Who, wanting that virtue which we call Honesty in all men, and that especial gift of God which we call Charity in Christian men; condemn, without hearing; and wound, without offence given: led thereunto by uncertain report only; which his *Majesty* truly acknowledgeth for the Author of all lies. *Blame no man* (saith Siracides) *before thou have inquired the matter:*

understand first, and then reform righteously. . . Rumour is without witness, without judge, malicious and deceivable. This vanity of vulgar opinion it was that gave *St Augustine* Argument to affirm, that he feared the praise of good men, and detested that of the evil. And herein no man hath given a better rule than this of *Seneca . . . Let us satisfy our own consciences, and not trouble ourselves with fame: be it never so ill, it is to be despised, so we deserve well.*

For myself, if I have in anything served my country, and prized it before my private; the general acceptation can yield me no other profit at this time, than doth a fair sunshine day to a Seaman after shipwreck; and the contrary no other harm than an outrageous tempest after the port attained. I know that I lost the love of many, for my fidelity towards Her, whom I must still honour in the dust; though further than the defence of Her excellent person I never persecuted any man. Of those that did it, and by what device they did it: He that is the Supreme Judge of all the world, hath taken the account; so as for this kind of suffering, I must say with *Seneca*, *Mala opinio*, *bene parta*, *delectat*.

As for other men: if there be any that have made themselves Fathers of that fame, which hath been begotten for them, I can neither envy at such their purchased glory, nor much lament mine own mishap in that kind; but content myself to say with *Virgil*, *Sic vos non vobis*, in many particulars.

To labour other satisfaction, were an effect of frenzy, not of hope: seeing it is not Truth, but Opinion, that can travel the world without a passport. For were it otherwise; and were there not as many internal forms of the mind as there are external figures of men; there were then some possibility, to persuade by the mouth of one Advocate, even Equity alone.

But such is the multiplying and extensive virtue of dead earth, and of that breath-giving life which God hath cast upon Slime and Dust: as that among those that were, of whom we read and hear, and among those that are, whom we see and converse with; every one hath received a several picture of face, and every one a diverse picture of mind; every one a form apart, every one a fancy and cogitation differing: there being nothing wherein Nature so much triumpheth, as in dissimilitude. From whence it cometh, that there is found so great diversity of opinions; so strong a contrariety of inclinations; so many natural and unnatural; wise, foolish; manly, and childish affections, and passions in Mortal Men. For it is not the visible fashion and shape of plants, and of reasonable Creatures, that makes the difference, of working in the one, and of condition in the other; but the form internal.

And though it hath pleased God, to reserve the Art of reading men's thoughts to himself: yet, as the fruit tells the name of the Trees; so do the outward works of men (so far as their cogitations are acted) give us whereof to guess at the rest. Nay, it were not hard to express the one by the other, very near the life: did not craft in many, fear in the most, and the world's love in all, teach every capacity, according to the compass it hath, to qualify and mask over their inward deformities for a time. Though it be also true. . . *No man can long continue masked in a counterfeit behaviour: the things that are forced for pretences, having no ground of truth, cannot long dissemble their own natures.* Neither can any man (saith *Plutarch*) so change himself, but that his heart may be sometime seen at his tongue's end.

In this great discord and dissimilitude of reasonable creatures, if we direct ourselves to the Multitude . . . *The common people are evil Judges of honest things*, and *whose wisdom* (saith Ecclesiastes) *is to be despised*; if to the better sort; every understanding hath a peculiar judgment, by which it both censureth other men, and valueth itself. And therefore unto me it will not seem strange, though I find these my worthless papers torn with Rats: seeing the slothful Censurers of all ages, have not spared to tax the Reverend Fathers of the Church,. with Ambition; the severest men to themselves, with Hypocrisy; the greatest lovers of Justice, with Popularity; and those of the truest valour and fortitude, with vainglory. But of these natures which lie in wait to find fault, and to turn good in to evil, seeing *Solomon* complained long since: and that the very age of the world renders it every day after other more malicious; I must leave the professors to their easy ways of reprehension, than which there is nothing of more facility.

To me it belongs in the first part of this preface, following the common and approved custom of those who have left the memories of time past to after ages; to give, as near as I can, the same right to History which they have done. Yet seeing therein I should but borrow other men's words; I will not trouble the Reader with the repetition. True it is, that among many other benefits, for which it hath been honoured; in this one it triumpheth over all human knowledge, that it hath given us life in our understanding, since the world itself had life and beginning, even to this day: yea it hath triumphed over time, which besides it, nothing but eternity hath triumphed over: for it hath carried our knowledge over the vast and devouring space of so many thousands of years, and given so fair and piercing eyes to our mind; that we plainly behold living now, as if we had lived then, that great world . . . *the wise work*, saith Hermes, *of a great God*, as it was then, when but new to itself. By it, I say, it is, that we live in the very time when it was created: we behold how it was governed: how it was covered with waters, and again repeopled: how Kings and Kingdoms have flourished and fallen; and for what virtue and piety God made prosperous; and for what vice and deformity he made wretched, both the one and the other. And it is not the least debt which we owe unto History, that it hath made us acquainted with our dead Ancestors; and, out of the depth and darkness of the earth, delivered us their memory and fame. In a word, we may gather out of History a policy no less wise than eternal; by the comparison and application of other men's forepassed miseries, with our own like errors and ill deservings.

But it is neither of Examples the most lively instructions, nor the words of the wisest men, nor the terror of future torments, that hath yet so wrought in our blind and stupefied minds; as to make us remember, that the justice of God doth require none other accuser, than our own consciences: which neither the false beauty of our apparent actions, nor all the formality, which (to pacify the opinions of men) we put on; can in any, or the least kind, cover from his knowledge. And so much did the Heathen wisdom confess, no way as yet qualified by the knowledge of a true God. If any (saith Euripides) *having in his life committed wickedness, think he can hide it from the everlasting gods, he thinks not well.*

To repeat God's judgments in particular, upon those of all degrees, which have played with his mercies; would require a volume apart: for the *Sea* of examples hath no bottom. The marks, set on private men, are with their bodies cast into the earth; and their fortunes, written only in the memories of those that lived with them: so as they who succeed, and have not seen the fall of others, do not fear their own faults. God's judgments upon the greater and greatest, have been left to posterity; first, by those happy hands which the Holy Ghost hath guided; and secondly, by their virtue, who have gathered the acts and ends of men, mighty and remarkable in the world. Now to point far off, and to speak of the conversion of angels into Devils, for Ambition: or of the greatest and most glorious Kings, who have gnawn the grass of the earth with beasts, for pride and ingratitude towards God: or of that wise working of Pharaoh, when he slew the infants of *Israel*, ere they had recovered their Cradles. Or of the policy of *Jezebel*, in covering the Murder of *Naboth* by a trial of the *Elders*, according to the Law: with many thousands of the like: what were it other, than to make an hopeless proof, that far off examples would not be left to the same far off respects, as heretofore? For who hath not observed, what labour, practice, peril, bloodshed, and cruelty, the Kings and Princes of the world have undergone, exercised, taken on them, and committed; to make themselves and their issues masters of the world? And yet hath *Babylon*, *Persia*, *Egypt*, *Syria*, *Macedon*, *Carthage*, *Rome*, and the rest, no fruit, flower, grass, nor leaf, springing upon the face of the Earth, of those seeds: No; their very roots and ruins do hardly remain . . . *All that the hand of man can make, is either overturned by the hand of man, or at length by standing and continuing consumed.* The reasons of whose ruins, are diversely given by those that ground their opinions on second causes. All Kingdoms and States have fallen (say the Politicians) by outward and foreign force, or by inward negligence and dissension, or by a third cause arising from both: Others observe, that the greatest have sunk down under their own weight; of which Livy hath a touch: *Eo crevit, ut magnitudine laboret sua*: Others, that the divine providence (which *Cratippus* objected to *Pompey*) hath set down the date and period of every estate, before their first foundation and erection. But hereof I will give myself a day over to resolve.

For seeing the first books of the following story, have undertaken the discourse of the first Kings and Kingdoms: and that it is impossible for the short life of a Preface, to travel after and overtake far off Antiquity, and to judge of it; I will, for the present, examine what profit hath been gathered by our own Kings, and their Neighbour Princes: who having beheld, both in divine and human letters, the success of infidelity, injustice, and cruelty; have (notwithstanding) planted after the same pattern.

True it is that the judgments of all men are not agreeable; nor (which is more strange) the affection of any one man stirred up alike with examples of like nature: but every one is touched most, with that which most nearly seemeth to touch his own private; or otherwise best suiteth with his apprehension. But the judgments of God are forever unchangeable; neither is he wearied by the long process of time, and won to give his blessing in one age, to that which he had cursed in another. Wherefore those that are wise, or whose wisdom, if it be not great, yet is true and well grounded; will be able to discern the bitter fruits of irreligious policy, as well among those examples that are found in ages removed far from the present, as in those of latter times. And that it may no less appear by evident proof, than by asseveration, that ill doing hath always been attended with ill success; I will here, by way of preface, run over some examples, which the work ensuing hath not reached.

Among our Kings of the *Norman* race, we have no sooner passed over the violence of the *Norman* Conquest, than we encounter with a singular and most remarkable example of God's justice, upon the children of *Henry* the First. For that King, when both by force, craft, and cruelty, he had dispossessed, overreached, and lastly made blind and destroyed his elder Brother *Robert* Duke of *Normandy*, to make his own sons lords of this land: God cast them all, Male and Female, Nephews and Nieces (*Maud* excepted) into the bottom of the Sea, with above a hundred and fifty others that attended them; whereof a great many were Noble, and of the King dearly beloved.

To pass over the rest, till we come to *Edward* the Second; it is certain that after the Murder of that King, the issue of blood then made, though it had some times of stay and stopping, did again break out; and that so often, and in such abundance, as all our Princes of the Masculine race (very few excepted) died of the same disease. And although the young years of *Edward* the Third, made his knowledge of that horrible fact no more than suspicious: yet in that he afterwards caused his own Uncle the Earl of *Kent* to die, for no other offence than the desire of his Brother's redemption, whom the earl as then supposed to be living; (the King making that to be treason in his Uncle, which was indeed treason in himself, had his Uncle's intelligence been true) this I say made it manifest, that he was not ignorant of what had passed, nor greatly desirous to have had it otherwise; though he caused *Mortimer* to die for the same.

This cruelty the secret and unsearchable judgment of God revenged, on the Grandchild of *Edward* the Third: and so it fell out, even to the last of that Line, that in the second or third descent they were all buried under the ruins of those buildings, of which the Mortar had been tempered with innocent blood. For *Richard* the Second, who saw, both his Treasurers, his Chancellor, and his Steward, with divers others of his Counsellors, some of them slaughtered by the people, others in his absence executed by his enemies; yet he always took himself for overwise, to be taught by examples. The Earls of *Huntingdon* and *Kent*, *Montague* and *Spencer*, who thought themselves as great politicians in those days, as others have done in these: hoping to please the King, and to secure themselves, by the Murder of *Gloucester*; died soon after, with many other their adherents, by the like violent hands; and far more shamefully than did that Duke. And as for the King himself (who, in regard of many deeds, unworthy of his Greatness, cannot be excused, as the disavowing himself by breach of Faith, Charters, Pardons, and Patents) he was in the Prime of his youth deposed; and murdered by his Cousin-german and vassal, *Henry* of *Lancaster*; afterwards *Henry* the Fourth.

This King, whose Title was weak, and his obtaining the Crown traitorous: who brake faith with the Lords at his landing, protesting to intend only the recovery of his proper Inheritance; brake faith with *Richard* himself; and brake Faith with all the Kingdom in Parliament, to whom he swore that the deposed King should live. After that he had enjoyed this Realm some few years, and in that time had been set upon on all sides by his Subjects, and never free from conspiracies and rebellions: he saw (if Souls immortal see and discern any things after the body's death) his Grandchild *Henry* the sixth, and his Son the Prince, suddenly, and without mercy, murdered: the possession of the Crown (for which he had caused so much blood to be poured out) transferred from his race; and by the Issues of his Enemies worn and enjoyed: Enemies, whom by his own practice he supposed, that he had left no less powerless, than the succession of the Kingdom questionless; by entailing the same upon his own Issues by Parliament. And out of doubt, human reason could have judged no otherwise, but that these cautious provisions of the Father, seconded by the valour and singular victories of his Son *Henry* the fifth, had buried the hopes of every Competitor, under the despair of all reconquest and recovery. I say, that human reason might so have judged: were not this passage of Casaubon also true . . . *A day, an hour, a moment, is enough to overturn the things, that seemed to have been founded and rooted in Adamant*.

Now for *Henry* the sixth, upon whom the great storm of his Grandfather's grievous faults fell, as it formerly had done upon *Richard* the grandchild of *Edward*: although he was generally esteemed for a gentle and innocent prince; yet as he refused the daughter of *Armignac*, of the house of *Navarre*, the greatest of the Princes of *France*, to whom he was affianced (by which match he might have defended his Inheritance in *France*) and married the Daughter of *Anjou*, (by which he lost all that he had in *France*) so as in condescending to the unworthy death of his Uncle of *Gloucester*, the main and strong pillar of the house of *Lancaster*; he drew on himself and this kingdom the greatest joint-loss and dishonour, that ever it sustained since the *Norman* Conquest. Of whom it may truly be said, which a Counsellor of his own spake of *Henry* the Third of *France* . . . *That he was a very gentle Prince: but his reign happened in a very unfortunate season*.

It is true, that *Buckingham* and *Suffolk* were the practisers and contrivers of the Duke's death: *Buckingham* and *Suffolk*, because the Duke gave instructions to their authority, which otherwise under the Queen had been absolute; the Queen, in respect of her personal wound, *spretaeque injuria formae*, because *Gloucester* dissuaded her marriage. But the fruit was answerable to the seed; the success to the Counsel. For after the cutting down of *Gloucester*, *York* grew up so fast, as he dared to dispute his right, both by arguments and arms; in which quarrel, *Suffolk* and *Buckingham*, with the greatest number of their adherents, were dissolved. And although for his breach of Oath by Sacrament, it pleased God to strike down *York*: yet his son the Earl of *March*, following the plain path which his Father had trodden out, despoiled *Henry* the Father, and *Edward*, the son, both of their lives and Kingdoms. And what was the end now of that politic Lady the Queen, other than this, that she lived to behold the wretched ends of all her partakers: that she lived to look on, while her Husband the King, and her only son the Prince, were hewn in sunder; while the Crown was set on his head that did it. She lived to see herself despoiled of her Estate, and of her moveables: and lastly, her Father, by rendering up to the Crown of France the Earldom of *Provence* and other places, for the payment of Fifty thousand crowns for her ransom, to become a stark beggar. And this was the end of that subtlety, which *Siracides* calleth *fine*, but *unrighteous*: for other fruit hath it never yielded since the world was.

And now it came to Edward the fourth's turn (though after many difficulties) to triumph. For all the Plants of Lancaster were rooted up; one only Earl of *Richmond* excepted: whom also he had once bought of the Duke of Britain, but could not hold him. And yet was not this of *Edward* such a plantation, as could anyway promise itself stability. For this *Edward* the king (to omit more than many of his other cruelties) beheld and allowed the slaughter, which *Gloucester*, *Dorset*, *Hastings*, and others, made of *Edward* the Prince in his own presence: of which tragical Actors, there was not one that escaped the judgment of God in the same kind. And He, which (besides the execution of his brother of *Clarence*, for none other offence than he himself had formed in his own imagination) instructed *Gloucester* to kill *Henry* the sixth, his predecessor; taught him also by the same Art to kill his own sons and Successors *Edward* and *Richard*. *For those Kings, which have sold the blood of others at a low rate; have but made the Market for their own enemies, to buy of theirs at the same price.*

To *Edward* the fourth succeeded *Richard* the Third, the greatest Master in mischief of all that forewent him: who although, for the necessity of his Tragedy, he had more parts to play, and more to perform in his own person, than all the rest; yet he so well fitted every affection that played with him, as if each of them had but acted his own interest. For he wrought so cunningly upon the affections of *Hastings*, and *Buckingham*, enemies to the Queen and to all her kindred: as he easily allured them to condescend, that *Rivers* and *Grey*, the King's maternal Uncle and half-brother, should (for the first) be severed from him: secondly, he wrought their consent to have them imprisoned, and lastly (for the avoiding of future inconvenience) to have their heads severed from their bodies. And having now brought those his chief instruments to exercise that common precept, which the Devil hath written on every post, namely, to depress those whom they had grieved, and to destroy those whom they had depressed; he urged that argument so far and so forcibly; as nothing but the death of the young king himself, and of his brother, could fashion the conclusion. For he caused it to be hammered into *Buckingham's* head, that, whensoever the king, or his brother, should have able years to exercise their power; they would take a most severe revenge of that cureless wrong, offered to their uncle and brother, *Rivers* and *Grey*.

But this was not his manner of reasoning with *Hastings*, whose fidelity to his master's sons was without suspect: and yet the Devil, who never dissuades by impossibility, taught him to try him. And so he did. But when he found by *Catesby*, who sounded him, that he was not fordable; he first resolved to kill him sitting in council: wherein having failed with his sword; he set the hangman upon him, with a weapon of more weight. And because nothing else could move his appetite; he caused his head to be stricken off, before he ate his dinner. A greater judgment of God, than this upon *Hastings*, I have never observed in any story. For the self same day that the Earl *Rivers*, *Grey*, and others, were (without trial of Law, or offence given) by *Hastings'* advice executed at *Pomfret*: I say *Hastings* himself in the same day, and (as I take it) in the same hour, in the same lawless manner had his head stricken off in the Tower of *London*: but *Buckingham* lived a while longer; and with an eloquent oration persuaded the *Londoners* to elect *Richard* for their king. And having received the Earldom of *Hereford* for reward, besides the high hope of marrying his daughter to the King's only son; after many grievous vexations of mind, and unfortunate attempts, being in the end betrayed and delivered up by his trustiest servant; he had his head severed from his body at *Salisbury*, without the trouble of any of his Peers. And what success had *Richard* himself after all these mischiefs and Murders, policies and counter-policies to Christian religion: and after such time, as with a most merciless hand he had pressed out the breath of his Nephews and Natural Lords; other than the prosperity of so short a life, as it took end, ere himself could well look over and discern it? The great outcry of innocent blood, obtaining at God's hands the effusion of his; who became a spectacle of shame and dishonour, both to his friends and enemies.

This cruel King, *Henry* the Seventh cut off; and was therein (no doubt) the immediate instrument of God's justice. A politic Prince he was if ever there were any, and who by the engine of his wisdom, beat down and overturned as many strong oppositions both before and after he ware the crown as ever King of England did: I say by his wisdom, because as he ever left the reins of his affections in the hands of his profit, so he always weighed his undertakings by his abilities, leaving nothing more to hazard than so much as cannot be denied in all human actions. He had well observed the proceedings of Louis the eleventh, whom he followed in all that was royal or royal-like, but he was far more just, and begun not their processes whom he hated or feared by the execution, as Louis did.

He could never endure any mediation in rewarding his servants, and therein exceeding wise, for whatsoever himself gave, he himself received back the thanks and the love, knowing it well that the affections of men (purchased by nothing so readily as by benefits) were trains that better became great Kings, than great subjects. On the contrary, in whatsoever he grieved his subjects, he wisely put it off on those, that he found fit ministers for such actions. Howsoever, the taking off, of *Stanley's* head, who set the Crown on his, and the death of the young Earl of *Warwick*, son to *George Duke* of *Clarence*, shows, as the success also did, that he held somewhat of the errors of his Ancestors, for his possession in the first line ended in his grandchildren, as that of *Edward* the Third and *Henry* the Fourth had done.

Now for king *Henry* the eighth. If all the pictures and Patterns of a merciless Prince were lost in the World, they might all again be painted to the life, out of the story of this King. For how many servants did he advance in haste (but for what virtue no man could suspect) and with the change of his fancy ruined again; no man knowing for what offence? To how many others of more desert gave he abundant flowers from whence to gather honey, and in the end of Harvest burnt them in the Hive? How many wives did he cut off, and cast off, as his fancy and affection changed? How many Princes of the blood (whereof some of them for age could hardly crawl towards the block) with a world of others of all degrees (of whom our common Chronicles have kept the account) did he execute? Yea, in his very death-bed, and when he was at the point to have given his account to God for the abundance of blood already spilt: he imprisoned the Duke of *Norfolk* the Father; and executed the Earl of *Surrey* the son; the one, whose deservings he knew not how to value, having never omitted any thing that concerned his own honour, and the King's service; the other, never having committed any thing worthy of his least displeasure: the one exceeding valiant and advised: the other, no less valiant than learned, and of excellent hope. But besides the sorrows which he heaped upon the Fatherless, and widows at home: and besides the vain enterprises abroad, wherein it is thought that he consumed more Treasure, than all our victorious Kings did in their several Conquests: what causeless and cruel wars did he make upon his own Nephew King *James* the Fifth? What Laws and Wills did he devise, to establish this Kingdom in his own issues? Using his sharpest weapons to cut off, and cut down those branches, which sprang from the same root that himself did. And in the end (notwithstanding these his so many irreligious provisions) it pleased God to take away all his own, without increase; though, for themselves in their several kinds, all Princes of eminent virtue. For these words of *Samuel* to *Agag* King of the *Amalekites*, have been verified upon many others: *As thy sword hath made other women childless: so shall thy mother be childless among other women*. And that blood, which the same King Henry affirmed, that the cold air of *Scotland* had frozen up in the North, God hath diffused by the sunshine of his grace: from whence His Majesty now living, and long to live, is descended. Of whom I may say it truly, that if all the malice of the world were infused into one eye: yet could it not discern in His life, even to this day, any one of those foul spots, by which the Consciences of all the forenamed Princes (in effect) have been defiled; nor any drop of that innocent blood on the sword of his justice, with which the most that forewent him, have stained both their hands and fame. And for this Crown of *England*; it may truly be avowed, that he hath received it even from the hand of God, and hath stayed the time of putting it on, howsoever he were provoked to hasten it: that he never took revenge of any man, that sought to put him beside it: that he refused the assistance of Her enemies, that wore it long, with as great glory as ever Princess did, that His Majesty entered not by a breach, nor by blood; but by the Ordinary gate, which his own right set open; and into which, by a general love and Obedience, he was received. And howsoever His Majesty's preceding title to this Kingdom, was preferred by many Princes (witness the Treaty of *Cambrai* in the year, 1559) yet he never pleased to dispute it, during the life of that renowned Lady, his Predecessor; no, notwithstanding the injury of not being declared Heir, in all the time of Her long reign.

Neither ought we to forget, or neglect our thankfulness to God for the uniting of the northern parts of Brittany to the south, to wit of Scotland to England: which though they were severed but by small brooks and banks, yet by reason of the long continued war, and the cruelties exercised upon each other, in the affection of the Nations, they were infinitely severed. This I say is not the least of God's blessings which His Majesty hath brought with him unto this land:

no, put all our petty grievances together, and heap them up to their height, they will appear but as a Molehill, compared with the Mountain of this concord. And if all the Historians since then; have acknowledged the uniting of the Red Rose, and the White, for the greatest happiness, (Christian Religion excepted) that ever this Kingdom received from God, certainly the peace between the two Lions of gold and gules, and the making them one, doth by many degrees exceed the former; for by it, besides the sparing of our british blood, heretofore and during the difference so often and abundantly shed, the state of England is more assured, the Kingdom more enabled to recover her ancient honour and rights, and by it made more invincible, than by all our former alliances, practices, policies and conquests. It is true that hereof we do not yet find the effect. But had the duke of Parma in the year 1588, joined the army which he commanded with that of Spain, and landed it on the south coast; and had his Majesty at the same time declared himself against us in the north: it is easy to divine what had become of the liberty of England, certainly we would then without murmur have bought this union at a far greater price than it hath since cost us.

It is true, that there was never any Commonweal or Kingdom in the world, wherein no man had cause to lament. Kings live in the world and not above it. They are not infinite to examine every man's cause, or to relieve every man's wants. And yet, in the latter, (though to his own prejudice) His Majesty hath had more compassion of other men's necessities, than of his own Coffers. Of whom it may be said, as of *Solomon*, *Dedit Deus Salomoni latitudinem cordis*: Which if other men do not understand with *Pineda*, to be meant by *Liberality*, but by *Latitude of knowledge*; yet may it be better spoken of His Majesty, than of any King that ever *England* had; who as well in Divine, as Human understanding, hath exceeded all that forewent him by many degrees.

I could say much more of the King's Majesty, without flattery: did I not fear the imputation of presumption, and withal suspect, that it might befall these papers of mine, (though the loss were little) as it did the pictures of *Queen Elizabeth*, made by unskilful and common Painters: which by her own Commandment, were knocked in pieces and cast into the fire. For ill Artists, in setting out the beauty of the external: and weak writers, in describing the virtues of the internal; do often leave to posterity, of well formed faces a deformed memory; and of the most perfect and Princely minds, a most defective representation. It may suffice, and there needs no other discourse; if the honest *Reader* but compare the cruel and turbulent passages of our former Kings, and of other their Neighbour Princes, (of whom for that purpose I have inserted this brief discourse) with *His Majesty's* temperate, revengeless, and liberal disposition: I say, that if the honest Reader weigh them justly, and with an even hand: and withal, but bestow every deformed child on his true Parent; he shall find, that there is no man which hath so just cause to complain, as the King himself hath.

Now as we have told the success of the trumperies and cruelties of our own Kings, and other great personages: so we find, that God is everywhere the same God. And as it pleased him to punish the usurpation, and unnatural cruelty of *Henry* the First, and of our third *Edward*, in their children for many generations: so dealt He with the sons of *Louis Debonaire*, the son of *Charles* the great, or *Charlemagne*. For after such time as *Debonaire* of *France*, had torn out the eyes of *Bernard* his Nephew, the son of *Pepin*, the eldest son of *Charlemagne*, and heir of the Empire, and then caused him to die in prison, as did our *Henry* to *Robert* his elder brother: there followed nothing but murders upon murders, poisonings, imprisonments, and civil war; till the whole race of that famous Emporer was extinguished.

And though *Debonaire*, after he had rid himself of his Nephew by a violent death; and of his Bastard Brothers by a civil death (having enclosed them with sure guard, all the days of their lives, within a Monastery) held himself secure from all opposition: yet God raised up against him (which he suspected not) his own sons, to vex him, to invade him, to take him prisoner, and to depose him; his own sons, with whom (to satisfy their ambition) he had shared his estate, and given them Crowns to wear, and Kingdoms to govern, during his own life. Yea, his eldest son *Lothaire* (for he had four, three by his first wife, and one by his second; to wit *Lothaire*, *Pepin*, *Louis*, and *Charles*) made it the cause of his deposition, that he had used violence towards his Brothers and Kinsmen; and that he had suffered his Nephew (whom he might have delivered) to be slain . . . saith the text . . . *Because he used violence to his Brothers and Kinsmen, and suffered his Nephew to be slain whom he might have delivered.*

Yet did he that which few Kings do; namely, repent him of his cruelty. For among many other things, which he performed in the General Assembly of the States, it follows . . . *After this he did openly confess himself to have erred, and following the example of the emperor* Theodosius *he underwent voluntary penance as well for his other offences, as for that which he had done against* Bernard *his own Nephew.*

This he did: and it was praiseworthy. *But the blood that is unjustly spilt, is not again gathered up from the ground by repentance. These Medicines, ministered to the dead, have but dead rewards.*

This King, as I have said, had Four Sons. To *Lothaire* his eldest he gave the Kingdom of *Italy*; as *Charlemagne*, his Father, had done to *Pepin* the Father of *Bernard*, who was to succeed him in the Empire. To *Pepin*, the second son, he gave the Kingdom of *Aquitaine*: to *Louis*, the Kingdom of *Bavier*: and to *Charles*, whom he had by a second wife, called *Judith*, the remainder of the Kingdom of *France*. But this second wife, being a Mother-in-law to the rest, persuaded *Debonaire* to cast his son *Pepin* out of *Aquitaine*; thereby to greaten *Charles*: which, after the death of his son *Pepin* he prosecuted to effect, against his Grandchild bearing the same name. In the mean while, being invaded by his son *Louis* of *Bavier*, he dies for grief.

Debonaire dead, *Louis* of *Bavier*, and *Charles*, afterwards called the *bald*, and their Nephew *Pepin* of *Aquitaine*, join in league against the emperor *Lothaire* their eldest Brother. They fight near to *Auxerre* the most bloody battle that ever was strucken in *France*: in which, the marvellous loss of Nobility, and men of war, gave courage to the *Saracens* to invade *Italy*; to the *Huns*, to fall upon *Almaine*; and to the *Danes*, to enter upon *Normandy*. *Charles* the *Bald* by treason seizeth upon his nephew *Pepin*, kills him in a Cloister, *Carloman* rebels against his father *Charles* the *Bald*, the father burns out the eyes of his son *Carloman*; *Bavier* invades the emporer *Lothaire* his Brother. *Lothaire* quits the Empire, he is assailed and wounded to the heart by his own conscience, for his rebellion against his Father and for his other cruelties, and dies in a Monastery. *Charles* the *Bald* the uncle oppresseth his Nephews the sons of Lothaire, he usurpeth the Empire to the prejudice of Louis of Bavier his elder Brother, Bavier's armies and his son *Carloman* are beaten, he dies of grief, and the Usurper *Charles* is poisoned by *Zedechias* a *Jew* his physician, his son *Louis le Beque* dies of the same drink. *Beque* had *Charles the Simple*, and two Bastards, *Louis* and *Carloman*; they rebel against their Brother, but the eldest breaks his Neck, the younger is slain by a wild Boar; the son of *Bavier* had the same ill destiny and brake his neck by a fall out of a Window in sporting with his companions: *Charles* the *Gross* becomes Lord of all that the sons of *Debonaire* held in *Germany*, wherewith not contented, he invades *Charles the Simple*, but being forsaken of his Nobility, of his wife, and of his understanding, he dies a distracted beggar. *Charles the Simple* is held in Wardship by *Eudes Major* of the palace, then by *Robert* the Brother of *Eudes*, and lastly being taken by the Earl of *Vermandois*, he is forced to die in the prison of *Peron*: *Louis* the son of *Charles the Simple* breaks his neck in Chasing a Wolf, and of the two sons of this *Louis*, the one dies of poison, the other dies in the prison of *Orleans*, after whom *Hugh Capet*, of another race, and a stranger to the *French*, makes himself King.

These miserable ends had the issues of *Debonaire*: who after he had once apparelled injustice with authority, his sons and successors took up the fashion; and wore that Garment so long without other provision, as when the same was torn from their shoulders, every man despised them as miserable and naked beggars. The wretched success they had (saith a learned Frenchman) shows . . . *that in the death of that Prince, to wit, of* Bernard *the son of* Pepin, *the true heir of* Charlemagne, *men had more meddling, than either God or Justice had.*

But to come nearer home; it is certain that *Francis* the first, One of the worthiest Kings (except for that fact) that ever the Frenchmen had, did never enjoy himself; after he had commended the destruction of the Protestants of *Mirandol* and *Cabrieres*, to the parliament of *Provence*, which poor people were thereupon burnt, and murdered; men, women, and children. It is true, that the said King *Francis* repented himself of the fact, and gave charge to Henry his son, to do justice upon the Murderers; threatening his son with God's judgments, if he neglected it. But this unseasonable care of his, God was not pleased to accept for payment. For after *Henry* himself was slain in sport by *Montgomery*; we all may remember what became of his four sons, *Francis*, *Charles*, *Henry*, and *Hercules*, Of which although three of them became Kings, and were married to beautiful and virtuous Ladies: yet were they, one after another, cast out of the world, without stock or seed. And notwithstanding their subtlety, and breach of faith; with all their Massacres upon those of the religion, and great effusion of blood; the Crown was set on his head, whom they all laboured to dissolve; the Protestants remain more in number than ever they were; and hold to this day more strong cities than ever they had.

Let us now see if God be not the same God in *Spain*, as in *England* and *France*. Towards whom we will look no farther back than to *Don Pedro* of *Castile*; in respect of which Prince, all the Tyrants of *Sicily*, our *Richard* the third, and the great *Ivan* Vasilowich of *Muscovy*, were but petty ones: this *Castilian*, of all Christian and Heathen Kings, having been the most merciless. For besides those of his own blood and Nobility which he caused to be slain in his own Court and Chamber, as *Sancho Ruis*, the great master of *Calatrava*, *Ruis Gonsales*, *Alphonso Tello*, and *Don John* of *Arragon*, whom he cut in pieces and cast into the streets, denying him Christian burial; I say besides these, and the slaughter of *Gomes Manriques*, *Diego Peres*, *Alphonso Gomes*, and the great commander of *Castile*; he made away the two Infants of *Arragon* his Cousin-germans, his brother *Don Frederick*, *Don John de la Cerde*, *Albuquerques*, *Nugnes de Guzman*, *Cornel*, *Cabrera*, *Tenorio*, *Mendes de Toledo*, *Guttiere* his great

Treasurer, and all his Kindred; and a world of others. Neither did he spare his two youngest brothers, innocent Princes: whom after he had kept in close prison from their Cradles, till one of them had lived sixteen years, and the other, fourteen; he murdered them there. Nay he spared not his Mother, nor his wife the Lady *Blanch* of *Bourbon*. Lastly as he caused the Archbishop of *Toledo*, and the Dean, to be killed of purpose to enjoy their treasures: so did he put to death *Mahomet Aben Alhamar* King of *Barbary*, with seven and thirty of his Nobility, that came unto him for succour, with a great sum of money, to levy (by his favour) some companies of soldiers to return withal. Yea he would needs assist the Hangman with his own hand, in the execution of the old King; insomuch as pope *Urban* declared him an enemy both to God and man. But what was his end? Having been formerly beaten out of his Kingdom, and reestablished by the valour of the *English Nation*, led by the famous Duke of *Lancaster*: he was stabbed to death by his younger Brother the Earl of *Astramara*, who dispossessed all his Children of their inheritance; which, but for the Father's injustice and cruelty, had never been in danger of any such thing.

. . . .

Oh by what plots, by what forswearings, betrayings, oppressions, imprisonments, tortures, poisonings, and under what reasons of State, and politic subtlety, have these forenamed Kings, both strangers and of our own Nation, pulled the vengeance of God upon themselves, upon theirs, and upon their prudent ministers! and in the end have brought those things to pass for their enemies, and seen an effect so directly contrary to all their own counsels and cruelties; as the one could never have hoped for themselves; and the other never have succeeded; if no such opposition had ever been made. God hath said it, and performed it ever . . . *I will destroy the wisdom of the wise*.

But what of all this? and to what end do we lay before the eyes of the living, the fall and fortunes of the dead: seeing the world is the same that it hath been; and the children of the present time, will still obey their parents? It is in the present time, that all the wits of the world are exercised. To hold the times we have, we hold all things lawful: and either we hope to hold them for ever; or at least we hope, that there is nothing after them to be hoped for. For, as we are content to forget our own experience, and to counterfeit the ignorance of our own knowledge, in all things that concern ourselves; or persuade ourselves, that God hath given us letters patents to pursue all our irreligious affections with a *non obstante*: so we neither look behind us what hath been, nor before us what shall be. It is true, that the quantity which we have, is of the body: we are by it joined to the earth; we are compounded of earth; and we inhabit it. The Heavens are high, far off and unsearchable: we have sense and feeling of corporal things; and of eternal grace, but by revelation. No marvel then that our thoughts are also earthly: and it is less to be wondered at, that the words of worthless men cannot cleanse them; seeing their doctrine and instruction, whose understanding the Holy Ghost vouchsafed to inhabit, have not performed it. For as the prophet *Isaiah* cried out long agone, *Lord, who hath believed our reports*? And out of doubt, as *Isaiah* complained then for himself and others; so are they less believed, every day after other. For although Religion, and the truth thereof, be in every man's mouth, yea in the discourse of every woman, who for the greatest number are but *Idols of vanity*: what is it other than an universal dissimulation? We profess that we know God: but by works we deny him. For Beatitude doth not consist in the knowledge of divine things, but in a divine life: for the Devils know them better than men. *Beatitudo non est divinorum cognitio, sed vita divina*. And certainly there is nothing more to be admired, and more to be lamented, than the private contention, the passionate dispute, the personal hatred, and the perpetual wars, massacres, and murders, for Religion among *Christians*: the discourse whereof hath so occupied the World, as it hath well near driven the practice thereof out of the world. Who would not soon resolve, that took knowledge but of the religious disputations among men, and not of their lives which dispute, that there were no other thing in their desires, than the purchase of Heaven; and that the World itself were but used as it ought, and as an Inn or place, wherein to repose ourselves in passing on towards our celestial habitation? When on the contrary, besides the discourse and outward profession, the soul hath nothing but hypocrisy. We are all (in effect) become Comedians in religion: and while we act in gesture and voice, divine virtues, in all the course of our lives we renounce our Persons, and the parts we play. For Charity, Justice, and Truth, have but their being *in terms*, like the Philosopher's *Materia prima*.

Neither is it that wisdom, which *Solomon* defineth to be the *Schoolmistress of the knowledge of God*, that hath valuation in the world: it is enough that we give it our good word; but the same which is altogether exercised in the service of the World, as the gathering of riches chiefly; by which we purchase and obtain honour, with the many respects which attend it.

These indeed be the marks which (when we have bent our consciences to the highest) we all shoot at. For the obtaining whereof it is true, that the care is our own; the care our own in this life, the peril our own in the future: and yet when we have gathered the greatest abundance, we ourselves enjoy no more thereof, than so much as belongs to one man. For the rest; he that had the greatest wisdom, and the greatest ability that ever man had, hath told us that this is the use: *When goods increase* (saith Solomon) *they also increase that eat them; and what good cometh to the Owners, but the beholding thereof with their eyes?* As for those that devour the rest, and follow us in fair weather: they again forsake us in the first tempest of misfortune, and steer away before the Sea and Wind; leaving us to the malice of our destinies. Of these, among a thousand examples, I will take but one out of Master *Dannet*, and use his own words: *Whilst the emperor* Charles *the fifth, after the resignation of his Estates, stayed at Flushing for wind, to carry him his last journey into Spain; he conferred on a time with* Seldius, *his brother* Ferdinand's *Ambassador, till the deep of the night. And when* Seldius *should depart: the emperor calling for some of his servants, and nobody answering him (for those that attended upon him, were some gone to their lodgings, and all the rest asleep) the Emperor took up the candle himself, and went before* Seldius *to light him down the stairs; and so did, notwithstanding all the resistance that* Seldius *could make. And when He was come to the stair's foot, he said thus unto him:* Seldius *remember this of* Charles *the Emperor, when he shall be dead and gone, that Him, whom thou hast known in thy time environed with so many mighty Armies, and Guards of soldiers, thou hast also seen alone, abandoned, and forsaken, yea even of his own domestical servants, &c. I acknowledge this change of Fortune to proceed from the mighty hand of God; which I will by no means go about to withstand.*

But you will say that there are some things else, and of greater regard than the former. The first, is the reverend respect that is held of great men, and the Honour done unto them by all sorts of people. And it is true indeed: provided, that an inward love for their justice and piety, accompany the outward worship given to their places and power; without which what is the applause of the Multitude, but as the outcry of an Herd of *Animals*, who without the knowledge of any true cause, please themselves with the noise they make? For seeing it is a thing exceeding rare, to distinguish Virtue and Fortune: the most impious (if prosperous) have ever been applauded; the most virtuous (if unprosperous) have ever been despised. For as Fortune's man rides the Horse, so Fortune herself rides the Man. Who, when he is descended and on foot: the Man taken from his Beast, and Fortune from the Man; a base groom beats the one, and a bitter contempt spurns the other, with equal liberty.

The second, is the greatening of our posterity, and the contemplation of their glory whom we leave behind us. Certainly, of those which conceive that their souls departed take any comfort therein, it may truly be said of them, which Lactantius spake of certain Heathen Philosophers, *quod sapientes sunt in re stulta*. For when our spirits immortal shall be once separate from our mortal bodies, and disposed by God: there remaineth in them no other joy of their posterity which succeed, than there doth of pride in that stone, which sleepeth in the Wall of a King's Palace; nor any other sorrow for their poverty, than there doth of shame in that, which beareth up a Beggar's cottage . . . *The dead though holy, know nothing of the living, no, not of their own children: for the souls of those departed, are not conversant with their affairs that remain.* And if we doubt of Saint *Augustine, we cannot of Job*; who tells us, *That we know not if our sons shall be honourable: neither shall we understand concerning them, whether they shall be of low degree.* Which *Ecclesiastes* also confirmeth: *Man walketh in a shadow, and disquieteth himself in vain: he heapeth up riches, and cannot tell who shall gather them. The living* (saith he) *know that they shall die, but the dead know nothing at all. For who can show unto man what shall be after him under the Sun?* He therefore accounted it among the rest of worldly vanities, to labour and travail in the world; not knowing after death, whether a fool or a wise man should enjoy the fruits thereof: *which made me* (saith he) *endeavour even to abhor mine own labour.* And what can other men hope, whose blessed or sorrowful estates after death God hath reserved? man's knowledge lying but in his hope; seeing the prophet Esay confesseth of the elect, that *Abraham is ignorant of us, and Israel knows us not*. But hereof we are assured, that the long and dark night of death: (of whose following day we shall never behold the dawn, till his return that hath triumphed over it) shall cover us over, till the world be no more. After which, and when we shall again receive Organs glorified and incorruptible, the seats of Angelical affections: in so great admiration shall the souls of the blessed be exercised, as they cannot admit the mixture of any second or less joy; nor any return of foregone and mortal affection, towards friends, kindred, or children. Of whom whether we shall retain any particular knowledge, or in any sort distinguish them: no man can assure us; and the wisest men doubt. But on the contrary; if a divine life retain any of those faculties, which the soul exercised in a mortal body; we shall not at that time so divide the joys of Heaven, as to cast any part thereof on the memory of their felicities which remain in the World. No; be their estates greater than ever the World gave, we shall (by the difference known unto us) even detest their consideration. And whatsoever comfort shall remain of all forepast, the same will consist in the charity, which we exercised living: and in that Piety, Justice, and firm Faith, for which it pleased the infinite mercy of God to accept of us, and receive us. Shall we therefore value honour and riches at nothing? and neglect them, as unnecessary and vain? certainly no. For that infinite wisdom of God, which hath distinguished his Angels by degrees: which hath given greater and less light, and beauty, to Heavenly bodies: which hath made differences between beasts and birds: created the Eagle and the fly, the Cedar and the Shrub: and among stones, given the fairest tincture to the Ruby, and the quickest light to the Diamond; hath also ordained Kings, Dukes or Leaders of the people, Magistrates, Judges, and other degrees among men. And as honour is left to posterity, for a mark and ensign of the virtue and understanding of their Ancestors: so, seeing *Siracides* preferreth Death before Beggary: and that titles, without proportionable estates, fall under the miserable succour of other men's pity, I account it foolishness to condemn such a care: provided, that worldly goods be well gotten, and that we raise not our own buildings out of other men's ruins. For as *Plato* doth first prefer the perfection of bodily health; secondly, the form and beauty; and thirdly, *Divitias nulla fraude quaesitas*: so Hieremie cries, *Woe unto them that erect their houses by unrighteousness, and their chambers without equity:* and Esay the same, *Woe to those that spoil, and were not spoiled.* And it was out of the true wisdom of *Solomon* that he commandeth us, *not to drink the wine of violence; not to lie in wait for blood; and not to swallow them up alive, whose riches we covet: for such are the ways* (saith he) *of every one that is greedy of gain.*

And if we could afford ourselves but so much leisure as to consider, that he which hath most in the world, hath, in respect of the world, nothing in it: and that he which hath the longest time lent him to live in it, hath yet no proportion at all therein, setting it either by that which is past when we were not, or by that time which is to come in which we shall abide for ever: I say, if both, to wit our proportion in the world, and our time in the world, differ not much from that which is nothing; it is not out of any excellency of understanding, that we so much prize the one, which hath (in effect) no being; and so much neglect the other, which hath no ending: coveting those mortal things of the world, as if our souls were therein immortal, and neglecting those things which are immortal, as if ourselves after the world were but mortal.

But let every man value his own wisdom, as he pleaseth. Let the Rich man think all fools, that cannot equal his abundance; the Revenger esteem all negligent, that have not trodden down their opposites; the Politician, all gross, that cannot merchandise their faith: yet when we once come in sight of the Port of death, to which all winds drive us; and when by letting fall that fatal Anchor, which can never be weighed again, the Navigation of this life takes end: then it is I say, that our own cogitations (those sad and severe cogitations, formerly beaten from us by our Health and Felicity) return again, and pay us to the uttermost for all the pleasing passages of our lives past. It is then that we cry out to God for mercy; then, when ourselves can no longer exercise cruelty towards others: and it is only then, that we are strucken through the soul with this terrible sentence, *that God will not be mocked*. For if according to Saint *Peter*, *the righteous scarcely be saved, and that God spared not his Angels*; where shall those appear, who, having served their appetites all their lives, presume to think, that the severe commandments of the All-powerful God were given but in sport; and that the short breath, which we draw when death presseth us, if we can but fashion it to the sound of *Mercy* (without any kind of satisfaction or amends) is sufficient? *O quam multi*, saith a reverend Father, *cum hac spe ad eternos labores et bella descendunt*: I confess that it is a great comfort to our friends, to have it said that we ended well: for we all desire (as *Balaam* did) *to die the death of the righteous*. But what shall we call a disesteeming, an opposing, or (indeed) a mocking of God; if those men do not oppose him, disesteem him, and mock him, that think it enough for God, to ask him forgiveness at leisure, with the remainder and last drawing of a malicious breath? For what do they otherwise, that die this kind of well-dying, but say unto God as followeth? We beseech thee, O God, that all the falsehoods, forswearings, and treacheries of our lives past, may be pleasing unto thee; that thou wilt for our sakes (that have had no leisure to do any thing for thine) change thy nature (though impossible) and forget to be a just God; that thou wilt love injuries and oppressions, call ambition wisdom, and charity foolishness. For I shall prejudice my son (which I am resolved not to do) if I make restitution; and confess myself to have been unjust (which I am too proud to do) if I deliver the oppressed. Certainly, these wise worldlings have either found out a new God; or have made One; and in all likelihood such a Leaden One, as *Lewis* the Eleventh ware in his Cap; which, when he had caused any that he feared, or hated, to be killed, he would take it from his head and kiss it: beseeching it to pardon him this one evil act more, and it should be the last, which, (as at other times) he did; when by the practice of a Cardinal and a falsified Sacrament, he caused the Earl of *Armagnac* to be stabbed to death; mockeries indeed fit to be used towards a Leaden, but not towards the ever-living God. But of this composition are all the devout lovers of the world, that they fear all that is dureless and ridiculous: they fear the plots and practices of their opposites, and their very whisperings: they fear the opinions of men which beat but upon shadows: they flatter and forsake the prosperous and unprosperous, be they friends or Kings: yea they dive under water, like Ducks, at every pebble stone, that's but thrown towards them by a powerful hand: and on the contrary, they show an obstinate and Giant-like valour, against the terrible judgments of the All-powerful God: yea they show themselves gods against God, and slaves towards men; towards men whose bodies and consciences are alike rotten.

Now for the rest: if we truly examine the difference of both conditions; to wit of the rich and mighty, whom we call fortunate; and of the poor and oppressed, whom we account wretched; we shall find the happiness of the one, and the miserable estate of the other, so tied by God to the very instant, and both so subject to interchange (witness the sudden downfall of the greatest Princes, and the speedy uprising of the meanest persons) as the one hath nothing so certain, whereof to boast; nor the other so uncertain, whereof to bewail itself. For there is no man so assured of his honour, of his riches, health, or life; but that he may be deprived of either or all, the very next hour or day to come . . . *What the evening will bring with it, it is uncertain. And yet ye cannot tell* (saith Saint James) *what shall be tomorrow. Today he is set up, and tomorrow he shall not be found; for he is turned into dust, and his purpose perisheth*. And although the air which compasseth adversity, be very obscure: yet therein we better discern God, than in that shining light which environeth worldly glory; through which, for the clearness thereof, there is no vanity which escapeth our sight. And let adversity seem what it will; to happy men, ridiculous, who make themselves merry at other men's misfortunes; and to those under the *cross*, grievous: yet this is true, that for all that is past, to the very instant, the portions remaining are equal to either. For be it that we have lived many years, *and* (according to Solomon) *in them all we have rejoiced;* or be it that we have measured the same length of days, and therein have evermore sorrowed: yet, looking back from our present being, we find both the one and the other, to wit, the joy and the woe, sailed out of sight; and death, which doth pursue us and hold us in chase, from our infancy, hath gathered it . . . *Whatsoever of our age is past, death holds it*. So as whosoever he be, to whom Fortune hath been a servant, and the Time a friend: let him but take the account of his memory (for we have no other keeper of our pleasures past) and truly examine what it hath reserved, either of beauty and youth, or foregone delights; what it hath saved, that it might last, of his dearest affections, or of whatever else the amorous Spring-time gave his thoughts of contentment, then unvaluable; and he shall find that all the art which his elder years have, can draw no other vapour out of these dissolutions, than heavy, secret, and sad sighs. He shall find nothing remaining, but those sorrows, which grow up after our fast-springing youth; overtake it, when it is at a stand; and overtop it utterly, when it begins to wither: insomuch as looking back from the very instant time, and from our now being; the poor, diseased, and captive creature, hath as little sense of all his former miseries and pains; as he, that is most blessed in common opinion, hath of his fore-passed pleasures and delights. For whatsoever is cast behind us, is just nothing: and what is to come, deceitful hope hath it. *Omnia quae ventura sunt, incerto jacent*. Only those few black Swans I must except: who having had the grace to value worldly vanities at no more than their own price; do, by retaining the comfortable memory of a well acted life, behold death without dread, and the grave without fear; and embrace both, as necessary guides to endless glory.

For myself, this is my consolation, and all that I can offer to others, that the sorrows of this life, are but of two sorts: whereof the one hath respect to God; the other, to the World. In the first we complain to God against ourselves, for our offences against him; and confess . . . *And thou O Lord art just in all that hath befallen us*. In the second we complain to ourselves against God: as if he had done us wrong, either in not giving us worldly goods and honours, answering our appetites: or for taking them again from us, having had them; forgetting that humble and just acknowledgment of *Job, The Lord hath given, and the Lord hath taken*. To the first of which Saint *Paul* hath promised blessedness; to the second, death. And out of doubt he is either a fool or ungrateful to God, or both, that doth not acknowledge, how mean soever his estate be, that the same is yet far greater, than that which God oweth him: or doth not acknowledge, how sharp soever his afflictions be, that the same are yet far less, than those which are due unto him. And if an Heathen wise man call the adversities of the world but *tributa vivendi*, the tributes of the living: a wise Christian man ought to know them, and bear them, but as the tributes of offending. He ought to bear them man-like, and resolvedly; and not as those whining soldiers do, *qui gementes sequuntur imperatorem*.

For seeing God, who is the Author of all our tragedies, hath written out for us, and appointed us all the parts we are to play: and hath not, in their distribution, been partial to the most mighty Princes of the world; that gave unto *Darius* the part of the greatest Emperor, and the part of the most miserable beggar, a beggar begging water of an Enemy, to quench the great drought of death;

that appointed *Bajazet* to play the *Grand Signior* of the *Turks* in the morning, and in the same day the *Footstool* of *Tamerlane* (both which parts *Valerian* had also played, being taken by *Sapores*) that made *Bellisarius* play the most victorious Captain, and lastly the part of a blind beggar; of which examples many thousands may be produced: why should other men, who are but of the least worms, complain of wrongs? Certainly there is no other account to be made of this ridiculous world, than to resolve, that the change of fortune on the great Theatre, is but as the change of garments on the less. For when on the one and the other, every man wears but his own skin; the Players are all alike. Now if any man, out of weakness, prize the passages of this world otherwise (for, saith *Petrarch*, *Magni ingenii est revocare mentem a sensibus*) it is by reason of that unhappy fantasy of ours, which forgeth in the brains of Man all the miseries (the corporal excepted) whereunto he is subject: therein it is, that Misfortune and Adversity work all that they work. For seeing Death, in the end of the Play, takes from all, whatsoever Fortune and Force takes from any one: it were a foolish madness in the shipwreck of worldly things, where all sinks but the Sorrow, to save it. That were, as *Seneca* saith . . . *to fall under Fortune, of all other the most miserable destiny*.

But it is now time to sound a retreat; and to desire to be excused of this long pursuit: and withal, that the good intent, which hath moved me to draw the picture of time past (which we call History) in so large a table, may also be accepted in place of a better reason.

. . . .

I have been already over long, to make any large discourse either of the parts of the following Story, or in mine own excuse; especially in the excuse of this or that passage; seeing the whole is exceeding weak and defective. Among the grossest, the unsuitable division of the books, I could not know how to excuse, had I not been directed to enlarge the building after the foundation was laid, and the first part finished. All men know that there is no great Art in the dividing evenly of those things, which are subject to number and measure. For the rest, it suits well enough with a great many Books of this age, which speak too much, and yet say little; *Ipsi nobis furto subducimur*; We are stolen away from ourselves, setting a high price on all that is our own. But hereof, though a late good Writer, make complaint, yet shall it not lay hold on me, because I believe as he doth; that whoso thinks himself the wisest man, is but a poor and miserable ignorant. Those that are the best men of war, against all the vanities and fooleries of the World, do always keep the strongest guards against themselves, to defend them from themselves, from self love, self estimation, and self opinion.

Generally concerning the order of the work, I have only taken counsel from the Argument. For of the *Assyrians*, which, after the downfall of *Babel* take up the first part, and were the first great Kings of the World, there came little to the view of posterity: some few enterprises, greater in fame than faith, of *Ninus* and *Semiramis* excepted.

It was the story of the *Hebrews*, of all before the *Olympiads*, that overcame the consuming disease of time; and preserved itself, from the very cradle and beginning to this day: and yet not so entire, but that the large discourses thereof (to which in many scriptures we are referred) are nowhere found. The Fragments of other Stories, with the actions of those Kings and Princes which shot up here and there in the same time I am driven to relate by way of digression: of which we may say with Virgil.

Apparent rari nantes in gurgite vasto;
They appear here and there floating in the great gulf of time.

To the same first Ages do belong the report of many Inventions therein found, and from them derived to us; though most of the Authors' Names have perished in so long a Navigation. For those Ages had their Laws; they had diversity of Government; they had Kingly rule; Nobility, Policy in war; Navigation; and all, or the most of needful Trades. To speak therefore of these (seeing in a general History we should have left a great deal of Nakedness, by their omission) it cannot properly be called a digression. True it is that I have also made many others: which, if they shall be laid to my charge, I must cast the fault into the great heap of human error. For seeing we digress in all the ways of our lives: yea seeing the life of man is nothing else but digression; I may the better be excused in writing their lives and actions. I am not altogether ignorant in the Laws of *History*, and of the *Kinds*.

The same hath been taught by many; but by no man better, and with greater brevity, than by that excellent learned Gentleman *Sir Francis Bacon*. Christian Laws are also taught us by the Prophets and Apostles; and every day preached unto us. But we still make large digressions; yea, the teachers themselves do not (in all) keep the path which they point out to others.

For the rest; after such time as the *Persians* had wrested the Empire from the *Chaldeans*, and had raised a great Monarchy, producing Actions of more importance than were elsewhere to be found: it was agreeable to the Order of Story to attend this Empire; whilst it so flourished, that the affairs of the nations adjoining had reference thereunto. The like observance was to be used towards the fortunes of *Greece*, when they again began to get ground upon the *Persians*, as also towards the affairs of *Rome*, when the *Romans* grew more mighty than the *Greeks*.

As for the *Medes*, the *Macedonians*, the *Sicilians*, the *Carthaginians*, and other *Nations*, who resisted the beginnings of the former Empires, and afterwards became but parts of their composition and enlargement; it seemed best to remember what was known of them from their several beginnings, in such times and places, as they in their flourishing estates opposed those Monarchies; which in the end swallowed them up. And herein I have followed the best Geographers: who seldom give names to those small brooks, whereof many, joined together, make great Rivers; till such time as they become united, and run in a main stream to the Ocean Sea. If the Phrase be weak, and the Style not every where like itself: the first, shows the legitimation and true Parent; the second, will excuse itself upon the Variety of Matter. For *Virgil*, who wrote his *Eclogues*, *gracili avena*, used stronger pipes when he sounded the wars of *Aeneas*. It may also be laid to my charge that I use divers *Hebrew* words in my first book, and elsewhere; in which language others may think, and I myself acknowledge it, that I am altogether ignorant; but it is true, that some of them I find in *Montanus*, others in Latin character in *S. Senensis*, and of the rest I have borrowed the interpretation of some of my learned friends. But say I had been beholden to neither, yet were it not to be wondered at, having had eleven years leisure to attain the knowledge of that, or of any other tongue, howsoever, I know that it will be said by many, that I might have been more pleasing to the Reader, if I had written the Story of mine own times; having been permitted to draw water as near the Well-head as another. To this I answer, that whosoever in writing a modern History, shall follow truth too near the heels, it may happily strike out his teeth. There is no Mistress or Guide, that hath led her followers and servants into greater miseries. He that goes after her too far off, loseth her sight, and loseth himself: and he that walks after her at a middle distance; I know not whether I should call that kind of course Temper or Baseness. It is true, that I never travailed after men's opinions, when I might have made the best use of them: and I have now too few days remaining, to imitate those, that either out of extreme ambition, or extreme cowardice, or both, do yet, (when death hath them on his shoulders) flatter the world between the bed and the grave. It is enough for me (being in that state I am) to write of the eldest times: wherein also why may it not be said, that in speaking of the past, I point at the present, and tax the vices of those that are yet living, in their persons that are long since dead; and have it laid to my charge. But this I cannot help, though innocent. And certainly if there be any, that, finding themselves spotted like the Tigers of old time, shall find fault with me for painting them over anew, they shall therein accuse themselves justly, and me falsely.

For I protest before the Majesty of God, that I malice no man under the Sun, Impossible I know it is to please all: seeing few or none are so pleased with themselves, or so assured of themselves, by reason of their subjection to their private passions; but they that seem diverse persons in one and the same day. *Seneca* hath said it, and so do I: *Unus mihi pro populo erat*: and to the same effect *Epicurus*, *Hoc ego non multis, sed tibi*; or (as it hath since lamentably fallen out) I may borrow the resolution of an ancient Philosopher, *Satis est unus, Satis est nullus*. For it was for the service of that inestimable Prince *Henry*, the successive hope, and one of the greatest of the Christian World, that I undertook this Work. It pleased him to peruse some part thereof, and to pardon what was amiss. It is now left to the world without a Master; from which all that is presented hath received both blows and thanks. *Eadem probamus, eadem reprehendimus: hic exitus est omnis judicii, in quo lis secundum plures datur*. But these discourses are idle. I know that as the charitable will judge charitably, so against those, *qui gloriantur in malitia*, my present adversity hath disarmed me. I am on the ground already; and therefore have not far to fall: and for rising again, as in the Natural privation there is no recession to habit; so it is seldom seen in the privation politic. I do therefore forbear to style my Readers *Gentle, Courteous*, and *Friendly*, thereby to beg their good opinions, or to promise a second and third volume (which I also intended) if the first receive grace and good acceptance. For that which is already done, may be thought enough; and too much: and it is certain, let us claw the Reader with never so many courteous phrases; yet shall we evermore be thought fools, that write foolishly. For conclusion; all the hope I have lies in this, that I have already found more ungentle and uncourteous Readers of my Love towards them, and well-deserving of them, than ever I shall do again. For had it been otherwise, I should hardly have had this leisure, to have made myself a fool in print.

From Book One of the History of the World

Chapter 1:15 Of Fortune: and of the reason of some things that seem to be by fortune, and against reason and Providence.

. . . But it may be objected, that if Fortune and Chance were not sometimes the causes of good and evil in men, but an idle voice, whereby we express success, how comes it then, that so many worthy and wise men depend upon so many unworthy and empty-headed fools; that riches and honour are given to external men, and without kernel: and so many learned, virtuous, and valiant men wear out their lives in poor and dejected estates. In a word there is no other inferior, or apparent cause, beside the partiality of man's affection, but the fashioning and not fashioning of ourselves according to the time wherein we live, for whosoever is most able, and best sufficient to discern, and hath withal an honest and open heart and loving truth, if Princes, or those that govern, endure no other discourse than their own flatteries, then I say such an one, whose virtue and courage forbiddeth him to be base and a dissembler, shall evermore hang under the wheel, which kind of deserving well and receiving ill, we always falsely charge Fortune withal. For whosoever shall tell any great man or Magistrate, that he is not just, the General of an Army, that he is not valiant, and great Ladies that they are not fair, shall never be made a Counsellor, a Captain, or a Courtier. Neither is it sufficient to be wise with a wise Prince, valiant with a valiant, and just with him that is just, for such a one hath no estate in his prosperity; but he must also change with the successor, if he be of contrary qualities, sail with the tide of the time, and alter form and condition, as the Estate or the Estate's Master changeth: Otherwise how were it possible, that the most base men, and separate from all imitable qualities, could so often attain to honour and riches, but by such an observant slavish course? These men having nothing else to value themselves by, but a counterfeit kind of wondering at other men, and by making them believe that all their vices are virtues, and all their dusty actions crystalline, have yet in all ages prospered equally with the most virtuous, if not exceeded them. For according to Menander . . . *Every fool is won with his own pride and others' flattering applause*: so as whosoever will live altogether out of himself, and study other men's humours, and observe them, shall never be unfortunate; and on the contrary, that man which prizeth truth and virtue (except the season wherein he liveth be of all these, and of all sorts of goodness fruitful) shall never prosper by the possession or profession thereof. It is also a token of a worldly wise man, not to war or contend in vain against the nature of the times wherein he liveth: for such a one is often the author of his own misery, but best it were to follow the advice, which the Pope gave the Bishops of that age, out of *Ovid*, while the Arian Heresy raged:

Dum furor in cursu est, currenti cede furori.
While fury gallops on the way,
Let no man fury's gallop stay.

And if *Cicero* (than whom that world begat not a man of more reputed judgment) had followed the counsel of his brother *Quintus . . . He might then have died the death of nature; and been with an untorn and undissevered body buried*; for, as *Petrarch* in the same place noteth: . . . *What more foolish than for him that despairs, especially of the effect, to be entangled with endless contentions*? Whosoever therefore will set before him *Machiavel's two marks to shoot at* (to wit) riches, and glory, must set on and take off a back of iron to a weak wooden bow, that it may fit both the strong and the feeble: for as he, that first devised to add sails to rowing vessels, did either so proportion them, as being fastened aloft, and towards the head of his Mast, he might abide all winds and storms, or else he sometime or other perished by his own invention: so that man which prizeth virtue for itself, and cannot endure to hoise and strike his sails, as the divers natures of calms and storms require, must cut his sails and his cloth, of mean length and breadth, and content himself with a slow and sure navigation, (to wit) a mean and free estate. But of this dispute of Fortune, and the rest, or of whatsoever Lords or Gods, imaginary powers, or causes, the wit (or rather foolishness) of man hath found out: let us resolve with *St Paul*, who hath taught us, that there is *but one God, the Father, of whom are all things, and we in him, and one Lord, Jesus Christ, by whom are all things, and we by him*; there are diversities of operations, but God is the same which worketh all in all.

Chapter 2:3 Of our base and frail bodies: and that the care thereof should yield to the immortal soul.

The external man God formed out of the dust of the earth, or according to the significance of the word, *Adam* or *Adamath*, of red earth, or, *ex limo terrae*, out of the slime of the earth, or a mixed matter of earth and water . . . *Not that God made an Image or Statue of clay, but out of clay, earth or dust God formed and made flesh, blood and bone, with all parts of man.*

That Man was formed of earth and dust, did *Abraham* acknowledge, when in humble fear he called unto God, to save *Sodom: Let not my Lord now be angry, if I speak, I, that am but dust and ashes: And in these houses of clay, whose foundation is in the dust, do our souls inhabit,* according to *Job*; and though our own eyes do everywhere behold the sudden and resistless assaults of death, and Nature assureth us by never-failing experience, and Reason by infallible demonstration, that our times upon the earth have neither certainty nor durability, that our bodies are but the Anvils of pain and diseases, and our Minds the Hives of unnumbered cares, sorrows, and passions; and that (when we are most glorified) we are but those painted posts, against which Envy and Fortune direct their darts; yet such is the true unhappiness of our condition, and the dark ignorance, which covereth the eyes of our understanding, that we only prize, pamper, and exalt this vassal and slave of death, and forget altogether (or only remember at our cast-away leisure) the imprisoned immortal Soul, which can neither die with the reprobate, nor perish with the mortal parts of virtuous men: seeing God's justice in the one, and his goodness in the other is exercised for evermore, as the ever-living subjects of his reward and punishment. But when is it that we examine this great account? never while we have one vanity left us to spend: we plead for titles, till our breath fail us; dig for riches, while our strength enableth us, exercise malice, while we can revenge; and then, when Time hath beaten from us both youth, pleasure, and health, and that nature itself hateth the house of old age, we remember with *Job*, that *we must go the way, from whence we shall not return, and that our bed is made ready for us in the dark*; and then I say, looking over-late into the bottom of our conscience which Pleasure and Ambition had locked up from us all our lives, we behold therein the fearful images of our actions past, and withal, this terrible inscription: *That God will bring every work into judgment, that man hath done under the Sun.*

But what examples have ever moved us? what persuasions reformed us? or what threatenings made us afraid? We behold other men's Tragedies played before us, we hear what is promised and threatened: but the world's bright glory hath put out the eyes of our minds; and these betraying lights (with which we only see) do neither look up towards termless joys, nor down towards endless sorrows, till we neither know, nor can look for any thing else, at the world's hands. Of which excellently *Marius Victor*:

. . .

Diseases, famine, enemies, in us no change have wrought,
What erst we were, we are; still in the same snare caught:
No time can our corrupted manners mend,
In Vice we dwell, in Sin that hath no end.

But let us not flatter our immortal souls herein: for to neglect God all our lives, and know that we neglect him, to offend God voluntarily, and know that we offend him, casting our hopes on the Peace, which we trust to make at parting, is no other than a rebellious presumption, and (that which is the worst of all) even a contemptuous laughing to scorn, and deriding of God, his laws, and precepts . . . *They hope in vain*, saith Bernard, *which in this sort flatter themselves with God's mercy*.

Chapter 2:5 That Man is (as it were) a little world: with a digression touching our mortality.

Man, thus compounded and formed by God, was an abstract or model, or brief Story of the Universal: in whom God concluded the creation, and work of the world, and whom he made the last and most excellent of his creatures, being internally endued with a divine understanding, by which he might contemplate and serve his Creator, after whose image he was formed, and endued with the powers and faculties of reason and other abilities, that thereby also he might govern and rule the world, and all other God's creatures therein. And whereas God created three sorts of living natures, (to wit) Angelical, Rational, and Brutal; giving to Angels an intellectual, and to Beasts a sensual nature, he vouchsafed unto man, both the intellectual of Angels, the sensitive of Beasts, and the proper rational belonging unto man; and therefore (saith *Gregory Nazianzene*:) . . . *Man is the bond* and chain *which tieth together both natures*: and because in the little frame of man's body there is a representation of the Universal, and (by allusion) a kind of participation of all the parts thereof, therefore was man called *Microcosmos*, or the little world . . . *God therefore placed in the earth the man whom he had made, as it were another world, the great and large world in the small and little world*: for out of earth and dust was formed the flesh of man, and therefore heavy, and lumpish; the bones of his body we may compare to the hard rocks and stones, and therefore strong and durable; of which *Ovid*:

. . . From thence our kind hard-hearted is, enduring pain and care,
Approving, that our bodies of a stony nature are.

His blood, which disperseth itself by the branches of veins through all the body, may be resembled to those waters, which are carried by brooks and rivers over all the earth; his breath to the air; his natural heat to the enclosed warmth, which the Earth hath in itself, which stirred up by the heat of the Sun, assisteth Nature in the speedier procreation of those varieties, which the Earth bringeth forth; our radical moisture, oil, or Balsamum (whereon the natural heat feedeth and is maintained) is resembled to the fat and fertility of the earth; the hairs of man's body, which adorns or overshadows it, to the grass, which covereth the upper face and skin of the earth; our generative power, to Nature, which produceth all things; our determinations, to the light, wandering, and unstable clouds, carried everywhere with uncertain winds; our eyes, to the light of the Sun and Moon, and the beauty of our youth, to the flowers of the Spring, which, either in a very short time, or with the Sun's heat dry up, and wither away, or the fierce puffs of wind blow them from the stalks; the thoughts of our mind; to the motion of Angels; and our pure understanding (formerly called *Mens*, and that which always looketh upwards) to those intellectual natures, which are always present with God; and lastly our immortal souls (while they are righteous) are by God himself beautified with the title of his own image and similitude: and although, in respect of God, there is no man just, or good, or righteous: (for . . . *Behold, he found folly in his Angels*, saith *Job*) yet with such a kind of difference, as there is between the substance, and the shadow, there may be found a goodness in man: which God being pleased to accept, hath therefore called man, the image and similitude of his own righteousness. In this also is the little world of man compared, and made more like the Universal (man being the measure of all things . . . saith *Aristotle* and *Pythagoras*) that the four complexions resemble the four Elements, and the seven Ages of man the seven Planets: whereof our Infancy is compared to the Moon, in which we seem only to live and grow, as Plants; the second age to *Mercury*, wherein we are taught and instructed; our third age to *Venus*, the days of love, desire, and vanity; the fourth to the *Sun*, the strong, flourishing, and beautiful age of man's life; the fifth to *Mars*, in which we seek honour and victory, and in which our thoughts travail to ambitious ends; the sixth age is ascribed to *Jupiter*, in which we begin to take account of our times, judge of ourselves, and grow to the perfection of our understanding; the last and seventh to *Saturn*, wherein our days are sad and overcast, and in which we find by dear and lamentable experience, and by the loss which can never be repaired, that of all our vain passions and affections past, the sorrow only abideth: our attendants are sicknesses, and variable infirmities; and by how much the more we are accompanied with plenty, by so much the more greedily is our end desired, whom when Time hath made unsociable to others, we become a burden to ourselves: being of no other use, than to hold the riches we have, from our successors. In this time it is, when (as aforesaid) we, for the most part, and never before, prepare for our eternal habitation, which we pass on unto, with many sighs, groans, and sad thoughts, and in the end, by the workmanship of death, finish the sorrowful business of a wretched life, towards which we always travail both sleeping and waking; neither have those beloved companions of honour and riches any power at all, to hold us any one day, by the promises of glorious entertainments; but by what crooked path soever we walk, the same leadeth on directly to the house of death: whose doors lie open at all hours, and to all persons. For this tide of man's life, after it once turneth and declineth, ever runneth with a perpetual ebb and falling stream, but never floweth again: our leaf once fallen, springeth no more; neither doth the Sun or the Summer adorn us again, with the garments of new leaves and flowers.

Redditur arboribus florens revirentibus aetas,
Ergo non homini, quod fuit ante, redit.

To which I give this sense,

The plants and trees made poor and old
By Winter envious,
The Spring-time bounteous
Covers again, from shame and cold:
But never Man repair'd again
His youth and beauty lost,
Though art, and care, and cost,
Do promise Nature's help in vain.

And of which Catullus Epigram 53,

Soles occidere et redire possunt:
Nobis cum semel occidit brevis lux,
Nox est perpetua una dormienda
The Sun may set and rise:
But we contrariwise
Sleep after our short light
One everlasting night.

For if there were any baiting place, or rest, in the course or race of man's life, then, according to the doctrine of the *Academics*, the same might also perpetually be maintained; but as there is a continuance of motion in natural living things, and as the sap and juice, wherein the life of Plants is preserved, doth evermore ascend or descend: so is it with the life of man, which is always either increasing towards ripeness and perfection, or declining and decreasing towards rottenness and dissolution.

Chapter 5:5 Of the long lives of the Patriarchs; and some of late memory.

. . . But besides the old age of the world, how far doth our education and simplicity of living differ from that old time? the tender bringing up of children, first fed and nourished with the milk of a strange Dug; an unnatural curiosity having taught all women (but the beggar) to find out Nurses, which necessity only ought to commend unto them: the hasty marriages in tender years, wherein Nature being but yet green and growing, we rent from her and replant her branches, while herself hath not yet any root sufficient to maintain her own top; and such half-ripe seeds (for the most part) in their growing up wither in the bud, and wax old even in their infancy. But above all things the exceeding luxuriousness of this gluttonous age, wherein we press nature with overweighty burdens, and finding her strength defective we take the work out of her hands, and commit it to the artificial help of strong waters, hot spices, and provoking sauces; of which *Lucan* hath these elegant Verses . . .

O wasteful Riot, never well content
With low-priz'd fare; hunger ambitious
Of cates by land and sea far fetched and sent:
Vain glory of a table sumptuous,
Learn with how little life may be preserved,
In Gold and Myrrh they need not to carouse,
But with the brook the people's thirst is served:
Who fed with bread and water are not starved.

The *Egyptians* affirm, that the longest time of man's life is an hundred years, because the heart in a perfect body waxeth and groweth to strength fifty years, and afterwards by the same degree decayeth and withereth. *Epigenes* findeth in his Philosophy, that the life of man may reach to the period of an hundred and twenty years and *Berosus* to an hundred and seventeen years. These opinions *Pliny* repeateth and reproveth, producing many examples to the contrary. In the last taxation, number and review of the eighth Region of *Italy*, there were found in the roll (saith *Pliny*) four and fifty persons of an hundred years of age: seven and fifty of an hundred and ten: two, of an hundred and five and twenty: four, of an hundred and thirty: as many that were an hundred and five and thirty, or an hundred and seven and thirty years old: and last of all three men of an hundred and forty: and this search was made in the times of *Vespasian* the Father and the Son.

The simple diet and temperate life of the *Essaeans* gave them long account of many years: so did it to the Secretaries of *Egyptian* ceremonies, to the *Persian's Magicians* and *Indian Brachmans*. The

Greeks affirm out of *Homer*, that *Nestor* lived three ages, and *Tiresias* six, *Sybilla* three hundred years, *Endymion* of the less *Asia*, little less: also *Masinissa* of *Numidia* lived very long, and *Dando* of *Illyria*. Among the kings of *Arcadia* many lived three hundred years (saith *Ephorus*) *Hellanicus* affirmeth of the *Epeians*, that some of them live full two hundred years: and so doth *Diodorus Siculus* of the *Egyptians*; and that these reports are not fabulous, *Josephus* bringeth many witnesses with himself, as *Marethon*, *Berosus*, *Mochus*, *Estius*, *Hieronymus*, *Aegyptius*, *Hecataeus*, *Ephorus*, and others. And *Anthony Fume* an Historian of good reputation reporteth, that in the year 1570 there was an *Indian* presented to *Solyman*, *General* of the *Turk's* Army, who had outlived three hundred years. I myself knew the old Countess of *Desmond* of *Inchiquin* in *Munster*, who lived in the year 1589, and many years since, who was married in *Edward* the fourth's time, and held her Jointure from all the Earls of *Desmond* since then; and that this is true, all the Noblemen and Gentlemen of *Munster* can witness. *Strozzius Cicogna*, out of *Torquemada Maffaeus*, and the like Authors, telleth of some that have not only far exceeded the term prescribed by *Epigenes*; but been repaired from the withered estate of decrepit age to fresh youth. But for length of life, if we note but the difference between the ability of men in those days wherein *Galen* the Physician lived, it may easily prove unto us what reeds we are in respect of those Cedars of the first age. For *Galen* did ordinarily let blood six pound weight, whereas we (for the most part) stop at six ounces. But to conclude this part, there are three things (not counting Constellations) which are the natural causes of a long and healthful life; (to wit) strong Parents, a pure and thin air, and temperate use of diet, pleasure, and rest: for those which are built of rotten timber, or mouldering stone, cannot stand long upright: on air we feed always and in every instant, and on meats but at times: and yet the heavy load of abundance, wherewith we oppress and overcharge Nature, maketh her to sink unawares in the midway; and therefore with a good constitution, a pure air, and a temperate use of those things which Nature wanteth, are the only friends and companions of a long life.

Chapter 5:8 That Heathenism and Judaism, after many wounds were at length about the same time under Julian miraculously confounded.

But all these are again vanished: for the inventions of mortal men are no less mortal than themselves. The Fire, which the *Chaldeans* worshipped for a God, is crept into every man's chimney, which the lack of fuel starveth, water quencheth, and want of air suffocateth: *Jupiter* is no more vexed with *Juno's* jealousies: Death hath persuaded him to chastity, and her to patience; and that Time which hath devoured itself, hath also eaten up both the bodies and images of him and his: yea, their stately Temples of stone and dureful Marble. The houses and sumptuous buildings erected to *Baal*, can nowhere be found upon the earth; nor any monument of that glorious Temple consecrated to *Diana*. There are none now in *Phoenicia*, that lament the death of *Adonis*; nor any in *Libya*, *Creta*, *Thessalia*, or elsewhere, that can ask counsel or help from *Jupiter*. The great god *Pan* hath broken his Pipes, *Apollo's* Priests are become speechless; and the Trade of riddles in Oracles, with the Devil's telling men's fortunes therein, is taken up by counterfeit *Egyptians*, and cozening *Astrologers*.

But it was long ere the Devil gave way to these his overthrows and dishonours: for after the Temple of *Apollo* at *Delphos* (one of his chief Mansions) was many times robbed, burnt, and destroyed; yet by his diligence the same was often enriched, repaired, and reedified again, till by the hand of God himself it received the last and utter subversion. For it was robbed of all the Idols and ornaments therein by the *Euboean Pirates*; Secondly, by the *Phlegians* utterly sacked: thirdly, by *Pyrrhus* the son of *Achilles*: fourthly, by the Army of *Xerxes*: fifthly, by the Captains of the *Phocenses*: sixthly, by *Nero*, who carried thence five hundred brasen images: all which were new made, and therein again set up at the common charge. But whatsoever was gathered between the time of *Nero* and *Constantine*, the Christian Army made spoil of, defacing as much as the time permitted them; notwithstanding all this it was again gloriously rebuilt, and so remained till such time as *Julian* the *Apostate* sent thither to know the success of his *Parthian* enterprise, at which time it was utterly burnt and consumed with fire from Heaven; and the image of *Apollo* himself, and all the rest of the Idols therein molten down and lost in the earth.

The like success had the *Jews* in the same *Julian's* time, when by his permission they assembled themselves to rebuild the Temple of *Jerusalem*: for while they were busied to lay the foundations, their buildings were overthrown by an Earthquake, and many thousands of the *Jews* were overwhelmed with the ruins, and others slain, and scattered by tempest and thunder: though *Am. Marcellinus* report it more favourably for the *Jews*, ascribing this to the nature of that element. For, saith he, *Allypius* and the Ruler of the Province of *Judea*, being by *Julian* busied in the reedifying of this Temple, flaming balls of fire issuing near the foundation, and oft consuming the workmen, made the enterprise frustrate.

Chapter 5:9 Of the last refuges of the Devil to maintain his Kingdom.

Now the Devil, because he cannot play upon the open stage of this world (as in those days) and being still as industrious as ever, finds it more for his advantage to creep into the minds of men; and inhabiting in the Temples of their hearts, works them to a more effectual adoration of himself than ever. For whereas he first taught them to sacrifice to Monsters, to dead stones cut into faces of beasts, birds, and other mixed Natures; he now sets before them the high and shining Idol of glory, the all-commanding Image of bright Gold. He tells them that Truth is the Goddess of dangers and oppressions: that chastity is the enemy of nature; and lastly, that as all virtue (in general) is without taste: so pleasure satisfieth and delighteth every sense: for true wisdom (saith he) is exercised in nothing else, than in the obtaining of power to oppress, and of riches to maintain plentifully our worldly delights. And if this *Arch-politician* find in his Pupils any remorse, any fear or feeling of God's future judgment, he persuades them that God hath so great need of men's souls, that he will accept them at any time, and upon any conditions: interrupting by his vigilant endeavours all offer of timeful return towards God, by laying those great blocks of rugged poverty, and despised contempt in the narrow passage leading to his divine presence. But as the mind of man hath two ports, the one always frequented by the entrance of manifold vanities; the other desolate and overgrown with grass, by which enter our charitable thoughts and divine contemplations: so hath that of death a double and twofold opening: worldly misery passing by the one, worldly prosperity by the other: at the entrance of the one we find our sufferings and patience, to attend us: (all which have gone before us to prepare our joys) at the other our cruelties, covetousness, licentiousness, injustice, and oppressions (the Harbingers of most fearful and terrible sorrow) staying for us. And as the Devil our most industrious enemy was ever most diligent: so is he now more laborious than ever: the long day of mankind drawing fast towards an evening, and the world's Tragedy and time near at an end.

Chapter 9:3 Of the good Government of the first Kings.

Now this first age After the flood, and after such time as the people were increased, and the families became strong, and dispersed into several parts of the world, was by ancient Historians called Golden: Ambition and Covetousness being as then but green, and newly grown up; the seeds and effects whereof were as yet but potential and in the blowth and bud. For while the Law of Nature was the rule of man's life, they then sought for no larger Territory than themselves could compass and manure: they erected no other magnificent buildings, than sufficient to defend them from cold and tempest: they cared for no other delicacy of fare, or curiosity of diet, than to maintain life: nor for any other apparel than to cover them from the cold, the Rain and the Sun.

And sure if we understand by that Age (which was called Golden) the ancient simplicity of our forefathers, this name may then truly be cast upon those elder times; but if it be taken otherwise, then, whether the same may be attributed more to any one time than to another, (I mean to one limited time and none else) it may be doubted. For good and golden Kings make good and golden Ages: and all times have brought forth of both sorts. And as the infancy of Empire, (when Princes played their prizes, and did then only woo men to obedience) might be called the golden Age: so may the beginning of all Princes' times be truly called golden, for be it that men affect honour it is then best purchased: or if honour affect men, it is then that good deservings have commonly the least impediments: and if ever Liberality overflow her banks and bounds, the same is then best warranted both by policy and example. But Age and Time do not only harden and shrink the openest and most *Jovial* hearts, but the experience which it bringeth with it layeth Princes' torn estates before their eyes, and (withal) persuadeth them to compassionate themselves. And although there be no Kings under the Sun whose means are answerable unto other men's desires; yet such as value all things by their own respects, do no sooner find their appetites unanswered, but they complain of alteration, and account the times injurious and iron. And as this falleth out in the reign of every King, so doth it in the life of every man, if his days be many: for our younger years are our golden Age; which being eaten up by time, we praise those seasons which our youth accompanied: and (indeed) the grievous alterations in ourselves, and the pains and diseases which never part from us but at the grave, make the times seem so differing and displeasing: especially the quality of man's nature being also such, as it adoreth and extolleth the passages of the former, and condemneth the present state how just soever . . . *It comes to pass* (saith Tacitus) *by the vice of our malignity, that we always extol the time past, and hold the present fastidious*: For it is one of the errors of wayward age . . . *that they are praisers of forepast times*, forgetting this advice of *Solomon*. *Say not then, Why is it that the former days were better than these? for thou dost not inquire wisely of this thing:* to which purpose *Seneca* . . . *Our ancestors have complained, we do complain, our children will complain, that good manners are gone, that wickedness doth reign, and all things grow worse and worse, and fall into all evil*. These are the usual discourses of Age and misfortune. But hereof what can we add to this of *Arnobius* . . . *Whatsoever is new, in time shall be made old: and the ancientest things when they took beginning were also new and sudden*. Wherefore not to stand in much admiration of these first times, which the discontentments of present times have made golden, this we may set down for certain, that as it was the virtue of the first Kings, which (after God) gave them Crowns: so the love of their people thereby purchased held the same Crowns on their heads. And as God gave the obedience of subjects to Princes: so (relatively) he gave the care and justice of Kings to the Subjects; having respect, not only to the Kings themselves, but even to the meanest of his Creatures . . . *The infinite goodness of God doth not attend any one only*: for he that made the small and the great, careth for all alike: and it is the care which Kings have of all theirs, which makes them beloved of all theirs; and by a general love it is, that Princes hold a general obedience: for . . . *All human power is rooted in the will or dispositions of men*.

From Book Two of the History of the World

Chapter 4:13 Of the several commandments of the Decalogue . . .

. . . The fourth of the second Table, is, that we shall not steal. And if that kind of violent robbery had been used in *Moses'* time, which many Ruffians practice nowadays in *England*, and to the dishonour of our Nation more in *England*, than in any Region of the world among *Christians*, out of doubt, he would have censured them by death, and not by restitution, though quadruple. For I speak not of the poor and miserable souls, whom hunger and extreme necessity enforceth, but of those detested Thieves, who, to maintain themselves Lordlike, assault, rob, and wound the Merchant, Artificer, and Labouring man, or break by violence into other men's houses, and spend in Bravery, Drunkenness, and upon Harlots, in one day, what other men sometimes have laboured for all their lives: impoverishing whole families: and taking the bread and food from the mouths of their children. And this Commandment might easily be observed, it would soon appear, if Princes would resolve, but for a few years to pardon none. For it is the hope of life, and the argument of sparing the first offence, that encourageth these Hell-hounds. And if every man may presume to be pardoned once, there is no state or commonwealth, but these men would in a short time impoverish or destroy it.

Chapter 13:7 Of Abimelech, Tholah, and Jair, and of the Lapithae, and of Theseus, Hippolytus, &c.

After the death of *Gideon*, *Abimelech* his base son begotten on a Concubine of the *Sechemites*, remembering what offers had been made to his father by the people, who desired to make him and his their perpetual Princes; and as it seemeth, supposing (notwithstanding his father's religious modesty) that some of his brethren might take on them the Sovereignty, practised with the inhabitants of *Sechem* (of which his mother was native) to make election of himself, who being easily moved with the glory, to have a King of their own, readily condescended: and the better to enable *Abimelech*, they borrowed 70 pieces of silver of their Idol *Baalberith*, with which treasure he hired a company of loose and desperate vagabonds, to assist his first detestable enterprise, to wit, the slaughter of his 70 brethren the sons of *Gideon*, begotten on his wives, of which he had many, of all which none escaped but *Jotham* the youngest, who hid himself from his present fury: all which he executed on one stone, a cruelty exceeding all that hath been written of in any age. Such is human ambition, a monster that neither feareth God (though all-powerful, and whose revenges are without date and for everlasting) neither hath it respect to nature, which laboureth the preservation of every being: but it rageth also against her, though garnished with beauty which never dieth, and with love that hath no end. All other passions and affections by which the souls of men are tormented, are by their contraries oftentimes restricted or qualified. But ambition, which begetteth very vice, and is itself the child and darling of *Satan*, looketh only towards the ends by itself set down, forgetting nothing (how fearful and inhuman soever) which may serve it: remembering nothing, whatsoever justice, piety, right or religion can offer and allege on the contrary. It ascribeth the lamentable affects of like attempts, to the error or weakness of the undertakers, and rather praiseth the adventure than feareth the like success. It was the first sin that the world had, and began in *Angels*: for which they were cast into hell, without hope of redemption. It was more ancient than man, and therefore no part of his natural corruption. The punishment also preceded his creation, yet hath the Devil which felt the smart thereof, taught him to forget the one as out of date, and to practise the other, as befitting every age, and man's condition.

Jotham the youngest of *Gideon's* sons having escaped the present peril, sought by his best persuasions to alienate the *Sechemites*, from the assisting of this merciless tyrant, letting them know, that those which were virtuous, and whom reason and religion had taught the safe and happy estate of moderate subjection, had refused to receive as unlawful, what others had not power to give, without direction from the King of Kings: who from the beginning (as to his own peculiar people) had appointed them by whom and how to be governed. This he taught them by the Olive, which contented itself with its fatness, the Fig-tree with sweetness, and the Vine with the good juice it had: the Bramble only, who was most base, cut down all the rest, and accepted the Sovereignty. He also foretold them by a Prophetical spirit, what should befall them in the end, and how a fire should come out of the Bramble, and consume the *Cedars* of *Libanon*.

Now (as it is an easy matter to call those men back whom rage without right led on) *Gaal* the son of *Ebed* withdrew the Citizens of *Sechem*, from the service of *Abimelech*: who therefore after some assaults entered the place, and mastered it; and in conclusion fired the town, wherein their Idol *Baalberith* was worshipped, and put all the people of all sorts to the slaughter. Lastly, in the assault of the Castle or Tower of *Teber*, himself was wounded in the head with a stone thrown over the wall by a woman, and finding himself mortally bruised, he commanded his own page to pierce his body, thereby to avoid the dishonour of being slain by so feeble a hand.

While *Abimelech* usurped the Government, the *Lapithae* and *Centaurs* made war against the Thebans. These nations were descended of *Apollo* and were the first in those parts that devised to manage horses, to bridle and to sit them: insomuch as when they first came down from the mountains of *Pindus*, into the plains, those which had never seen horsemen before, thought them creatures compounded of men and horses; so did the *Mexicans* when *Ferdinando Cortes* the *Spaniard* first invaded that Empire.

After the death of *Abimelech*, *Thola* of *Issachar* governed *Israel* 23 years, and after him *Jair* the *Gileadite* 22 years, who seemeth to be descended of *Jair* the son of *Manasse*, who in Moses' time conquered a great part of *Gilead*, and called the same after his own name, *Haboth Jair*. For to this *Jair* there remained thirty of those Cities, which his ancestor had recovered from the *Amorites*. Of these Judges, because there is nothing else written, it is an argument that during all their times, *Israel* lived without disturbance and in peace.

When *Jair* judged *Israel*, *Priamus* began to reign in *Troy*, who at such time as *Hercules* sacked *Ilium*, was carried away captive with his sister *Hesione* into *Greece*, and being afterwards redeemed for ransom, he rebuilt and greatly strengthened, and adorned *Troy*; and so far enlarged his Dominions, as he became the supreme Lord in effect of all *Asia* the Less. He married *Hecuba* the daughter of *Cisseus* King of *Thrace*, and had in all (saith *Cicero*) fifty sons, whereof seventeen by *Hecuba*, of whom *Paris* was one; who attempting to recover his aunt *Hesione*, took *Helena* the wife of *Menelaus*, the cause of the war which followed.

Theseus the tenth King of *Athens*, began likewise to reign in the beginning of *Jair*: some writers call him the son of *Neptune* and *Aethra*: but *Plutarch* in the Story of his life finds him begotten by *Aegeus*, of whom the *Grecian* sea between it and *Asia* the less took name. For when *Minos* had mastered the *Athenians*, so far, as he forced them to pay him seven of their sons every year for tribute, whom he enclosed within a *Labyrinth*, to be devoured by the monster *Minotaur*: because belike the sons of *Taurus*, which he begat on *Pasiphae* the Queen, had the charge of them: Among these seven *Theseus* thrust himself, not doubting by his valour to deliver the rest, and to free his country of that slavery occasioned for the death of *Androgeus*, *Minos* his son.

And having possessed himself of *Ariadne's* affection, who was *Minos'* daughter, he received from her a bottom of thread, by which he conducted himself through all the crooked and inextricable turnings of the *Labyrinth*, made in all like that of the City of *Crocodiles* in *Egypt*; by mean whereof, having slain *Minotaur*, he found a ready way to return. But whereas his father *Aegeus* had given order, that if he came back with victory and in safety, he should use a white sail in sign thereof, and not that mournful black sail, under which they had left the port of *Athens*. This instruction being either forgotten or neglected, *Aegeus* descrying the ship of *Theseus* with a black sail cast himself over the rocks into the sea, afterward called of his name *Aegeum*.

One of the first famous acts of *Theseus* was the killing of *Scyron*, who kept a passage between *Megara* and the *Peloponnesian Isthmus*, and threw all whom he mastered into the sea, from the high rocks. Afterward he did the like to *Cercyon*, by wrestling, who used by that Art to kill others. He also rid the Country of *Procrustes*, who used to bend down the strong limbs of two trees, and fastened by cords such as he took, part of them to one and part to the other bough, and by their springing back tare them asunder. So did he root out *Periphetes* and other mischievous thieves and murderers. He overthrew the army of the *Amazons*, who after many victories and vastations, entered the Territory of *Athens*. *Theseus* having taken their Queen *Hippolyta* prisoner, begat on her *Hippolytus*; with whom afterward his mother-in-law *Phaedra*, falling in love, and he refusing to abuse his father's bed, *Phaedra* persuaded *Theseus* that his son offered to force her: after which it is feigned that *Theseus* besought *Neptune* to revenge this wrong of his son's, by some violent death. *Neptune*, taking a time of advantage sent out his Sea-Calves, as *Hippolytus* passed by the sea-shore, and so affrighted his horses, as casting the Coach over, he was (by being entangled therein) torn in pieces. Which miserable and undeserved destiny, when *Phaedra* had heard of, she strangled herself. After which it is feigned, that *Diana* entreated *Aesculapius* to set *Hippolytus* his pieces together, and to restore him to life: which done, because he was chaste, she led him with her into *Italy*, to accompany her in her hunting and field sports.

It is probable that *Hippolytus*, when his father sought his life, thinking to escape by Sea, was affronted thereat, and received many wounds in forcing his passage and escape; which wounds *Aesculapius*, to wit, some skilful Physician, or Chirurgeon healed again, after which he passed into *Italy*, where he lived with *Diana*, that is the life of a hunter, in which he most delighted. But of these ancient profane Stories, *Plutarch* saith well, that as *Cosmographers* in their descriptions of the world, where they find many vast places whereof they know nothing, fill the same with strange beasts, birds, and fishes, and with *Mathematical* lines, so do the *Grecian* Historians and Poets, embroider and intermix the tales of ancient times, with a world of fictions and fabulous discourses. True it is, that *Theseus* did many great things in imitation of *Hercules*, whom he made his pattern, and was the first that gathered the *Athenians*, from being dispersed in thin and ragged villages: in recompense whereof, and for devising them laws to live under, and in order, he was by the beggarly, mutable, and ungrateful multitude, in the end banished: some say *per Ostracismum*, by the

Law of Lots, or names written on shells, which was a device of his own . . .

Chapter 19:6 A conjecture of the causes hindering the reunion of Israel with Juda . . .

. . . On the other side, such of the kings of *Israel* as perished by treason (which were seven of the twenty) were all slain by conspiracy of the great men, who aspired by treason to the Crown: the people being so far from embruing their hands in the blood of their Sovereigns, that (after *Nadab*) they did never forbear to revenge the death of their Kings, when it lay in their power; nor approve the good success of treason, unless fear compelled them. So that the death of two Kings, being throughly revenged upon other two, namely the death of *Elah* and *Zacharia*, upon *Zimri* and *Shallum*, who traitorously got and usurped, for a little while, their places; only three of the seven remain, whose ends how the people took, it may be doubtful. Though indeed it is precisely said of the slaughter, committed on *Ahab's* children by *Jehu*, that the people durst not fight with him that did it, because they *were exceedingly afraid*: and the same fear might be in them at the death of *Peka*, whose history (as others of that time) is cursorily passed over. The like may be pronounced, and more absolutely, of the Kings of *England*, that never any of them perished by fury of the people, but by treason of such as did succeed them, neither was there any motive urging so forcibly the death of King *Edward* and king *Richard* when they were in prison, as fear lest the people should stir in their quarrel. And certainly (howsoever all that the law calls treason, be interpreted, as tending finally to the King's destruction) in those treasonable insurrections of the vulgar, which have here most prevailed, the fury of the multitude hath quenched itself with the blood of some great Officers; no such rebellions, howsoever wicked and barbarous otherwise, thirsting after the ruin of their natural Sovereign, but rather forbearing the advantages gotten upon his royal person: which if any man impute unto gross ignorance, another may more charitably, and I think, more truly, ascribe to a reverent affection. Wherefore that fable of *Briareus*, who, being loosened by *Pallas*, did with his hundred hands give assistance to *Jupiter*, when all the rest of the Gods conspired against him, is very fitly expounded by Sir *Francis Bacon*, as signifying, that Monarchs need not to fear any curbing of their absoluteness by mighty subjects, as long as by wisdom they keep the hearts of the people, who will be sure to come in on their side. Though indeed the Story might very well have borne the same interpretation, as it is rehearsed by *Homer*, who tells us that *Pallas* was one of the conspiracy, and that *Thetis* alone did mar all their practice, by loosening *Briareus*. For a good form of government sufficeth by itself to retain the people, not only without assistance of a laborious Wit, but even against all devices of the greatest and shrewdest politicians: every Sheriff and Constable, being sooner able to arm the multitude, in the King's behalf, than any over-weening rebel how mighty soever, can against him . . .

Chapter 20:6 How Ahazia perished with the house of Ahab: and how that Family was destroyed by Jehu.

. . . The King's Palace was joining to the wall, by the gate of the City, where *Jezabel* might soon be advertised of this calamity, if she did not with her own eyes behold it. Now it was high time for her to call to God for mercy, whose judgment, pronounced against her long before, had overtaken her, when she least expected it. But she, full of indignation, and proud thoughts, made herself ready in all haste, and painted her face, hoping with her stately and imperious looks to daunt the Traitor, or at least to utter some *Apophthegm*, that should express her brave spirit, and brand him with such a reproach as might make him odious for ever. Little did she think upon the hungry dogs, that were ordained to devour her, whose paunches the *stibium* with which she besmeared her eyes, would more offend, than the scolding language wherewith she armed her tongue, could trouble the ears of him that had her in his power. As *Jehu* drew near she opened her window, and looking out upon him, began to put him in mind of *Zimri*, that had not long enjoyed the fruits of his treason, and murder of the King his Master. This was in mere human valuation stoutly spoken, but was indeed a part of miserable folly, as are all things, howsoever laudable, if they have an ill relation to *God the Lord of all*. Her own *Eunuchs* that stood by and heard her, were not affected so much as with any compassion of her fortune; much less was her enemy daunted with her proud spirit. When *Jehu* saw that she did use the little remainder of her life in seeking to vex him; he made her presently to understand her own estate, by deeds and not by words. He only called to her servants to know which of them would be of his side, and soon found them ready to offer their service, before the very face of their proud Lady. Hereupon he commanded them to cast her down headlong: which immediately they performed without all regard of her greatness and estate, wherein she had a few hours before shined so gloriously in the eyes of men; of men that considered not the judgments of God that had been denounced against her.

So perished this accursed woman by the rude hands of her own servants, at the commandment of her greatest enemy, that was yesterday her subject, but now her Lord; and she perished miserably struggling in vain with base grooms, who contumeliously did hale and thrust her, whilst her insulting enemy sat on horseback, adding indignity to her grief by scornfully beholding the shameful manner of her fall, and trampling her body under foot. Her dead carcass that was left without the walls was devoured by dogs, and her very memory was odious. Thus the vengeance of God rewarded her Idolatry, murder, and oppression, with slow, but sure payment, and full interest.

Chapter 21:6 A digression, wherein is maintained the liberty of using conjecture in histories.

Thus much concerning the person of *Joash*, from whom, as from a new root, the tree of *David* was propagated into many branches. In handling of which matter, the more I consider the nature of this History, and the diversity between it and others, the less me thinks, I need to suspect mine own presumption, as deserving blame, for curiosity in matter of doubt, or boldness in liberty of conjecture. For all Histories do give us information of human counsels and events, as far forth as the knowledge and faith of the writers can afford; but of God's will, by which all things are ordered, they speak only at random, and many times falsely. This we often find in profane writers, who ascribe the ill success of great undertakings to the neglect of some impious rites, whereof indeed God abhorred the performance as vehemently, as they thought him to be highly offended with the omission. Hereat we may the less wonder, if we consider the answer made by the *Jews* in *Egypt* unto *Jeremy* the prophet reprehending their idolatry. For, howsoever the written Law of *God* was known unto the people, and his punishments laid upon them for contempt thereof were very terrible, and even then but newly executed; yet were they so obstinately bent unto their own wills, that they would not by any means be drawn to acknowledge the true cause of their affliction. But they told the prophet roundly, that they would worship the *Queen of Heaven*, as they and their fathers, their Kings and their Princes had used to do; *For then* (said they) *had we plenty of victuals, and were well, and felt no evil*: adding that all manner of miseries were befallen them, since they left off the service of the *Queen of Heaven*. So blind is the wisdom of man, in looking into the counsel of God, which to find out there is no better nor other guide than his own written will not perverted by vain additions.

But this History of the Kings of *Israel* and *Juda* hath herein a singular prerogative above all that have been written by the most sufficient of merely human authors: it setteth down expressly the true, and first causes of all that happened; not in imputing the death of *Ahab* to his overforwardness in battle; the ruin of his family, to the security of *Jeroboam* in *Jezreel*; nor the victories of *Hazael* to the great commotions raised in *Israel*, by the coming of *Jehu*; but referring all unto the will of God, I mean, to his revealed will: from which that his hidden purposes do not vary, this story, by many great examples, gives most notable proof. True it is that the concurrence of second causes with their effects, is in these books nothing largely described, nor perhaps exactly in any of those Histories that are in these points most copious. For it was well noted by that worthy Gentleman Sir *Philip Sidney*, that Historians do borrow of Poets, not only much of their ornament, but somewhat of their substance. Informations are often false, records not always true, and notorious actions commonly insufficient to discover the passions, which did set them first on foot. Wherefore they are fain (I speak of the best, and in that which is allowed: for to take out of *Livy* every one circumstance of *Claudius* his journey against *Asdrubal* in *Italy*, fitting all to another business, or any practice of that kind, is neither Historical nor Poetical) to search into the particular humours of Princes, and of those which have governed their affections, or the instruments by which they wrought, from whence they do collect the most likely motives, or impediments of every business; and so figuring, as near to the life as they can imagine, the matter in hand, they judiciously consider the defects in council, or obliquity in proceeding.

Yet all this, for the most part, is not enough to give assurance, howsoever it may give satisfaction. For the heart of man is unsearchable: and Princes, howsoever their intents be seldom hidden from some of those many eyes which pry both into them, and into such as live about them; yet sometimes either by their own close temper, or by some subtle mist, they conceal the truth from all reports. Yea, many times the affections themselves lie dead, and buried in oblivion, when the preparations which they begat, are converted to another use. The industry of an Historian, having so many things to weary it, may well be excused, when finding apparent cause of things done, it forbeareth to make further search; though it often fall out, where sundry occasions work to the same end, that one small matter in a weak mind is more effectual, than many that seems far greater. So comes it many times to pass that great fires, which consume whole houses or Towns, begin with a few straws, that are wasted or not seen; when the flame is discovered, having fastened upon some wood-pile, that catcheth all about it. Questionless it is that the war commenced by *Darius* and pursued by *Xerxes* against the *Greeks*, proceeded from a desire of the *Persians* to enlarge their Empire: howsoever the enterprise of the *Athenians* upon *Sardes*, was noised abroad as the ground of that quarrel: yet *Herodotus* telleth us, that the wanton desire of Queen *Atossa* to have the *Grecian* dames her bondwomen, did first move *Darius* to prepare for this war before he had received any injury; and when he did not yet so much desire to get more, as to enjoy what was already gotten.

I will not here stand to argue whether *Herodotus* be more justly reprehended by some, or defended by others, for alleging the vain appetite, and secret speech of the Queen in bed with her husband, as the cause of those great evils following; this I may boldly affirm, (having I think, in every estate some sufficient witnesses) that matter of much consequence, founded in all seeming upon substantial reasons, have issued indeed from such petty trifles, as no Historian would either think upon, or could well search out.

Therefore it was a good answer that *Sixtus Quintus* the Pope made to a certain Friar, coming to visit him in his Popedom, as having long before in his meaner estate been his familiar friend. This poor Friar, being emboldened by the Pope to use his old liberty of speech, adventured to tell him, that he very much wondered how it was possible for his holiness, whom he rather took for a direct honest man than any cunning politician, to attain unto the Papacy; in compassing of which all the subtlety (said he) of the most crafty brains, find work enough: and therefore the more I think upon the art of the conclave, and your unaptness thereto, the more I needs must wonder. Pope *Sixtus* to satisfy the plain dealing Friar, dealt with him again as plainly, saying, Hadst thou lived abroad as I have done, and seen by what folly this world is governed, thou wouldst wonder at nothing.

Surely, if this be referred unto those exorbitant engines, by which the course of affairs is moved; the Pope said true. For the wisest of men are not without their vanities, which requiring and finding mutual toleration, work more closely, and earnestly, than right reason either needs or can. But if we lift up our thoughts to that supreme governor, of whose Empire all that is true, which by the Poet was said of *Jupiter*. . .

> Who rules the duller earth, the wind-swoln streams,
> The civil Cities, and th' infernal realms,
> Who th' host of heaven and the mortal band
> Alone doth govern by his just command.

Then shall we find the quite contrary. In him there is no uncertainty nor change; he forseeth all things, and all things disposeth to his own honour; He neither deceiveth nor can be deceived, but continuing one and the same for ever, doth constantly govern all creatures by that law, which he hath prescribed and will never alter. The vanities of man beguile their vain contrivers, and the prosperity of the wicked, is the way leading to their destruction: yea, this broad and headlong passage to hell, is not so delightful as it seemeth at the first entrance, but hath growing in it, besides the poisons which infect the soul, many cruel thorns deeply wounding the body, all which, if any few escape, they have only this miserable advantage of others, that their descent was the more swift and expedite. But the service of God is the path guiding us to perfect happiness, and hath in it a true, though not complete felicity, yielding such abundance of joy to the conscience, as doth easily countervail all afflictions whatsoever: though indeed those brambles that sometimes tear the skin of such as walk in this blessed way, do commonly lay hold upon them at such time as they sit down to take their ease, and make them wish themselves at their journey's end, in presence of their Lord whom they faithfully serve, in whose *presence is the fullness of joy, and at whose right hand are pleasures for evermore*.

Wherefore it being the end and scope of all History, to teach by example of times past, such wisdom as may guide our desires and actions, we should not marvel though the *Chronicles of the Kings of Juda and Israel*, being written by men inspired with the Spirit of God, instruct us chiefly, in that which is most requisite for us to know, as the means to attain unto true felicity, both here, and hereafter, propounding examples which illustrate this infallible rule, *The fear of the Lord is the beginning of Wisdom*. Had the expedition of *Xerxes* (as it was foretold by *Daniel*) been written by some Prophet after the captivity: we may well believe that the counsel of God therein, and the execution of his righteous will, should have occupied either the whole, or the principal room in that narration. Yet had not the purpose of *Darius*, the desire of his wife, and the business at *Sardes*, with other occurrents, been the less true, though they might have been omitted, as the less material: but these things it had been lawful for any man to gather out of profane Histories, or out of circumstances otherwise appearing, wherein he should not have done injury to the sacred writings, as long as he had forborne to derogate from the first causes, by ascribing to the second more than was due.

Such, or little different, is the business that I have now in hand: wherein I cannot believe that any man of judgment will tax me as either fabulous or presumptuous. For he doth not feign, that rehearseth probabilities as bare conjectures; neither doth he deprave the text, that seeketh to illustrate and make good in human reason, those things, which authority alone, without further circumstances, ought to have confirmed in every man's belief. And this may suffice in defence of the liberty, which I have used in conjectures, and may hereafter use when occasion shall require, as neither unlawful, nor misbeseeming an Historian.

Chapter 23:4 Of the Assyrian Kings . . .

. . . I neither do reprehend the boldness of *Torniellus*, in conjecturing, nor the modesty of *Scaliger* and *Sethus Calvisius*, in forbearing to set down as warrantable, such things as depend only upon likelihood. For things, whereof the perfect knowledge is taken away from us by Antiquity, must be described in History, as Geographers in their Maps described those Countries, whereof as yet there is made no true discovery, that is, either by leaving some part blank, or by inserting the Land of Pigmies, Rocks of lodestone, with Headlands, Bays, great Rivers, and other particularities, agreeable to common report, though many times controlled by following experience, and found contrary to truth. Yet indeed the ignorance growing from distance of place allows not such liberty to a Describer, as that which ariseth from the remediless oblivion of consuming time. For it is true that the Poet saith. . .

Nor Southern heat, nor Northern snow
That freezing to the ground doth grow,
The subject Regions can fence,
And keep the greedy Merchant thence.
The subtle Shipmen way will find,
Storm never so the Seas with wind.

Therefore the fictions (or let them be called conjectures) painted in maps do serve only to mislead such discoverers as rashly believe them; drawing upon the publishers, either some angry curses, or well deserved scorn; but to keep their own credit, they cannot serve always. To which purpose I remember a pretty jest of *Don Pedro de Sarmiento*, a worthy Spanish Gentleman, who had been employed by his King in planting a Colony upon the Straits of *Magellan*: for when I asked him, being then my Prisoner, some question about an Island in those straits, which me thought, might have done either benefit or displeasure to his enterprise, he told me merrily, that it was to be called the *Painter's Wife's Island*: saying, that whilst the fellow drew that Map, his wife sitting by, desired him to put in one Country for her; that she, in imagination, might have an Island of her own. But in filling up the blanks of old Histories, we need not be so scrupulous. For it is not to be feared, that time should run backward, and by restoring the things themselves to knowledge, make our conjectures appear ridiculous: What if some good Copy of an ancient Author could be found, showing (if we have it not already) the perfect truth of these uncertainties? would it be more shame to have believed in the mean while *Annius* or *Torniellus*, than to have believed nothing. Here I will not say, that the credit, which we give to *Annius*, may chance otherwhiles to be given to one of those Authors whose names he pretendeth. Let it suffice, that in regard of authority, I had rather trust *Scaliger* or *Torniellus* than *Annius*; yet him than them, if his assertion be more probable, and more agreeable to approved Histories than their conjecture, as in this point it seems to me; it having moreover gotten some credit, by the approbation of many, and those not meanly learned.

To end this tedious disputation; I hold it a sure course in examination of such opinions, as have once gotten the credit of being general, so to deal as *Pacuvius* in *Capua* did with the multitude, finding them desirous to put all the Senators of the City to death. He locked the Senators up within the State-house, and offered their lives to the People's mercy; obtaining thus much, that none of them should perish, until the Commonalty had both pronounced him worthy of death, and elected a better in his place. The condemnation was hasty; for as fast as every name was read, all the Town cried, Let him die: but the execution required more leisure; for in substituting another, some notorious vice of the Person, or baseness of his condition, or insufficiency of his quality, made each new one that was offered to be rejected; so that finding the worse and less choice, the further and the more that they sought, it was finally agreed, that the old should be kept for lack of better.

Chapter 24:5 Of the beginnings of Rome, and of Romulus' birth and death.

. . . Now of Romulus' begetting, of his education and preservation, it is said, That he had *Rhea* for his mother, and *Mars* was supposed to be his father; that he was nursed by a Wolf, found and taken away by *Faustula*, a Shepherd's wife. The same unnatural nursing had *Cyrus*, the same incredible fostering had *Semiramis*; the one by a Bitch, the other by Birds. But, as *Plutarch* saith, it is like enough that *Amulius* came covered with armour to *Rhea*, the mother of *Romulus*, when he begat her with child: and therein it seemeth to me that he might have two purposes; the one, to destroy her, because she was the daughter and heir of his elder brother, from whom he injuriously held the

Kingdom; the other to satisfy his appetite, because she was fair and goodly. For she being made a Nun of the Goddess *Vesta*, it was death in her, by the Law, to break her chastity. I also find in *Fauchet* his *Antiquitez de Gaule*, that *Merovee*, King of the *Francs*, was begotten by a monster of the Sea: but *Fauchet* says, *Let them believe it that list; Il le croira qui voudra:* also of *Alexander*, and of *Scipio African*, there are poetical inventions: but to answer these imaginations in general, it is true, that in those times, when the World was full of this barbarous Idolatry, and when there were as many Gods as there were Kings, or passions of the mind, or as there were of vices and virtues; then did many women greatly born, cover such slips as they made by protesting to be forced by more than human power: so did *Oenone* confess to *Paris*, that she had been ravished by *Apollo*. And *Anchises* boasted that he had known *Venus*. But *Rhea* was made with child by some man of War, or other, and therefore called *Mars*, the God of battle, according to the sense of the time. *Oenone* was overcome by a strong wit, and by such a one as had those properties ascribed to *Apollo*. The Mother of *Merovee* might fancy a Sea Captain to be gotten with young by such a one: as the daughter of *Inachus* fancied, according to *Herodotus*. *Aeneas* was a bastard and begotten upon some fair Harlot, called for her beauty *Venus*, and was therefore the child of lust, which is *Venus*. *Romulus* was nursed by a Wolf, which was *Lupa* or *Lupina*, for the Courtesans in those days were called Wolves, *quae nunc* (saith Halicarnassaeus) *honestiori vocabulo amicae appellantur, which are now by an honester name called friends*. It is also written, that *Romulus* was in the end of his life taken up into heaven, or rather out of the world by his Father *Mars*, in a great storm of thunder, and lightning: so was it said that *Aeneas* vanished away by the River *Numicus*: but thereof *Livy* also speaketh modestly; for he rehearseth the other opinion, that the storm was the fury of the Senators, but seemeth to adhere partially to this taking up; and many Authors agree that there was an unnatural darkness, both at his birth and at his death, and that he might be slain by thunder and lightning, it is not unlikely. For the Emperor *Anastasius* was slain with lightning, so was *Strabo*, the Father of *Pompey* slain with a thunder-bolt: so *Carus* the Emperor (who succeeded *Probus*) whilst he lodged with his Army upon the river *Tigris*, was there slain with lightning. But a *Mars* of the same kind might end him that began him; for he was begotten by a man of War, and by violence destroyed. And that he dies by violence (which destiny followed most of the *Roman* emperors) it appeareth by *Tarquinius Superbus*; who was but the seventh King after him: who when he had murdered his father-in-law, commanded that he should not be buried, for (said he) *Romulus* himself died and was not buried. But let *Halicarnassaeus* end this dispute: whose words are these: *They* (saith he) *who draw nearest to the truth, say that he was slain by his own Citizens; and that his cruelty in punishments of offenders, together with his arrogancy, were the cause of his slaughter. For it is reported that both when his mother was ravished, whether by some man, or by a God, the whole body of the sun was eclipsed, and all the earth covered with darkness like unto night, and that the same did happen at his death.*

Such were the birth and death of *Romulus*; whose life historified by *Plutarch*, doth contain (besides what is here already spoken of him) the conquest of a few miles which had soon been forgotten, if the *Roman* greatness built upon that foundation, had not given it memory in all ages following, even unto this day. A valiant man he was, very strong of body, patient of travail, and temperate in diet, as forbearing the use of wine and delicacies: but his raging ambition he knew not how to temper which caused him to slay his brother, and neglect revenge the death of *Tatius* his companion in the Kingdom, that he himself might be Lord alone in those narrow Territories. He reigned seven and thirty years; first alone, then with *Tatius*, and after his death single, till he was slain, as is already showed: after which time the Sovereignty fell into the hands of *Numa*, a man to him unknown, and more Priestlike than Kinglike: wherein *Rome* itself in her later times hath somewhat resembled this King. For having long been sole Governess till *Constantinople* shared with her: afterwards, when as the *Greek* Emperor was crushed by foreign enemies, and the *Latins* despoiled of Imperial power, she fell into the subjection of a Prelate, swelling by degrees from the Sheephook to the Sword, and therewith victorious to excessive magnificence, from whence by the same degrees it fell, being driven from luxury to defensive arms, and therein having been unfortunate, at length betakes herself again to the Crosier's staff.

From Book Three of the History of the World

Chapter 1:11 Of the later time of Nebuchadnezzar; his buildings, madness, and death.

Of the time which this great *Monarch* spent in quiet, I think there are no monuments extant; save those which we find among the prophecies of *Daniel*. Among these we may reckon his great works at *Babylon*, wherewith he pleased himself so well, that he brake out into these glorious words: *Is not this great Babel that I have built for the house of the Kingdom, by the might of my power, and for the honour of my majesty?* Surely if those things be true that are by *Josephus* rehearsed of him out of *Berosus* and *Megasthenes*, he might well delight himself with the contemplation of such goodly and magnificent buildings. For it is said, that he fortified *Babylon* with a triple wall; that besides other stately works, he raised those huge arches wherewith were borne up the high Orchards, hanging as were in the air, and equalling the tops of Mountains; which most sumptuous frame, that outlasted all the remainder of the *Assyrian*, and all the *Persian* Empire, is said to have been reared, and finished in fifteen days.

But of all this, and other his magnificence, we find little else recorded, than that (which indeed is most profitable for us to consider) his overvaluing of his own greatness abased him unto a condition, inferior to the poorest of men. And not undeservedly fell these judgments of God upon him. For whereas God had honoured him, not only with many victories, and much happiness in his own life, but with a discovery of things to come after him, yea and had approved the certainty of his dream, by the miraculous reducing of it into his memory, and interpretation thereof by *Daniel* the Prophet; he nevèrtheless became so forgetful of God, whose wonderful power he had seen and acknowledged, that he caused a golden Image to be set up and worshipped: ordaining a cruel death as reward unto them that should dare to disobey his Kingly will and pleasure, which was utterly repugnant to the law of him that is the *King of kings*. Hereof *St Jerome* hath well noted. . . *A hasty forgetfulness of the truth, that he who so lately had worshipped* (Daniel) *the servant of God, as if he had been God himself, should now command a Statua to be erected unto himself, wherein himself might be worshipped as God*. From this impiety it pleased God to reclaim him, by the strange and wonderful delivery of those blessed Saints out of the fiery furnace, who being thrown into it bound, for refusing to commit Idolatry, were assisted by an Angel; preserved from all harm of the fire; loosened from their bands; and finally called out with gracious words, and restored to their former honour, by the King: who amazed at the miracle, made a decree tending to the honour of God, which by erection of his image he had violated. Yet this devotion of *Nebuchadnezzar* was not so rooted in him, that it could bring forth fruit answerable to his hasty zeal. Therefore was he forewarned by God in a dream of the terrible judgment hanging over his head, which *Daniel* expounding, advised him to *break off his sin by righteousness, and his iniquity by mercy towards the poor, that there might be an healing of his error.* Hereby it seems that injustice and cruelty were the faults, for which he was threatened, but this threatening sufficed not unto his reformation. For that so great a *Monarch* should be driven from among men (according to the tenor of the dream and interpretation) yea compelled to dwell with the beasts of the field, and made to eat grass as the Oxen, was a thing so incredible in man's judgment, that easily it might be thought an idle dream, and much more easily be forgotten at the year's end. One whole year's leisure to repent was given to this haughty Prince: which respite of the execution may seem to have bred in him a forgetfulness of God's sentence. For at the end of twelve months, walking in the royal palace of *Babel*, he was so overjoyed and transported with a vain contemplation of his own seeming happiness, that without all fear of God's heavy judgment pronounced against him, he uttered those lofty words before rehearsed, in vaunting of the Majestical works which he had reared, as well beseeming his majestical person. But his high speeches were not fully ended, when a voice from heaven, telling him that his Kingdom was departed from him, rehearsed over unto him the sentence again, which was fulfilled upon him the very same hour.

That *Solomon* and many other Princes and great ones have taken delight in their own buildings, it cannot any way be doubted; yet I do not remember that ever I have read of any, that were punished for rejoicing in works of this kind (though it is hard in joy, or any passion of the mind to keep a just measure) excepting only this *Nebuchadnezzar*.

The like may be said of *David*: for other (and some very godly) Kings have mustered all their forces to the very last man; but few or none have been known to have been punished as *David* was. Surely I not only hold it lawful to rejoice in those good things wherewith God hath blessed us; but a note of much unthankfulness to entertain them with a sullen and unfeeling disposition. Yet as all human affections, wherein due reference to God is wanting, are no better than obscure clouds, hindering the influence of that blessed light, which clarifies the soul of man, and predisposeth it unto the brightness of eternal felicity; so that insolent joy, which man in the pride of his vain imagination conceiveth of his own worth, doth above all other passions blast our minds, as it were with lightning, and make us to reflect our thoughts upon our seeming inherent greatness, forgetting the whilst him, to whom we are indebted for our very being. Wherefore these *mala mentis gaudia*; *the evil joys of the mind*, were not unaptly, by the Prince of Latin Poets, bestowed in the entrance of *Hell*, and placed further inward than sorrows, cares, and fears; not far from the iron Cabins of the *Furies*. And certainly it is no unlikely token of vengeance near at hand, when these unreasonable flushes of proud and vain joy, do rage in a mind, that should have been humbled with a just repentance and acknowledgment of ill deserving.

This was verified upon *Nebuchadnezzar*, whose punishment was singular and unexampled. For he ran among beasts in the fields and woods, where for seven years he lived, not only as a salvage man, but as a salvage beast, for a beast he thought himself *secundum suum imaginationem*, as *Thomas* noteth, and therefore fed himself in the same manner, and with the same food that beasts do; not that he was changed in figure external according to *Mediana*, insomuch as he appeared a beast to other men's eyes, as St *Jerome* in the Life of *Hilarius* (how true God knows) speaks of a woman that appeared to all other men's sight a Cow, but to *Hilarius* only a woman; neither was he changed as *Iphigenia* the daughter of *Agamemnon* was said to be into a Hind, nor made a Monster as *Dorotheus* and *Epiphanius* dreamed: but according to St *Jerome's* exposition of these words . . . *When he saith that his sense was restored unto him, he showeth that he had not lost his human shape, but his understanding*. Seven years expired, it pleased God to restore *Nebuchadnezzar* both to his understanding, and his estate, for which he acknowledged and praised God all the rest of his life, confessing his power and everlasting being; that he was the Lord of heaven and earth, and wrought without resistance what he pleased in both; that his works were all truth, and his ways righteous . .

Chapter 1:13 . . . *the quality and death of Balthasar*.

. . .This may suffice to show, that they who are said to have succeeded *Evilmerodach* in the Kingdom, might indeed have so done, though not when he held it in his own right. Of *Balthasar* who was his Son and Heir, we find, that he had such conditions, as God permitteth to be in a King for the ruin of the people. He was from his young years of a mischievous nature; having in his Father's time slain a Noble young man that should have married his sister, only for spite and envy to see him kill two wild beasts in hunting, at which himself having thrown his Javelin had missed them. Another great Lord he had gelded, because a Gentlewoman, commending his beauty, said it were a happy woman that should be his wife. Such barbarous villainies caused many which had loved his Father (as a good and gracious, though unfortunate Prince) to revolt from him unto the enemy as soon as he was King. Neither do I find that he performed any thing worthy of record, but as a Coward and a Fool he lost all; sitting still, and not once daring to give battle to them that daily took somewhat from him; Yet carelessly feasting when danger had hemmed him in on every side, and when death arrested him by the hands of those whom he had wronged in his Father's life. So the end of him was base and miserable; for he died as a fool taken in unexcusable security, yet had not that happiness (such as it is) of a death free from apprehension of fear, but was terrified with a dreadful vision, which had showed his ruin not many hours before, even whilst he was drinking in that wine, which the swords of his insulting enemies drew out of him, together with his latest blood. It is therefore in this place enough to say of him, That after a dishonourable reign of seventeen years, he perished like a beast, and was slain as he deserved.

Chapter 6:2 Xerxes' army entertained by Pythius; his cutting off mount Athos from the continent; his bridge of boats over the Hellespont; and the discourse between him and Artabanus upon the view of his army.

When this world of an Army was throughly furnished, he caused all the Nations of which it was compounded to make their *Rendezvous* and repair at *Sardis* in *Lydia*. And when he had assembled to the number of seventeen hundred thousand foot, as he entered the body of *Celaenas*, he was by one *Pythius* the *Lydian* entertained, who out of his Flocks and Herds of Cattle gave food to *Xerxes* and his whole Army. The Feast ended, he also presented him with two thousand Talents of Silver, and in Gold four Millions, wanting seven thousand of the *Persian Darici*, which make so many of our marks.

The King overcome with the exceeding liberality of *Pythius*, did not only refuse his treasure offered, but commanded that seven thousand *Darici* should be given him to make up his four Millions; of which, so many thousands were wanting when he made the present. But soon after, when *Pythius* besought him to spare one of his five sons from his attendance into *Greece* (because himself was old, and had none whom he could so well trust as his own son) *Xerxes* most barbarously caused the young man, for whom his father sought exemption, to be sundered into two parts, commanding that the one half of his carcass should be laid on the right, and the other half on the left hand of the common way by which the army marched.

Two things he commanded to be done before he came to the Sea-side. The one was a passage for Galleys to be cut behind Mount *Athos*, making the same (with the half Island or Headland, whereon it stood) to be an entire Island, sundering thereby from the Continent of *Thrace* five Cities, besides the Mountain and the *Chersonesus*, or Neck of Land itself: a work of more ostentation than of use, and yet an enterprise of no great wonder, the Valley which held it to the Continent having but twelve furlongs (which make about a mile and half) to cut through, and the ditch being broad enough only for two Galleys to pass in front. The Cities so severed from the main, were *Dion*, *Olophyxus*, *Acrothoon*, *Thysus*, and *Cleonae*.

He also gave order, that a Bridge upon Boats should be made over the *Hellespont* between *Abidos* and *Sestos*, the Sea there having a mile of breadth, wanting an eighth part; which after finishing, was by a Tempest torn asunder and dissevered; wherewith *Xerxes* being more enraged than discouraged, commanded those to be slain that were masters of the work, and caused six hundred threescore and fourteen Galleys to be coupled together, thereon to frame a new Bridge; which, by the art and industry of the *Phoenicians* was so well anchored to resist both winds blowing into and from the *Euxine* Sea, as the same being well boarded and railed, the whole Army of seventeen hundred thousand foot, and fourscore thousand Horse, with all the Mules and Carriages, passed over it into *Europe* in seven days and seven nights, without intermission. This transportation of Armies did *Caesar* afterward use: And *Caligula* that mad Emperor, in imitation of *Xerxes* his bridge, did build the like.

The Bridge finished, and the Army brought near to the Sea side, *Xerxes* took a view of all his Troops assembled in the Plains of *Abidos*, being carried up and seated on a place overtopping the Land round about it, and the Sea adjoining: and after he had gloried in his own happiness, to behold and command so many Nations, and so powerful an Army and Fleet, he suddenly (notwithstanding) burst out into tears, moved with this contemplation, That in one hundred years there should not any one survive of that marvellous multitude: the cause of which sudden change of passion when he uttered to *Artabanus* his uncle, *Artabanus* spake to the King to this effect: That which is more lamentable than the dissolution of this great Troop within that number of years by the King remembered, is, That the life itself which we enjoy is yet more miserable than the end thereof: for in those few days given us in the world, there is no man among all these, nor elsewhere, that ever found himself so accompanied with happiness, but that he oftentimes pleased himself better with the desire and hope of death than of living; the incident calamities, diseases, and sorrows whereto mankind is subject, being so many and inevitable, that the shortest life doth oftentimes appear unto us over-long; to avoid all which, there is neither refuge nor rest, but in desired death alone.

With this melancholy discourse *Xerxes* being not much pleased, prayed *Artabanus* not to overcast those joys which they had now in pursuit with sad remembrances. And holding still a doubtful conceit, that *Artabanus* utterly condemned the invasion of *Greece*, against which he had formerly given many strong reasons, desired him to deal freely with him, Whether he were returned to his first resolution, that the enterprise of *Greece* could not be prosperous? Or whether, according to the change of mind put into him by his late Vision, he was confident of good success? *Artabanus* notwithstanding that he assured himself of the King's resolution to go on, and dared not by any new Arguments to batter the great purpose itself, yet he told the King, That there were two things which marvellously affrighted him, and which the King should find, as he feared, to be most adverse; to wit, the Sea and the Land: The Sea, because it had nowhere in that part of the world any Port capable of so great a Fleet; insomuch, as if any tempest should arise, all the Continent of *Greece* could hardly receive them, nor all the Havens thereof afford them any safety: and therefore when such shelter shall be wanting unto them, he prayed him to understand, that in such a case of extremity men are left to the will and disposition of Fortune, and not Fortune to the will and disposition of men. The Land, besides other incommodities, will be found by so much the more an enemy, by how much the unsatiate desire of man to obtain more and more thereof, doth lead him forward: for were there no man found to give resistance, yet the want of means to feed such an Army, and the Famine, which cannot be prevented, will, without any other violence offered, disenable and consume it. By these Arguments *Artabanus* hoped to have diverted *Xerxes*, not daring perchance to utter what indeed he most feared; to wit, the overthrow of the Army itself both by Sea and Land, which soon after followed. These Cautions were exceeding weighty, if *Xerxes* his obstinancy had not misprised them. For to invade by Sea upon a perilous Coast, being neither in possession of any Port, nor succoured by any party, may better fit a Prince presuming on his fortune, than enriched with understanding. Such was the enterprise of *Philip* the Second upon England in the year 1588, who had belike never heard of this Counsel of *Artabanus* to *Xerxes*, or forgotten it.

Now concerning the second point, it was very likely, that *Xerxes* his Army, which could not have less in it than two millions of Souls, besides his beasts for Service and Carriage, should after a few days suffer famine, and, using *Machiavel's* words, *Mourire sans cousteo, die without a knife*. For it was impossible for *Greece*, being a ragged, strait, and mountainous Country, to yield food (besides what served themselves) for twenty hundred thousand strangers, whom they never meant to entertain but with sharpened points of their weapons, destroying withal whatsoever they could not well enclose and defend. Nay, if we may believe *Herodotus*, the army of *Xerxes*, being reviewed at *Thermopylae*, consisted of five millions, two hundred eighty-three thousand two hundred twenty men, besides Laundresses, Harlots, and Horses, and was therefore likely to endure a speedy famine.

The effect of *Xerxes* his answer was, That it was impossible to provide for all things; and that whosoever should enterprise any great matter, if he gave the hearing to all that could be objected of accidental inconveniences, he should never pursue the same farther than the dispute and consultation: which if his predecessors, the *Persian* Kings, had done, they had never grown to that greatness, or possessed so many Kingdoms and Nations as they now did, and therefore concluded, That great enterprises were never undertaken without great perils. Which resolution of *Xerxes* was not to be condemned, if any necessity had enforced him to that war. But seeing the many Nations newly conquered, which he already commanded, were more than could be constrained to obedience any longer than the powerful prosperity of the *Persians* endured, and that *Greece* were separated by the sea from the rest of *Xerxes'* Dominions (of whose resolution his father *Darius* had made a dear experience) the fruit of this war was answerable to the plantation, and the success and end agreeable to the weak counsel whereon it was grounded. Furthermore, those millions of men which he transported, and yet in his own judgment not sufficient (for he gathered in marching on, all the strength of *Thrace* and *Macedon*) were an argument, that he rather hoped to fear the *Greeks* by the fame of his numbers, than that he had any confidence in their valour and resolution, whom he conducted. For it is wisely said of those unaccountable multitudes . . . *They are great in bulk, but weak in force, and rather a luggage than an aid*.

Besides, as it was impossible to marshal such a world of men in one Army, so the divers Nations, speaking divers Languages, bred the same confusion among the *Persian* commanders when they came to fight, as it did to the builders of *Babel*, when they came to work. Whereas if *Xerxes* had of his five millions compounded ten Armies of fifty thousand chosen soldiers in each, and sent them yearly into *Greece* well victualled and furnished, he had either prevailed by the sword, or forced them to forsake their territory, or brought them in obedience by necessity and famine, which cannot be resisted. But while *Xerxes* resolved to cut down the banks of *Greece*, and to let in a sea of men upon them, he was deceived both in his own hopes, and in their hearts whom he employed, and beaten by the *Greeks*, both by Land and Sea; yea, he himself, conducted by his fear, fled shamefully into *Asia*. A great part of his Army was buried in *Greece*: the remainder whereof, which wintered in *Thessaly*, and led by *Mardonius*, who persuaded the Enterprise, was in the Summer following utterly defeated, and himself slain.

Chapter 6:11 Of the barbarous quality of Xerxes . . .

Xerxes lay at *Sardis*, not far from the place of this battle; but little mind had he to revenge either this or other his great losses, being wholly given over to the love of his Brother's Wife: with whom when he could not prevail by entreaty, nor would obtain his desire by force, because he respected much his Brother her husband, he thought it best to make a match between his own son *Darius*, and the Daughter of this Woman; hoping by that means to find occasion of such familiarity, as might work out his desire. But whether it were so, that the chastity of the Mother did still reject him, or the beauty of her Daughter allure him; he soon after fell in love with his Son's wife, being a vicious Prince, and as ill able to govern himself in peace, as to guide his Army in War. This young Lady having once desired the King to give her the Garment which he then wore, being wrought by his own Wife; caused the Queen thereby to perceive her husband's conversation with her, which she imputed, not so much to the beauty of her Daughter-in-law, as to the cunning of her Mother, against whom thereupon she conceived extreme hatred. Therefore at a Royal feast, wherein the custom was that the King should grant every request, she craved that the wife of *Masistes*, her husband's Brother, the young Lady's Mother, might be given into her disposition. The barbarous King, who might either have reformed the abuse of such a custom, or have deluded the importunate cruelty of his Wife, by threatening herself with the like, to whatsoever she should inflict upon the innocent Lady, granted the request; and sending for his brother persuaded him to put away the Wife which he had, and take one of his Daughters in her stead. Hereby it seems, that he understood how villainously that poor Lady should be entreated, whom he knew to be virtuous, and whom himself had loved. *Masistes* refused to put her away; alleging his own love, her deserving, and their common Children, one of which was married to the King's Son, as reasons important to move him to keep her. But in most wicked manner *Xerxes* reviled him; saying, That he now should neither keep the Wife which he had, nor have his Daughter whom he had promised unto him. *Masistes* was much grieved with these words, but much more, when returning home, he found his Wife most butcherly mangled by the Queen *Amestris*, who had caused her Nose, Lips, Ears, and Tongue to be cut off, and her Breasts in like manner, which were cast unto Dogs. *Masistes* enraged with this villainy, took his way with his children, and some Friends, towards *Bactria*, of which Province he was Governor, intending to rebel and avenge himself. But *Xerxes* understanding his purpose, caused an Army to be levied, which cut him off by the way, putting him and all his Company to the sword. Such was the tyrannical condition of the *Persian* government; and such are generally the effects of Luxury when it is joined with absolute power.

Yet of *Xerxes* it is noted that he was a Prince of much virtue. And therefore *Alexander* the Great, finding an Image of his overthrown, and lying upon the ground, said, That he doubted, whether, in regard of his virtue, he should again erect it, or, for the mischief done by him to *Greece*, should let it lie. But surely whatsoever his other good qualities were, he was foolish, and was a coward, and consequently merciless. . .

From Book Four of The History of the World

Chapter 1:1 What kings reigned in Macedon before Philip.
. . . But, as it commonly falleth out with every man of mark in the world, that they underfall, and perish, by the hands and arms, which they least fear; so fared it at this time with the Greeks. For of *Philip of Macedon* (of whom we are now to speak) they had so little regard, as they grew even then more violent in devouring each other, when the fast growing greatness of such a Neighbouring King, should, in regard of their own safety, have served them for a strong argument of union and accord. But the glory of their *Persian* victories, wherewith they were pampered and made proud, taught them to neglect all Nations but themselves, and the rather to value at little the power and purposes of the *Macedonians*, because those Kings and States, which sat nearer them than they did, had in the time of *Amyntas*, the Father of *Philip*, so much weakened them, and won upon them, that they were not (as the *Grecians* persuaded themselves) in any one age, likely to recover their own, much less to work any wonders against their borderers. And, indeed, it was not in their Philosophy to consider, That all great alterations are storm-like, sudden, and violent; and that it is then overlate to repair the decayed and broken banks, when great Rivers are once swollen, fast running, and enraged. No, the *Greeks* did rather employ themselves in breaking down those defences, which stood between them and this inundation: than seek to rampire and reinforce their own fields, which by the Level of reason they might have found to have lain under it. It was therefore well concluded by Orosius . . . *The Cities of Greece lost their command, by striving each of them to command all* . . .

Chapter 1:5 Of the Olynthian war. The ambitious practices of Philip.
From hence *Philip* resolved to invade *Phocis* itself, but the *Athenians* did not favour his entrance into those parts, and therefore with the help of the *Lacedaemonians* they retrenched his passage at the Straits of *Thermopylis*. Whereupon he returned into *Macedon*, and after the taking of *Micyberne*, *Torone*, and other Towns, he quarrelled with the *Olynthians*, whom not long before he had wooed to his alliance, and bought his peace of them. For the *Olynthians* were very strong, and had evermore both braved and beaten the *Macedonians*. It is said that *Philip* having put to death *Archelaus* his half-brother (for *Amyntas* had three sons by *Eurydice* the mother of *Philip*, and three other sons by *Gygaea*; but *Philip's* elder brothers by the same Mother being dead, he determined to rid himself also of the rest) the two

younger held themselves within *Olynthus*; and that the receiving of them by the *Olynthians* was the cause of the war, *Justin* affirmeth. But just quarrels are balanced by just Princes, for to this King all things were lawful that might any way serve his turn; all his affections and passions, how diverse soever in other men, were in his ambition swallowed up, and thereinto converted. For he neither forbare the murder of his own brothers, the breach of faith, the buying of other men's fidelity, he esteemed no place strong where his Ass laden with gold might enter, Nor any City or State unconquerable, where a few of the greatest, to be made greater, could lose the sense of other men's sorrow and subjection. And because he thought it vain to practise the winning of *Olynthus*, till he had enclosed all the power they had within their own walls, he entered their Territory, and by the advantage of a well-compounded and trained Army, he gave them two overthrows ere he sat down before the City itself: which done, he bought *Euthicrates* and *Lasthenes* from their people, and from the service of their Country and Commonweal, by whose treason he entered the Town, slew his brothers therein, sacked it, and sold the Inhabitants for slaves by the drum. By the spoil of their place he greatly enriched himself, and had treasure sufficient to buy in other Cities withal, which he daily did. For so was he advised by the Oracle in the beginning of his undertaking, *That he should make his assaults with silver spears*: whereupon Horace well and truly said. . .

> By gifts the Macedon clave Gates asunder,
> And Kings envying his estate brought under.

And it is true that he won more by corruption and fraud than he did by force. For as he had in all the principal Cities of *Greece* his secret workers (which way of Conquest was well followed by *Philip* the second of *Spain*:) so, when in the contention between the Competitors for the Kingdom of *Thrace* he was chosen the Arbitrator, he came not to the Council accompanied with Piety and Justice, but with a powerful Army, and having beaten and slain both kings, gave sentence for himself, and made the Kingdom his own.

Chapter 1:9 What good foundations of Alexander's greatness were laid by Philip. Of his laudable qualities, and issue.

. . . Of this Prince it is hard to judge, whether his ambition had taught him the exercise of more vices, than Nature, and his excellent Education had enriched him with virtues. For besides that He was Valiant, Wise, Learned, and Master of his Affections, he had this savour of Piety, that he rather laboured to satisfy those that were grieved, than to suppress them, Whereof (among many other) we find a good example in his dealing with *Arcadion*, and *Nicanor*; whom, when for their evil speech of *Philip*, his familiars persuaded him to put to death; He answered them, That first it ought to be considered, whether the fault were in them that gave him ill language, or in himself; Secondly, that it was in every man's own power to be well spoken of; and this was shortly proved, for after *Philip* had relieved their necessities, there were none within his Kingdom that did him more honour than they did. Whereupon he told those that had persuaded him to use Violence, that he was a better Physician for evil speech than they were.

His *Epistles* to *Alexander* his son are remembered by *Cicero*, and *Gellius*; and by *Dion*: and by *Chrysostom* exceedingly commended. His Stratagems are gathered by *Polyaenus* and *Frontinus*, his wise sayings by *Plutarch*. And albeit he held *Macedon* as in his own right all the time of his reign, yet was he not the true and next Heir thereof; for *Amyntas* the son of his Brother *Perdiccas* (of whom he had the protection during his infancy) had the right. This *Amyntas* he married to his daughter *Cyna*, who had by him a Daughter called *Eurydice*, who was married to *Philip's* base son *Aridaeus*, her Uncle by the mother's side: both which *Olympias*, *Philip's* first Wife, and Mother to *Alexander* the Great, put to death; *Aridaeus* by extreme torments; *Eurydice* she strangled.

Philip had by this *Olympias* the daughter of *Neoptolemus*, King of the *Molossians*, (of the race of *Achilles*) *Alexander* the Great, and *Cleopatra*. *Cleopatra* was married to her Uncle *Alexander*, King of *Epirus*, and was after her brother *Alexander's* death slain at *Sardis* by the commandment of *Antigonus*.

By *Audata*, an *Illyrian*, his second wife, he had *Cyna*, married as is showed before.

By *Nicasipolis*, the sister of *Jason*, Tyrant of *Pheres*, he had *Thessalonica*, whom *Cassander*, after he had taken *Pidna*, married, but she was afterward by her Father-in-law *Antipater* put to death.

By *Cleopatra*, the Niece of *Attalus*, he had *Caranus*, whom others call *Philip*; him *Olympias*, the Mother of *Alexander* the Great, caused to be roasted to death in a copper pan. Others lay this murder on *Alexander* himself. By the same *Cleopatra* he had likewise a daughter, called *Europa*, whom *Olympias* also murdered at the Mother's breast.

By *Phila* and *Meda* he had no issue.

He had also two concubines, *Arsinoe*, whom, after he had gotten with child, he married to an obscure man, called *Lagus*, who bare *Ptolomy*, King of *Egypt*, called the son of *Lagus*, but esteemed the son of *Philip*; by *Philinna*, his second Concubine, a public Dancer, he had *Aridaeus*, of whom we shall have much occasion to speak hereafter.

Chapter 2:3 A digression concerning the defence of hard passages. Of things following the battle of Granick.

The winning of this passage did greatly encourage the *Macedonians*, and brought such terror upon all those of the lesser *Asia*, as he obtained all the Kingdoms thereof without a blow, some one or two Towns excepted. For in all invasions where the Nations invaded have once been beaten upon a great advantage of the place as in defence of Rivers, Straits, and Mountains, they will soon have persuaded themselves, that such an enemy, upon equal terms and even ground, can hardly be resisted. It was therefore *Machiavel's* counsel, that he which resolveth to defend a passage, should with his ablest force oppose the Assailant. And to say truth, few Regions of any great circuit are so well fenced, that Armies, of such force as may be thought sufficient to conquer them, can be debarred all entrance, by the natural difficulty of the ways. One passage or other is commonly left unguarded: if all be defended, then must the forces of the Country be distracted, and yet lightly, some one place will be found that is defended very weakly. How often have the *Alps* given way to armies, breaking into *Italy*? Yea, where shall we find that ever they kept out an invader? Yet are they such, as (to speak briefly) afflict with all difficulties those that travel over them; but they give no security to those that lie behind them: for they are of too large extent. The Towns of *Lombardy* persuaded themselves that they might enjoy their quiet, when the Warlike Nation of the *Switzers* had undertaken to hinder *Francis* the *French* King from descending into the Duchy of *Milan*: but whilst these Patrons of *Milan*, whom their own dwelling in those mountains had made fittest of all other for such a service, were busied in custody of the *Alps*; *Francis* appeared in *Lombardy*, to so much the greater terror of the Inhabitants, by how much the less they had expected his arrival. What shall we say of those Mountains, which lock up whole Regions in such sort, as they leave but one Gate open? The Straits, or (as they were called) the Gates of *Taurus* in *Cilicia*, and those of *Thermopylae*, have seldom been attempted, perhaps because they were thought impregnable: but how seldom (if ever) have they been attempted in vain? *Xerxes*, and long after him, the *Romans* forced the entrance of *Thermopylae*; *Cyrus* the younger, and after him *Alexander*, found the Gates of *Cilicia* wide open; how strongly soever they had been locked and barred, yet were those countries open enough to a fleet that should enter on the back side. The defence of Rivers how hard a thing it is, we find examples in all histories that bear good witness. The deepest have many Fords; the swiftest and broadest may be passed by Boats, in case it be found a matter of difficulty to make a Bridge. He that hath men enough to defend all the length of his own bank, hath also enough to beat his enemy; and may therefore do better to let him come over, to his loss, than by striving in vain to hinder the passage, as a matter tending to his own disadvantage, fill the heads of his Soldiers with an opinion, that they are in ill case, having their means of safeguard taken from them, by the skill and valour of such as are too good for them. Certainly if a River were sufficient defence against an Army, the Isle of *Mona*, now called *Anglesea*, which is divided from North-Wales by an arm of the Sea; had been safe enough against the *Romans*, invading it under conduct of *Julius Agricola*. But he wanting, and not meaning to spend the time in making vessels to transport his forces, did assay the fords. Whereby he so amazed the enemies attending for ships and such like provision by Sea, that surely believing nothing could be hard or invincible to men, which came so minded to War, they humbly entreated for peace, and yielded the Island. Yet the *Britains* were men stout enough; the *Persians* very dastards.

It was therefore wisely done of *Alexander*, to pass the River of *Granick* in face of the enemy; not marching higher to seek an easier way, nor labouring to convey his men over it by some safer means. For having beaten them upon their own ground, he did thereby cut off no less of their reputation, than of their strength, leaving no hope of succour to the partakers and followers of such unable Protectors.

Soon after this victory he recovered *Sardis*, *Ephesus* the Cities of the *Trallians* and *Magnesia*, which were rendered unto him. The Inhabitants of which, with the people of the Country, he received with great grace, suffering them to be governed by their own laws. For he observed it well . . . *It is commodious unto such as lay the foundations of a new Sovereignty to have the fame of being merciful*. He then by *Parmenio* won *Miletus*, and by force mastered *Halicarnassus*, which, because it resisted obstinately, he rased to the ground. From thence he entered into *Caria*, where *Ada*, the Queen, who had been cast out of all that she held (except the city of *Alinda*) by *Darius* his lieutenants, presented herself unto him, and adopted him her son and successor; which *Alexander* accepted in so gracious part as he left the whole Kingdom to her disposing. He then entered into *Lycia*, and *Pamphylia*, and obtained all the Sea coasts, and subjecting unto him *Pisidia*, he directed himself towards *Darius* (who was said to be advanced towards him with a marvellous Army) by the way of *Phrygia*: For all the Province of *Asia* the less, bordering upon the Sea, his first victory laid under his feet.

While he gave order for the government and settling of *Lycia*, and *Pamphylia*, he sent *Cleander* to raise some new Companies in *Peloponnesus*, and marching towards the North, he entered *Celenas*, seated on the River *Maeander*, which was abandoned unto him, the Castle only holding out, which also after forty days was given up; for so long time he gave them to attend succour from *Darius*. From *Celenas* he passed on through *Phrygia* towards the *Euxine* Sea, till he came to a city called *Gordium*, the Regal seat, in former times, of King *Midas*. In this City it was that he found the *Gordian* knot, which when he knew not how to undo, he cut it asunder with his sword. For there was an ancient prophecy did promise to him that could untie it, the Lordship of all *Asia*; whereupon *Alexander*, not respecting the manner how, so it were done, assumed to himself the fulfilling the prophecy, by hewing it in pieces.

But before he turned from this part of *Asia* the less towards the East, he took care to clear the Sea coast on his back, and to thrust the *Persians* out of the Islands of *Lesbos*, *Scio*, and *Coos*, the charge whereof he committed unto two of his Captains, giving them such order as he thought to be most convenient for that service; and delivering unto them fifty talents to defray the charge; and withal out of his first spoil gotten, he sent threescore talents more to *Antipater* his Lieutenant in *Greece*, and *Macedon*. From *Celenas* he removed to *Ancyra*, now called *Anguori*, standing on the same River of *Sangarius* which runneth through *Gordium*: there he mustered his Army, and then entered *Paphlagonia*, whose people submitted themselves unto him, and obtained freedom of tribute: where he left *Catus* Governor with one Regiment of *Macedonians* lately arrived.

Here he understood of the death of *Memnon* Darius' Lieutenant, which heartened him greatly to pass on towards him, for of this only Captain he had more respect than of all the multitude by *Darius* assembled, and of all the Commanders he had besides. For so much hath the spirit of some one man excelled, as it hath undertaken and effected the alteration of the greatest States and Commonweals, the erection of Monarchies, the conquest of Kingdoms and Empires guided handfuls of men against multitudes of equal bodily strength, contrived victories beyond all hope and discourse of reason, converted the fearful passions of his own followers into magnanimity, and the valour of his enemies into cowardice; such spirits have been stirred up in sundry Ages of the world, and in divers parts thereof, to erect and cast down again, to establish and to destroy, and to bring all things, Persons and States; to the same certain ends, which the infinite spirit of the *Universal*, piercing, moving, and governing all things hath ordained. Certainly the things that this King did were marvellous, and would hardly have been undertaken by any man else: and though his father had determined to have invaded the lesser *Asia*, it is like enough that he would have contended himself with some part thereof, and not have discovered the river of *Indus*, as this man did. The swift course of victory, wherewith he ran over so large a portion of the World, in so short a space, may justly be imputed unto this, That he was never encountered by an equal spirit, concurring with equal power against him. Hereby it came to pass that his actions being limited by no greater opposition, than Desert places, and the mere length of tedious journeys could make, were like the *Colossus* of Rhodes, not so much to be admired for the workmanship, though therein also praiseworthy, as for the huge bulk. For certainly the things performed by *Xenophon*, discover as brave a spirit as *Alexander's*, and working no less exquisitely, though the effects were less material, as were also the forces and power of command, by which it wrought. But he that would find the exact pattern of a noble Commander, must look upon such as *Epaminondas*, that encountering worthy Captains, and those better followed than themselves, have by their singular virtue overtopped their valiant enemies, and still prevailed over those, that would not have yielded one foot to any other. Such as these are do seldom live to obtain great Empires. For it is a work of more labour and longer time, to master the equal forces of one hardy and well ordered State, than to tread down and utterly subdue a multitude of servile Nations, compounding the body of a gross unwieldy Empire. Wherefore these *Parvo Potentes*, men that with little have done much upon enemies of like ability, are to be regarded as choice examples of worth; but great Conquerors, to be rather admired for the substance of their actions, than the exquisite managing: exactness and greatness concurring so seldom, that I can find no instance of both in one, save only that brave *Roman Caesar*.

Having thus far digressed, it is now time that we return unto our Eastern Conqueror; who is travelling hastily towards *Cilicia*, with a desire to recover the Straits thereof before *Darius* should arrive there. But first making a despatch into *Greece*, he sent to those Cities, in which he reposed most trust, some of the *Persian* Targets which he had recovered in his first battle; upon which, by certain inscriptions, he made them partakers of his victory. Herein he well advised himself; for he that doth not as well impart of the honour which he gaineth in the Wars, as he doth of the spoils, shall never be long followed by those of the better sort. For men which are either well born or well bred, and have more of wealth than of reputation, do as often satisfy themselves with the purchase of glory; as the weak in fortune, and strong in courage, do with the gain of gold and silver.

The Governor of *Cilicia* hearing of *Alexander* coming on, left some Companies to keep the Straits, which were indeed very defensible; and withal, as *Curtius* noteth, he began over-late to prize and put in execution the Counsel of *Memnon*: who in the beginning of the Wars advised him to waste all the provisions for Men and Horse, that could not be lodged in strong places, and always to give ground to the invader, till he found some such notable advantage as might assuredly promise him the obtaining of victory. For the fury of an invading Army is best broken, by delays, change of diet, and want, eating sometimes too little, and sometimes too much, sometimes reposing themselves in beds, and more oftener on the cold ground. These and the like sudden alterations bring many diseases upon all Nations out of their own Countries. Therefore if *Darius* had kept the *Macedonians* but a while from meat and sleep, and refusing to give or take battle, had wearied them with his light horse, as the *Parthians* afterward did the *Romans*; he might perchance have saved his own life, and his estate: For it was one of the greatest encouragements given by *Alexander* to the *Macedonians*, in the third and last fatal battle, that they were to fight with all the strength of *Persia* at once.

Xerxes, when he invaded *Greece* and fought abroad, in being beaten, lost only his men; but *Darius* being invaded by the *Greeks*, and fighting at home, by being beaten, lost his Kingdom: *Pericles*, though the *Lacadaemonians* burnt all in *Attica* to the Gates of *Athens*, yet could not be drawn to hazard a battle: for the invaded ought evermore to fight upon the advantage of time and place. Because we read Histories to inform our understanding by the examples therein found, we will give some instances of those that have perished by adventuring in their own Countries to charge an invading Army. The *Romans*, by fighting with *Hannibal*, were brought to the brink of their destruction.

Pompey was well advised for a while, when he gave *Caesar* ground, but when by the importunity of his Captains he adventured to fight at *Pharsalia*, he lost the battle, lost the freedom of *Rome*, and his own life.

Ferdinand, in the Conquest of *Naples*, would needs fight a battle with the *French* to his confusion, though it was told him by a man of sound judgment, that those Counsels which promise surety in all things, are honourable enough.

The Constable of *France* made frustrate the mighty preparations of *Charles* the Fifth, when he invaded *Provence*, by wasting the Country and forbearing to fight; so did the Duke of *Alva* weary the *French* in *Naples*, and dissolve the boisterous Army of the Prince of *Orange* in the low Countries.

The *Liegers*, contrary to the advice of their General, would needs fight a battle with the *Bourgonians*, invading their Country, and could not be persuaded to linger the time, and stay their advantage; but they lost eight and twenty thousand upon the place. *Philip* of *Valois* set upon King *Edward* at *Cressy*, and King *John* (when the *English* were well near tired out, and would in short time by an orderly pursuit have been wasted to nothing) constrained the black Prince with great fury, near *Poitiers*, to join battle with him: But all men know what lamentable success these two *French* Kings found. *Charles* the Fifth of *France* made another kind of *Fabian*-Warfare; and though the *English* burnt and wasted many places, yet this King held his resolution to forbear blows, and followed his advice which told him, That the *English* could never get his inheritance by smoke; and it is reported by *Bellay* and *Herrault*, that King *Edward* was wont to say of this *Charles*, that he won from him the Duchy of *Guien* without ever putting on his Armour.

But where God hath a purpose to destroy, wise men grow short lived, and the charge of things is committed unto such as either cannot see what is for their good, or know not how to put in execution any sound advice. The course which *Memnon* had propounded, must in all appearance of reason have brought the *Macedonian* to a great perplexity, and made him stand still a while at the Straits of *Cilicia*, doubting whether it were more shameful to return, or dangerous to proceed. For had *Cappadocia* and *Pàphlagonia* been wasted whilst *Alexander* was far off; and the Straits of *Cilicia* been defended by *Arsenes*, Governor of that Province, with the best of his forces: hunger would not have suffered the enemy, to stay the trial of all means that might be thought upon, of forcing that passage; or if the place could not have been maintained, yet might *Cilicia* at better leisure have been so thoroughly spoiled, that the heart of his Army should have been broken, by seeking out miseries with painful travail.

But *Arsenes* leaving a small number to defend the Straits, took the best of his Army with him, to waste, and spoil the Country; or rather, as may seem, to find himself some work, by pretence of which he might honestly run further away from *Alexander*. He should rather have adventured his person in custody of the Straits, whereby he might perhaps have saved the Province; and in the mean time, all that was in the fields, would have been conveyed into strong Towns. So should his Army, if it were driven from the place of advantage, have found good entertainment within walled Cities, and himself with his horsemen have had the less work in destroying that little which was left abroad. Handling the matter as he did, he gave the *Cilicians* cause to wish for *Alexander's* coming, and as great cause to the Keepers of the passage not to hinder it. For cowards are wise in apprehending all forms of danger. These Guardians of the Straits, hearing that *Arsenes* made all haste to join himself with *Darius*, burning down all as he went, like one despairing of the defence, began to grow circumspect, and to think that surely their General, who gave as lost the Country behind their backs, had exposed themselves unto certain death, as men that were good for nothing else, but to dull the *Macedonian* swords. Wherefore, not affecting to die for their Prince and Country (which honour they saw that *Arsenes* himself could well forbear) they speedily followed the footsteps of their General, gleaning after his Harvest. Thus *Alexander* without labour got both the entrance of *Cilicia*, abandoned by the cowardice of his Enemies, and the whole Province that had been alienated from the *Persian* side by their indiscretion.

Chapter 2:4 Of the unwarlike army levied by Darius against Alexander. The unadvised courses which Darius took in this expedition. He is vanquished at Issus; where his Mother, Wife, and Children are made prisoners . . .

In the mean season *Darius* approached; who (as *Curtius* reports) had compounded an Army of more than two hundred and ninety thousand Soldiers, out of divers Nations; *Justin* musters them at three hundred thousand Foot, and a hundred thousand Horse; *Plutarch* at six hundred thousand.

The manner of his coming on, as *Curtius* describes it, was rather like a masquer than a man of War, and like one that took more care to set out his glory and riches, than to provide for his own safety, persuading himself, as it seemed, to beat *Alexander* with pomp and sumptuous Pageants. For before the Army there was carried the holy fire which the *Persians* worshipped, attended by their *Priests*, and after them three hundred and threescore and five young men, answering the number of the days of the year, covered with Scarlet; then the Chariot of *Jupiter* drawn with white Horses, with their Riders clothed in the same colour, with rods of gold in their hands; And after it, the Horse of the Sun: Next after these followed ten sumptuous Chariots, inlaid and garnished with silver and gold, and then the Vanguard of their horse, compounded of twelve several Nations, which the better to avoid confusion, did hardly understand each other's language, and these marshalled in the head of the rest, being beaten, might serve very fitly to disorder all that followed them; in the tail of these Horses the Regiment of foot marched, with the *Persians* called immortal, because if any died the number was presently supplied: and these were armed with chains of gold, and their coats with the same metal embroidered, whereof the sleeves were garnished with pearl, baits, either to catch the hungry *Macedonians* withal, or to persuade them that it were great incivility to cut and deface such glorious garments. But it was well said . . . *Let no man think that he exceedeth those in valour, whom he exceedeth in gay garments, for it is by men armed with fortitude of mind, and not by the apparel they put on, that enemies are beaten*. And it was perchance from the *Roman Papyrius* that this advice was borrowed, who when he fought against the *Samnite* in that fatal battle, wherein they all sware either to prevail or die, thirty thousand of them having apparelled themselves in white garments, with high crests and great plumes of feathers, bade the *Roman* Soldiers to lay aside all fear. . . *For these plumed crests would wound nobody, and the Roman pile would bore holes in painted and gilded shields*.

To second this Court-like company, fifteen thousand were appointed more rich and glittering than the former, but apparelled like Women (belike to breed the more terror) and these were honoured with the Title of the King's Kinsmen. Then came *Darius* himself, the Gentlemen of his Guard-robe riding before his Chariot, which was supported with the Gods of his Nation, cast and cut in pure gold; these the *Macedonians* did not serve, but they served their turns of these, by changing their massy bodies into thin portable and current coin. The head of this Chariot was set with precious stones, with two little golden Idols, covered with an open-winged Eagle of the same metal: The hinder part being raised high whereon *Darius* sat, had a covering of inestimable value. This Chariot of the King was followed with ten thousand Horsemen, their Lances plated with silver, and their heads gilt; which they meant not to imbrue in the *Macedonian* blood, for fear of marring their beauty. He had for the proper Guard of his person two hundred of the blood Royal, blood too Royal and precious to be spilt by any valorous adventure, (I am of opinion that two hundred sturdy fellows, like the *Switzers*, would have done him more service) and these were backed with thirty thousand footmen, after whom again were led four hundred spare horses for the King, which if he had meant to have used he would have marshalled somewhat nearer him.

Now followed the Rearward, the same being led by *Sisygambis* the King's Mother, and by his Wife, drawn in glorious Chariots, followed by a great train of Ladies, their attendants on horseback, with fifteen Waggons of the King's children and the wives of the Nobility, waited on by two hundred and fifty Concubines, and a world of Nurses, and *Eunuchs*, most sumptuously apparelled, By which it should seem that *Darius* thought that the *Macedonians* had been *Comedians* or *Tumblers*: for this troop was far fitter to behold those sports than to be present at battles. Between these and a company of slight-armed slaves, with a world of Valets, was the King's treasure, charged on six hundred Mules, and three hundred Camels, brought, as it proved, to pay the *Macedonians*. In this sort came this *May-game-King* into the field, encumbered with a most unnecessary train of Strumpets, attended with troops of divers Nations, speaking divers languages, and for their numbers impossible to be marshalled, and for the most part so effeminate, and so rich in gold and in garments, as the same could not but have encouraged the nakedest Nation of the world against them. We find it in daily experience that all discourse of magnanimity, of National Virtue, of Religion, of Liberty, and whatsoever else hath been wont to move and encourage virtuous men, hath no force at all with the common Soldier, in comparison of spoil and riches, The rich ships are boarded upon all disadvantages, the rich Towns are furiously assaulted, and the plentiful Countries willingly invaded. Our *English* Nations have attempted many places in the *Indies*, and run upon the *Spaniards* headlong, in hope of their Royals of plate, and Pistolets, which had they been put to it upon the like disadvantages in *Ireland*, or in any poor Country, they would have turned their Pieces and Pikes against their Commanders, contesting that they had been brought without reason to the Butchery and slaughter. It is true that war is made willingly, and for the most part with good success, that is ordained against the richest Nations; for as the needy are always adventurous, so plenty is wont to shun peril, and men that have well to live, do rather study how to live well, I mean wealthily, than care to die (as they call it) honourably . . . *No man makes haste to the market, where there is nothing to be bought but blows.*

Now if *Alexander* had beheld this preparation before his consultation with his Soothsayers, he would have satisfied himself by the outsides of the *Persians*, and never have looked into the entrails of Beasts for success. For leaving the description of this second battle, (which is indeed nowhere well described, neither for the confusion and hasty running away of the *Asians* could it be) we have enough by the slaughter that was made of them, and by the few that fell of the *Macedonians*, to inform us what manner of resistance was made. For if it be true that threescore thousand *Persian* footmen were slain in this battle, with ten thousand of their horsemen, Or (as *Curtius* saith) an hundred thousand footmen, with the same number of horsemen, and besides this slaughter, forty thousand taken prisoners, while of *Alexander's* army there miscarried but two hundred and fourscore of all sorts, of which numbers *Arianus* and other Historians cut off almost the one half: I do verily believe that this small number rather died with the over-travail and pains-taking in killing their enemies, than by any strokes received from them. And surely if the *Persian* Nation (at this time degenerate, and the basest of the World) had had any savour remaining of the ancient valour of their forefathers; they would never have sold so good cheap, and at so vile a price, the Mother, the Wife, the Daughters, and other the King's children; had their own honour been valued by them at nothing, and the King's safety and his estate at less. *Darius* by this time found it true that *Charidemus* a banished *Grecian* of *Athens* had told him, when he made a view of his Army about *Babylon*, to wit, That the multitude which he had assembled of divers Nations, richly attired, but poorly armed, would be found more terrible to the Inhabitants of the country, whom in passing by they would devour, than to the *Macedonians*, whom they meant to assail; who being all old and obedient Soldiers, embattled in gross squadrons, which they call their *Phalanx*, well covered with Armour for defence, and furnished with weapons for offence of great advantage, would make so little account of his delicate *Persians*, loving their ease and their palate, being withal ill-armed and worse disciplined, as except it would please him to entertain (having so great abundance of treasure to do it withal) a sufficient number of the same *Grecians*, and so to encounter the *Macedonians* with men of equal courage, he would repent him overlate, as taught by the miserable success like to follow.

But this discourse was so unpleasing to *Darius* (who had been accustomed to nothing so much as to his own praises, and to nothing so little as to hear truth;) as he commanded that this poor *Grecian* should be presently slain: who while he was a sundering in the Tormentor's hand, used this speech to the King, That *Alexander*, against whom he had given this good counsel, should assuredly revenge his death, and lay deserved punishment upon *Darius* for despising his advice.

It was the saying of a Wise man . . . *That Prince's safety is in a desperate case, whose ears judge all that is profitable to be too sharp, and will entertain nothing that is unpleasant.*

For liberty in counsel is the life and essence of counsel . . .

Darius did likewise value at nothing the Advice given him by the *Grecian* soldiers that served him, who entreated him not to fight in the Straits; but had they been Counsellors and directors in that War, as they were underlings and commanded by others, they had with the help of a good troop of horsemen been able to have opposed the fury of *Alexander*, without any assistance of the *Persian* footmen. For when *Darius* was overthrown with all his cowardly and confused rabble, those *Grecians*, under their Captain *Amyntas*, held firm, and marched away in order in despite of the vanquishers. Old Soldiers are not easily dismayed: we read in Histories ancient and modern, what brave retreats have been made by them, though the rest of the Army in which they have served hath been broken.

At the battle of *Ravenna* where the Imperials were beaten by the *French*, a squadron of *Spaniards*, old Soldiers, came off unbroken and undismayed; whom when *Gaston de Foix*, Duke of *Nemours*, and Nephew to *Louis* the twelfth, charged, as holding the victory not entire by their escape, he was overturned and slain in the place. For it is truly said of these men, who, by being acquainted with dangers fear them not, That . . . *They go about the business itself, how hard soever it be, not standing to consider of the danger, which the mischief hanging over their heads may bring:* and as truly of those that know the wars but by hearsay . . . *They have ability enough, and to spare, till dangers appear; but when peril indeed comes, they get them gone.*

These *Grecians* also that made the retract, advised *Darius* to retire his Army into the plain of *Mesopotamia*, to the end that *Alexander* being entered into those large fields and great Champaigns, he might have environed the *Macedonians* on all sides with his multitude; and withal they counselled him to divide that his huge Army into parts, not committing the whole to one stroke of Fortune, whereby he might have fought many battles, and have brought no greater numbers at once than might have been well marshalled and conducted. But this counsel was so contrary to the cowardly affections of the *Persians*, as they persuaded *Darius* to environ the *Grecians* which gave the advice, and to cut them in pieces as Traitors. The infinite wisdom of God doth not work always by one, and the same way, but very often in the alteration of Kingdoms and Estates, by taking understanding from the Governors, so as they can neither give nor discern of Counsels. For *Darius* that would needs fight with *Alexander* upon a straitened piece of ground, near unto the city of *Issus*, where he could bring no more hands to fight than *Alexander* could, (who by the advice of *Parmenio* stayed there, as in a place of best advantage) was utterly overthrown, his Treasure lost, his Wife, Mother, and Children (whom the *Grecians* his followers had persuaded him to leave in *Babylon*, or elsewhere) taken prisoners, and all their train of Ladies spoiled of their rich Garments, Jewels, and Honour. It is true, that both the Queen, with her Daughters, who had the good hap to be brought to *Alexander's* presence, were entertained with all respect due unto their birth, their Honours preserved, and their Jewels and rich Garments restored unto them; and though *Darius*' Wife was a most beautiful Lady, and his Daughters of excellent form, Yet *Alexander* mastered his affections towards them all: only it is reported out of *Aristobolus* the Historian, That he embraced the Wife of the valiant *Memnon*, her Husband lately dead, who was taken flying from *Damascus* by *Parmenio*, at which time the Daughters of *Ochus*, who reigned before *Darius*, and the Wives and Children of all the nobility of *Persia* in effect, fell into captivity; At which time also *Darius'* Treasure (not lost at *Issus*) was seized, amounting to six thousand and two hundred talents of coin, and of *Bullion* five hundred talents, with a world of riches besides.

Darius himself leaving his brother dead, with divers other of his chief Captains (casting the Crown from his head) hardly escaped . . .

Chapter 2:7 Alexander wins Egypt, and makes a journey to the Temple of Hammon.

From *Jerusalem Alexander* turned again towards *Egypt*, and entered it, where *Darius* his lieutenant, *Astaces*, received him and delivered into his hand the City of *Memphis*, with eight hundred talents of treasure, and all other the King's riches. By this we see that the King of *Persia*, who had more of affection than of judgment, gave to the valiantest man he had but the command of one City, and to the veriest coward the government of all *Egypt*. When he had set things in order in *Egypt*, he began to travail after *Godhead*, towards *Jupiter Hammon*, so foolish had prosperity made him. He was to pass over the dangerous and dry sands, where, when the water which he brought on his Camels' back was spent, he could not but have perished, had not a marvellous shower of rain fallen upon him, when his Army was in extreme despair. All men that know *Egypt*, and have written thereof, affirm, That it never rains there; but the purposes of the Almighty God are secret, and he bringeth to pass what it pleaseth him; for it is also said, That when he had lost his way in those vast deserts, that a flight of Crows flew before the Army, who making faster wing when they were followed, and fluttering slowly when the Army was cast back, guided them over those pathless sands to *Jupiter's* temple.

Arrianus, from the report of *Ptolomy*, the son of *Lagus*, says, That he was led by two Dragons, both which reports may be alike true; But many of these wonders and things prodigious are feigned by those that have written the story of *Alexander*, as that an Eagle lay hovering directly over his head at the battle of *Issus*; That a Swallow flew about his head when he slept, and could not be feared from him, till it had wakened him, at *Halicarnassus*, foreshowing the treason of *Aeropus*, practised by *Darius* to have slain him; That from the iron bars of which the *Tyrians* made their defensive engines, when *Alexander* besieged them, there fell drops of blood; and that the like drops were found in a loaf of bread, broken by a *Macedonian* Soldier, at the same time; That a Turf of earth fell on his shoulder, when he lay before *Gaza*, out of which there flew a Bird into the air. The *Spaniards* in the conquest of the West *Indies* have many such pretty tales; telling how they have been assisted in battle, by the presence of our *Lady*, and by *Angels* riding on white horses, with the like *Romish* miracles, which I think themselves do hardly believe. The strangest thing that I have read of in this kind being certainly true, was, That the night before the battle of *Novara*, all the Dogs which followed the *French* Army, ran from them to the *Switzers*, leaping and fawning upon them, as if they had been bred and fed by them all their lives, and in the morning following, *Trivulzi* and *Tremoville*, Generals for *Louis* the twelfth, were by these *Imperial Switzers* utterly broken and put to ruin.

The place of this idol of *Jupiter Hammon* is ill described by *Curtius*, for he bounds it by the *Arabian Troglodytes* on the south, between whom and the territory of *Hammon*, the Region *Thebais*, or the superior *Egypt*, with the Mountains of *Libya*, and the River of *Nilus*, are interjacent, and on the North he joins it to a Nation, called *Nassamones*, who bordering the Sea shore, live (saith he) upon the spoils of shipwreck, whereas the Temple or Grove of this Idol hath no Sea near it by two hundred miles and more, being found on the South part of *Libya*; these *Nassamones* being due West from it, in the South part of *Marmarica*.

When *Alexander* came near the place, he sent some of his Parasites before him to practise the Priests attending the Oracle, That their answer might be given in all things, agreeable to his mad ambition, who affected the title of *Jupiter's* son. And so he was saluted *Son of Jupiter* by the Devil's Prophet, whether prepared before to flatter him, or rather (as some think) defective in the *Greek* tongue; For whereas he meant to say *O pai dion*, he said *O pai dios*, that is; *O son of Jupiter*, instead of, *O dear son*: for which Grammatical error he was richly rewarded, and a rumour presently spread, that the great *Jupiter* had acknowledged *Alexander* for his own.

He had heard that *Perseus* and *Hercules* had formerly consulted with this Oracle, The one when he was employed against *Gorgon*, The other against *Anteus* and *Busiris*; and seeing these men had derived themselves from the Gods, why might not he? By this it seems, that he hoped to make his followers and the world fools, though indeed he made himself one, by thinking to cover from the World's knowledge his vanities and vices; and the better to confirm his followers in the belief of his Deity, he had practised the Priests to give answer to such as consulted with the Oracle, that it should be pleasing to *Jupiter* to honour *Alexander* as his son.

Who this *Ammon* was, and how represented, either by a boss carried in a Boat, or by a Ram, or a Ram's head; I see that many wise men have troubled themselves to find out; but, as *Arrianus* speaks of *Dionysius*, or *Liber pater* (who lived saith St. *Augustine* in *Moses'* time,) . . . *We must not over curiously search into the fables, which the Ancients have written of their Gods.*

But this is certain and notable, that after the Gospel began to be preached in the World, the Devil in this and in all other Idols became speechless. For that this *Hammon* was neglected in the time of *Tiberius Caesar*, and in the time of *Trajan* altogether forgotten, *Strabo* and *Plutarch* witness. . .

Chapter 2:12 How Alexander came to Persepolis, and burnt it.

From *Susa Alexander* leadeth his Army toward *Persepolis*, and when he sought to pass those Mountains which sunder *Susiana* and *Persia*, he was soundly beaten by *Ariobarzenes*, who defended against him those Straits, called *Pylae Persidis*, or *Susoeidae*; and after the loss of many Companies of his *Macedonians*, he was forced to save himself by retreat, causing his foot to march close together, and to cover themselves with their Targets from the stones tumbled on them from the Mountain top. Yet in the end he found out another path, which a *Lycian*, living in that Country, discovered unto him, and came thereby suddenly in view of *Ariobarzenes*, who being enforced to fight upon even ground, was by *Alexander* broken, whereupon he fled to *Persepolis*, but (after that they of *Persepolis* had refused to receive him) he returned and gave a second charge upon the *Macedonians*, wherein he was slain. In like manner did king *Francis* the first, in the year 1515, find a way over the *Alps*, the *Switzers* undertaking to defend all the passages, who, if their footmanship had not saved them upon the King's descent on the other side, they had been ill paid for their hard lodging on those Hills.

Four thousand *Greeks*, saith *Curtius*, (*Justin* numbers them but at eight hundred) having been taken prisoners by the *Persians*, presented themselves to *Alexander* now in sight of *Persepolis*. These had the barbarous *Persians* so maimed and defaced, by cutting off their Hands, Noses, Ears, and other Members, as they could no way have been known to their countrymen, but by their voices; to each of these *Alexander* gave three hundred Crowns, with new garment, and such Lands as they liked to live upon.

Tiridates, one of *Darius* his falsehearted *Grandees*, hearing of *Alexander's* approach, made him know that *Persepolis* was ready to receive him, and prayed him to double his pace, because there was a determination in the people to spoil the King's treasure. This City was abandoned by many of her Inhabitants upon *Alexander's* arrival, and they that stayed followed the worst counsel, for all was left to the liberty of the Soldiers, to spoil and kill at their pleasure, There was no place in the world at that time, which, if it had been laid in balance with *Persepolis,* would have weighed it down. *Babylon*, indeed, and *Susa*, were very rich, but in *Persepolis* lay the bulk and main store of the *Persians*. For after the spoil that had been made of money, curious plate, bullion, Images of gold and silver, and other jewels, there remained to *Alexander* himself one hundred and twenty thousand talents. He left the same number of three thousand *Macedonians* in *Persepolis*, which he had done in *Susa*, and gave the same formal honour to the Traitor *Tiridates*, that he had done to *Abulites*: but he that had the trust of the place was *Nicarides*, a creature of his own. The body of his Army he left here for thirty days, of which the Commanders were *Parmenio* and *Craterus*, and with a thousand horse and certain troops of chosen foot, he would needs view in the Winter time those parts of *Persia* which the Snow had covered, a fruitless and foolish enterprise, but as *Seneca* says. . . *He hath not a will to go, but he is unable to stand still*. It is said and spoken in his praise, That when his Soldiers cried out against him, because they could not endure the extreme frost, and make way but with extreme difficulty through the snow, that *Alexander* forsook his horse, and led them the way. But what can be more ridiculous than to bring other men into extremity, thereby to show how well himself can endure it? His walking on foot did no otherwise take off their weariness, that followed him, than his sometime forbearing to drink did quench their thirst, that could less endure it. For mine own little judgment I shall rather commend that Captain, that makes careful provision for those that follow him, and that seeks wisely to prevent extreme necessity, than those witless arrogant fools, that make the vaunt of having endured equally with the common Soldier, as if that were a matter of great glory and importance.

We find in all the wars that *Caesar* made, or the best of the *Roman* Commanders, that the provision of victuals was their first care. For it was a true saying of *Coligni*, Admiral of *France*; *That whoso will shape that beast* (meaning War) *must begin with his belly*.

But *Alexander* is now returned to *Persepolis*, where those Historians that were most amorous of his virtues, complain, that the opinion of his valour, of his liberality, of his clemency towards the vanquished, and all other his Kingly conditions, were drowned in drink; That he smothered in carousing cups all the reputation of his actions past, and that by descending, as it were, from the reverend Throne of the greatest King into the company and familiarity of base Harlots, he began to be despised, both of his own and all other Nations. For being persuaded, when he was inflamed with wine, by the infamous Strumpet *Thais*, he caused the most sumptuous and goodly Castle and City of *Persepolis*, to be consumed with fire, notwithstanding all the arguments of *Parmenio* to the contrary, who told him that it was a dishonour to destroy those things by the persuasions of others, which by his proper virtue and force he had obtained; and that it would be a most strong persuasion to the *Asians*, to think hardly of him, and thereby alien their hearts: For they might well believe that he which demolished the goodliest Ornaments they had, meant nothing less than (after such vastation) to hold their possession. *Fere vinoleniam crudelitas sequitur; Cruelty doth commonly follow drunkenness*: For so it fell out soon after, and often, in *Alexander*.

Chapter 2:13 The treason of Bessus against Darius. Darius his death.
About this time he received a new supply of Soldiers out of *Cilicia*, and goes on to find *Darius* in *Media*, *Darius* had there compounded his fourth and last Army, which he meant to have increased in *Bactria*, had he not heard of *Alexander's* coming on, with whom (trusting to such companies as he had, which was numbered at thirty or forty thousand) he determined once again to try his fortune. He therefore calls together his Captains and Commanders, and propounds unto them his resolution, who being desperate of good success used silence for a while. *Artabazus*, one of his eldest men of War, who had sometime lived with *Phillip* of *Macedon*, brake the ice, and protesting that he could never be beaten by any adversity of the king's, from the faith which he had ever owed him, with firm confidence, that all the rest were of the same disposition (whereof they likewise assured *Darius* by the like protestation) he approved the King's resolution. Two only, and those the greatest, to wit, *Naburzanes*, and *Bessus*, whereof the latter was Governor of *Bactria*, had conspired against their Master, and therefore advised the King to lay a new foundation for the War, and to pursue it by some such person for the present, against whom neither the Gods nor Fortune had in all things declared themselves to be an enemy: this preamble *Naburzanes* used, and in conclusion advised the election of his fellow Traitor *Bessus*, with promise that, the wars ended, the Empire

should again be restored to *Darius*. The King swollen with disdain pressed towards *Naburzanes* to have slain him, but *Bessus* and the *Bactrians* whom he commanded being more in number than the rest, withheld him. In the mean while *Naburzanes* withdrew himself, and *Bessus* followed him, making their quarter apart from the rest of the Army. *Artabazus*, the King's faithful servant, persuaded him to be advised, and serve the time, seeing *Alexander* was at hand, and that he would at least make show of forgetting the offence made, which the King, being of a gentle disposition willingly yielded unto. *Bessus* makes his submission and attends the King, who removes his Army. *Patron*, who commanded a Regiment of four thousand *Greeks*, which had in all the former battles served *Darius* with great fidelity, and always made the retreat in spite of the *Macedonians*, offered himself to guard his person, protesting against the treason of *Bessus*, but it was not in his destiny to follow their advice, who from the beginning of the War gave him faithful counsel, but he inclined still to *Bessus*, who told him, that the *Greeks* with *Patron* their Captain were corrupted by *Alexander*, and practised the division of his faithful servants. *Bessus* had drawn unto him thirty thousand of the Army, promising them all those things, by which the lovers of the world and themselves, are wont to be allured, to wit, riches, safety, and honour.

Now the day following *Darius* plainly discovered the purposes of *Bessus*, and being overcome with passion, as thinking himself unable to make head against these ungrateful and unnatural Traitors, he prayed *Artabazus* his faithful servant to depart from him, and to provide for himself. In like sort he discharged the rest of his attendants, all save a few of his *Eunuchs*; for his guards had voluntarily abandoned him, His *Persians* being most base cowards, durst not undertake his defence against the *Bactrians*, notwithstanding that they had four thousand *Greeks* to join with them, who had been able to have beaten both Nations. But it is true, that him, which forsakes himself, no man follows. It had been far more manlike and Kinglike, to have died in the head of those four thousand *Greeks*, which offered him the disposition of their lives, (to which *Artabazus* persuaded him) than to have lain bewailing himself on the ground, and suffering himself to be bound like a slave by those ambitious Monsters that laid hand on him, whom neither the consideration of his former great estate, nor the honours he had given them, nor the trust reposed in them, nor the world of benefits bestowed on them, could move to pity: no, nor his present adversity, which above all things should have moved them, could pierce their viperous and ungrateful hearts. Vain it was indeed to hope it, for infidelity hath no compassion.

Now *Darius*, thus forsaken, was bound and laid in a Cart, covered with hides of beasts, to the end that by any other ornament he might not be discovered; and to add despite and derision to his adversity, they fastened him with chains of gold, and so drew him on among their ordinary carriages and Carts. For *Bessus* and *Nabarzanes* persuaded themselves to redeem their lives and the Provinces they held either by delivering him a prisoner to *Alexander*, or if that hope failed, to make themselves Kings by his slaughter, and then to defend themselves by force of Arms. But they failed in both. For it was against the nature of God, who is most just, to pardon so strange villainy, yea though against a Prince purely Heathenish, and an Idolater.

Alexander having knowledge that *Darius* was retired towards *Bactria*, and durst not abide his coming, hasted after him with a violent speed, and because he would not force his footmen beyond their powers, he mounted on horseback certain selected Companies of them, and best armed, and with six thousand other Horse, rather ran than marched after *Darius*. Such as hated the treason of *Bessus*, and secretly forsook him, gave knowledge to *Alexander* of all that had happened, informing him of the way that *Bessus* took, and how near he was at hand; for many men of worth daily ran from him. Hereupon *Alexander* again doubled his pace, and his Vanguard being discovered by *Bessus* his rear, *Bessus* brought a horse to the Cart, where *Darius* lay bound, persuading him to mount thereon, and to save himself. But the unfortunate King refusing to follow those that had betrayed him, they cast Darts at him, wounded him to death, and wounded the beasts that drew him, and slew two poor servants that attended his person. This done, they all fled that could, leaving the rest to the mercy of the *Macedonian* swords.

Polystratus, a *Macedonian*, being by pursuit of the vanquished pressed with thirst, as he was refreshing himself with some water that he had discovered, espying a Cart with a Team of wounded beasts breathing for life, and not able to move, searched the same, and therein found *Darius* bathing in his own blood. And by a *Persian* captive which followed this *Polystratus*, he understood that it was *Darius*, and was informed of this barbarous Tragedy. *Darius* also seemed greatly comforted (if dying men ignorant of the living God can be comforted) that he cast not out his last sorrows unheard, but that by this *Macedonian*, *Alexander* might know and take vengeance on those Traitors, which had dealt no less unworthily than cruelly with him, recommending their revenge to *Alexander* by this Messenger, which he besought him to pursue, not because *Darius* had desired it, but for his own honour, and for the safety of all that did, or should after wear Crowns. He also, having nothing else to present, rendered thanks to *Alexander* for the Kingly grace used towards his Wife, Mother, and Children, desiring the immortal Gods to submit unto him the Empire of the whole world. As he was thus speaking, impatient death pressing out his few remaining spirits, he desired water, which *Polystratus* presented him, after which he lived but to tell him, that of all the best things that the world had, which were lately in his power, he had nothing remaining but his last breath, wherewith to desire the Gods to reward his compassion.

Chapter 2:23 Of Alexander's person and qualities.

Howsoever it were, *Alexander's* former cruelties cannot be excused, no more than his vanity to be esteemed the son of *Jupiter*, with his excessive delight in drink and drunkenness, which others make the cause of his fever and death. In that he lamented his want of enterprising, and grieved to consider what he should do when he had conquered the World, *Augustus Caesar* found just cause to deride him, as if the well-governing of so many Nations and Kingdoms, as he had already conquered, could not have offered him matter more than abundant, to busy his brains withal. That he was both learned and a lover of learning, it cannot be doubted: Sir *Francis Bacon*, in his first book of the advancement of learning, hath proved it sufficiently. His liberality I know not how to praise, because it exceeded proportion. It is said, That when he gave a whole City to one of his Servants, He to whom it was given, did out of modesty refuse it, as disproportionable to his fortune: to whom *Alexander* replied, That he did not enquire what became him to accept, but the King to give: of which *Seneca* . . . *It seems a brave and royal speech, whereas indeed it is very foolish. For nothing simply considered by itself beseems a man. We must regard that, to whom, when, why, where, and the like; without which considerations no act can be approved. Let honours be proportioned unto the persons: for whereas virtue is ever limited by measure, the excess is as faulty as the defect.*

For his Person, it is very apparent, That he was as valiant as any man, a disposition taken by itself, not much to be admired; For I am resolved that he had ten thousand in his Army as daring as himself. Surely, if adventurous nature were to be commended simply, we should confound that virtue with the hardiness of Thieves, Ruffians, and mastiff Dogs. For certainly it is no way praiseworthy but in daring good things, and in the performance of those lawful enterprises, in which we are employed for the service of our Kings and Commonweals.

If we compare this great Conqueror with other Troublers of the World, who have bought their glory with so great destruction, and effusion of blood, I think him far inferior to *Caesar*, and many other that lived after him, seeing he never undertook any warlike Nation, the naked *Scythians* excepted, nor was he ever encountered with any Army of which he had not a most mastering advantage, both of weapons and of Commanders, every one of his Father's old Captains by far exceeding the best of his Enemies. But it seemeth, Fortune and Destinies (if we may use those terms) had found out and prepared for him, without any care of his own, both heaps of Men, that willingly offered their necks to the yoke, and Kingdoms that invited and called in their own Conquerors. For conclusion, we will agree with *Seneca*, who speaking of *Philip* the Father, and *Alexander* the Son, gives this judgment of them . . . *That they were no less plagues to mankind, than an overflow of waters, drowning all the level; or some burning drought, whereby a great part of living creatures is scorched up.*

From Book Five of the History of the World

Chapter 1:1 . . . That neither the Macedonian nor the Roman soldier, was of equal valour to the English.

. . . Whether the *Roman* or the *Macedonian*, were in those days the better Soldier, I will not take upon me to determine: though I might, without partiality, deliver mine own opinion, and prefer that Army, which followed not only *Philip* and *Alexander*, but also *Alexander's* Princes after him, in the greatest dangers of all sorts of war; before any, that *Rome* either had, or in long time after did send forth. Concerning fortune, who can give a rule that shall always hold? *Alexander* was victorious in every battle that he fought: and the *Romans* in the issue of every war. But forasmuch as *Livy* hath judged this a matter worthy of consideration; I think it a great part of Rome's good fortune, that *Alexander* came not into *Italy*: where, in three years after his death, the two *Roman* Consuls, together with all the power of that State, were surprised by the *Samnites*, and enforced to yield up their arms. We may therefore permit *Livy* to admire his own *Romans*, and to compare with *Alexander* those Captains of theirs, which were honoured sufficiently, in being thought equal to his followers: that the same conceit should blind our judgment, we cannot permit without much vanity.

Now in deciding such a controversy, methinks it were not amiss, for an *Englishman*, to give such a sentence between the *Macedonians* and *Romans*, as the *Romans* once did (being chosen Arbitrators) between the *Ardeates* and *Aricini*, that strove about a piece of land; saying, that it belonged unto neither of them, but unto the *Romans* themselves.

If therefore it be demanded, whether the *Macedonian*, or the *Roman*, were the best Warrior? I will answer, the *Englishmen*. For it will soon appear, to any that shall examine the noble acts of our Nation in war, that they were performed by no advantage of weapon; against no savage or unmanly people; the enemy being far superior unto us in numbers, and all needful provisions, yea as well trained as we, or commonly better, in the exercise of war.

In what sort *Philip* won his Dominion in *Greece*; what manner of men the *Persians* and *Indians* were; whom *Alexander* vanquished; as likewise of what force the *Macedonian Phalanx* was, and how well appointed, against such arms as it commonly encountered: any man, that hath taken pains to read the foregoing story of them, doth sufficiently understand. Yet was this *Phalanx* never, or very seldom, able to stand against the *Roman* Armies: which were embattled in so excellent a form, as I know not, whether any Nation besides them have used, either before or since. The *Roman* weapons likewise, both offensive and defensive, were of greater use, than those which any other Nation hath served, before the fiery instruments of Gun-powder were known. As for the enemies, with which *Rome* had to do; we find, that they, which did overmatch her in numbers, were as far overmatched by her, in weapons; and that they, of whom she had little advantage in arms, had as little advantage of her in multitude. This also (as *Plutarch* well observeth) was a part of her happiness; that she was never overlaid, with two great wars at once.

Hereby it came to pass, that having at first increased her strength, by accession of the *Sabines*; having won the State of *Alba*, against which she adventured her own self, as it were in wager, upon the heads of three Champions: and having thereby made herself Princess of *Latium*: she did afterwards, by long war, in many ages, extend her Dominion over all *Italy*. The *Carthaginians* had well near oppressed her: but their Soldiers were Mercenary; so that for want of proper strength, they were easily beaten at their own doors. The *Aetolians*, and with them all, or the most of *Greece*, assisted her against *Philip* the *Macedonian*: he being beaten, did lend her his help, to beat the same *Aetolians*. The wars against *Antiochus*, and other *Asiatics*, were such as gave to *Rome* small cause of boast, though much of joy: for those opposites were as base of courage, as the lands which they held were abundant of riches. *Sicil*, *Spain*, and all *Greece* fell into her hands by using her aid, to protect them against the *Carthaginians* and *Macedonians*.

I shall not need to speak of her other conquests: it was easy to get more when she had gotten all this. It is not my purpose to disgrace the *Roman* valour (which was very noble) or to blemish the reputation of so many famous victories: I am not so idle. This I say; that among all their wars, I find not any, wherein their valour hath appeared, comparable to the *English*. If my judgment seem over partial; our wars in *France* may help to make it good.

First therefore it is well known; that *Rome* (or perhaps all the world besides) had never any so brave a Commander in war, as *Julius Caesar*: and that no *Roman* army, was comparable unto that, which served under the same *Caesar*. Likewise, it is apparent that this gallant Army, which had given fair proof of the *Roman* courage, in good performance of the *Helvetian* war, when it first entered into *Gaul*; was nevertheless utterly disheartened, when *Caesar* led it against the *Germans*. So that we may justly impute, all that was extraordinary in the valour of Caesar's men, to their long exercise, under so good a Leader, in so great a war. Now let us in general, compare with the deeds done by these best of *Roman* Soldiers, in their principal service; the things performed in the same Country, by our common *English* Soldier, levied in haste, from following the Cart, or sitting in the shop-stall: so shall we see the difference. Herein will we deal fairly, and believe *Caesar*, in relating the acts of the *Romans*: but will call the *French* Historians to witness, what actions were performed by the *English*. In *Caesar's* time, *France* was inhabited by the *Gauls*, a stout people, but inferior to the *French*, by whom they were subdued; even when the *Romans* gave them assistance. The Country of *Gaul* was rent in sunder (as *Caesar* witnesseth) into many Lordships: some of which were governed by petty Kings, others by the multitude, none ordered in such sort as might make it appliable to the nearest Neighbour. The factions were many, and violent: not only in general through the whole Country, but between the petty States, yea in every City, and almost in every house. What greater advantage could a Conqueror desire? Yet there was a greater. *Ariovistus*, with his *Germans*, had overrun the Country, and held much part of it in a subjection, little different from mere slavery: yea, so often had the *Germans* prevailed in war upon the *Gauls*, that the *Gauls* (who had sometimes been the better Soldiers) did hold themselves no way equal to those daily Invaders. Had *France* been so prepared unto our *English* Kings, *Rome* itself, by this time, and long ere this time, would have been ours. But when King *Edward* the third began his war upon *France*, he found the whole Country settled in obedience to one mighty King; a King whose reputation abroad, was no less, than his puissance at home; under whose Ensign, the King of *Bohemia*, did serve in person; at whose call, the *Genoese*, and other Neighbour States, were ready to take arms: finally, a King unto whom one Prince gave away his Dominion, for love; another sold away a goodly City and Territory for money. The Country lying so open to the *Roman*, and being so well fenced against the *English*; it is noteworthy, not who prevailed most therein (for it were mere vanity to match the *English* purchases, with the *Roman* conquest) but whether of the two gave the greater proof of military virtue. *Caesar* himself doth witness, that the *Gauls* complained of their own ignorance in the Art of war, and that their own hardiness was overmastered, by the skill of their enemies. Poor men, they admired the *Roman* Towers and Engines of battery, raised and planted against their walls, as more than human works. What greater wonder is it, that such a people was beaten by the *Roman*; than that the *Caribes*, a naked people, but valiant, as any under the sky, are commonly put to the worse by small numbers of *Spaniards*? Besides all this, we are to have regard, of the great difficulty that was found, in drawing all the *Gauls*, or any great part of them, to one head, that with joint forces they might oppose their assailants: as also the much more difficulty, of holding them long together. For hereby it came to pass, that they were never able to make use of opportunity: but sometimes compelled to stay for their fellows; and sometimes driven, to give or take battle, upon extreme disadvantages, for fear, lest their Companies should fall asunder: as indeed, upon any little disaster, they were ready to break, and return every one to the defence of his own. All this, and (which was little less than all this) great odds in weapon, gave to the *Romans*, the honour of many gallant victories. What such help? or what other worldly help, than the golden mettle of their Soldiers, had our *English* Kings against the *French*? Were not the *French* as well experienced in feats of War? Yea, did they not think themselves therein our superiors? Were they not in arms, in horse, and in all provision, exceedingly beyond us? Let us hear, what a *French* writer saith, of the inequality that was between the *French* and *English*, when their king *John* was ready to give the onset, upon the *Black Prince*, at the battle of *Poitiers*: *John had all advantages over Edward, both of number, force, show, Country, and conceit (the which is commonly a consideration of no small importance in worldly affairs) and withal, the choice of all his horsemen (esteemed then the best in Europe) with the greatest and wisest Captains of his whole Realm.* And what could he wish more?

I think, it would trouble a *Roman* antiquary, to find the like example in their Histories; the example, I say, of a King, brought prisoner to *Rome*, by an Army of eight thousand, which he had surrounded with forty thousand, better appointed, and no less expert warriors. This I am sure of; that neither *Syphax* the *Numidian*, followed by a rabble of half Scullions, as *Livy* rightly terms them, nor those cowardly Kings *Perseus* and *Gentius*, are worthy patterns. All that have read of *Cressy* and *Agincourt*, will bear me witness, that I do not allege the battle of *Poitiers*, for lack of other, as good examples of the *English* virtue: the proof whereof hath left many a hundred better marks, in all quarters of *France*, than ever did the valour of the *Romans*. If any man impute these victories of ours to the long Bow, as carrying further, piercing more strongly, and quicker of discharge than the *French* Cross-bow, my answer is ready; that in all these respects, it is also, (being drawn with a strong arm) superior to the Musket; yet is the Musket a weapon of more use. The Gun and the Cross-bow, are of like force, when discharged by a Boy or Woman, as when by a strong Man; weakness, or sickness, or a sore finger, makes the long Bow unserviceable. More particularly, I say, that it was the custom of our Ancestors to shoot, for the most part, *point blank*: and so shall he perceive, that will note the circumstances of almost any one battle. This takes away all objection: for when two Armies are within the distance of a Butt's length, one flight of arrows, or two at the most, can be delivered, before they close. Neither is it in general true, that the long Bow reacheth farther, or that it pierceth more strongly than the Cross-bow: But this is the rare effect, of an extraordinary arm; whereupon can be grounded no common rule. If any man ask, How then came it to pass, that the *English* won so many great battles, having no advantage to help him? I may, with best commendation of modesty, refer him to the *French* Historian: who relating the victory of our men at *Crevant*, where they passed a bridge, in face of the enemy, useth these words: *The English comes with a conquering bravery, as he, that was accustomed to gain everywhere, without any stay: he forceth our guard, placed upon the bridge, to keep the passage.* Or I may cite another place of the same Author, where he tells, how the *Britons*, being invaded by *Charles* the eighth, King of *France*, thought it good policy, to apparel a thousand and two hundred of their own men in *English* Cassocks; hoping that the very sight of the *English* red Cross, would be enough to terrify the *French*. But I will not stand to borrow of the *French* historians (all which, excepting *De Serres*, and *Paulus Aemilius*, report wonders of our Nation) the proposition which first I undertook to maintain; *That the military virtue of the English, prevailing against all manner of difficulties, ought to be preferred before that of Romans, which was assisted with all advantages that could be desired.* If it be demanded; Why then did not our Kings finish the conquest, as *Caesar* had done? my answer may be (I hope without offence) that our Kings were like to the race of the *Aeacidae*, of whom the old Poet *Ennius* gave this note . . . *They were more warlike than politic.* Whoso notes their proceedings, may find that none of them went to work like a Conqueror, save only King *Henry* the fifth, the course of whose victories, it pleased God to interrupt by his death. But this question is the more easily answered, if another be first made. Why did not the *Romans* attempt the conquest of *Gaul*, before the time of *Caesar*? why not after the *Macedonian* war? why not after the third *Punic*, or after the *Numantian*? At all these times they had good leisure; and then especially had they both leisure, and fit opportunity, when under the conduct of *Marius*, they had newly vanquished the *Cimbri*, and *Teutones*, by whom the Country of *Gaul* had been piteously wasted. Surely, the words of *Tully* were true; that with other Nations, the *Romans* fought for Dominion; with the *Gauls*, for preservation of their own safety.

Therefore they attempted not the conquest of *Gaul*, until they were Lords of all other Countries, to them known. We on the other side, held only the one half of our own Island; the other half being inhabited by a Nation (unless perhaps in wealth and numbers of men somewhat inferior) every way equal to ourselves; a Nation, anciently and strongly allied to our enemies the *French*, and in that regard enemy to us. So that our danger lay both before and behind us; and the greater danger at our backs; where commonly we felt, always we feared, a stronger invasion by land, than we could make upon *France*, transporting our forces over Sea.

It is usual, with men, that have pleased themselves, in admiring the matters which they find in ancient Histories; to hold it a great injury done to their judgment, if any take upon him, by way of comparison, to extol the things of later ages. But I am well persuaded, that as the divided virtue of this our Island, hath given more noble proof of itself; than under so worthy a Leader, that *Roman* Army could do, which afterwards could win *Rome*, and all her Empire, making *Caesar* a *Monarch*; so hereafter, by God's blessing, who hath converted our greatest hindrance, into our greatest help, the enemy that shall dare to try our forces, will find cause to wish, that avoiding us, he had rather encountered as great a puissance, as was that of the *Roman* Empire. But it is now high time, that laying aside comparisons, we return to the rehearsal of deeds done: wherein we shall find, how *Rome* began, after *Pyrrhus* had left *Italy*, to strive with *Carthage* for Dominion, in the first *Punic* war.

Chapter 1:2 *The estate of Carthage, before it entered into war with Rome.*
The city of *Carthage* had stood above six hundred years, when first it began to contend with *Rome*, for the mastery of *Sicil*. It forewent *Rome* one hundred and fifty years in antiquity of foundation: but in the honour of great achievements, it excelled far beyond this advantage of time. For *Carthage* had extended her Dominion in *Africa* itself, from the west part of *Cyrene*, to the straits of *Hercules*, about one thousand and five hundred miles in length, wherein stood three hundred Cities. It had subjected all *Spain*, even to the *Pyrenean* Mountains, together with all the *Islands* in the *Mediterranean Sea*, to the west of *Sicil*, and of *Sicil* the better part. It flourished about seven hundred and thirty year, before the destruction thereof by *Scipio*: who besides other spoils, and all that the Soldiers reserved, carried thence four hundred and seventy thousand weight of silver, which make of our money (if our pounds differ not) fourteen hundred and ten thousand pound sterling. So as this glorious City, ran the same fortune, which many other great ones have done, both before and since. The ruin of the goodliest pieces of the world, foreshows the

dissolution of the whole.

About one hundred years after such a time as it was cast down, the Senate of *Rome* caused it to be rebuilt: and by *Gracchus* it was called *Junonia*: it was again and again abandoned and repeopled, taken and retaken; by *Genesericus* the *Vandal*, by *Belisarius* under *Justinian*, by the *Persians*, by the *Egyptians*, and by the *Mahometans*. It is now nothing. The seat thereof was exceeding strong: and, while the *Carthaginians* commanded the Sea, invincible. For the Sea compassed it about, saving that it was tied to the main by a neck of land; which passage had two mile and more of breadth (*Appian* saith three mile, and one furlong) by which we may be induced, to believe the common report, that the City itself, was above twenty mile in compass; if not that of *Strabo*, affirming the circuit to have been twice as great.

It had three walls, without the wall of the City; and between each of those, three or four streets, with vaults under ground, of thirty foot deep, in which they had place for three hundred Elephants, and all their food. Over these they had stables for four thousand horse, and Granaries for all their provender. They had also lodging in these streets, between these outwalls for four thousand horsemen and twenty thousand footmen, which (according to the discipline used now by those of *China*) never pestered the City. It had towards the South part, the Castle of *Byrsa*; to which *Servius* gives two and twenty furlongs in compass, that make two mile and a half. This was the same piece of ground, which *Dido* obtained of the *Libyans*, when she got leave to buy only so much land of them, as she could compass with an Ox hide. On the west side it had also the salt Sea, but in the nature of a standing pool; for a certain arm of Land, fastened to the ground, on which the City stood, stretched itself towards the west continent, and left but seventy foot open for the Sea to enter. Over this standing Sea was built a most sumptuous *Arsenal*, having their ships and galleys riding under it.

The form of their Commonweal resembled that of *Sparta*, for they had titulary Kings, and the *Aristocratical* power of Senators. But (as *Regius* well observeth) the people in the later times usurped too great authority in their Councils. This confusion in government, together with the trust that they reposed in hired Soldiers, were helping causes of their destruction in the end. Two other more forcible causes of their ruin, were their avarice and their cruelty. Their avarice was showed both in exacting from their Vassals (besides ordinary tributes) the one half of the fruits of the earth; and in conferring of great Offices, not upon gentle and merciful persons, but upon those who could best tyrannize over the people, to augment their treasures. Their cruelty appeared, in putting them to death without mercy, that had offended through ignorance. The one of these rendered them odious to their vassals, whom it made ready, upon all occasions, to revolt from them: the other did break the spirits of their Generals, by presenting, in the heat of their actions abroad, the fear of a cruel death at home. Hereby it came to pass, that many good Commanders of the *Carthaginian* forces, after some great loss received, have desperately cast themselves, with all that remained under their charge, into the throat of destruction; holding it necessary, either to repair their losses quickly, or to ruin all together: and few of them have dared, to manage their own best projects, after that good form, wherein they first conceived them, for fear lest the manner of their proceeding should be misinterpreted: It being the *Carthaginian* rule, to crucify, not only the unhappy Captain, but even him, whose bad counsel had prosperous event. . .

Chapter 1:4.i Of the Island of Sicil . . . and the first Inhabitants thereof. . . . It may perchance seem strange to the Reader, that in all ancient story, he finds one and the same beginning of Nations, after the flood; and that the first planters of all parts of the World, were said to be mighty and Giantlike men; and that, as *Phoenicia*, *Egypt*, *Libya*, and *Greece*, had *Hercules*, *Orestes*, *Antaeus*, *Typhon*, and the like; as *Denmark* had *Starchaterus*, remembered by *Saxo Grammaticus*; as *Scythia*, *Brittany*, and other Regions, had Giants for their first Inhabitants; so this Isle of *Sicil* had her *Laestrygones* and *Cyclops*. This discourse I could also reject for feigned and fabulous; did not *Moses* make us know, that the *Zamzummims*, *Emims*, *Anakims*, and *Og* of *Basan*, with others, which sometime inhabited the Mountains and Deserts of *Moab*, *Ammon*, and *Mount Seir*, were men of exceeding strength and stature, and of the races of Giants; and were it not, that *Tertullian*, *St Augustine*, *Nicephorus*, *Procopius*, *Isidore*, *Pliny*, *Diodore*, *Herodotus*, *Solinus*, *Plutarch*, and many other Authors, have confirmed the opinion. Yea, *Vesputius*, in his second Navigation into *America*, hath reported, that himself hath seen the like men in those parts. Again, whereas the selfsame is written of all Nations, that is written of any one; as touching their simplicity of life, their mean fare, their feeding on acorns and roots, their poor cottages, the covering of their bodies, with the skins of beasts, their hunting, their arms, and weapons, and their warfare, their first passages over great Rivers, and arms of the Sea, upon rafts of trees, tied together; and afterward, their making boats, first, of twigs and leather, then of wood; first, with Oars, and then with sail; that they esteemed as Gods, the first finders out of Arts; as of Husbandry, of Laws, and of

Policy: it is a matter, that makes me neither to wonder at, nor to doubt of it. For they all lived in the same newness of time, which we call *Old time*, and had all the same want of his instruction, which (after the Creator of all things) hath by degrees taught all Mankind. For other teaching had they none, that were removed far off from the *Hebrews*, who inherited the knowledge of the first Patriarchs, than that from variable effects they began, by time and degrees, to find out the causes: from whence came Philosophy Natural; as the Moral did from disorder and confusion, and the Law from cruelty and oppression.

But it is certain, that the Age of *Time* hath brought forth stranger and more incredible things, than the Infancy. For we have now greater Giants, for vice and injustice, than the World had in those days, for bodily strength; for cottages, and houses of clay and timber, we have raised Palaces of stone; we carve them, we paint them, and adorn them with gold; insomuch as men are rather known by their houses, than their houses by them; we are fallen from two dishes, to two hundred; from water, to wine and drunkenness; from the covering of our bodies with the skins of beasts, not only to silk and gold, but to the very skins of men. But to conclude this digression, *Time* will also take revenge of the excess, which it hath brought forth . . . *Long time brought forth, longer time increased it, and a time, longer than the rest, shall overthrow it.*

Chapter 1:6 . . . *Of Sea fight in general.*

. . . Certainly, he that will happily perform a fight at Sea, must be skilful in making choice of Vessels to fight in: he must believe, that there is more belonging to a good man of war, upon the waters, than great during; and must know, that there is a great deal of difference, between fighting loose or at large, and grappling. The Guns of a slow ship pierce as well, and make as great holes, as those in a swift. To clap ships together, without consideration, belongs rather to a mad man, than to a man of war: for by such an ignorant bravery was *Peter Strossie* lost at the *Azores*, when he fought against the *Marquis of Santa Cruz*. In like sort had the Lord *Charles Howard*, Admiral of *England*, been lost in the year 1588, if he had not been better advised, than a great many malignant fools were, that had found fault with his demeanour. The *Spaniards* had an Army aboard them; and he had none: they had more ships than he had, and of higher building and charging; so that, had he entangled himself with those great and powerful Vessels, he had greatly endangered this Kingdom of *England*. For twenty men upon the defences, are equal to an hundred that board and enter; whereas then, contrariwise, the *Spaniards* had an hundred, for twenty of ours, to defend themselves withal. But our Admiral knew his advantage, and held it: which had he not done, he had not been worthy to have held his head. Here to speak in general of Sea fight (for particulars are fitter for private hands, than for the Press) I say, That a fleet of twenty ships, all good sailers, and good ships, have the advantage, on the open Sea, of an hundred as good ships, and of slower sailing. For if the fleet of an hundred sail keep themselves near together, in a gross squadron; the twenty ships, charging them upon any angle, shall force them to give ground, and to fall back upon their next fellows: of which so many as entangle, are made unserviceable, or lost. Force them they may easily, because the twenty ships, which give themselves scope, after they have given one broadside of Artillery, by clapping into the wind, and staying, they may give them the other: and so the twenty ships batter them in pieces with a perpetual volley; whereas those, that fight in a troop, have no room to turn, and can always use but one and the same beaten side. If the fleet of an hundred sail give themselves any distance, then shall the lesser fleet prevail, either against those that are arear and hindmost, or against those, that by advantage of over-sailing their fellows keep the wind: and if upon a Lee-shore, the ships next the wind be constrained to fall back into their own squadron, then it is all to nothing, that the whole fleet must suffer shipwreck, or render itself. That such advantage may be taken upon a fleet of unequal speed, it hath been well enough conceived in old time; as by that Oration of *Hermocrates* in *Theucydides*, which he made to the *Syracusians*, when the *Athenian* invaded them, it may easily be observed.

Of the Art of War by Sea, I had written a Treatise, for the Lord *Henry*, *Prince of Wales*; a subject, to my knowledge, never handled by any man, ancient or modern: but God hath spared me the labour of finishing it, by his loss; by the loss of that brave Prince; of which, like an Eclipse of the Sun, we shall find the effects hereafter. Impossible it is to equal words and sorrows; I will therefore leave him in the hands of God that hath him. *Curae leves loquuntur, ingentes stupent.*

Chapter 2:2.i Of Tyranny, and how tyrants are driven to use help of mercenaries.

Here let us rest a while, as in a convenient breathing place: whence we may take prospect of the subject, over which we travail. Behold a tyrannical City, persecuted by her own mercenaries with a deadly war. It is a common thing, as being almost necessary, that a tyranny should be upheld by mercenary forces: it is common that mercenaries should be false: and it is common, that all war, made against

Tyrants, should be exceeding full of hate and cruelty. Yet we seldom hear, that the ruin of a Tyranny is procured or sought, by those that were hired to maintain the power of it: and seldom or never do we read of any war, that hath been prosecuted with such inexpiable hatred, as this that is now at hand.

That which we properly call Tyranny, is *A violent form of government, not respecting the good of the subject, but only the pleasure of the Commander*. I purposely forbear to say, that it is the unjust rule of one over many; for very truly doth *Cleon* in *Theucydides* tell the *Athenians*, that their dominion over their subjects was none other than a mere tyranny; though it were so, that they themselves were a great City, and a Popular estate. Neither is it peradventure greatly needful, that I should call this form of commanding, *violent*: since it may well and easily be conceived, that no man willingly performs obedience, to one regardless of his life and welfare; unless himself be either a mad man, or (which is little better) wholly possessed with some extreme passion of love. The practice of tyranny, is not always of a like extremity: for some Lords are more gentle, than others, to their very slaves; and he that is most cruel to some, is mild enough towards others, though it be but for his own advantage. Nevertheless, in large Dominions, wherein the Ruler's discretion cannot extend itself, unto notice of the difference which might be found between the worth of several men; it is commonly seen, that the taste of sweetness, drawn out of oppression, hath so good a relish, as continually inflames the Tyrant's appetite, and will not suffer it to be restrained with any limits of respect. Why should he seek out bounds, to prescribe unto his desires, who cannot endure the face of one so honest, as may put him in remembrance of any moderation? It is much that he hath gotten, by extorting from some few: by sparing none, he should have riches in goodly abundance. He hath taken a great deal from every one: but every one could have spared more. He hath wrung all their purses, and now he hath enough: but (as Covetousness is never satisfied) he thinks that all this is too little for a stock, though it were indeed a good yearly Income. Therefore he deviseth new tricks of robbery, and is not better pleased with the gains, than with the Art of getting. He is hated for this; and he knows it well: but he thinks by cruelty to change hatred into fear. So he makes it his exercise, to torment and murder all, whom he suspecteth: in which course, if he suspect none unjustly, he may be said to deal craftily; but if Innocency be not safe, how can all this make any Conspirator to stand in fear, since the Traitor is no worse rewarded, than the quiet man? Wherefore he can think upon none other security, than to disarm all his Subjects; to fortify himself within some strong place; and for defence of his Person and state, to hire as many lusty Soldiers as shall be thought sufficient. These must not be of his own Country: for if not every one, yet some one or other, might chance to have a feeling of the public misery. This considered, he allures unto him a desperate rabble of strangers, the most unhonest that can be found; such as have neither wealth nor credit at home, and will therefore be careful to support him, by whose only favour they are maintained. Now lest any of these, either by detestation of his wickedness, or (which in wicked men is most likely) by promise of greater reward, than he doth give, should be drawn to turn his sword against the Tyrant himself: they shall all be permitted to do as he doth; to rob, to ravish, to murder, and to satisfy their own appetites, in most outrageous manner; being thought so much the more assured to their Master, by how much the more he sees them grow hateful to all men else, Considering in what Age, and in what Language I write; I must be fain to say, that these are not dreams; though some *Englishmen* perhaps, that were unacquainted with History, lighting upon this leaf, might suppose this discourse to be little better. This is to show, both how tyranny grows to stand in need of mercenary Soldiers, and how those Mercenaries are, by mutual obligation, firmly assured unto the Tyrant.

ii That the tyranny of a City over her Subjects is worse, than the tyranny of one man: and that a tyrannical City must likewise use mercenary Soldiers. Now concerning the tyranny, wherewith a City or State oppresseth her Subjects; it may appear some ways to be more moderate, than that of one man: but in many things it is more intolerable. A City is jealous of her Dominion; but not (as is one man) fearful of her life: the less need hath she therefore, to secure herself by cruelty. A City is not luxurious in consuming her treasures; and therefore needs the less, to pluck from her Subjects. If war, or any other great occasion, drive her to necessity, of taking from her Subjects more than ordinary sums of money: the same necessity makes either the contribution easy, or the taking excusable. Indeed, no wrongs are so grievous and hateful, as those that are insolent. *Remember* (saith *Caligula* the Emperor, to his Grandmother *Antonia*) *that I may do what I list, and to whom I list*: these words were accounted horrible, though he did her no harm. And *Juvenal* reckons it, as the complement of all torments, inflicted by a cruel *Roman* Dame upon her slaves; that whilst she was whipping them, she painted her face, talked with her Gossips, and used all signs of neglecting what those wretches felt. Now seeing that the greatest grievances, wherewith a domineering

State offendeth her Subjects, are free from all sense of indignity: likely it is, that they will not extremely hate her, although desire of liberty make them weary of her Empire. In these respects it is not needful, that she should keep a Guard of licentious cut-throats, and maintain them in all villainy, as a *Dionysius* or *Agathocles* must do: her own Citizens are able to terrify, and to hold perforce in obedience, all malcontents. These things, considered alone by themselves, may serve to prove, That a City is scarce able to deserve the name of a Tyranness, in the proper signification.

All this notwithstanding, it shall appear, That the miseries, wherewith a Tyrant loadeth his people, are not so heavy, as the burdens imposed by a cruel City. Not without some appearance of truth, it may be said, that Lust, and many other private passions, are no way incident to a City or Corporation. But to make this good, we shall have need to use the help of such distinctions, as the Argument in hand doth not require. Was not *Rome* lascivious, when *Cato* was fain to rise and leave the theatre, to the end, that the reverend regard of his gravity, might not hinder the people, from calling for a show of naked Courtesans, that were to be brought upon the open stage? By common practice, and general approved custom, we are to censure the quality of a whole State; not by the private virtue or vice, of any one man; nor by metaphysical abstraction, of *the universal* from *the singular*; or of *the Corporation* from *those of whom it is compounded*. I say therefore (as I have said elsewhere) That it were better to live under one pernicious Tyrant, than under many thousands. The reasons, proving this, are too many to set down: but few may suffice. The desires of one man, how inordinate soever, if they cannot be satisfied, yet they may be wearied; he is not able to search all corners; his humour may be found and soothed; age, or good advice, yea or some unexpected accident, may reform him: all which failing, yet is there hope, that his Successor may prove better. Many Tyrants have been changed into worthy Kings; and many have ill used their ill-gotten Dominion, which, becoming hereditary to their posterity, hath grown into the most excellent form of Government, even a lawful Monarchy. But they that live under a tyrannical City, have no such hope: their Mistress is immortal, and will not slacken the reins, until they be pulled out of her hands; and her own mouth receive the bridle of a more mighty Charioteer. This is woeful: yet their present sufferings make them less mindful of the future. New flies, and hungry ones, fall upon the same sore, out of which others had already sucked their fill. A new Governor comes yearly among them, attended by all his poor kindred and friends, who mean not to return home empty to their hives, without a good lading of wax and honey. These fly into all quarters, and are quickly acquainted with every man's wealth, or whatsoever else, in all the Province, is worthy to be desired. They know all a man's enemies, and all his fears: becoming themselves, within a little space, the enemies that he feareth most. To grow into acquaintance with these masterful guests, in hope to win their friendship, were an endless labour (yet it must be undergone) and such as every one hath not means to go about: but, were this effected, what availeth it? The love of one Governor is purchased with gifts: the Successor of this man, he is more loving than could be wished, in respect of a fair Wife or Daughter: then comes the third, perhaps of the contrary faction at home, a bitter enemy to both his foregoers, who seeks the ruin of all that have been inward with them. So the miseries of this tyranny are not simple; but interlaced (as it were) with the calamities of civil war. The *Romans* had a Law *De Repetundis*, or *Of Recovery*, against extorting Magistrates: yet we find, that it served not wholly to restrain their Provincial Governors; who presuming on the favour of their own Citizens, and of their kindred and friends at home, were bold in their Provinces, to work all these enormities rehearsed; though somewhat the more sparingly, for fear of judgment. If the subjects of *Rome* groaned under such oppressions; what must we think of those, that were vassals unto *Carthage*? The *Romans* imposed no burdensome tribute; they loved not to hear, that their Empire was grievous; they condemned many noble Citizens, for having been ill Governors. At *Carthage* all went quite contrary: the rapines newly devised by one Magistrate, served as precedents to instruct another; every man resolved to do the like, when it should fall to his turn; and he was held a noble statesman, whose robberies had been such, as might afford a good share to the common treasure. Particular examples of this *Carthaginian* practice, are not extant: the government of *Verres* the *Roman*, in *Sicil*, that is livelily set out by *Tully*, may serve to inform us, what was the demeanour of these *Punic Rulers*, who stood in fear of no such condemnation, as *Verres* underwent. By prosecuting this discourse, I might infer a more general Proposition: That a City cannot govern her subject Provinces so mildly, as a King: but it is enough to have showed, That the tyranny of a City is far more intolerable, than that of any one most wicked man.

Suitable to the cruelty of such Lords is the hatred of their subjects: and again, suitable to the hatred of the subjects, is the jealousy of their Lords. Hence it followed, that, in wars abroad, the *Carthaginians* durst use the service of *African* soldiers; in *Afric* itself, they had rather be beholding to others, that were farther fetched. For the same purpose did *Hannibal*, in the second *Punic* war, shift his mercenaries out of their own Countries . . . *That the Africans might serve in Spain, the Spaniards in Afric, being each of them like to prove the better Soldiers, the farther they were from home, as if they were obliged by mutual pledges*. It is disputable, I confess, whether these *African*, and *Spanish* hirelings, could properly be termed *Mercenaries*; for they were subject unto *Carthage*, and carried into the field, not only by reward, but by duty. Yet seeing their duty was no better than enforced, and that it was not any love to the State, but mere desire of gain, that made them fight; I will not nicely stand upon propriety of a word, but hold them, as *Polybius* also doth, no better than *Mercenaries*.

iii The dangers growing from the use of mercenary Soldiers, and foreign Auxiliaries.

The extreme danger, growing from the employment of such Soldiers, is well observed by *Machiavel*; who showeth, that they are more terrible to those whom they serve, than to those against whom they serve. They are seditious, unfaithful, disobedient, devourers, and destroyers of all places and countries, whereinto they are drawn; as being held by no other bond, than their own commodity. Yea, that which is most fearful among such hirelings, is, that they have often, and in time of greatest extremity, not only refused to fight, in their defence, who have entertained them, but revolted unto the contrary part; to the utter ruin of those Princes and States, that have trusted them. These Mercenaries (saith *Machiavel*) which filled all *Italy*, when *Charles* the *Eighth* of *France* did pass the *Alps*, were the cause that the said *French* King won the Realm of *Naples*, with his Buckler without a sword. Notable was the example of *Sforza*, the Father of *Francis Sforza*, Duke of *Milan*; who being entertained by Queen *Joan* of *Naples*, abandoned her service on the sudden; and forced her to put herself into the hands of the King of *Arragon*. Like unto his father was *Francis Sforza*, Duke of *Milan*: who, being entertained by the *Milanese*, forced them to become his slaves; even with the same Army which themselves had levied for their own defence. But *Lodovick Sforza*, the son of this *Francis*, by the just judgment of God, was made a memorable example unto posterity, in losing his whole estate by the treachery of such faithless Mercenaries as his own father had been. For, having waged an Army of *Switzers*, and committed his Duchy, together with his person, into their hands; he was by them delivered up unto his enemy the *French* king, by whom he was enclosed in the Castle of *Loches* to his dying day.

The like inconvenience is found in using the help of foreign Auxiliaries. We see, that when the Emporer of *Constantinople* had hired ten thousand *Turks*, against his neighbour Princes; he could never, either by persuasion or force, set them again over Sea upon *Asia* side: which gave beginning to the *Christian* servitude, that soon after followed. *Alexander*, the son of *Cassander*, sought aid of the great *Demetrius*: but *Demetrius*, being entered into his Kingdom, slew the same *Alexander* who had invited him, and made himself King of *Macedon*. *Syracon* the *Turk* was called into *Egypt* by *Sanar* the *Soldan*, against his Opposite: but this *Turk* did settle himself so surely in *Egypt*, that *Saladin* his Successor became Lord thereof; and of all the *Holy Land*, soon after. What need we look about for examples of this kind? Every Kingdom, in effect, can furnish us. The *Britons* drew the *Saxons* into this our Country; and *Mac Murrough* drew the *English* into *Ireland*; but the one and the other soon became Lords of those two Kingdoms . . .

iv . . . That in man's nature there is an affection breeding tyranny, which hindereth the use and benefit of . . . moderation.

. . . The moderate use of sovereign power being so effectual, in assuring the people unto their Lords, and consequently, in the establishment or enlargement of Dominion: it may seem strange, that the practice of tyranny, whose effects are contrary, hath been so common in all ages. The like, I know, may be said of all Vice and Irregularity whatsoever. For it is less difficult (whosoever think otherwise) and more safe, to keep the way of Justice and Honesty, than to turn aside from it; yet commonly our passions lead us into by-paths. But where Lust, Anger, Fear, or any the like Affection, seduceth our reason; the same unruly appetite either bringeth with it an excuse, or at leastwise taketh away all cause of wonder. In tyranny it is not so: forasmuch as we can hardly descry the passion, that is of force to insinuate itself into the whole tenor of a Government. It must be confessed, that lawless desires have bred many Tyrants: yet so, that these desires have seldom been hereditary, or long lasting; but have ended commonly with the Tyrant's life, sometimes before his death; by which means the Government hath been reduced to a better form. In such cases, the saying of *Aristotle* holds, *That Tyrannies are of short continuance*. But this doth not satisfy the question in hand. Why did the *Carthaginians* exercise Tyranny? why did the *Athenians*? why have many other Cities done the like? If in respect of their general good; how could they be ignorant, that this was an ill course for the safety of the Weal public? If they were led hereunto by any affection; what was that affection, wherein so many thousand citizens, divided and subdivided within themselves by factions, did all concur, notwithstanding the much diversity of temper, and the vehemency of private hatred among them? Doubtless, we must be fain to say, That Tyranny is, by itself, a Vice distinct from others. A Man, we know, is *Animal politicum*, apt, even by Nature, to command, or to obey; every one in his proper degree. Other desires of Mankind, are common likewise unto brute beasts; and some of them, to bodies wanting sense: but the desire of rule belongeth unto the nobler part of reason; whereunto is also answerable an aptness to yield obedience. Now as hunger and thirst are given by nature, not only to Man and Beast, but unto all sorts of Vegetables, for the sustentation of their life; as Fear, Anger, Lust, and other Affections are likewise natural, in convenient measure, both unto mankind, and to all creatures that have sense, for the shunning or repelling of harm, and seeking after that which is requisite: even so is this desire of ruling or obeying, engrafted by Nature in the race of Man, and in Man only as a reasonable creature, for the ordering of his life, in a civil form of justice. All these inbred qualities are good and useful. Nevertheless, Hunger and Thirst are the Parents of Gluttony and Drunkenness, which, in reproach, are called beastly, by an unproper term: since they grow from appetites, found in less worthy creatures than beasts, and are yet not so common in beasts, as in men. The effects of Anger, and of such other Passions as descend no lower than unto brute beasts, are held less vile; and perhaps not without good reason: yet are they more horrible, and punished more grievously, by sharper Laws, as being in general more pernicious. But as no corruption is worse, than of that which is best; there is not any Passion, that nourisheth a vice more hurtful unto Mankind, than that which issueth from the most noble root, even the depraved Affection of ruling. Hence arise those two great mischiefs, of which hath been an old question in dispute, whether be the worse; That all things, or That nothing, should be lawful. Of these a dull spirit, and overladen by fortune, with power, whereof it is not capable, occasioneth the one; the other proceedeth from a contrary distemper, whose vehemency the bounds of Reason cannot limit. Under the extremity of either, no country is able to subsist: yet the defective dulness, that permitteth any thing will also permit the execution of Law, to which, mere necessity doth enforce the ordinary Magistrate; whereas Tyranny is more active, and pleaseth itself in the excess, with a false colour of justice. Examples of stupidity, and unaptness to rule, are not very frequent, though such natures are everywhere found: for this quality troubles not itself in seeking Empire; or if by some error of fortune, it encounter therewithal, (as when *Claudius*, hiding himself in a corner, found the Empire of *Rome*) some friend or else a wife, is not wanting to supply the defect, which also cruelty doth help to shadow. Therefore this Vice, as a thing unknown, is without a name. Tyranny is more bold, and feareth not to be known, but would be reputed honourable: for it is *prosperum et felix scelus, a fortunate mischief*, as long as it can subsist. *There is no reward or honour* (saith *Peter Charron*) *assigned to those, that know how to increase, or to preserve human nature: all honours, greatness, riches, dignities, empires, triumphs, trophies, are appointed for those, that know how to afflict, trouble, or destroy it. Caesar* and *Alexander*, have unmade and slain, each of them, more than a million of men: but they made none, nor left none behind them. Such is the error of Man's judgment, in valuing things according to common opinion. But the true name of *Tyranny*, when it grows to ripeness, is none other, than *Ferity*: the same that *Aristotle* saith to be worse than any vice. It exceedeth indeed all other vices, issuing from the Passions incident both to Man, and Beast; no less than Perjury, Murder, Treason, and the like horrible crimes, exceed in villainy, the faults of Gluttony and drunkenness, that grow from more ignoble appetites. Hereof *Sciron*, *Procrustes*, and *Pityocamptes*, that used their bodily force to the destruction of Mankind, are not better examples, than *Phalaris*, *Dionysius* and *Agathocles*, whose mischievous heads were assisted by the hands of detestable Ruffians. The same barbarous desire of Lordship, transported those old examples of *Ferity*, and these latter Tyrants, beyond the bounds of reason: neither of them knew the use of Rule, nor the difference between Freemen, and slaves.

The rule of the husband over the wife, and of parents over their children, is natural, and appointed by God himself; so that it is always, and simply, allowable and good. The former of these, is, as the dominion of Reason over Appetite; the latter is the whole authority, which one free man can have over another. The rule of a King is no more, nor none other, than of a common Father over his whole country: which he that knows what the power of a Father is, or ought to be, knows to be enough. But there is a greater, and more Masterly rule, which God gave unto *Adam*, when he said; *Have dominion over the fish of the Sea, and over the fowl of the air, and over every living thing that moveth upon the earth*: which also he confirmed unto *Noah*, and his children, saying, *The fear of you, and the dread of you, shall be upon every beast of the earth, and upon every fowl of the air, upon all that moveth upon the earth, and upon all the fishes of the Sea; into your hands are they delivered.* He who gave this dominion to Man, gave also an aptitude to use it. The execution of this power hath since extended itself, over a great part of Mankind. There are indeed no small numbers of men, whose disability to govern themselves, proves them, according unto *Aristotle's* doctrine, to be naturally slaves.

Yet find I not in Scripture any warrant to oppress men with bondage: unless the lawfulness thereof be sufficiently intimated, where it is said, That a man shall not be punished for the death of a servant, whom he hath slain by correction, if the servant live a day or two, because *he is his money*; or else by the captivity of the *Midianitish* girls, which were made bondslaves, and the Sanctuary had a part of them for *the Lord's tribute*. Doubtless the custom hath been very ancient: for *Noah* laid this curse upon *Canaan*, that he should be a *servant of servants*; and *Abraham* had of *Pharaoh*, among other gifts, *menservants, and maidservants*, which were none other than slaves. Christian Religion is said to have abrogated this old kind of servility: but surely, they are deceived, that think so. Saint *Paul* desired the liberty of *Onesimus*, whom he had won unto *Christ*: yet wrote he for this unto *Philemon*, by way of request, craving it as *a benefit*, not urging it as a duty. Agreeable hereto is the direction, which the same Saint *Paul* giveth unto servants: *Let every man abide in the same calling wherein he was called: art thou called, being a servant? care not for it, but if thou mayest be made free, use it rather.* It is true, that Christian Religion hath procured liberty unto many; not only in regard to piety, but for that the Christian Masters stood in fear, of being discovered by their slaves, unto the persecutors of religion. *Mahomet* likewise by giving liberty to his followers, drew many unto his impiety: but whether he forbade it, as unlawful, unto his sectators, to hold one another of them in bondage, I cannot tell; save that by the practice of the *Turks* and *Moors*, it seems he did not. In *England* we had many bond-servants, until the times of our last civil wars: and I think that the Laws concerning *Villainage* are still in force, of which the latest are the sharpest. And now, since slaves were made free, which were of great use and service, there are grown up a rabble of Rogues, Cutpurses, and other the like Trades; slaves in Nature, though not in Law.

But whether this kind of dominion be lawful, or not; *Aristotle* hath well proved, that it is natural. And certainly we find not such a latitude of difference, in any creature, as in the nature of man: wherein (to omit the infinite distance in estate, of the elect and reprobate) the wisest excel the most foolish, by far greater degree, than the most foolish of men doth surpass the wisest of beasts. Therefore when Commiseration hath given way to Reason; we shall find, that Nature is the ground even of Masterly power, and of servile obedience, which is thereto correspondent. But it may be truly said, that some countries have subsisted long, without the use of any servility; as also it is true, that some countries have not the use of any tame cattle. Indeed the affections which uphold civil rule, are (though more noble) not so simply needful, unto the sustentation either of our kind, as are Lust, and the like; or of every one, as are hunger and thirst; which notwithstanding are the lowest in degree. But where most vile and servile dispositions, have liberty to show themselves begging in the streets; there may we more justly wonder, how the dangerous toil of seafaring men can find enough to undertake them, than how the swarm of idle vagabonds should increase, by access of those, that are weary of their own more painful condition. This may suffice to prove, that in Mankind there is found, ingrafted even by Nature, a desire of absolute dominion: whereunto the general custom of Nations doth suscribe; together with the pleasure which most men take in flatterers, that are the basest of slaves.

This being so, we find no cause to marvel how Tyranny hath been so rife in all ages, and practised, not only in the single rule of some vicious Prince, but ever by consent of whole Cities and Estates: since other vices have likewise gotten ahead, and borne a general sway; notwithstanding that the way of virtue be more honourable, and commodious. Few there are that have used well the inferior Passions: how then can we expect, that the most noble affections should not be disordered? In the government of wife and children, some are utterly careless, and corrupt all by their dull connivancy: others, by masterly rigour, hold their own blood under condition of slavery. To be a good Governor is a rare commendation; and to prefer the Weal public above all respects whatsoever, is the Virtue justly termed *Heroical*. Of this Virtue, many Ages afford not many examples. *Hector* is named by *Aristotle*, as one of them; and deservedly, if this praise be due to extraordinary height of fortitude, used in defence of a man's own country. But if we consider that a love of the general good cannot be perfect, without reference unto the *fountain of all goodness*: we shall find, that no Moral virtue, how great soever, can, by itself, deserve the commendation of *more than Virtue*, as the *Heroical* doth. Wherefore we must search the Scriptures, for patterns hereof; such, as *David*, *Josaphat*, and *Josais* were. Of Christian Kings if there were many such, the world would soon be happy. It is not my purpose to wrong the worth of any, by denying the praise where it is due; or by preferring a less excellent. But he that can find a King, religious, and zealous in God's cause, without enforcement either of adversity, or of some regard of state; a procurer of the general peace and quiet; who not only useth his authority, but adds the travail of his eloquence, in admonishing his Judges to do justice; by the vigorous influence of whose Government civility is infused, even into those places, that have been the dens of savage Robbers and Cutthroats; one that hath quite abolished a slavish *Brehon* Law, by which an whole Nation of his subjects were held in bondage; and one, whose higher virtue and wisdom doth make the praise, not only of Nobility and other ornaments, but of abstinence from the blood, the wives, and the goods, of those that are under his power, together with a world of chief commendations belonging unto some good Princes, to appear less regardable: he, I say, that can find such a King, findeth an example, worthy to add unto virtue an honourable title, if it were formerly wanting. Under such a King, it is likely by God's blessing, that a land shall flourish, with increase of Trade, in countries before unknown; that Civility and Religion shall be propagated, into barbarous and heathen countries; and that the happiness of his subjects, shall cause the Nations far off removed, to wish him their Sovereign. I need not add hereunto, that all the actions of such a King, even his bodily exercises, do partake of virtue: since all things tending to the preservation of his life and health, or to the mollifying of his cares, (who, fixing his contemplation upon God, seeketh how to imitate the unspeakable goodness, rather than the inaccessible majesty, with both of which himself is endued, as far as human nature is capable) do also belong to the furtherance of that common good, which he procureth. Lest any man should think me transported with admiration, or other affection, beyond the bounds of reason: I add hereunto, that such a King is nevertheless a man must die, and may err: yet wisdom and fame shall set him free, from *error*, and from *death*, both with and without the help of *time*. One thing I may not omit, as a singular benefit (though there be many other besides) redounding unto this King, as the fruit of his goodness. The people that live under a pleasant yoke, are not only loving to their Sovereign Lord, but free of courage, and no greater in muster of men, than of stout fighters, if need require: whereas on the contrary, he that ruleth as over slaves, shall be attended, in time of necessity, by slavish minds, neither loving his person, nor regarding his or their own honour. Cowards may be furious, and slaves outrageous, for a time: but among spirits that have once yielded unto slavery, universally it is found true, that *Homer* saith, *God bereaveth a man of half his virtue that day, when he casteth him into bondage*.

Chapter 2:3 How the war against the mercenaries was diversely managed by Hanno and Amilcar, with variable success. The bloody counsels of the

Mercenaries; and their final destruction.

. . . The fame of this victory, together with the diligence of *Amilcar* in pursuing it, caused many Towns revolted, partly by fear, partly by force, to return to their former obedience. Yet was not *Matho* wanting to himself, in this dangerous time. He sent about *Numidia* and *Afric*, for new supplies; admonishing the people, now or never to do their best, for the recovery of their freedom; he persuaded *Spendius*, and *Autaritus* that was Captain of the *Gauls*, to wait upon *Amilcar*, and always to keep the higher grounds, or at least the foot of some hill, where they might be safe from the Elephants; and he himself continued to press the Town of *Hippagreta* with an hard siege. It was necessary for *Amilcar*, in passing from place to place, as his business required, to take such ways as there were: for all the country lay not level. Therefore *Spendius*, who still coasted him, had once gotten a noble advantage of ground: the *Carthaginians* lying in a Plain, surrounded with hills, that were occupied by the Mercenaries, with their *Numidian* and *African* succours. In this difficulty; the fame of *Amilcar* his personal worth did greatly benefit his country. For *Naravasus*, a young gentleman commanding over the *Numidians*, was glad of this occasion serving to get the acquaintance and love of so brave a man, which he much desired: and therefore came unto *Amilcar*, signifying his good affection to him, with offer to do him all service. *Amilcar* joyfully entertained this friend; promised unto him his own daughter in marriage; and so won from the enemies two thousand horse, that following *Naravasus* turned unto the *Carthaginian's* side. With this help he gave battle unto *Spendius*; wherein the *Numidian* laboured to approve his own valour, to his new friend. So the victory was great: for there were slain ten thousand of *Spendius* his fellows, and four thousand taken prisoners, but *Spendius* himself, with *Autaritus* the *Gaul*, escaped to do more mischief. *Amilcar* dealt very gently with his prisoners; pardoning all offences past, and dismissing as many, as were unwilling to become his followers; yet with condition, that they should never more bear arms against the *Carthaginians*; threatening to take sharp revenge upon all, that should break this Covenant.

This humanity was vehemently suspected by *Matho*, *Spendius*, and *Autaritus*, as tending to win from them, the hearts of their soldiers. Wherefore they resolved to take such order, that not a man among them should dare, to trust in the good nature of *Amilcar*, nor to hope for any safety, whilst *Carthage* was able to do him hurt. They counterfeited letters of advertisement, wherein was contained, that some of their company, respective only of their private benefit, and careless of the general good, had a purpose to betray them all unto the *Carthaginians*, with whom they held intelligence; and that it was needful, to look well unto *Gesco*, and his companions, whom these traitors had a purpose to enlarge. Upon this Theme *Spendius* makes an Oration to the soldiers, exhorting them to fidelity; and showing with many words, that the seeming humanity of *Amilcar*, toward some, was none other than a bait, wherewith to entrap them all at once together; as also telling them, what a dangerous enemy *Gesco* would prove, if he might escape their hands. While he is yet in the midst of his tale; were letters come, to the same purpose. Then steps forth *Autaritus*, and speaks his mind plainly: saying, that it were the best, yea the only way, for the common safety, to cut off all hope of reconciliation with *Carthage*; that if some were devising to make their own peace, it would go hard with those, that had a care of the war; that it were better to make an end of *Gesco* his life, than to trouble themselves with looking to his custody; that by such a course everyone should be engaged in the present Action, as having none other hope left, than in victory alone; finally, that such as would speak here-against, were worthy to be reputed Traitors. This *Autaritus* was in great credit with the Soldiers, and could speak sundry languages, in such sort that he was understood by all. According to his motion therefore it was agreed, that *Gesco*, and all the other prisoners, should forthwith be put to horrible death, by torments. Nevertheless there were some, that for love of *Gesco*, sought to alter this intended cruelty; but they were forthwith stoned to death, as a Document unto others; and so the Decree was put in execution. Neither were they herewithal contented; but further ordained, that all *Carthaginian* prisoners which they took, should be served in like sort: and that the subjects or friends of *Carthage*, should lose their hands, and so be sent home; which rule they observed ever afterwards.

Of this cruelty I need say no more, than that it was most execrable ferity. As for the counsel of using it, it was like unto the counsel of *Achitophel; All Israel shall hear, that thou art abhorred of thy father; then shall the hands of all that are with thee, be strong*. Such are the fruits of desperation. He that is past all hope of pardon, is afraid of his own fellows, if they be more innocent; and to avoid the punishment of less offences, committeth greater. The cowardice of offenders, and the revengeful spirits of those that have been wronged, are breeders of this desperation: to which may be added, some deficiency of Laws, in distinguishing the punishments of malefactors, according to the degree of their several crimes. A coward thinks all provisions too little, for his own security. *If Phocas be a coward* (said the emperor *Mauritius*) *then he is murderous*. To be steadfast and sure, in taking revenge; is thought a point of honour, and a defensative against new injuries. But wrongfully: for it is opposite to the rule of *Christianity*; and such a quality discovered, makes them deadly enemies, who otherwise would have repented, and sought to make amends, for the wrong done in passion. This was it, which wrought so much woe to the *Carthaginians*; teaching *Matho*, and his *Africans*, to suspect even their gentleness, as the introduction to extreme rigour. Like unto the errors of Princes and Governors, are the errors of Laws. Where one and the same punishment, is awarded unto the less offence, and unto the greater, he that hath adventured to rob a man, is easily tempted to kill him, for his own security.

Against these inconveniences, Mercy and Severity, used with due respect, are the best remedies. In neither of which *Amilcar* failed. For as long as these his own soldiers were any way likely to be reclaimed, by gentle courses; his humanity was ready to invite them. But when they were transported with beastly outrage, beyond all regard of honesty and shame, he rewarded their villainy with answerable vengeance; casting them unto wild beasts to be devoured . . .

Chapter 3:1 The wars of Hannibal in Spain . . . War proclaimed between Rome and Carthage.

. . . In conclusion, the *Carthaginian* Senate moved the *Roman* Ambassadors, to deliver unto them in plain terms the purpose of those that sent them, and the worst of that, which they had long determined against them: as for the *Saguntines*, and the confining of their Armies within *Iberus*; those were but their pretences. Whereupon Q. *Fabius* gathering up the skirt of his Gown, as if somewhat had been laid in the hollow thereof, made this short reply: I have here (quoth he) in my Gown-skirt both Peace and War: make you (my Masters of the Senate) election of these two, which of them you like best, and purpose to embrace. Hereat all cried out at once; Even which of them you yourself have a fancy to offer us. Marry then (quoth *Fabius*) take the War, and share it among you. Which all the Assembly willingly accepted.

This was plain dealing. To wrangle about pretences, when each part had resolved to make war, it was merely frivolous. For all these disputes of breach of peace, have ever been maintained by the party unwilling, or unable to sustain the war. The rusty sword, and the empty purse, do always plead performance of covenants. There have been few Kings or States in the World, that have otherwise understood the obligation of a Treaty, than with the condition of their own advantage: and commonly (seeing peace between ambitious Princes, and States, is but a kind of breathing) the best advised have rather begun with the sword, than with the trumpet. So dealt the *Arragonois* with the *French* in *Naples*; *Henry* the second, of *France*, with the *Imperials*, when he wrote to *Brisac*, to surprise as many places as he could, ere the war brake out, *Don John*, with the *Netherlands*; and *Philip* the second, of *Spain* with the *English*, when in the great Embargo he took all our ships and goods in his Ports.

But *Hannibal*, besides the present strength of *Carthage*, and the common feeling of injuries received from these enemies, had another private and hereditary desire, that violently carried him against the *Romans*. His father *Amilcar*, at what time he did sacrifice, being ready to take his journey into *Spain*, had solemnly bound him by oath, to pursue them with immortal hatred, and to work them all possible mischief, as soon as he should be a man, and able. *Hannibal* was then about nine years old, when his father caused him to lay his hand upon the Altar, and make this vow: so that it was no marvel, if the impression were strong in him.

That it is inhuman, to bequeath hatred in this sort, as it were by Legacy, it cannot be denied. Yet for mine own part, I do not much doubt, but that some of those Kings, with whom we are now in peace, have received the like charge from their Predecessors, that as soon as their coffers shall be full, they shall declare themselves enemies to the people of *England*.

Chapter 3:4 Scipio the Roman Consul overcome by Hannibal at Ticinum. Both of the Roman consuls beaten by Hannibal, in a great battle at Trebia.

Five months *Hannibal* had spent in his tedious journey from *Carthagena*; what great muster he could make, when he had passed the *Alps*, it is not easily found. Some reckon his foot at an hundred thousand, and his horse at twenty thousand; others report them to have been only twenty thousand foot, and six hundred horse. *Hannibal* himself, in his Monument which he raised, in the Temple of *Juno Lacinia*, agreeth with the latter sum. Yet the *Gauls*, *Ligurians*, and others that joined with him, are likely to have mightily increased his Army, in short space. But when he marched Eastward from the banks of Rhodanus, he had with him eight and thirty thousand foot, and eight thousand horse; of which all, save those remembered by himself in the Inscription of his Altar in *Juno's* Temple, are like to have perished, by diseases, enemies, Rivers, and Mountains; which mischiefs had devoured, each, their several shares.

Having newly passed the *Alps*, and scarce refreshed his wearied Army in the country of *Piedmont*; he sought to win the friendship of the *Taurini*, who lay next in his way. But the *Taurini* held war at that time with the *Insubrians*, which were his good friends; and refused (perhaps for the same cause) his amity. Wherefore he assaulted their Town; and won it by force in three days. Their spoil served well to hearten his Army; and their calamity, to terrify the Neighbour places. So the *Gauls*, without more ado, fell unto his side: many for fear, many for good-will, according to their former inclination. This disposition ran through the whole Country: which joined, or was all in readiness to join, with the *Carthaginians*; when the news of *Scipio* the Consul his arrival, made some to be more advised, than the rest. The name of the *Romans* was terrible in those quarters; what was in the *Carthaginians*, experience had not yet laid open. Since therefore the *Roman* Consul was already gotten through the most defensible passages, ere any speech had been heard of his approach; many sat still, for very fear, who else would fain have concluded a League with these new-come friends; and some, for greater fear, offered their service against the *Carthaginians*, whom nevertheless they wished well to speed.

This wavering affection of the Province, whereinto they were entered, made the two Generals hasten to the trial of a battle. Their meeting was at *Ticinum*, now called *Pavia*; where each of them wondered at the other's great expedition: *Hannibal* thinking it strange, that the Consul, whom he had left behind him on the other side of the *Alps*, could meet him in the face, before he had well warmed himself in the Plains; *Scipio* admiring the strange adventure of passing those Mountains, and the great spirit of his Enemy. Neither were the Senate at *Rome* little amazed, at *Hannibal's* success, and sudden arrival. Wherefore they despatched a Messenger in all haste unto *Sempronius*, the other Consul, that was then in *Sicilia*; giving him to understand hereof; and letting him further know, that whereas he had been directed to make the war in *Africa*, it was now their pleasure that he should forbear to prosecute any such attempt, but that he should return the Army under his charge, with all possible speed, to save *Italy* itself. According to this order, *Sempronius* sent off his Fleet from *Lilybaeum*; with direction to land the Army at *Ariminum*, a Port Town not far from Ravenna: quite another way from *Carthage*, whither he was making haste. In the meanwhile, *Scipio* and *Hannibal* were come so near, that fight they must, ere they could part asunder. Hereupon, both of them prepared the minds of their Soldiers, by the best arguments they had: unto which *Hannibal* added the Rhetoric of a present example, that he showed upon certain prisoners of the *Savoyans*, which he brought along with him, fitted for the purpose, into *Italy*. For these, having been no less miserably fettered and chained, than sparingly fed; and withal so often scourged on their naked bodies, as nothing was more in their desire, than to be delivered from their miseries by any kind of present death; were brought into the middle of the Army: where it was openly demanded, which of them would fight hand to hand with some other of his Companions, till the one of them were slain; with condition, being the Victor, to receive his liberty, and some small reward. This was no sooner propounded, than all of them together accepted the offer. Then did *Hannibal* cause lots to be cast, which of them should enter the List, with such weapons, as the Chieftains of the *Gauls* were wont to use in single combats. Every one of these unhappy men wished, that his own lot might speed; whereby it should at least be his good fortune, to end his miseries by death, if not, to get a reward by victory. That couple, whose good hap it was to be chosen, fought resolvedly: as rather desiring, than fearing death; and having none other hope, than in vanquishing. Thus were some few couples matched, it skilled not how equally; for all these poor creatures were willing, upon whatsoever uneven terms, to rid themselves out of slavery. The same affection that was in these Combatants, and in their fellows which beheld them; wrought also upon the *Carthaginians*, for whom the spectacle was ordained. For they deemed happy, not only him, that by winning the victory had gotten his liberty, together with an horse and armour: but even him also, who being slain in fight had escaped that miserable condition, unto which his Companions were returned. Their General perceiving what impression this dumb show had wrought in them; began to admonish them of their own condition, speaking to this effect. That he had laid before them an example of their own estates: seeing the time was at hand, wherein they were all to run the same fortune, that these slaves had done: all to live victorious and rich; or all to die, or (which these prisoners esteemed far more grievous) to live in a perpetual slavery: That none of them all, in whom was common sense, could promise to himself any hope of life by flight; since the Mountains, the Rivers, the great distance from their own Countries, and the pursuit of merciless Enemies, must needs retrench all such impotent imaginations. He therefore prayed them to remember, that they, who had even now praised the fortune both of the Victor, and of the vanquished, would make it their own case; seeing there was never any in the world, appointed with such a resolution, that had ever been broken, or beaten by their enemies. On the contrary, he told them, that the *Romans*, who were to fight upon their own soil, and in view of their own Towns; who knew as many ways to save themselves by flight, as they had bodies of men to fight withal, could no way entertain such a resolution as theirs: seeing the same necessity, (to which nothing seems impossible) did no way press them, or constrain them. In this sort did *Hannibal*, with one substantial argument. *That there was no mean, between Victory and Death*, encourage his Companions. For (saith a great Captain of *France*) . . . *the commodity of a retreat, doth greatly advance a flat running away*.

Scipio, on the other side, after that he had given order for the laying of a bridge over the River of *Ticinus*, did not neglect to use the best arguments and reasons he could, to encourage the Army he led: putting them in mind of the great conquests and victories of their Ancestors; against how many Nations they had prevailed; and over how many Princes, their Enemies, they had triumphed. As for this Army commanded by *Hannibal*, although it were enough to tell them, that it was no better than of *Carthaginians*, whom in their late war they had so often beaten, by Land and Sea; yet he prayed them withal to consider, that at this time it was not only so diminished in numbers, as it rather seemed a troop of *Brigands* and *Thieves*, than an Army like to encounter the *Romans*; but so weather-beaten, and starved, as neither the men, nor horses, had strength or courage to sustain the first charge that should be given upon them. Nay (said he) ye yourselves may make judgment what daring they have now remaining, after so many travails and miseries; seeing when they were in their best strength, after they had passed the *Roan*, their horsemen were not only beaten by ours, and driven back to the very Trenches of their Camp, but *Hannibal* himself, fearing our approach, ran headlong towards the *Alps*: thinking it a less dishonour, to die there by frost, famine, and precipitation, than by the sharp swords of the *Romans*, which had so often cut down his people, both in *Africa*, and in *Sicil*.

It was not long after this, ere the two Generals met: each being far advanced before the gross of his Army, with his Horse; and the *Roman* having also with him some light-armed foot, to view the ground, and the enemy's countenance. When they discovered the approach one of the other; *Scipio* sent before him his horsemen of the *Gauls*, to begin the fight, and bestowing his Darters in the void ground between their troops, to assist them: himself with his *Roman* men at arms, following softly in good order. The *Gauls* (whether desirous to try the mettle of the *Carthaginians*, or hoping thereby to get favour of the *Romans*) behaved themselves courageously, and were as courageously opposed. Yet their foot that should have aided them, shrank at the first brunt, or rather fled cowardly away, without casting a Dart; for fear of being trodden down by the enemy's horse. This notwithstanding the *Gauls* maintained the fight, and did more hurt than they received: as presuming that they were well backed. Neither was the Consul unmindful to relieve them: their hardiness deserving his aid; and the hasty flight of those that should have stood by them, admonishing him that it was needful. Wherefore he adventured himself so far, that he received a dangerous wound; and had been left in the place, if his son (afterward surnamed *Africanus*) had not brought him off: though others give the honour of his rescue, to a *Ligurian* slave. Whilst the *Romans* were busied in helping their Consul; an unexpected storm came driving at their backs, and made them look about how to help themselves. *Hannibal* had appointed his *Numidian* light horse, to give upon the *Romans* in flank, and to compass them about, whilst he with his men at arms sustained their charge, and met them in the face. The *Numidians* performed this very well: cutting in pieces the scattered foot, that ran away at the first encounter; and then falling on the backs of those, whose looks were fastened upon *Hannibal* and *Scipio*. By this impression the *Romans* were shuffled together, and routed: so that they all betook them to their speed, and left unto their enemies the honour of the day.

When *Scipio* saw his horse thus beaten, and the rest of his Army thereby greatly discouraged; he thought it a point of wisdom, having lost so many of his Fleet upon the first puff of wind, to take Port with the rest, before the extremest of the tempest overtook him. For he saw by the lowering morning, what manner of day it was likely to prove. Therefore his battle of foot being yet unbroken, he in a manner stole the retreat; and recovered the bridge over *Ticinus*, which he had formerly built. But notwithstanding all the haste that he made, he left six hundred of his Rear behind him: who were the last that should have passed, and stayed to break the bridge. Herein he followed this rule of a good man of war . . . *If a General of an Army, by some unprosperous beginnings doubt the success; or find his Army fearful or wavering; it is more profitable to steal a safe retreat, than to abide the uncertain event of battle.*

It was two days after, ere *Hannibal* could pass the River; *Scipio* the whilst refreshing his men, and easing himself of his wound in *Placentia*. But as soon as *Hannibal* presented his Army before the Town, offering battle to the *Romans*, who durst not accept it, nor issue forth of their camp; the *Gauls*, that hitherto had followed *Scipio* for fear, gathered out of his fear courage to forsake him. They thought that now the long desired time was come, in which better Chieftains and Soldiers than *Aneroestus*, *Britomarus*, and the *Gessates* were come to help them: if they had the hearts to help themselves. Wherefore the same night they fell upon the *Roman* camp; wounded and slew many; especially of those guards that kept watch at the gate; with whose heads in their hands, they fled over to the *Carthaginians*, and presented their service. *Hannibal* received them exceeding courteously, and dismissed them to their own places: as men likely to be of more use to him, in persuading the rest of the Nation to become his Confederates, than in any other service at the present.

About the fourth watch of the night following, the Consul stole a retreat, as he had done before; but not with the like ease and security. *Hannibal* had a good eye upon him; and ere he could get far, sent the *Numidians* after him: following himself with all his Army. That night the *Romans* had received a great blow, if the *Numidians*, greedy of spoil, had not stayed to ransack their camp; and thereby given time to all, save some few in Rear, that were slain or taken, to pass the River of *Trebia*, and save themselves. *Scipio*, being both unable to travel by reason of his wound, and withal finding it expedient to attend the coming of his fellow Consul; encamps himself strongly upon the banks of *Trebia*. Necessity required that he should so do; yet this diminished his reputation. For every day, more and more of the *Gauls* fell to the *Carthaginian* side; among whom came in the *Boii*, that brought with them the *Roman* Commissioners, which they had taken in the late Insurrection. They had hitherto kept them as Pledges, to redeem their own Hostages; but now they deliver them up to *Hannibal*, as tokens and pledges of their affections towards him; by whose help they conceived better hope of recovering their own men and lands. In the meanwhile, *Hannibal*, being in great scarcity of victuals, attempted the taking of *Clastidium*, a Town wherein the *Romans* had laid up all their store and munition. But there needed no force; a *Brundusian*, whom the *Romans* had trusted with keeping it, sold it for a little money.

The news of these disasters, brought to *Rome*, filled the Senate and People, rather with a desire of hasty revenge, than any great sorrow for their loss received; seeing that, in a manner, all their foot, wherein their strength and hope consisted, were as yet entire. They therefore hasted away *Sempronius*, that was newly arrived, towards *Ariminum*, where the Army, by him sent out of *Sicil*, awaited his coming. He therefore hasted thither; and from thence he marched speedily towards his Colleague; who attended him upon the banks of *Trebia*. Both the Armies being joined in one, the Consuls devised about that which remained to be done: *Sempronius* receiving from *Scipio* the relation of what had passed since *Hannibal's* arrival; the fortune of the late fight; and by what error or misadventure the *Romans* were therein foiled: which *Scipio* chiefly laid on the revolt and treason of the *Gauls*.

Sempronius, having received from *Scipio* the state of the affairs in those parts; sought by all means to try his fortune with *Hannibal* before *Scipio* were recovered of his wounds, that thereby he might purchase to himself the sole glory of the victory, which he already, in his imagination, certainly obtained. He also feared the election of the new Consuls; his own time being well near expired. But *Scipio* persuaded the contrary; objecting the unskilfulness of the new-come Soldiers: and withal gave him good reason, to assure him, that the *Gauls*, naturally unconstant, were upon terms of abandoning the party of the *Carthaginians*; those of them inhabiting between the Rivers of *Trebia*, and *Po*, being already revolted. *Sempronius* knew all this as well as *Scipio*: but, being both guided and blinded by his ambition, he made haste to find out the dishonour, which he might otherwise easily have avoided. This resolution of *Sempronius* was exceeding pleasing to *Hannibal*, who feared nothing so much as delay and loss of time. For the strength of his Army, consisting in strangers, to wit, in *Spaniards*, and *Gauls*; he no less feared the change of affection in the one, than the impatiency of the other: who being far from their own home, had many passions moving them to turn their faces towards it. To further the desire of *Sempronius*, it fell out so, that about the same time, the *Gauls* inhabiting near unto *Trebia*, complained of injuries done by the *Carthaginians*. They did not supply *Hannibal* with necessities, as he supposed that they might have done; although he daily reprehended their negligence, telling them, that for their sakes, and to set them at liberty, he had undertaken this Expedition. Seeing therefore how little they regarded his words, he was bold to be his own Carver; and took from them by force, as much as he needed of that which they had. Hereupon they fly to the *Romans* for help: and, to make their tale the better, say that this wrong is done them, because they refused to join with *Hannibal*. *Scipio* cared not much for this: he suspected their falsehood, and was assured of their mutability. But *Sempronius* affirmed, that it stood with the honour of *Rome*, to preserve the Confederates from suffering injury: and that hereby might be won the friendship of all the *Gauls*. Therefore he sent out a thousand horse: which coming unlooked for upon *Hannibal* his foragers, and finding them heavy loaden, cut many of them in pieces, and chased the rest even into their own camp. This indignity made the *Carthaginians* sally out against them: who caused them to retire faster than they came. *Sempronius* was ready to back his own men; and repelled the enemies. *Hannibal* did the like. So that at length, all the *Roman* Army was drawn forth; and a battle ready to be fought, if the *Carthaginian* had not refused it.

This victory (for so the Consul would have it called) made the *Romans* in general desirous to try the main chance in open field: all the persuasions of *Scipio* to the contrary notwithstanding. Of this disposition *Hannibal* was advertised by the *Gauls*, his spies, that were in the *Roman* Camp. Therefore he bethought himself how to help forward the victory, by adding some stratagem to his forces. He found in the hollow of a watercourse, overgrown with high reed, a fit trench to cover an ambush. Thereinto he cast his brother *Mago*, with a thousand choice horse, and as many foot. The rest of his Army, after they had well warmed, and well fed themselves, in their camp, he led into the field, and marched towards the Consul. Early in the morning, he had sent over *Trebia* some companies of *Numidian* light horse: to brave the enemy, and draw him forth to a bad dinner, ere he had broken his fast. *Sempronius* was ready to take any opportunity to fight: and therefore not only issued out of his camp, but forded the River of *Trebia*, in a most cold and miserable day; his foot being wet almost to the arm-holes: which, together with the want of food, did so enfeeble and cool their courages, as they wanted force to handle the arms they bare. Strong they were in foot, as well of their own Nation, as of the *Latins*: having of the one, sixteen, of the other, twenty thousand. The mass of these they ranged in a gross Battalion, guarded on the flanks with three thousand horse: thrusting their light-armed, and Darters, in loose troops in the head of the rest, in the nature of a Vanguard. The *Carthaginian* numbers of foot, were in a manner equal to their enemies; in horse, they had by far the better, both in number and goodness. When therefore the *Roman* horse, ranged on the flanks of their foot, were broken by the *Numidians*; when their foot were charged both in front and flank, by the *Spaniards*, *Gauls*, and *Elephants*; when finally the whole Army was unawares pressed in the Rear, by *Mago* and his two thousand, that rose out of their place of ambush: then fell the *Romans* by heaps, under the enemies' swords; and being beaten down, as well fighting in disorder, as flying towards the River, by the horsemen that pursued them, there escaped no more of six and thirty thousand, than ten thousand of all sorts, Horse and Foot.

Three great errors *Sempronius* committed, of which every one deserved to be recompensed with the loss that followed. The first was, that he fought with *Hannibal* in a Champaign, being by far inferior in horse, and withal thereby subject to the *African* Elephants, which in enclosed or uneven grounds, and woodlands, would have been of no use. His second error was, that he made no discovery of the place upon which he fought; whereby he was grossly overreached, and ensnared, by the ambush which *Hannibal* had laid for him. The third was, that he drenched his footmen with empty stomachs, in the River of *Trebia*, even in a most cold and frosty day, whereby in effect they lost the use of their limbs. For, as one saith well, *There is nothing more inconvenient and perilous, than to present an Army, tired with travel, to an enemy fresh and fed; since where the strength of body faileth, the generosity of mind is but as an unprofitable vapour.*

The broken remainder of the *Roman* Army, was collected by *Scipio*, who got therewith into *Placentia*; stealing away the same night, which was exceeding rainy, from the *Carthaginians*; who either perceived him not, because of the showers; or would not perceive him, because they were overwearied. *Sempronius* escaped with extreme danger; flying through the Country that was overrun by the enemy's horse. He was attended by more, than were requisite in a secret flight, yet by fewer, than could have made resistance, if the enemy had met with him. Nevertheless he got away, and came to *Rome*, where he did his office in choosing new Consuls for the year following: and then returned into his Province, with a fresh supply against *Hannibal*.

Chapter 3:8 . . . *The great battle of Cannae.*

. . . When he had said this; his brother *Mago* came to him, whom he had sent to view the countenance of the Enemy. *Hannibal* asked him, what news; and what work they were likely to have with these *Romans*? Work enough (answered *Mago*) for they are an horrible many. As horrible a many as they are (thus *Hannibal* replied) I tell thee brother, that among them all, search them never so diligently, thou shalt not find one man, whose name is *Mago*. With that he fell a laughing, and so did all that stood about him: which gladded the soldiers, who thought their General would not be so merry, without great assurance. Whether it were so, that *Hannibal*, in the pride of his victories already gotten, valued one *Mago* above many thousand *Romans*; or whether he intimated, that the *Romans* were no less troubled with thinking upon *Mago* and his Companions, than was *Mago* with beholding their huge multitude; or whether he meant only to correct the sad mood of his brother with a jest, and show himself merry unto the Soldiers: this his answer was more manly, than was the relation of his discoverer. But if *Hannibal* himself had been sent forth by *Mago*, to view the *Romans*, he could not have returned with a more gallant report in his mouth, than that which Captain *Gam*, before the battle of *Agincourt*, made unto our King *Henry* the fifth: saying, that of the *Frenchmen*, there were enough to be killed; enough to be taken prisoners; and enough to run away. Even such words as these, or such pleasant jests as this of *Hannibal*, are not without their moment; but serve many times, when battle is at hand, to work upon such passions, as must govern more of the business: especially, where other needful care is not wanting; without which they are but vain boasts.

In this great day, the *Carthaginian* excelled himself; expressing no less perfection of his military skill, than was greatness in his spirit and undertakings. For to omit the commodiousness of the place, into which he had long before conceived the means to draw his enemies to battle, He marshalled his Army in such convenient order, that all hands were brought to fight, where every one might do best service. His Darters, and Slingers of the *Baleares*, he sent off before him, to encounter with the *Roman Velites*. These were loose troops, answerable in a manner to those, which we call now by a *French* name *Enfans perdus*; but when we used our own terms, *the forlorn hope*. The gross of his Army following them he ordered thus. His *Africans*, armed after the *Roman* manner, with the spoils which they had gotten at *Trebia*, *Thrasymene*, or elsewhere; and well trained in the use of those weapons, that were of more advantage, than those wherewith they had formerly served; made the two wings, very deep in File. Between these he ranged his *Gauls* and *Spaniards*, armed, each after their own Country manner; their shields alike, but the *Gauls* using long broadswords, that were forcible in a downright stroke; the *Spaniards*, short and well-pointed blades, either to strike or thrust; the *Gauls*, naked from their navel upwards, as confident in their own fierceness; the *Spaniards*, wearing white cassocks embroidered with purple. This medley of two Nations, differing as well in habit and furniture, as in quality, made a gallant show; and terrible, because strange. The *Gauls* were strong of body, and furious in giving charge; but soon wearied, as accustomed to spend their violence at the first brunt, which disposition all that come of them have inherited to this day. The *Spaniards* were less eager, but more wary; neither ashamed to give ground, when they were over-pressed; nor afraid to return, and renew the fight, upon any small encouragement. As the roughness of the one, and patience of the other, served mutually to reduce each of them to a good and firm temper; so the place which they held in this battle, added confidence jointly unto them both. For they saw themselves well and strongly flanked with *Carthaginians* and other *Africans*; whose name was grown terrible in *Spain*, by their Conquests; and in *Gaul*, by this their present war. Since therefore it could not be feared, that any great calamity should fall upon them, whilst the wings on either side stood fast: these Barbarians had no cause to shrink, or forbear to employ the utmost of their hardiness, as knowing that the Enemy could not press far upon them, without further engaging himself than discretion would allow. Hereunto may be added that great advantage, which the *Carthaginian* had in horse: by which he was able, if the worst had happened, to make a good retreat. The effect of contraries is many times alike. Desperation begetteth courage; but not greater, nor so lively, as doth assured Confidence. *Hannibal* therefore caused these *Gauls* and *Spaniards* to advance; leaving void the place wherein they stood, and into which they might fall back, when they should be overhardly pressed. So, casting them into the form of a Crescent, He made them as it were his Vanguard: the two points of this great half Moon, that looked toward the empty space from which he had drawn it, being narrow and thin, as serving only to guide it orderly back, when need should require; the foremost part of the Ring, swelling out toward the enemies, being well strengthened and thickened against all impression. The circle hereof seemeth to have been so great, that it shadowed the *Africans*, who stood behind it: though such figures, cut in brass, as I have seen of this Battle, present it more narrow; with little reason, as shall anon appear: as also in the same figures it is omitted, That any Companies of *Africans*, or others, were left in the Rear, to second the *Gauls* and *Spaniards*, when they were driven to retreat; though it be manifest, that *Hannibal* in person stood between the last ranks of his long battalions, and in the head of his rear, doubtless well accompanied with the choice of his own Nation. Between the left battalion and the River *Aufidus* were the *Gauls* and *Spanish* horse, under the command of *Asdrubal*: On the right wing, toward the wide Plains, was *Hanno* (*Livy* saith *Maharbal*) with the *Numidian* light horse. *Hannibal* himself, with his brother *Mago*, had the leading of the Rear. The whole sum of *Hannibal's* Army in the field this day, was ten thousand horse, and forty thousand foot; his enemies having two to one against him in foot; and He, five to three against them in horse.

The *Roman* Army was marshalled in the usual form; but somewhat more narrow, and deep, than was accustomed; perhaps, because this had been found convenient against the *Carthaginians* in the former war. It was indeed no bad way of resistance against Elephants to make the Ranks *thick and short*, but the Files long; as also to strengthen well the Rear, that it might stand fast compacted as a wall, under shelter whereof the disordered troops might re-ally themselves. Thus much it seems, that *Terentius* had learned of some old Soldiers; and therefore he now ordered his Battles accordingly, as meaning to show more skill, than was in his understanding. But the *Carthaginians* had here no Elephants with them in the field: their advantage was in Horse; against which, this manner of embattling was very unpıofitable, forasmuch as their charge is better sustained in front, than upon a long flank. As for *Aemilius*; it was not his day of command; He was but an Assistant; and in such cases it happens often, that wise men yield for very weariness unto the more contentious. Upon the right hand, and toward the River, were the *Roman* horsemen, under the Consul *Paulus*: On the left wing, was *C. Terentius Varro* the other Consul, with the rest of the horse, which were of the *Latins*, and other Associates: *Cn. Servilius* the former year's Consul, had the leading of the battle. The Sun was newly risen, and offended neither part; the *Carthaginians* having their faces Northward; the *Romans* toward the South.

After some light skirmish, between the *Roman Velites* and *Hannibal* his Darters and slingers of the *Baleares*: *Asdrubal* brake upon the Consul *Paulus*, and was roughly encountered; not after the manner of service on horseback, used in those times, wheeling about *Alman-like*; but each giving on in a right line, Pouldron to Pouldron, as having the River on the one hand; so that there was no way left, but to pierce and break through. Wherefore they not only used their Lances and Swords; but rushing violently amongst the Enemies, grasped one another: and so, their horses running from under them, fell many to the ground; where starting up again, they began to deal blows like footmen. In conclusion, the *Roman* horse were overborne, and driven by plain force to a staggering recoil. This the Consul *Paulus* could not remedy. For *Asdrubal*, with his boisterous *Gauls* and *Spaniards*, was not to be resisted by these *Roman* Gentlemen, unequal both in number, and in horsemanship. When the battles came to joining, the *Roman* Legionaries found work enough, and somewhat more than enough, to break that great Crescent, upon which they first fell: so strongly, for the while, did the *Gauls* and *Spanish* foot make resistance. Wherefore the two points of their battle drew towards the midst, by whose aid, these Opposites were forced to disband, and fly back to their first place. This they did in great haste and fear: and were with no less haste, and folly, pursued. Upon the *Africans*, that stood behind them, they needed not to fall foul; both for that there was void room enough; and forasmuch as the Rear, or Horns of this Moon, pointed into the safe retreat, where *Hannibal* with his *Carthaginians* was ready to reinforce them, when time should require. In this hasty retreat, or flight, of the *Gauls* and *Spaniards*; it happened, as was necessary, that they who had stood in the limb or utter compass of the half Moon, made the innermost or concave surface thereof (disordered and broken though it were) when it was forced to turn the inside outward: the horns or points thereof, as yet, untouched, only turning round, and recoiling very little. So the *Romans*, in pursuing them, were enclosed in an half circle; which they should not have needed greatly to regard (for that the sides of it were exceeding thin and broken; and the bottom of it, none other than a throng of men routed, and seeming unable to make resistance) had all the enemy's foot been cast into this one great body, that was in a manner dissolved. But whilst the Legions, following their supposed victory, rushed on upon those that stood before them, and thereby unwittingly engaged themselves deeply within the principal strength of the Enemies, hedging them in on both hands; the two *African* Battalions on either side advanced so far, that, getting beyond the Rear of them, they enclosed them, in a manner, behind: and forward they could not pass far, without removing *Hannibal* and *Mago*; which made that way the least easy. Hereby it is apparent, That the great Crescent, before spoken of, was of such extent, as covered the *Africans*; who lay behind it undiscerned, until now. For it is agreed, that the *Romans* were thus empaled *unawares*; and that they behaved themselves, as men that thought upon no other work, than what was found them by the *Gauls*. Neither is it credible, that they would have been so mad, as to run headlong, with the whole bulk of their Army, into the throat of slaughter; had they seen those weapons bent against them at the first, which when they did see, they had little hope to escape. Much might be imputed to their heat of fight, and rashness of inferior Captains: but since the Consul *Paulus*, a man so expert in war, being vanquished in horse, had put himself among the Legions; it cannot be supposed, that he and they did wilfully thus engage themselves. *Asdrubal*, having broken the troops of *Roman* horse, that were led by the Consul *Paulus*, followed upon them along the River side, beating down, and killing, as many as he could, (which were almost all of them) without regard of taking prisoners. The Consul himself was either driven upon his own Legions, or willingly did cast himself among them; as hoping by them to make good the day, notwithstanding the defeat of his horse. But he failed of this his expectation. Nevertheless he cheered up his men as well as he could, both with comfortable words, and with the example of his own stout behaviour: beating down, and killing many of the enemies with his own hand. The like did *Hannibal* among his *Carthaginians*, in the same part of the battle; and with better success. For the Consul received a blow from a sling, that did him great hurt: and though a troop of *Roman* Gentlemen, riding about him, did their best to save him from further harm; yet was he so hardly laid at, that he was compelled, by wounds and weakness, to forsake his horse. Hereupon all his company alighted, thinking that the Consul had given order so to do: as in many battles the *Roman* men at arms had left their horses, to help their foot in distress. When *Hannibal* (for he was near at hand) perceived this, and understood that the Consul had willed his horsemen to dismount; He was very glad of it, and pleasantly said, *I had rather he would have delivered them unto me, bound hand and foot*: meaning, that he had them now almost as safe, as if they were so bound. All this while *C. Terentius Varro*, with the horse of the Associates, in the left wing, was marvellously troubled by *Hanno* (or *Maharbal*) and the *Numidians*: who beating up and down about that great sandy Plain, raised a foul dust; which a strong South wind, blowing there accustomarily, drave into the eyes and mouths of the *Romans*. These, using their advantage both of number and lightness, wearied the Consul and his followers exceedingly: neither giving, nor sustaining any charge, but continually making offers, and wheeling about. Yet at the first they seemed to promise him an happy day of it. For when the battles were even ready to join; five hundred of these *Numidians* came pricking away from their fellows, with their shields cast behind their backs, (as was the manner of those which yielded) and, throwing down their arms, rendered themselves. This was good luck to begin withal, if there had been good meaning. *Varro* had not leisure to examine them; but caused them, unweaponed as they were, to get them behind the Army, where he bade them rest quietly till all was done. These crafty adventurers did as he bade them, for a while; till they found opportunity to put in execution the purpose, for which they had thus yielded. Under their Jackets they had short swords and poniards; besides which, they found other scattered weapons about the field, of such as were slain, and therewithal flew upon the hindmost of the *Romans*, whilst all eyes and thoughts were bent another way: so that they did great mischief, and raised yet a greater terror. Thus *Hannibal*, in a plain level ground, found means to lay an ambush at the back of his enemies. The last blow, that ended all fight and resistance, was given by the same hand which gave the first. *Asdrubal*, having in short space broken the *Roman* troops of horse, and cut in pieces all, save the Company of *Aemilius* that rushed into the gross of his foot, and a very few besides, that recovered some narrow passage, between the River and their own Battalions; did not stay to charge upon the face of the Legions, but fell back behind the Rear of his own, and fetching about, came up to the *Numidians*: with whom he joined, and gave upon *Terentius*. This fearful cloud, as it showed at the first appearance what weather it had left behind it, on the other side: so did it prognosticate a dismal storm unto those, upon whom it was ready now to fall. Wherefore *Terentius* his followers, having wearied themselves much in doing little, and seeing more work toward, than they could hope to sustain; thought it the best way, to avoid the danger by present flight. The Consul was no less wise than they, in apprehending the greatness of his own peril; nor more desperate, in striving to work impossibilities: it being impossible, when so many shrank from him, to sustain the impression alone, which he could not have endured with their assistance. Now he found that, it was one thing to talk of *Hannibal* at *Rome*; and another, to encounter him. But of this; or of ought else, excepting hasty flight, his present leisure would not serve him to consider. Close at the heels of him and his flying troops, followed the light *Numidians*: appointed by *Asdrubal* unto the pursuit, as fittest for that service. *Asdrubal* himself, with the *Gauls* and *Spanish* horse, compassing about, fell upon the backs of the *Romans*; that were ere this hardly distressed, and in a manner surrounded on all parts else. He brake them easily; who before made ill resistance, being enclosed, and laid at on every side, not knowing which way to turn. Here began a pitiful slaughter: the vanquished multitude thronging up and down, they knew not whither or which way, whilst every one sought to avoid those enemies, whom he saw nearest. Some of the *Roman* Gentlemen that were about *Aemilius*, got up to horse, and saved themselves: which though it is hardly understood how they could do; yet I will rather believe it, than suppose that *Livy* so reporteth, to grace thereby his History with this following tale. *Cn. Cornelius Lentulus, galloping along by a place where he saw the Consul sitting all bloodied upon a stone, entreated him to rise and save himself; offering him assistance and horse. But Paulus refused it; willing Lentulus to shift for himself, and not to lose time: saying, That it was not his purpose to be brought again into judgment by the People, either as an accuser of his Colleague, or as guilty himself of that day's loss. Further he willed Lentulus to commend him to the Senate, and in particular to Fabius: willing them to fortify Rome, as fast and well as they could; and telling Fabius, that He lived and died mindful of his wholesome counsel.* These words (peradventure) or some to like purpose, the Consul uttered to *Lentulus*, either when against his will he was drawn to that Battle, or when he beheld the first defeat of his Horse; at what time he put himself in the head of his Legions. For I doubt not, but *Hannibal* knew what he said a good while before this; when he thought the Consul and his troop, in little better case than if they had been bound. The whole Gross of the *Romans*, was enclosed indeed as within a sack; whereof the *African* Battalions made the sides; the *Spaniards*, *Gauls*, and *Hannibal* with his *Carthaginians*, the bottom; and *Asdrubal* with his horse, closed up the mouth: in which part, they first of all were shuffled together, and began the Rout, wherein all the rest followed. *Aemilius* therefore, who could not sit his horse, whilst the battle yet lasted, and whilst the spaces were somewhat open, by which he might have withdrawn himself; was now (had he never so well been mounted) unable to fly, having in his way so close a throng of his own miserable followers, and so many heaps of bodies, as fell apace in that great Carnage. It sufficeth unto his honour, That in the Battle he fought no less valiantly, than he had warily before, both abstained himself, and dissuaded his fellow Consul, from fighting at all. If, when the day was utterly lost, it had lain in his power to save his own life, unto the good of his Country, never more needing it; I should think, that he either too much disesteemed himself; or being too faintly minded, was weary of the World, and his unthankful Citizens. But if such a resolution were praiseworthy in *Aemilius*, as proceeding out of *Roman* valour; then was the *English* virtue of the Lord *John Talbot*, *Viscount Lisle*, son to that famous *Earl* of *Shrewsbury*, who died in the Battle of *Chastillon*, more highly to be honoured. For *Aemilius* was old, grievously, if not mortally, wounded, and accountable for the overthrow received: *Talbot* was in the flower of his youth, unhurt, easily able to have escaped, and not answerable for that day's misfortune, when he refused to forsake his father; who foreseeing the loss of the battle, and not meaning to stain his actions past by flying in his old age, exhorted this his noble son to be gone, and leave him.

In this terrible overthrow died all the *Roman* foot, save two or three thousand who (as *Livy* saith) escaped into the lesser camp; whence, the same night, about six hundred of them brake forth, and joining with such of those in the greater camp, as were willing to try their fortune, conveyed themselves away ere morning, about four thousand foot, and two hundred horse, partly in whole troops, partly dispersed, into *Cannusium*: the next day, the *Roman* Camps, both less and greater, were yielded unto *Hannibal* by those that remained in them. *Polybius* hath no mention of this escape: only he reports, that the ten thousand, whom *Aemilius* had left on the West side of *Aufidus* (as was showed before) to set upon the camp of *Hannibal*, did as they were appointed; but ere they could effect their desire, which they had well near done, the battle was lost: and *Hannibal*, coming upon them with his victorious Army, a great number of these did fly; and thereby escaped, whilst their fellows, making defence in vain, retired into their camp, and held the Enemy busied. For about *two Legions* they were (perhaps not half full, but made up by addition of others, whose fault or fortune was like) that having served at *Cannae*, were afterwards extremely disgraced by the State of *Rome*, for that they had abandoned their Companions fighting. Of the *Roman* horse what numbers escaped, it is uncertain: but very few they were that saved themselves in the first charge, by getting behind the River; and *Terentius* the Consul recovered *Venusia*, with threescore and ten at the most in his company. That he was so ill attended, it is no marvel; for *Venusia* lay many miles off to the Southward; so that his nearest way thither, had been through the midst of *Hannibal's* Army, if the passage had been open. Therefore it must needs be, that when once he got out of sight, he turned up some by-way; so disappointing the *Numidians* that hunted *contre*. Of such as could not hold pace with the Consul, but took other ways, and were scattered over the fields; two thousand, or thereabouts, were gathered up by the *Numidians*, and made prisoners: the rest were slain, all save three hundred; who dispersed themselves in flight, as chance led them, and got into sundry Towns. There died in this great battle of *Cannae*, besides *L. Aemilius Paulus* the Consul; two of the *Roman* Questors or Treasurers, and one and twenty Colonels or Tribunes of the Soldiers, fourscore Senators, or such as had borne office, out of which they were to be chosen into the Senate. Many of these were of especial mark, as having been *Aediles*, *Praetors*, or *Consuls*: among whom was *Cn. Servilius*, the last year's Consul, and *Minutius*, late Master of the horse. The number of prisoners, taken in this battle, *Livy* makes no greater than three thousand foot, and three hundred horse: too few to have defended, for the space of one half hour, both the *Roman* camps; which yet the same *Livy* saith, to have been over-cowardly yielded up. We may therefore do better, to give credit unto one of the prisoners, whom the same Historian shortly after introduceth speaking in the Senate, and saying, That they were no less than eight thousand. It may therefore be, that these three thousand were only such as the Enemy spared, when the fury of Execution was past: but to these must be added about five thousand more, who yielded in the greater camp, when their company were either slain or fled. So the reckoning falls out right: which the *Romans*, especially the Consul *Varro*, had before cast up (as we say) without their Host; nothing so chargeable, as now they find it. On the side of *Hannibal* there died some four thousand *Gauls*, fifteen hundred *Spaniards* and *Africans*, and two hundred horse, or thereabouts: a loss not sensible, in the joy of so great a victory; which if he had pursued, as *Maharbal* advised him, and forthwith marched away towards *Rome*; it is little doubted but that the War had presently been at an end. But he believed not so far in his own prosperity; and was therefore told, That *he knew how to get, not how to use a victory*.

Chapter 3:14 . . . The journey of Hannibal to the gates of Rome. Capua taken by the Romans.

. . . *Hannibal*, having passed over *Vulturnus*, burnt up all his boats; and left nothing that might serve to transport the Enemy, in case he should offer to pursue or coast him. Then hasted he away toward *Rome*; staying no longer in any one place than he needs must. Yet found he the bridges over *Liris* broken down, by the people of *Fregellae*: which as it stopped him a little on his way; so it made him the more grievously to spoil their lands, whiles the bridges were in mending. The nearer he drew to *Rome*, the greater waste he made: his *Numidians* running before him; driving the Country, and killing or taking multitudes of all sorts and ages, that fled out of all parts round about. The messengers of these news came apace, one after another, into the City; some few bringing true advertisements; but the most of them reporting the conceits of their own fear. All the streets, and Temples in *Rome*, were pestered with women, crying and praying, and rubbing the Altars with their hair, because they could do none other good. The Senators were all in the great Market, or place of Assembly; ready to give their advice, if it were asked, or to take directions given by the Magistrates. All places of most importance were stuffed with soldiers: it being uncertain, upon which part *Hannibal* would fall. In the midst of this trepidation, there came news that *Q. Fulvius*, with part of the Army from *Capua*, was hastening to defence of the City. The Office of a Proconsul did expire, at his return home, and entry into the Gates of *Rome*. Wherefore, that *Fulvius* might lose nothing by coming into the City in time of such need, an Act was passed, That He should have equal power with the Consuls, during his abode there. He and *Hannibal* arrived at *Rome*, one soon after another: *Fulvius* having been long held occupied in passing over *Vulturnus*; and *Hannibal* receiving impediments in his journey, as much as the Country was able to give. The Consuls, and *Fulvius*, encamped without the Gates of *Rome*; attending the *Carthaginian*. Thither they called the Senate: and as the danger grew nearer and greater; so took they more careful and especial order, against all occurrences. *Hannibal* came to the river *Anio* or *Anien*, three miles from the Town: whence He advanced with two thousand Horse, and rode along a great way under the walls; viewing the site thereof, and considering how he might best approach it. But He either went, or (as the *Roman* Story saith) was driven away; without doing, or receiving any hurt. Many tumults rose in this while among the people; but were suppressed by care and diligence of the Senators. Above the rest, one accident was both troublesome, and not without peril. Of *Numidians* that had shifted side, and fallen (upon some displeasures) from *Hannibal* to the *Romans*, there were some twelve hundred then in *Rome*: which were appointed by the Consuls, to pass through the Town, from the Mount *Aventine* to the Gate *Collina*, where it was thought that their service might be useful, among broken ways, and Garden walls lying in the suburbs. The faces of these men, and their furniture, wherein they differed not from the followers of *Hannibal*; bred such mistaking, as caused a great uproar among the people: all crying out, that *Aventine* was taken, and the enemy gotten within the walls. The noise was such, that men could not be informed of the truth: and the streets were so full of cattle, and husbandmen, which were fled thither out of the Villages adjoining, that the passage was stopped up: and the poor *Numidians* pitifully beaten from the house-tops, with stones and other weapons that came next to hand, by the desperate multitude, that would have run out at the gates, had it not been certain who lay under the walls. To remedy the like inconveniences, it was ordained, *That all which had been Dictators, Consuls, or Censors, should have authority as Magistrates, till the Enemy departed*. The day following, *Hannibal* passed over *Anien*, and presented battle to the *Romans*, who did not wisely if they undertook it. It is said, that a terrible shower of rain, caused both *Romans* and *Carthaginians* to return into their several Camps: and that this happened two days together, the weather breaking up, and clearing, as soon as they were departed asunder. Certain it is, that *Hannibal*, who had brought along with him no more than ten days' provision, could not endure to stay there, until his victuals were all spent. In which regard, the *Romans* if they suffered him to waste his time and provisions, knowing that he could not abide there long, did as became well-advised men: if they offered to fight with him, and either had the better, or were parted (as is said) by some accident of weather; the commendations must be given to their fortune. The terror of *Hannibal's* coming to the City, how great soever it was at the first, yet after some leisure, and better notice taken of his forces, which appeared less than the first apprehension had formed them, was much and soon abated. Hereunto it helped well, that at the same time, the supply appointed for *Spain*, after the death of the two *Scipios*, was sent out of the town, and went forth at one gate, whilst the *Carthaginian* lay before another. In all *Panic terrors*, as they are called, whereof there is either no cause known or no cause answerable to the greatness of the sudden consternation; it is a good remedy, to do something quite contrary to that which the danger would require, were it such, as men have fashioned it in their amazed conceits. Thus did *Alexander* cause his soldiers to disarm themselves, when they were all on a sudden in a great fear of they knew not what. And thus did *Clearchus* pacify a foolish uproar in his Army, by proclaiming a reward unto him, that could tell who had sent the Ass into the Camp. But in this present example of the *Romans*, appears withal a great magnanimity: whereby they sustained their reputation and augmented it no less, than by this bold attempt of *Hannibal* it might seem to have been diminished. Neither could they more finely have checked the glorious conceits of their Enemies, and taken away the disgrace of that fear, which clouded their valour at his first coming; than by making such demonstrations, when once they had recovered spirit, how little they esteemed him. To this purpose therefore that very piece of ground on which the *Carthaginian* lay encamped, was sold in *Rome*: and sold it was nothing under the value, but at as good a rate, as if it had been in time of peace. This indignity coming to his ear, incensed *Hannibal* so much, that he made Port-sale of the Silversmiths' shops, which were near about the Market or Common place in *Rome*; as if his own title to the houses within the Town, were no whit worse, than any *Roman* Citizen's could be unto that piece of ground, whereon he raised his Tent. But this counter-practice was nothing worth. The *Romans* did seek to manifest that assurance, which they justly had conceived; *Hannibal*, to make show of continuing in an hope, which was already past. His victuals were almost spent: and of those ends, that he had proposed unto himself, this journey had brought forth none other, than the fame of his much daring. Wherefore he brake up his camp: and doing what spoil he could in the *Roman* Territory, without sparing religious places, wherein wealth was to be gotten, He passed like a Tempest over the Country; and ran toward the Eastern Sea so fast, that he had almost taken the city of *Rhegium* before his arrival was feared or suspected. As for *Capua* he gave it lost: and is likely to have cursed the whole faction of *Hanno*, which thus disabled him to relieve that fair City; since he had no other way to vent his grief.

Q. *Fulvius* returning back to *Capua*, made Proclamation anew, that whoso would yield, before a certain day, might safely do it. This, and the very return of *Fulvius*, without any more appearance of *Hannibal*, gave the *Capuans* to understand that they were abandoned, and their case desperate. To trust the *Roman* pardon proclaimed, every man's conscience of his own evil deserts, told him that it was a vanity: and some faint hope was given, by *Hanno* and *Bostar*, Captains of the *Carthaginian* Garrison within the Town, that *Hannibal* should come again; if means could only be found, how to convey such letters unto him, as they would write. The carriage of the letters was undertaken, by some *Numidians*: who running, as fugitives, out of the Town, into the *Roman* camp, waited fit opportunity to make an escape thence with their packets. But it happened, ere they could convey themselves away, that one of them was detected by an Harlot following him out of the Town; and the letters of *Bostar* and *Hanno*, were taken and opened; containing a vehement entreaty unto *Hannibal*, that he would not thus forsake the *Capuans* and them. For (said they) we came not hither to make war against *Rhegium* and *Tarentum*, but against the *Romans*: whose Legions wheresoever they lie, there also should the *Carthaginian* Army be ready to attend them; and by taking of such course, have we gotten those victories at *Trebia*, *Thrasymene*, and *Cannae*. In fine, they besought him, that he would not dishonour himself, and betray them to their enemies, by turning another way: as if it were his only care, that the City should not be taken in his full view: promising, to make a desperate sally, if he would once more adventure to set upon the *Roman* camp. Such were the hopes of *Bostar* and his fellow. But *Hannibal* had already done his best: and now began to faint under the burden of that war, wherein (as afterward he protested) he was vanquished by *Hanno* and his Partisans in the *Carthaginian* Senate, rather than by any force of *Rome*. It may well be, as a thing incident in like cases, that some of those which were besieged in *Capua*, had been sent over by the *Hannonians*, to observe the doings of *Hannibal*, and to check his proceedings. If this were so; justly might they curse their own malice, which had cast them into this remediless necessity. Howsoever it were, the letters directed unto *Hannibal* fell (as is showed) into the *Roman* Proconsuls' hands; who cutting off the hands of all such counterfeit fugitives, as carried such messages, whipped them back into the Town. This miserable spectacle brake the hearts of the *Campans*: so that the Multitude crying out upon the Senate, with menacing terms, caused them to assemble, and consult, about the yielding up of *Capua* unto the *Romans*. The bravest of the Senators, and such as a few years since had been the most forward in joining with *Hannibal*, understood well enough whereunto the matter tended. Wherefore one of them invited the rest home to supper: telling them, that when they had made good cheer, he would drink to them such an health, as should set them free from that cruel revenge, which the Enemy sought upon their bodies. About seven and twenty of the Senators that were there, that liking well of this motion, ended their lives together, by drinking poison. All the rest, hoping for more mercy than they had deserved, yielded simply to discretion. So one of the Town-gates was set open: whereat a *Roman* Legion with some other companies, entering, disarmed the Citizens; apprehended the *Carthaginian* Garrison; and commanded all the

Senators of *Capua* to go forth into the *Roman* camp. At their coming thither, the Proconsuls laid irons upon them all: and commanding them to tell what store of gold and silver they had at home, sent them into safe custody; some to *Cales*, others to *Theanum*. Touching the general Multitude; they were reserved unto the discretion of the Senate; yet so hardly used by *Fulvius* in the meanwhile, that they had little cause of hope or comfort in this adversity. *App. Claudius* was brought even to the point of death, by the wound which he had lately received: yet was he not inexorable to the *Campans*; as having loved them well in former times, and having given his daughter in marriage to that *Pacuvius*, of whom we spake before. But this facility of his Colleague, made *Fulvius* the more hasty in taking vengeance: for fear, lest upon the like respects, the *Roman* Senate might prove more gentle, than he thought behoveful to the common safety, and honour of their state. Wherefore he took the pains, to ride by night unto *Theanum*, and from thence to *Cales*: where he caused all the *Campan* prisoners to suffer death; binding them to stakes, and scourging them first a good while with rods; after which he struck off their heads.

This terrible example of vengeance, which the *Carthaginians* could not hinder, made all Towns of *Italy* the less apt to follow the vain hope of the *Campans*: and bred a general inclination, to return upon good conditions to the *Roman* side. The *Atellans*, *Calatines*, and *Sabatines*, people of the *Campans*, that in the former change had followed the fortune of *Capua*, made also now the like submission, for very fear, and want of ability to resist. They were therefore used with the like rigour, by *Fulvius*: who dealt so extremely with them all, that he brought them into desperation. Wherefore some of their young Gentlemen, burning with fire of revenge, got into *Rome*: where they found means by night time, to set on fire so many houses, that a great part of the City was like to have been consumed. The beginning of the fire in divers places at once, argued that it was no casualty. Wherefore liberty was proclaimed unto any slave, and other sufficient reward unto any free man, that should discover who those Incendiaries were. Thus all came out: and the *Campans*, being detected by a slave of their own (to whom, above his liberty promised, was given about the sum of an hundred marks) had the punishment answerable to their deserts. *Fulvius* hereby being more and more incensed against this wretched people, held them in a manner as prisoners within their walls: and this extreme severity caused them at length to become Suppliants unto the *Roman* Senate; that some period might be set unto their miseries. That whereupon the Senators resolved in the end, was worse than all which they had suffered before. Only two poor women in *Capua* (of which one had been an Harlot) were found not guilty of the late rebellion. The rest were, some of them, with their wives and children sold for slaves, and their goods confiscated; others laid in prison, and reserved to further deliberation: but the generality of them, commanded to depart out of *Campania* by a certain day; and confined unto several places, as it best liked the angry Victors. As for the Town of *Capua*, it was suffered to stand, in regard of the beauty and commodious site: but no corporation, or form of polity, was allowed to be therein; only a *Roman* Provost was every year sent, to govern over those that should inhabit it, and to do justice. This was the greatest act, and most important, hitherto done by the people of *Rome*, after many great losses in the present war. After this, the glory of *Hannibal* began to shine with a more dim light than before: his oil being far spent; and that, which should have revived his flame, being unfortunately shed; as shall be told in place convenient.

Chapter 3:15 How the Carthaginians, making a party in Sardinia and Sicil, held war against the Romans in those Islands, and were overcome.

. . . Immediately began the siege, which endured longer than the *Romans* had expected. The quick and easy winning of *Leontium* did put *Marcellus* in hope, that so long a circuit of walls, as compassed *Syracuse*, being manned with no better kind of Soldiers, than those with whom he had lately dealt, would in some part or other, be taken at the first assault. Wherefore he omitted no violence or terror in the very beginning; but did his best, both by Land and Sea. Nevertheless all his labour was disappointed; and his hope of prevailing by open force, taken from him by the ill success of two or three of the first assaults. Yet was it not the virtue of the Defendants, or any strength of the City; that bred such despair of hasty victory. But there lived at that time in *Syracuse*, *Archimedes* the noble Mathematician: who at the request of *Hiero* the late King, that was his kinsman, had framed such engines of war, as being in this extremity put in use, did more mischief to the *Romans* than could have been wrought by the Cannon, or any instruments of Gunpowder; had they in that age been known. This *Archimedes* discoursing once with *Hiero*, maintained, That it were possible to remove the whole earth out of the place wherein it is, if there were some other earth, or place of sure footing, whereon a man might stand. For proof of this bold assertion, he performed some strange works; which made the King entreat him to convert his study unto things of use; that might preserve the City from danger of enemies. To such Mechanical works *Archimedes*, and the Philosophers of those times, had little affection. They held it an injury done unto the liberal sciences, to submit learned Propositions, unto the workmanship, and gain, of base handicrafts men. And of this opinion *Plato* was an author: who greatly blamed some Geometricians; that seemed unto him to profane their science, by making it vulgar. Neither must we rashly task a man so wise as *Plato*, with the imputation of supercilious austerity, or affected singularity in his reprehension. For it hath been the unhappy fate of great inventions, to be vilified, as idle fancies, or dreams, before they were published: and being once made known, to be undervalued; as falling within compass of the meanest wit; and things, that every one, could well have performed. Hereof (to omit that memorable example of *Columbus* his discovery, with the much different sorts of neglect, which he underwent before and after it) in a familiar and most homely example, we may see most apparent proof. He that looks upon our *English Brewers*, and their Servants, that are daily exercised in the Trade; will think it ridiculous to hear one say, that the making of Malt, was an invention, proceeding from some of an extraordinary knowledge in natural Philosophy. Yet is not the skill of the inventors any whit the less, for that the labour of workmanship grows to be the Trade of ignorant men. The like may be said of many handicrafts: and particularly in the Printing of Books; which being devised, and bettered, by great Scholars, and wise men, grew afterward corrupted by those, to whom the practice fell; that is, by such, as could slubber things easily over, and feed their workmen at the cheapest rate. In this respect therefore, the Alchemists, and all others, that have, or would seem to have any secret skill, whereof the publication might do good unto mankind; are not without excuse of their close concealing. For it is a kind of injustice, that the long travails of an understanding brain, beside the loss of time, and other expense, should be cast away upon men of no worth; or yield less benefit unto the Author of a great work, than to mere strangers; and perhaps his enemies. And surely, if the passion of Envy have in it any thing allowable and natural, as have Anger, Fear, and other the like Affections: it is in some such case as this; and serveth against those, which would usurp the knowledge, wherewith God hath denied to endue them. Nevertheless, if we have regard unto common charity, and the great affection that every one ought to bear unto the generality of mankind, after the example of him that *suffereth his Sun to shine upon the just and unjust*: it will appear more commendable in wise men, to enlarge themselves, and to publish unto the world, those good things that lie buried in their own bosoms. This ought specially to be done, when a profitable knowledge hath not annexed to it some dangerous cunning, that may be perverted by evil men to a mischievous use. For if the secret of any rare *Antidote*, contained in it the skill of giving some deadly and irrecoverable poison: better it were, that such a jewel remain close in the hands of a wise and honest man; than being made common, bind all men to use the remedy, by teaching the worst men how to do mischief. But the works which *Archimedes* published, were such as tended to very commendable ends. They were engines, serving unto the defence of *Syracuse*; not fit for the *Syracusians* to carry abroad, to the hurt and oppression of others. Neither did he altogether publish the knowledge, how to use them, but reserved so much to his own direction; that after his death more of the same kind were not made, nor those of his own making were employed by the *Romans*. It sufficed unto this worthy man, that he had approved, even unto the vulgar, the dignity of his Science, and done especial benefit unto his Country. For to enrich a Mechanical trade, or teach the art of murdering men, it was besides his purpose . . .

. . . By the treason of Mercius, the *Roman* Army was let into possession of all *Syracuse*: wherein, the booty that it found, was said to have been no less, than could have been hoped for, if they had taken *Carthage* itself; that maintained war by Land and Sea against them. All the goodly works and Imageries, wherewith *Syracuse* was marvellously adorned, were carried away to *Rome*; and nothing left untouched; save only the houses of those banished men, that had escaped from *Hippocrates* and *Epicedes*, into the *Roman* camp. Among other pitiful accidents; the death of *Archimedes*, was greatly lamented, even by *Marcellus* himself. He was so busy about his Geometry, in drawing figures, that he hearkened not to the noise, and uproar in the City: no, nor greatly attended the rude Soldier that was about to kill him. *Marcellus* took heavily the death of him; and caused his body to be honourably buried. Upon his Tomb (as he had ordained in his lifetime) was placed a Cylinder and a Sphere, with an inscription of the proportion between them; which he first found out. An Invention of so little use, as this may seem, pleased that great Artist better, than the devising of all those engines, that made him so famous. Such difference is between the judgment of learned men, and of the vulgar sort. For many an one would think the money lost, that had been spent upon a son, whose studies, in the University had brought forth such a fruit, as the proportion between a Sphere and a Cylinder.

Chapter 6:2 The death of Philipoemen, Hannibal, and Scipio. That the military profession is of all other the most unhappy: notwithstanding some examples, which may seem to prove the contrary.

. . . In this year also (as good Authors have reported) to accompany *Philopoemen* and *Hannibal*, died *Scipio* the *African*: these being, all of them, as great Captains as ever the world had; but not more famous, than unfortunate. Certainly, for *Hannibal*, whose Tragedy we have now finished, had he been the Prince of the *Carthaginians*, and one who by his authority might have commanded such supplies, as the War which he undertook, required; it is probable, that he had torn up the *Roman* Empire by the roots. But he was so strongly crossed by a cowardly and envious Faction at home; as his proper virtue, wanting public force to sustain it, did lastly dissolve itself in his own, and in the common misery of his Country and Commonweal.

Hence it comes, to wit, from the envy of our equals, and jealousy of our Masters, be they Kings, or Commonweals, That there is no Profession more unprosperous than that of Men of War, and great Captains, being no Kings. For besides the envy and jealousy of men; the spoils, rapes, famine, slaughter of the innocent, vastation, and burnings, with a world of miseries laid on the labouring man, and so hateful to God, as with good reason did *Monluc* the Marshal of *France* confess, *That were not the mercies of God infinite, and without restriction, it were in vain for those of his profession to hope for any portion of them: seeing the cruelties, by them permitted and committed, were also infinite.* Howsoever, this is true, That the victories, which are obtained by many of the greatest Commanders, are commonly either ascribed to those that serve under them, to Fortune, or to the cowardice of the Nation against whom they serve. For the most of others, whose virtues have raised them above the level of their inferiors, and have surmounted their envy: yet have they been rewarded in the end, either with disgrace, banishment, or death. Among the *Romans* we find many examples hereof; as *Coriolanus*, *M. Livius*, *L. Aemilius*, and this our *Scipio*, whom we have lately buried. Among the *Greeks* we read of not many, that escaped these rewards. Yea long before these times, it was a Legacy that *David* bequeathed unto his victorious Captain *Joab*. With this fare *Alexander* feasted *Parmenio*, *Philotas*, and others; and prepared it for *Antipater* and *Cassander*. Hereto *Valentinian* the Emperor invited *Aetius*: who, after many other victories, overthrew *Attila* of the *Huns*, in the greatest battle, for the well fighting and resolution of both Armies, that ever was strucken in the world; for there fell of those that fought, besides runaways, an hundred and fourscore thousand. Hereupon it was well and boldly told unto the Emperor by *Proximus*, That in killing of *Aetius*, he had cut off his own right hand with his left: for it was not long after that *Maximus* (by whose persuasion *Valentinian* slew

Aetius) murdered the Emperor, which he never durst attempt, *Aetius*, living. And besides the loss of that Emperor, it is true, That with *Aetius*, the glory of the Western Empire was rather dissolved, than obscured. The same unworthy destiny, or a far worse, had *Belisarius*; whose undertakings and victories were so difficult and glorious, as after-ages suspected them for fabulous. For he had his eyes torn out of his head by *Justinian*; and he died a blind beggar. *Narses* also, to the great prejudice of *Christian* Religion, was disgraced by *Justin*. That Rule of *Cato* against *Scipio*, hath been well observed in every age since then, to wit, That the Commonweal cannot be accounted free, which standeth in awe of any one man. And hence have the *Turks* drawn another Principle, and indeed a *Turkish* one, That every warlike Prince should rather destroy his greatest men of war, than suffer his own glory to be obscured by them. For this cause did *Bajazet* the Second despatch *Bassa Acomat*; *Selim* strangle *Bassa Mustapha* ; and most of those Princes bring to ruin the most of their *Viziers*. Of the *Spanish* Nation, the great *Gonsalvo*, who drave the *French* out of *Naples*; and *Ferdinando Cortes*, who conquered *Mexico*; were crowned with nettles, not with Laurel. The Earls of *Egmond* and *Horn*, had no heads left them to wear garlands on. And that the great Captains of all Nations, have been paid with this copper coin; there are examples more than too many. On the contrary it may be said, That many have acquired the State of Princes, Kings, and Emperors, by their great ability in matter of war. This I confess. Yet it must be had withal, in consideration, that these high places have been given, or offered, unto very few, as rewards of their military virtue; though many have usurped them, by the help and favour of those Armies which they commanded. Neither is it unregardable, That the Tyrants which have oppressed the liberty of free Cities: and the lieutenants of Kings or Emperors, which have traitorously cast down their Masters, and stepped up into their seats; were not all of them good men of war: but have used the advantage of some commotion; or many of them, by base and cowardly practices, have obtained those dignities, which undeservedly were ascribed to their personal worth. So that the number of those, that have purchased absolute greatness by the greatness of their warlike virtue; is far more in seeming, than in deed. *Phocas* was a soldier, and by the help of the soldiers, he got the Empire from his lord *Mauritius*: but he was a coward; and with a barbarous cruelty, seldom found in any other than cowards, he slew first the children of *Mauritius*, a Prince that never had done him wrong, before his face, and after them *Mauritius* himself. This his bloody aspiring was but as a debt, which was paid unto him again by

Heraclius: who took from him the Imperial Crown, unjustly gotten; and set it on his own head. *Leontius* laid hold upon the emperor *Justin*, cut off his nose and ears, and sent him into banishment: but God's vengeance rewarded him with the same punishment, by the hands of *Tiberius*; to whose charge he had left his own men of war. *Justin*, having recovered forces, lighted on *Tiberius*, and barbed him after the same fashion. *Philippicus*, commanding the forces of *Justin*, murdered both the Emperor and his son. *Anastasius*, the vassal of his new Tyrant, surprised his Master *Philippicus*, and thrust out both his eyes. But with *Anastasius*, *Theodosius* dealt more gently: for having wrested the Sceptre out of his hands, he enforced him to become a Priest. It were an endless, and a needless work to tell, how *Leo* rewarded this *Theodosius*; how many others have been repaid with their own cruelty, by men alike ambitious and cruel; or how many hundreds, or rather thousands, hoping of Captains to make themselves Kings, have by God's justice miserably perished in the attempt. The ordinary, and perhaps the best way of thriving, by the practice of arms, is to take what may be gotten by the spoil of Enemies, and the liberality of those Princes and Cities, in whose service one hath well deserved. But scarce one of a thousand have prospered by this course. For that observation, made by *Solomon*, of unthankfulness in this kind, hath been found belonging to all Countries and Ages: *A little City, and few men in it, and a great King came against it, and compassed it about, and builded Forts against it: And there was found a poor and wise man therein, and he delivered the City by his wisdom: but none remembered this poor man.* Great Monarchs are unwilling to pay great thanks, lest thereby they should acknowledge themselves to have been indebted for great benefits: which the unwiser sort of them think to savour of some impotency in themselves. But in this respect they are oftentimes cozened and abused: which proves that weakness to be in them indeed, whereof they so gladly shun the opinion. Contrariwise, free Estates are bountiful in giving thanks; yet so, as those thanks are not of long endurance. But concerning other profit which their Captains have made, by enriching themselves with the spoil of the enemy, they are very inquisitive to search into it, and to strip the well-deservers out of their gettings: yea most injuriously to rob them of their own, upon a false supposition: that even they whose hands are most clean from such offences, have purloined somewhat from the common Treasury. Hereof I need not to produce examples: that of the two *Scipios* being so lately recited.

In my late Sovereign's time, although for the wars, which for her own safety she was constrained to undertake, her Majesty had no less cause to use the service of Martial men both by Sea and land, than any of her Predecessors for many years had, yet, according to the destiny of that profession, I do not remember, that any of hers, the Lord Admiral excepted, her eldest and most prosperous Commander, were either enriched, or otherwise honoured, for any service by them performed. And that her Majesty had many advised, valiant, and faithful men, the prosperity of her affairs did well witness, who in all her days never received dishonour, by the cowardice or infidelity of any Commander by herself chosen and employed.

For as all her old Captains by Land died poor men, as *Malbey*, *Randol*, *Drewry*, *Reade*, *Wilford*, *Layton*, *Pellam*, *Gilbert*, *Cunstable*, *Bourchier*, *Barkeley*, *Bingham*, and others; so those of a later and more dangerous employment, whereof *Norice* and *Vere* were the most famous, and who have done as great honour to our Nation (for the means they had) as ever any did: those (I say) with many other brave Colonels, have left behind them (besides the reputation which they purchased with many travails and wounds) nor title nor estate to their posterity. As for the *Lord Thomas Burrough*, and *Peregrine Berty Lord Willoughby* of *Eresby*, two very worthy and exceeding valiant Commanders, they brought with them into the world their Titles and Estates.

That her Majesty in the advancement of her Men of war did sooner believe other men than herself, a disease unto which many wise Princes, besides herself, have been subject, I say that such a confidence, although it may seem altogether to excuse her Noble Nature, yet can it not but in some sort accuse her of weakness. And exceeding strange it were, were not the cause manifest enough, that where the prosperous Actions are so exceedingly prized, the Actors are so unprosperous, and so generally neglected. The cause, I say, which hath wrought one and the same effect in all times, and among all Nations, is this, that those which are nearest the person of Princes (which martial men seldom are) can with no good grace commend, or at least magnify a Profession far more noble than their own, seeing therein they should only mind their Masters of the wrong they did unto others, in giving less honour and reward to men of far greater deserving, and of far greater use than themselves.

But his Majesty hath already paid the greatest part of that debt. For besides the relieving by Pensions all the poorer sort, he hath honoured more Martial men than all the Kings of *England* have done for this hundred years.

He hath given a *Coronet* to the Lord *Thomas Howard* for his chargeable and remarkable service, as well in the year 1588, as at

Cadiz, the *Islands*, and in our own Seas; having first commanded as a Captain, twice Admiral of a Squadron, and twice Admiral in chief. His Majesty hath changed the Baronies of *Montjoy* and *Burley* into Earldoms, and created *Sidney* Viscount, *Knollys*, *Russel*, *Carew*, *Danvers*, *Arundel* of Warder, *Gerald*, and *Chichester*, Barons, for their governments and services in the *Netherlands*, *France*, *Ireland*, and elsewhere.

Chapter 6:8 . . . The Battle of Pydna. Perseus his flight. He forsakes his kingdom: which hastily yields to Aemilius. Perseus at Samothrace. He yields himself to the Roman Admiral; and is sent prisoner to Aemilius.

. . . Now concerning the Battle; *Aemilius* was throughly persuaded, that the King meant to abide it: for that otherwise he would not have stayed at *Pydna*, when as a little before, his leisure served to retire whither he listed, the *Romans* being further off. In regard of this, and perhaps of the tokens appearing in the Sacrifices, the Consul thought that he might wait upon advantage, without making any great haste. Neither was it to be neglected, that the morning Sun was full in the *Romans'* faces: which would be much to their hindrance all the forenoon. Since therefore *Perseus* kept his ground, that was commodious for the *Phalanx*, and *Aemilius* sent forth part of his men to bring in Wood and Fodder; there was no likelihood of fighting that day. But about ten of the clock in the morning, a small occasion brought to pass that, which whereto neither of the Generals had over earnest desire. A horse brake loose at watering; which two or three of the *Roman* soldiers followed into the river, wading after him up to the knees. The King's men lay on the further bank; whence a couple of *Thracians* ran into the water, to draw this horse over to their own side. These fell to blows, as in a private quarrel; and one of the *Thracians* was slain. His countrymen seeing this, hasted to revenge their fellow's death, and followed those that had slain him over the river. Hereupon company came in, to help on each part, until the number grew such, as made it past a fray, and caused both the armies to be careful of the event. In fine, each of the Generals placed his men in order of battle, accordly as the manner of his Country, and the arms wherewith they served, did require. The ground was a flat level, save that on the sides a few hillocks were raised here and there; whereof each part might take what advantage it could. The *Macedonians* were the greater number, the *Romans* the better soldiers, and better appointed. Both the King and the Consul encouraged their men with lively words: which the present condition could bountifully afford. But the King having finished his Oration, and sent on his men, withdrew himself into *Pydna*: there to do sacrifice, as he pretended, unto *Hercules*. It is the less marvel, that he durst adventure battle, since he had bethought himself of such a stratagem, whereby to save his own person. As for *Hercules*, he liked not the sacrifice of a coward: whose unseasonable devotion could be no better than hypocrisy. For he that will pray for a good Harvest, ought also to Plough, Sow, and Weed his Ground. When therefore the king returned to the battle, he found it no better than lost: and he, in looking to his own safety, caused it to be lost altogether, by beginning the flight. The acts of this day, such as we find recorded, are, that the *Roman* Elephants could do no manner of good; That the *Macedonian Phalanx* did so stoutly press onwards, and beat off all which came before it, as *Aemilius* was thereat much astonished; That the *Peligni* rushing desperately on the *Phalanx*, were overborne, many of them slain, and the squadrons following them so discouraged herewith, as they retired apace towards an hill. These were the things that fell out adverse to the *Romans*; and which the Consul beholding, is said to have rent his coat-armour for grief. If the King with all his power of horse, had in like manner done his devoir; the victory might have been his own. That which turned the fortune of the battle, was the same which doubtless the Consul expected, even from the beginning: the difficulty, or almost impossibility, of holding the *Phalanx* long in order. For whilst some of the *Romans'* small battalions pressed hard upon one part of it, and others recoiled from it; it was necessary (if the *Macedonians* would follow upon those which were put to the worse) that some files having open way before them, should advance themselves beyond the rest that were held at a stand. This coming so to pass, admonished the Consul, what was to be done. The long pikes of the *Macedonians* were of little use, when they were charged in flank by the *Roman* Targetiers; according to direction given by *Aemilius*, when he saw the front of the Enemy's great battle become unequal, and the ranks in some places open, by reason of the unequal resistance which they found. Thus was the use of the *Phalanx* proved unavailable against many small squadrons, as it had been formerly in the battle of *Cynoscephalae*: yea, this form of embattling was found unserviceable against the other, by reason, that being not everywhere alike distressed, it would break of itself; though here were little such inconvenience of ground, as had been at *Cynoscephalae*.

Perseus, when he saw his battle begin to rout, turned his bridle presently, and ran amain towards *Pella*. All his horse escaped, in a manner untouched, and a great number followed him; the little harm they had taken, witnessing the little good service which they had done. As for the poor foot; they were left to the mercy of the Enemy: who slew above twenty thousand of them; though having little cause to be furious, as having lost, in that battle, only some four score, or six score men at the most. Some of the foot, escaping from the execution, overtook the king and his company in a wood; where they fell to railing at the horsemen, calling them cowards, traitors, and such other names, till at length they fell to blows. The King was in doubt lest they had ill meaning to himself: and therefore turned out of the common way, being followed by such as thought it good. The rest of the company dispersed themselves: every one as his own occasions guided him. Of those that kept along with their King, the number began within a while to lessen. For he fell to devising upon whom he might lay the blame of that day's misfortune, which was most due to himself: thereby causing those that knew his nature to shrink away from him, how they could. At his coming to *Pella*, he found his Pages and household servants, ready to attend him, as they had been wont. But of his great men that had escaped from the battle, there was none appearing in the Court. In this melancholic time, there were two of his Treasurers that had the boldness to come to him, and tell him roundly of his faults. But in reward of their unseasonable admonitions, he stabbed them both to death. After this, none whom he sent for would come at him. This boded no good. Wherefore standing in fear, lest they that refused to come at his call, should shortly dare some greater mischief; he stole out of *Pella* by night. Of his friends he had with him only *Evander* (who had been employed to kill *Eumenes* at *Delphi*) and two other. There followed him likewise about five hundred *Cretans*; more for love of his money, than of him. To these he gave of his plate, as much as was worth about fifty talents, though shortly he cozened them of some part thereof; making show as if he would have redeemed it; but never paying the money. The third day after the battle he came to *Amphipolis*; where he exhorted the townsmen to fidelity, with tears; and his own speech being hindered by tears, appointed *Evander* to speak what himself would have uttered. But the *Amphipolitans* made it their chief care, to look well to themselves. Upon the first fame of the overthrow, they had emptied the town of two thousand *Thracians* that lay there in garrison: sending them forth under colour of a gainful employment, and shutting the gates after them. And now to be rid of the King; they plainly bade *Evander* be gone. The King hearing this, had no mind to tarry: but embarking himself and the treasure which he had there, in certain vessels that he found in the river *Strymon*; passed over to the Isle of *Samothrace*: where he hoped to live safe, by privilege of the religious sanctuary therein.

These miserable shifts of the King made it the less doubtful, how all the kingdom fell into the power of *Aemilius*, within so few days after his victory. *Pydna* which was nearest at hand, was the last that yielded. About six thousand of the soldiers, that were of sundry Nations, fled out of the battle into that Town; and prepared for defence: the confused rabble of so many strangers hindering all deliberation and consent. *Hippius* who had kept the passage over *Ossa* against *Martius*, with *Pantauchus*, who had been sent Ambassador to *Gentius* the *Illyrian*, were the first that came in; yielding themselves and the Town of *Beroea*, whither they had retired out of the battle. With the like message came others from *Thessalonica*, from *Pella*, and from all the Towns of *Macedon*, within two days: the loss of the head bereaving the whole body of all sense and strength. Neither did they of *Pydna* stand out any longer, when they knew that the King had forsaken his Country: but opened their gates upon such terms, that the sack of it was granted to the *Roman* army. *Aemilius* sent abroad into the Country, such as he thought meetest, to take charge of other Cities: he himself marching towards *Pella*. He found in *Pella* no more than three hundred talents; the same whereof *Perseus* had lately defrauded the *Illyrian*. But within a little while he shall have more.

It was soon understood, that *Perseus* had taken Sanctuary, in the Temple at *Samothrace*: his own letters to the Consul, confirming the report. He sent these letters by persons of such mean condition; that his case was pitied, for that he wanted the service of better men. The scope of his writing was, to desire favour: which though he begged in terms ill beseeming a King; yet since the inscription of his Epistle was, *King Perseus to the Consul Paulus*; the Consul, who had taken from him his Kingdom, and would not allow him to retain the Title, refused to make answer thereunto. So there came other letters, as humble as could be expected: whereby he craved and obtained, that some might be sent to confer with him about matters of his present estate. Nevertheless in this conference, he was marvellous earnest, that he might be allowed to retain the name of King. And to this end it was perhaps, that he had so carefully preserved his treasure, unto the very last: flattering himself with such vain hopes as these; That the *Romans* would neither violate a Sanctuary, nor yet neglect those great riches in his possession; but compound with him for money, letting him have his desire to live at ease, and be called King. Yea it seems that he had indeed, even from the beginning, a desire to live in this Isle of *Samothrace*: both for that in one of his consultations about the war he was dehorted by his friends from seeking to exchange his

Kingdom of *Macedon*, for such a paltry Island; and for that he offered to lay up the money which *Eumenes* demanded, in the holy Temple that was there. But he finds it otherwise. They urge him to give place unto necessity, and without more ado, to yield to the discretion and mercy of the people of *Rome*. This is so far against his mind, that the conference breaks off without effect. Presently there arrives at *Samothrace Cn. Octavius*, the *Roman* Admiral, with his fleet: who assays, as well by terrible threats, as by fair language, to draw the King out of his lurking hole, wherein, for fear of imprisonment, he had imprisoned himself. When all would not serve, a question was moved to the *Samothracians*; How they durst pollute their Temple, by receiving into it one that had violated the like holy privilege of Sanctuary, by attempting the murder of King *Eumenes* at *Delphi*? This went to the quick. The *Samothracians*, being now in the power of the *Romans*, take this matter to heart; and send word to the King, That *Evander*, who lives with him in the Temple, is accused of an impious fact committed at *Delphi*, whereof unless he can clear himself in judgment, he must not be suffered to profane that holy place, by his abiding in it. The reverence borne to his Majesty, now past, makes them forbear to say, that *Perseus* himself is charged with the same crime. But what will this avail, when the minister of the fact being brought into judgment, shall (as is to be feared) appeach the author? *Perseus* therefore willeth *Evander* to have consideration of the little favour that can be expected at the *Romans*' hand, who are like to be presidents and overseers of this judgment: so as it were better to die valiantly, since none other hope remains, than hope to make good an ill cause; where, though he had a good plea, yet it could not help him. Of this motion *Evander* seems to like well: and either kills himself, or hoping to escape thence, by deferring the time as it were to get poison wherewith to end his life, is killed by the King's commandment. The death of this man, who had stuck to *Perseus* in all times of need, makes all the King's friends that remained hitherto, to forsake him: so as none are left with him, save his wife and children, with his Pages. It is much to be suspected, that they which leave him upon this occasion, will tell perilous tales, and say, That the king hath lost the privilege of this holy Sanctuary, by murdering *Evander* therein. Or if the *Romans* will affirm so much, who shall dare to gainsay them? Since therefore there is nothing but a point of formality, and even that also liable to dispute, which preserves him from captivity; he purposeth to make an escape, and fly, with his Treasures, unto *Cotys* his good friend, into *Thrace*. *Oroandes*, a *Cretan*, lay at *Samothrace* with one ship; who easily was persuaded to waft the King thence. With all secrecy the King's money, as much as could be so conveyed, was carried aboard by night; and the King himself, with his wife and children (if rather it were not true, that he had with him only *Philip* his elder son, who was only by adoption his son, being his brother by nature) with much ado got out at a window by a rope, and over a mud wall. At his coming to the Sea side, he found no *Oroandes* there: the *Cretan* had played a *Cretan* trick, and was gone with the money to his own home. So it began to wax clear day, whilst *Perseus* was searching all along the shore: who had stayed so long about this, that he might fear to be intercepted ere he could recover the Temple. He ran therefore amain towards his lodging: and thinking it not safe to enter it the common way, lest he should be taken; he hid himself in an obscure corner. His Pages missing him, ran up and down making enquiry: till *Octavius* made proclamation, That all the King's Pages, and *Macedonians* whatsoever, abiding with their master in *Samothrace*, should have their lives and liberty, with all to them belonging, which they had either in that Isle, or at home in *Macedon*, conditionally, That they should presently yield themselves to the *Romans*. Hereupon they all came in. Likewise *Ion*, a *Thessalonian*, to whom the King had given the custody of his children, delivered them up to *Octavius*. Lastly, *Perseus* himself, with his son *Philip*, accusing the gods of *Samothrace*, that had no better protected him; rendered himself, and made the *Roman* victory complete. If he had not trusted in those gods of *Samothrace*, but employed his whole care in the defence of *Macedon*, without other hope of living than of reigning therein; he might well have brought this War to an happier end. Now, by dividing his cogitations, and pursuing at once, those contrary hopes of saving his Kingdom by arms, and himself by flight; he is become a spectacle of misery, and one among the number of those Princes, that have been wretched by their own default. He was presently sent away to *Aemilius*; before whom he fell to the ground so basely, that he seemed thereby to dishonour the victory over himself, as gotten upon one of abject quality, and therefore the less to be esteemed. *Aemilius* used to him the language of a gentle Victor: blaming him, though mildly, for having, with so hostile a mind, made War upon the *Romans*. Hereto good answer might have been returned by one of better spirit. As for *Perseus*, he answered all with a fearful silence. He was comforted with hope of life, or (as the Consul termed it) almost assurance; for that such was the mercy of the People of *Rome*. After these good words, being invited to the Consul's Table, and respectively entreated, he was committed prisoner to Q. *Aelius*.

Such end had this *Macedonian* War, after four years continuance: and such end therewithal had the Kingdome of *Macedon*; the glory whereof, that had sometime filled all parts of the World then known, was now translated unto *Rome*.

Chapter 6:12 . . . The end of Perseus and his children. The instability of Kingly Estates. The triumphs of Paulus, Anicius, and Octavius. With the Conclusion of the Work.

. . . As for those unhappy Kings, *Perseus* and *Gentius*, they were led through *Rome*, with their children and friends, in the Triumphs of *Aemilius* and *Anicius*. *Perseus* had often made suit to *Aemilius*, that he might not be put to such disgrace: but he still received one scornful answer, That it lay in his own power to prevent it; whereby was meant, that he might kill himself. And surely, had he not hoped for greater mercy than he found, he would rather have sought his death in *Macedon*, than have been beholding to the courtesy of his insolent enemies for a wretched life. The issue of the *Roman* clemency, whereof *Aemilius* had given him hope, was no better than this: After that he, and his fellow King, had been led in chains through the streets, before the Chariots of their triumphing Victors, they were committed to prison, wherein they remained without hope of release. It was the manner, that when the Triumpher turned his Chariot up towards the Capitol, there to do sacrifice, he should command the captives to be had away to prison, and there put to death: so as the honour of the Vanquisher, and misery of those that were overcome, might be both together at the utmost. This last sentence of death was remitted unto *Perseus*: yet so, that he had little joy of his life; but either famished himself, or (for it is diversely reported) was kept watching perforce by those that had him in custody; and so died for want of sleep. Of his sons, two died; it is uncertain how. The youngest called *Alexander* (only in name like unto the Great, though destined sometimes perhaps by his father, unto the fortunes of the Great) became a Joiner, or Turner, or, at his best preferment, a Scribe under the *Roman* Officers. In such poverty ended the Royal House of *Macedon*: and it ended on the sudden; though some eight score years after the death of that Monarch, unto whose ambition this whole Earth seemed too narrow.

If *Perseus* had known it before, that his own son should one day be compelled to earn his living by handiwork, in a painful Occupation; it is like, that he would not, as in a wantonness of Sovereignty, have commanded those poor men to be slain, which had recovered his treasures out of the sea, by their skill in the feat of diving. He would rather have been very gentle, and would have considered, that the greatest oppressors, and the most undertrodden wretches, are all subject unto One high Power, governing all alike with absolute command. But such is our unhappiness; instead of that blessed counsel, *Do as ye would be done unto*, a sentence teaching all moderation, and pointing out the way to felicity; we entertain that arrogant thought, *I will be like to the Most High*: this is, I will do what shall please myself. One hath said truly . . .

> Even they that have no murd'rous will,
> Would have it in their power to kill.

All, or the most, have a vain desire of ability to do evil without control: which is a dangerous temptation unto the performance. God, who best can judge what is expedient, hath granted such power to very few: among whom also, very few there are, that use it not to their own hurt. For who sees not, that a Prince, by racking his Sovereign authority to the utmost extent, enableth (besides the danger to his own person) some one of his own sons or nephews to root up all his progeny? Shall not many excellent Princes, notwithstanding their brotherhood, or other nearness in blood, be driven to flatter the Wife, the Minion, or perhaps the Harlot, that governs one, the most unworthy of his whole house, yet reigning over all? The untimely death of many Princes, which could not humble themselves to such flattery; and the common practice of the *Turkish* Emperors, to murder all their brethren, without expecting till they offend; are too good proofs hereof. Hereto may be added, That the heir of the same *Roger Mortimer*, who murdered most traitorously and barbarously King *Edward* the second; was, by reason of a marriage, proclaimed, in time not long after following, heir apparent to the Crown of *England*: which had he obtained, then had all the power of *Edward* fallen into the race of his mortal enemy, to exercise the same upon the Line of that unhappy King. Such examples of the instability whereto all mortal affairs are subject; as they teach moderation, and admonish the transitory Gods of Kingdoms, not to authorize, by wicked precedents, the evil that may fall on their own posterity: so do they necessarily make us understand, how happy that Country is, which hath obtained a King able to conceive and teach, That God *is the sorest and sharpest Schoolmaster, that can be devised, for such Kings, as think this world ordained for them, without controlment to turn it upside down at their own pleasure.*

Now concerning the triumph of *L. Aemilius Paulus*; it was in all points like unto that of *T. Quintius Flaminius*: though far more glorious, in regard of the King's own person, that was led along therein, as part of his own spoils; and in regard likewise both of the Conquest and of the Booty. So great was the quantity of Gold and

Silver carried by *Paulus* into the *Roman* Treasury, that from thenceforth, until the civil Wars, which followed upon the death of *Julius Caesar*, the Estate had no need to burden itself with any Tribute. Yet was this noble Triumph likely to have been hindered by the soldiers; who grudged at their General, for not having dealt more bountifully with them. But the Princes of the Senate overruled the People and Soldiers herein, and brought them to reason by severe exhortations. Thus *Paulus* enjoyed as much honour of his victory as men could give. Nevertheless, it pleased God to take away from him his two remaining sons, that were not given in adoption: of which, the one died five days before the Triumph; the other, three days after it. This loss he bore wisely: and told the People, That he hoped to see the Commonwealth flourish in a continuance of prosperity; since the joy of his victory was requited with his own private calamity, instead of the public.

About the same time *Octavius* the Admiral, who had brought *Perseus* out of *Samothrace*: and *Anicius* the Praetor, who had conquered *Illyria*, and taken King *Gentius* prisoner; made their several triumphs. The glory of which magnificent spectacles; together with the confluence of Embassages from all parts; and Kings, either visiting the Imperial City, or offering to visit her, and do their duties in person; were enough to say unto *Rome, Sume superbiam, Take upon thee the Majesty, that thy deserts have purchased.*

By this which we have already set down, is seen the beginning and end of the three first Monarchies of the world; whereof the Founders and Erectors thought, that they could never have ended. That of *Rome* which made the fourth, was also at this time almost at the highest. We have left it flourishing in the middle of the field; having rooted up, or cut down, all that kept it from the eyes and admiration of the world. But after some continuance, it shall begin to lose the beauty it had; the storms of ambition shall beat her great boughs and branches one against another; her leaves shall fall off, her limbs wither, and a rabble of barbarous Nations enter the field, and cut her down.

Now these great Kings, and conquering Nations, have been the subject of those ancient Histories, which have been preserved, and yet remain among us; and withal of so many tragical Poets, as in the persons of powerful Princes and other mighty men have complained against Infidelity, Time, Destiny, and most of all against the Variable success of worldly things, and Instability of Fortune. To these undertakings the greatest Lords of the world have been stirred up, rather by the desire of *Fame*, which plougheth up the Air, and soweth in the Wind; than by the affection of bearing rule, which draweth after it so much vexation, and so many cares. And that this is true, the good advice of *Cineas* to *Pyrrhus* proves. And certainly, as Fame hath often been dangerous to the living, so is it to the dead of no use at all; because separate from knowledge. Which were it otherwise, and the extreme ill bargain of buying this lasting discourse, understood by them which are dissolved; they themselves would then rather have wished, to have stolen out of the world without noise; than to be put in mind, that they have purchased the report of their actions in the world, by rapine, oppression and cruelty, by giving in spoil the innocent and labouring soul to the idle and insolent. and by having emptied the Cities of the world of their ancient Inhabitants, and filled them again with so many and so variable sorts of sorrows.

Since the fall of the *Roman Empire* (omitting that of the Germans, which had neither greatness nor continuance) there hath been no State fearful in the East, but that of the *Turk*; nor in the West any Prince that hath spread his wings far over his nest, but the *Spaniard*; who since the time that *Ferdinand* expelled the *Moors* out of *Granada*, have made many attempts to make themselves Masters of all Europe. And it is true, that by the treasures of both *Indies*, and by the many Kingdoms which they possess in *Europe*, they are at this day the most powerful. But as the *Turk* is now counterpoised by the *Persian*, so instead of so many Millions as have been spent by the *English*, *French*, and *Netherlands* in a defensive war, and in diversions against them, it is easy to demonstrate, that with the charge of two hundred thousand pound continued but for two years or three at the most, they may not only be persuaded to live in peace, but all their swelling and overflowing streams may be brought back into their natural channels and old banks. These two Nations, I say, are at this day the most eminent, and to be regarded; the one seeking to root out the Christian Religion altogether, the other the truth and sincere profession thereof, the one to join all *Europe* to *Asia*, the other the rest of all *Europe* to *Spain*.

For the rest, if we seek a reason of the succession and continuance of this boundless ambition in mortal men, we may add to that which hath been already said; That the Kings and Princes of the world have always laid before them, the actions, but not the ends, of those great Ones which preceded them. They are always transported with the glory of the one, but they never mind the misery of the other, till they find the experience in themselves. They neglect the advice of God, while they enjoy life, or hope it; but they follow the counsel of Death, upon his first approach. It is he that puts into man all the wisdom of the world, without speaking a word; which God with all the words of his Law, promises, or threats, doth not infuse. *Death* which hateth and destroyeth man, is believed; God, which hath made him and loves him, is always deferred: *I have considered* (saith *Solomon*) *all the works that are under the Sun, and behold, all is vanity and vexation of spirit*: but who believes it, till Death tells it us? It was Death, which opening the conscience of *Charles* the fifth, made him enjoin his son *Philip* to restore *Navarre*; and King *Francis* the first of *France*, to command that justice should be done upon the Murderers of the Protestants in *Merindol* and *Cabrieres*, which till then he neglected. It is therefore Death alone that can suddenly make man to know himself. He tells the proud and insolent, that they are but Abjects, and humbles them at the instant; makes them cry, complain, and repent, yea, even to hate their forepassed happiness. He takes the account of the rich, and proves him a beggar; a naked beggar, which hath interest in nothing, but in the gravel that fills his mouth. He holds a Glass before the eyes of the most beautiful, and makes them see therein, their deformity and rottenness; and they acknowledge it.

O eloquent, just and mighty Death! whom none could advise, thou hast persuaded; that none hath dared, thou hast done; and whom all the world hath flattered, thou only hath cast out of the world and despised: thou hast drawn together all the far stretched greatness, all the pride, cruelty, and ambition of man, and covered it all over with these two narrow words, *Hic jacet*.

Lastly, whereas this Book, by the title it hath, calls itself *The first part of the General History of the World*, implying a *Second*, and *Third* Volume; which I also intended, and have hewn out; besides many other discouragements, persuading my silence; it hath pleased God to take that glorious *Prince* out of the world, to whom they were directed; whose unspeakable and never enough lamented loss, hath taught me to say with Job, *Versa est in Luctum Cithara mea, et Organum meum in vocem flentium*.

Letters

To Sir Robert Cecil: July 1592

I pray be a mean to her Majesty for the signing of the bills for the guards' coats, which are to be made now for the Progress, and which the Clerk of the Check hath importuned me to write for.

My heart was never broken till this day, that I hear the Queen goes away so far off — whom I have followed so many years with so great love and desire, in so many journeys, and am now left behind her, in a dark prison all alone. While she was yet near at hand, that I might hear of her once in two or three days, my sorrows were the less: but even now my heart is cast into the depth of all misery. I that was wont to behold her riding like Alexander, hunting like Diana, walking like Venus, the gentle wind blowing her fair hair about her pure cheeks, like a nymph; sometime sitting in the shade like a Goddess; sometime singing like an angel; sometime playing like Orpheus. Behold the sorrow of this world! Once amiss, hath bereaved me of all. O Glory, that only shineth in misfortune, what is become of thy assurance? All wounds have scars, but that of fantasy; all affections their relenting, but that of womankind. Who is the judge of friendship, but adversity? Or when is grace witnessed, but in offences? There were no divinity, but by reason of compassion; for revenges are brutish and mortal. All those times past — the loves, the sithes, the sorrows, the desires, can they not weigh down one frail misfortune? Cannot one drop of gall be hidden in so great heaps of sweetness? I may then conclude, *Spes et fortuna, valete*. She is gone, in whom I trusted, and of me hath not one thought of mercy, nor any respect of that that was. Do with me now, therefore, what you list. I am more weary of life than they are desirous I should perish; which if it had been for her, as it is by her, I had been too happily born.

Yours, not worthy any name or title,

W.R.

To Sir Robert Cecil: written at sea, ?1594

I am sorry to be now so near that my letters may come to your hands. But this unfortunate year is such as those that were ready and at sea two months before us are beaten back again and distressed. This long stay hath made me a poor man, the year far spent, and what shall become of us, God knows. The body is wasted with toil, the purse with charge, and all things worn. Only the mind is indifferent to good fortune or adversity.

There is no news from hence worth the writing. If I were more fortunate, I should be the more worth the commanding; as I am, you may dispose of me; and thus, for the present, I leave you to all good fortune, and my self *quo me Fortuna retrudet*.

Yours ever to do you service,
W. Ralegh

[PS] I pray be gracious to my friends in my absence, and not too credulous. And further that you will be pleased, if any of my officers be suitors unto you in my behalf, that you will vouchsafe your favour towards them. I pray excuse me to my lord your father, having nothing worth his reading to write of.

To Sir Robert Cecil: on the death of Cecil's wife, 1596–7

Because I know not how you dispose of yourself, I forbear to visit you, preferring your pleasure before mine own desire. I had rather be with you now than at any other time, if I could thereby either take off from you the burden of your sorrows, or lay the greater part thereof on mine own heart. In the meantime I would but mind you of this, that you should not overshadow your wisdom with passion, but look aright into things as they are.

There is no man sorry for death itself, but only for the time of death; every one knowing that it is a bond never forfeited to God. If then we know the same to be certain and inevitable, we ought withal to take the time of his arrival in as good part as the knowledge; and not to lament at the instant of every seeming adversity, which, we are assured, have been on the way towards us from the beginning. It appertaineth to every man of a wise and worthy spirit to draw together into sufferance the unknown future of the known present; looking no less with the eyes of the mind than those of the body — the one beholding afar off, and the other at hand — that those things of this world in which we live be not strange unto us, when they approach, as to feebleness, which is moved with novelties. But that, like true men, participating immortality, and know our destinies to be of God, we do then make our estates and wishes, our fortunes and desires, all one.

It is true that you have lost a good and virtuous wife, and myself an honourable friend and kinswoman. But there was a time when she was unknown to you, for whom you then lamented not. She is now no more yours, nor of your acquaintance, but immortal, and not needing of knowing your love or sorrow. Therefore you shall but grieve for that which now is as then it was when not yours, only bettered by the difference in this, that she hath passed the wearisome journey of this dark world, and hath possession of her inheritance.

She hath left behind her the fruit of her love, for whose sake you ought to care for yourself, that you leave them not without a guide, and not by grieving to repine at His will that gave them you, or by sorrowing to dry up your own times that ought to establish them.

I believe it that sorrows are dangerous companions, converting bad into evil and evil into worse, and do no other service than multiply harms. They are the treasures of weak hearts and of the foolish. The mind that entertaineth them is as the earth and dust whereon sorrows and adversities of the world do, as the beasts of the field, tread, trample, and defile. The mind of man is that part of God which is in us, which, by how much it is subject to passion, by so much it is farther from Him that gave it us. Sorrows draw not the dead to life, but the living to death. And, if I were myself to advise myself in the like, I would never forget my patience till I saw all and the worst of evils, and so grieve for all at once, lest, lamenting for some one, another might not remain in the power of Destiny of greater discomfort.

Yours ever beyond the power of words to utter,

W. Ralegh

To Lady Ralegh: the night before he expected to be put to death, 1603

You shall now receive, dear wife, my last words in these my last lines; my love I send you, that you may keep it when I am dead, and my counsel, that you may remember it when I am no more. I would not with my last will present you with sorrows, dear Bess. Let them go into the grave with me and be buried in the dust. And, seeing it is not the will of God that ever I shall see you in this life, bear my destruction gently, and with a heart like thy self.

First, I send you all the thanks my heart can conceive, or my pen express, for your many troubles and cares taken for me, which, though they have not taken effect as you wished, yet my debt is to you never the less; but pay it I never shall in this world.

Secondly, I beseech you, for the love you bare me living, that you do not hide yourself many days, but by your travail seek to help your miserable fortunes, and the right of your poor child. Your mourning cannot avail me that am but dust.

You shall understand that my lands were conveyed to my child *bona fide*. The writings were drawn at midsummer was twelve months; my honest cousin Brett can testify as much, and Dalberry too can remember somewhat therein. And I trust my blood will quench their malice that desire my slaughter, and that they will not also seek to kill you and yours with extreme poverty. To what friend to direct thee I know not, for all mine have left me in the true time of trial; and I plainly perceive that my death was determined from the first day. Most sorry I am, as God knows, that being thus surprised with death, I can leave you no better estate: I meant you all my office of wines, or that I could purchase by selling it, half my stuff and jewels — but some few for my boy. But God hath prevented all my determinations, the great God that worketh all in all. If you can live free from want, care for no more, for the rest is but vanity. Love God, and begin betimes to repose yourself on Him. Therein you shall find true and lasting riches, and endless comfort. For the rest, when you have travailed and wearied your thoughts on all sorts of worldly cogitations, you shall sit down by sorrow in the end. Teach your son also to serve and fear God, while he is young, that the fear of God may grow up in him. Then will God be a husband unto you, and a father unto him; a husband and a father which can never be taken from you.

Bailey oweth me £200 and Adrian £600. In Jersey, also, I have much owing me. The arrearages of the wines will pay my debts; and, howsoever, for my soul's health, I beseech you pay all poor men.

When I am gone, no doubt you shall be sought unto by many, for the world thinks that I was very rich. But take heed of the pretences of men, and of their affections, for they last but in honest and worthy men. And no greater misery can befall you in this life than to become a prey, and after to be despised. I speak it, God knows, not to dissuade you from marriage — for that will be best for you, both in respect of God and the world. As for me, I am no more yours, nor you mine. Death hath cut us asunder; and God hath divided me from the world, and you from me.

Remember your poor child for his father's sake, who chose you and loved you in his happiest times.

Get those letters, if it be possible, which I writ to the Lords, wherein I sued for my life; but God knoweth that it was for you and yours that I desired it. But it is true that I disdain myself for begging it. And know it, dear wife, that your son is the child of a true man, and one, who in his own respect, despiseth Death, and all his misshapen and ugly forms.

I cannot write much. God knows how hardly I steal this time when all sleep, and it is time to separate my thoughts from the world. Beg my dead body, which living was denied you, and either lay it at Sherborne, if the land continue, or in Exeter church, by my father and mother. I can write no more. Time and Death call me away.

The everlasting, infinite, powerful, and inscrutable God, that almighty God, that is goodness itself, mercy itself, the true life and light, keep you and yours, and have mercy on me, and teach me to forgive my persecutors and false accusers; and send us to meet in His glorious kingdom. My true wife, farewell. Bless my poor boy. Pray for me. My true God hold you both in his arms.

Written with the dying hand of sometime thy husband, but now, alas, overthrown

yours that was; but now not my own.

W: R:

To Lady Ralegh: 22 March, 1618

I was loath to write, because I knew not how to comfort you; and God knows, I never knew what sorrow meant till now. All that I can say to you is, that you must obey the will and providence of God; and remember that the Queen's majesty bare the loss of Prince Henry with a magnanimous heart, and the Lady Harington of her only son. Comfort your heart, dearest Bess, I shall sorrow for us both. I shall sorrow the less because I have not long to sorrow, because not long to live. I refer you to Mr Secretary Winwood's letter, who will give you a copy of it, if you send for it. Therein you shall know what hath passed. I have written that letter, for my brains are broken, and it is a torment for me to write, and especially of misery. I have desired Mr Secretary to give my Lord Carew a copy of his letter. I have cleansed my ship of sick men, and sent them home. I hope God will send us somewhat ere we return. Commend me to all at Lothbury. You shall hear from me, if I live, from the Newfoundland, where I mean to make clean my ships and revictual, for I have tobacco enough to pay for it. The Lord bless and comfort you, that you may bear patiently the death of your valiant son.

22d of March, from the Isle of Christopher,

Yours,

W. Ralegh

[PS] I protest before the majesty of God, that as Sir Francis Drake and Sir John Hawkins died heartbroken when they failed of their enterprise, I could willingly do the like, did I not contend against sorrow for your sake, in hope to provide somewhat for you, and to comfort and relieve you. If I live to return, resolve yourself that it is the care for you that hath strengthened my heart. It is true that Keymis might have gone directly to the mine, and meant it. But, after my son's death, he made them to believe he knew not the way, and excused himself upon the want of water in the river, and, counterfeiting many impediments, left it unfound. When he came back, I told him that he had undone me, and that my credit was lost for ever.

He answered, that when my son was lost and that he left me so weak that he resolved not to find me alive, he had no reason to enrich a company of rascals, who, after my son's death, made no account of him. He farther told me that the English sent up into Guiana could hardly defend the Spanish town of St. Thomas which they had taken, and therefore for them to pass through thick woods it was impossible; and more impossible to have victuals brought them into the mountains. And it is true that the governor, Diego Polempque, and four other captains being slain, of which my son Wat slew one; Plessington, Wat's sergeant, and John of Morocco, one of his men, slew other two. I say five of them slain in the entrance of the town, the rest went off in a whole body, and took more care to defend the passages to their mines (of which they had three within a league of the town, besides a mine that was about five miles off) than they did of the town itself.

Yet Keymis, at the first, was resolved to go to the mine; but when he had come to the bank-side to the land, he had two of his men slain outright from the bank, and six other hurt, and Captain Thornix shot in the head, of which wound, and the accidents thereof, he hath pined away these twelve weeks.

Now when Keymis came back and gave me the former reasons which moved him not to open the mine — the one, the death of my son; the second, the weakness of the English, and their impossibilities to work and be victualled; a third, that it were a folly to discover it for the Spaniards; and last, both my weakness and my being unpardoned — and that I rejected all these arguments, and told him that I must leave him to himself, to resolve it to the king and the State, he shut up himself into his cabin, and shot himself with a pocket pistol, which brake one of his ribs; and finding that it had not prevailed, he thrust a long knife under his short ribs up to the handle, and died. Thus much I have writ to Mr Secretary, to whose letters I refer you. But because I think my friends will rather hearken after you than any other to know the truth, I did after the sealing break open your letter again, to let you know in brief the state of that business, which I pray you impart to my Lord of Northumberland, and Sil. Scory, and to Sir John Leigh.

For the rest, there was never poor man so exposed to the slaughter as I was; for being commanded upon my allegiance to set down, not only the country, but the very river by which I was to enter it, to name my ships, number my men, and my artillery — this was sent by the Spanish ambassador to his master, the King of Spain. The king wrote his letters to all parts of the Indies, especially to the governor Polemque of Guiana, El Dorado, and Trinidado; of which the first letter bare date the 19th of March, 1617, at Madrill, when I had not yet left the Thames; which letter I have sent Mr Secretary. I have also two other letters of the king's which I reserve, and of the council. The king also sent a commission to levy 300 soldiers out of his garrisons of Nuevo Reigno de Granadoes or Porto Rico, with ten pieces of brass ordnance to entertain us. He also prepared an armada by sea to set upon us. It were too long to tell you how we were preserved. If I live, I shall make it known. My brains are broken, and I cannot write much. I live yet, and I have told you why. Whitney, for whom I sold my plate at Plymouth, and to whom I gave more credit and countenance than all the captains of my fleet, ran from me at Granadoes, and Woolaston with him; so as I am now but five ships, and one of those I have sent home — my fly-boat — and in her a rabble of idle rascals, which I know will not spare to wound me; but I care not. I am sure there is never a base slave in the fleet hath taken the pains and care that I have done; hath slept so little and travailled so much. My friends will not believe them; and for the rest I care not. God in heaven bless you and strengthen your heart.

Your
W. Ralegh

Lady Ralegh to Sir Nicholas Carew, 30 October, 1618

I desire, good brother, that you will be pleased to let me bury the worthy body of my noble husband, Sir Walter Ralegh, in your church at Beddington, where I desire to be buried. The Lords have given me his dead body, though they denied me his life. This night he shall be brought you with two or three of my men. Let me hear presently. God hold me in my wits.

Notes

Introduction

1 Ralegh describes himself as a 'very ill footman' in the *Discovery of Guiana*, and apologizes for his lack of Hebrew knowledge towards the end of the Preface to the *History of the World*.
2 In *The Arte of English Poesie* (1589), Bk I, ch. 31.
3 The quotations come from a sonnet Spenser wrote 'To the right honourable and valorous knight, Sir Walter Ralegh', and from the introduction to Book III of *The Faerie Queene*.
4 In *Forms of Discovery* (New York, 1967), p. 23.
5 In *Elizabethan Poetry*, ed. J. R. Brown and B. Harris (London, 1960), p. 89.
6 In 'The Poetry of Ralegh', *Rev. Eng. Lit.*, I (1960), p. 19.
7 In her *Muses Library* edition of the poems (London, 1951), p. 140.
8 Drummond reported Jonson as having claimed that he had written a draft of the Punic war narrative which Ralegh 'altered and set in his book'.
9 See George Bruner Parks, *Richard Hakluyt and the English Voyages* (New York, 1928), pp. 138–9.
10 A Theban general who died fighting the Spartans in 362 BC.
11 See *The Letters and Speeches of Oliver Cromwell*, ed. S. C. Lomas (New York, 1904), vol. 2, p. 54.
12 In Arnold's inaugural lecture at Oxford he contrasted Thucydides' introduction to the *Peloponnesian War* with Ralegh's *History*, entirely to the latter's detriment.
13 For an account of Ralegh's influence on Milton, see George Wesley Whiting, *Milton's Literary Milieu* (New York, 1964), pp. 15–35.
14 Ralegh's own phrase, in the *History*, I, 2:2.

Poems

In commendation of 'The Steel Glass' 'The Steel Glass' (1576) is a poem by George Gascoigne. Ralegh praises the sardonic tone of Gascoigne's satire (an early model for 'The Lie'?); and his general admiration for the poet is borne out by his adoption of Gascoigne's motto for himself: 'Tam marti quam mercurio' ('as much a soldier as an artist').
4 *percase* perhaps
13 *censure* judgment

An epitaph upon Sir Philip Sidney Sidney died at Zutphen in 1586. This poem was first published in *The Phoenix Nest* (1593).
11 *seeled* blindfold
17 Philip II of Spain was Sidney's godfather.
20 *sort* consort
26 *treat* deal: Sidney acted as the royal ambassador to the Emperor Rudolf.
32 i.e. Elizabeth I
43 *dure* last
52 *spright* spirit
57 The Spanish Count Hannibal Gonzago also died at Zutphen. See the *History* below, pp. 257–8 for Ralegh's account of the deaths of Scipio and Hannibal in the same year.

A farewell to false Love The first four stanzas are from William Byrd's *Psalmes, Sonets, and songs* (1588); the fifth is supplied in *MS. Rawlinson Poetry 85.*
25 *sith* since
trains courses of action
27 *bewrayed* betrayed

The excuse From *The Phoenix Nest*; there are many manuscript copies.

Praised be Diana's fair and harmless light From *The Phoenix Nest*. Diana, the goddess of the moon, is an image of Elizabeth I.
10 *in aye* for ever
18 *Circes* Circe, the sorceress who transformed men into beasts.

Like to a hermit poor From *The Phoenix Nest*; this is a translation from the French poet Desportes. For the French original and another Elizabethan translation, by Thomas Lodge, see Agnes Latham's 'Muses Library' edition of Ralegh's poems, p. 107. Set to music by Ferrabosco, this became one of the most popular seventeenth century songs: one of Pepys' acquaintances talks of the impossibility of introducing 'good music' into England, 'nay, says "Hermit poor" and "Chevy Chase" was all the music we had' (12 Feb. 1667).
3 *recure* heal
10 *stay* stand firm

Farewell to the Court From *The Phoenix Nest*. The title comes from a version of the poem in *Le Prince d'Amour* (1660). Ralegh quotes the refrain of this poem in 'The Ocean to Cynthia', 120–4; and in the *History*, see below, p. 155.

A vision upon 'The Faerie Queene' This and another sonnet were printed at the end of the first edition of Spenser's poem (1590). Spenser describes Ralegh's visit to him in Ireland in *Colin Clouts come home againe*, which he dedicated to Ralegh.
1 *Laura* the addressee of Petrarch's love poems.

The advice From *Le Prince d'Amour*, where it is attributed to W.R. There are two anonymous manuscript versions, both of which describe it as addressed to one of Elizabeth's maids of honour, Anne Vavasour.

The nymph's reply From *Englands Helicon* (1600). This the best known of the many answers to Marlowe's poem 'The passionate Shepheard to his love', its last line echoing Marlowe's opening line 'Come live with me and be my love'.
14 *poesies* combining, as was common, the senses of *poesy* and *posy*.

A poesy to prove affection is not love From Francis Davison's *A Poetical Rhapsody* (1602). *Affection* has a stronger sense here than in modern usage, its meaning extending as far as 'passion' and 'lust'. It is one of Ralegh's key words in poetry and prose.
1 *conceit* infatuation: the poem uses *affection*, *desire*, and *conceit* virtually as synonyms.
4 *his* i.e. conceit's
29 *fond* foolish

Sir Walter Ralegh to Queen Elizabeth From *MS. Additional 22602* (Brit. Mus.). There are many manuscript versions of this poem, most of which conflate it with a longer poem, 'Wrong not, dear Empress of my Heart' probably by Robert Ayton. See Charles B. Gullans, 'Ralegh and Ayton: The Disputed Authorship of "Wrong Not Sweete Empress of My Heart" ', *Stud. Bib.*, XIII, 1960.

Nature, that washed her hands in milk From *MS. Harley 6917*, where it is titled 'A Poem of Sir Walter Rawleighs'; there are other manuscript versions, and the final stanza, with an added couplet, makes up the last poem in this selection.
26 *discovers* often appears as *discolours* in other mss. versions.

As you came from the holy land From *MS. Rawlinson Poetry 85*. For the kind of popular ballad this is based on, cp. Ophelia's song in *Hamlet* (IV.v.22): 'How should I your true-love know/From another one?/By his cockle hat and staff,/And his handle shoon'.
31 *when he list* when he wishes to be
33 *dureless* ephemeral
40 *conceits* fantasies
41 *true* a ms. addition

If Cynthia be a Queen The first of the Cynthia poems in *MS. Hatfield* (Cecil Papers, 144), all in Ralegh's own hand. For an attempt to explicate this poem, see A. M. Buckan, 'Ralegh's *Cynthia* — Facts or Legend', *Mod. Lang. Q.*, I, 1940.

My body in the walls captived From *MS. Hatfield*, where it comes between 'If Cynthia be a Queen' and 'The Ocean to Cynthia'. Biographical readings date it in 1592, when Ralegh was in the Tower because of the Queen's jealousy at his affair with Elizabeth Throckmorton. Such a reading makes *her* in line 4 refer at least as much to Elizabeth I as to *envy* in line 2.
6 *erst* before

The Ocean to Cynthia From *MS. Hatfield*. This is the poem of Ralegh's (or part of it) which Spenser three times refers to; in the *Faerie Queene's* sonnet of dedication to Ralegh, the introduction to Book III of *The Faerie Queene*, and in *Colin Clouts come home again* (1595). In this last poem he describes Ralegh as 'the shepherd of the sea', and describes his poem like this:

> His song was all a lamentable lay,
> Of great unkindness, and of usage hard,
> Of Cynthia the Lady of the sea,
> Which from her presence faultless him debarred. (164–7)

Cynthia is clearly Elizabeth I; and the poem, as Spenser indicates, is a sustained complaint at the way she has treated Ralegh. Whether there were twenty books before this one (or ten, because there is doubt whether the number in the title should be read as 21st or 11th) is unknown; but since this fragment has no narrative structure it is impossible to envisage what they might have contained. For attempts to explicate what has survived, see in particular: Donald Davie, 'A Reading of "The Ocean's Love to Cynthia" ', in *Elizabethan Poetry*, ed. J. R. Brown and B. Harris (London, 1960); Joyce Horner, 'The Large Landscape: A Study of Certain Images in Ralegh', *Essays in Crit*. V, 1955; and Michael L. Johnson, 'Some Problems of Unity in Sir Walter Ralegh's *The Oceans Love to Cynthia*', *Stud. in Eng. Lit.*, XIV, 1974. See also K. Duncan-Jones, 'The Date of Ralegh's "21th and Last Book of the Ocean to Scinthia" ', *Rev. of Eng. Stud*. n.s. XXI, 1970, for the view that Ralegh wrote the poem in the last years of his life.

The poem is normally divided into four (and some three) line stanzas: I have preferred an arrangement as close to its ms. form as possible. Stanza division makes it neater to look at but it impedes the cumulative effect of the complaint.

37 *invention* source of creation
40 *transpersant* piercing through everything
49 *sithes* sighs
95 *weal* prosperity
112 *angelic* the ms. has 'angellike': perhaps the modernization should be *angel-like*.
116 *embalmed* anointed
123–4 From *Farewell to the Court*, see above, p. 30.
125 *sorrowful success* the sorrow which will follow
129 *recure* remedy
192 *vade* fade
199 *dure* last
201 *wounders* perhaps could be modernized to *wonders*, but cp. l. 197.
232 It is possible that *lives* also governs *thrall* (and should therefore be modernized as *lives*').
250 *reaves* steals
271 *Belphoebe* a character in *The Faerie Queene*, here representing Diana, Elizabeth, and the moon.
341 *sith* since
351 *sithing* sighing
365 *painful* produced by effort

447 Perhaps should be modernized as *injury's effect.*
471 *sorrow-worren* sorrow-worn
473 *rind* the original reads *vinde*
490 *erst* before
505 *brast* broken

The beginning of the 22nd Book From *MS. Hatfield*; the title is Ralegh's own. He reworked this fragment into the first draft of the *Petition to Queen Anne*, above p. 60.

Now we have present made This poem was first published by George Seddon in *The Illustrated London News*, 28 February 1953. It was discovered in a vellum-bound commonplace book, which also contains geographical notes, maps, and a library list. The handwriting has been identified as Ralegh's. The subject of the poem seems to be the death of Elizabeth I.
4 *vade* fade
10 *lasteth* the ms. may well read *lusteth*
18 *quintessential* most pure
19 *heavens* is the object of *binds*, not the subject.
24 *Or* this is certainly the ms. reading, but *our* would fit better.
29 *indite* write

The lie From the 1611 edition of Francis Davison's *A Poetical Rhapsody*. There are many ms. versions of the poem, and it was first printed in the 1608 edition of Davison's collection. A good number of the manuscript versions attribute the poem to Ralegh, often with substantial additions or variations in their text. I have made the following emendations to Davison's text: 1.64 *so* instead of *too*; 1.70 *preferreth* instead of *preferred*; 1.75 *although* instead of *but*. These all have ms. support. *To give the lie* means to accuse someone to his face of a falsehood.
16 *a faction* i.e. a seditious party; some texts have *affection*, a very possible reading, given Ralegh's fondness for the word.
25 *brave it* show off
33 *metes* measures out
44 *tickle* precarious
50 *prevention* anticipation

To his son From *MS. Additional 22229* (Brit. Mus.). The title is the one given in two other manuscript versions of the poem. In place of the couplet, one of these (*MS. Malone 19*) reads simply 'God bless thee child'.

The passionate man's pilgrimage From *Diaphantus, or The Passions of Love . . . By An. Sc. Gentleman. Whereunto is added, The passionate mans Pilgrimage . . .* (1604). For a strong argument that this poem is not by Ralegh, but must instead be by a Catholic poet, see P. Edwards, 'Who wrote "The passionate man's pilgrimage"?', *Eng. Lit. Renaiss.*, 4, 1974, 83–97. There are many manuscript versions, with many possible variant readings; some have subtitles indicating that this was written the day before Ralegh's intended execution in 1603.

1 *scallop-shell* the pilgrim's badge: the rest of the stanza lists other items taken on pilgrimage.
3 *scrip* wallet
5 *gage* pledge
7 *balmer* both anointer and embalmer seem to be senses at work here.
9 *white palmer* a *palmer* is a pilgrim; some versions of the poem have *quiet* instead of *white*.
25 *suckets* sweets
42 *angels* one of the commonest Elizabethan puns, on the gold coin called an angel.
48 *proceeder* one involved in the process of law
49 *movest* propose as a motion to the court
50 *palms* note the pun: a different kind of *palmer*
55 *stroke* a pun here too: the stroke of noon and the stroke of the axe.

On the life of man From Orlando Gibbons' *The First Set of Madrigals and Mottets* (1612). Five manuscript versions assign the poem to Ralegh; more than twenty have it as anonymous or as the work of other poets. There is a huge number of variant readings in these mss. (e.g. several have *tragedy* instead of *comedy* in line 4, *scorching sun* in line 7, and *not in jest* instead of *that's no jest* in line 10.
2 *division* as a musical term, in which a succession of long notes is modulated into several short ones.
3 *tiring houses* dressing-rooms

To the translator of Lucan From Sir Arthur Gorges' *Lucans Pharsalia* (1614). This sonnet prefaces Gorges' translation of Lucan. Gorges was Ralegh's cousin, and his companion on the expedition to the Azores in 1597. In the couplet Ralegh plays on the two senses of *translation*: one the rendering into English, the other the reincarnation of Lucan in the person of Gorges.

Translations from the 'History of the World' Ralegh's *History* is studded with fine translations from classical writers, equal in quality with the best Renaissance translations. Further examples can be seen in the selections from the *History*, on pp. 153, 156, 157, 171, 173, 187.

First draft of the petition to Queen Anne From *MS. Additional 27407* (Brit. Mus.) Agnes Latham takes this to be an intermediate stage between the Hatfield fragment of the *22nd Book of the Ocean to Cynthia* and the next poem, *The Petition to Queen Anne*.

Petition to the Queen, 1618 From *MS. Drummond*, in Drummond's hand. Agnes Latham suggests 1603 as a date more relevant to the detail in the poem.
14 *descrived* described
34–5 *the miss/Of her we had* i.e. Elizabeth I

Even such is Time From *Cinq Cents de Colbert, 467*, in the Bibliothèque Nationale, transcribed by H. Bibas in the *Times Literary Supplement*, 13

October 1932. There are many manuscript versions, with variant readings and titles, most of the latter referring the poem to the night before Ralegh's execution. The poem is made up of the final stanza of *Nature that washed her hands in milk*, with the change of the first three words (for 'Oh cruel Time') and the addition of the final couplet.

The last fight of the Revenge:
Ralegh's account of Grenville's rash battle against a Spanish fleet in the late summer of 1591 was his first piece of published prose, appearing anonymously in the same year. It was attributed to Ralegh by Richard Hakluyt when he reprinted it in his collection of voyages in 1599. The text here follows the original edition.

p. 65 [title] *this last summer* Hakluyt changes this to *the last of August 1591*.
Grenville Ralegh's spelling is *Grinvile*.
advisoes counsels
240 sail Hakluyt corrects to *140 sail*.
Argosies . . . Carracks . . . Florentines . . . Hulks large, lightly-armed merchant vessels
Galliass a heavy, low built vessel, impelled by sails and oars
squibs fireships

66 *Cockboat* a small ship's boat
billets piece of wood used for fuel
the bark Ralegh a ship built by Ralegh in 1583

67 *pestered* in disorder
rummaging putting the cargo in order
Admiral the chief ship
the master the ship's master, i.e. navigation officer
on his weather bow to the windward of him
sprang their luff brought their ship's head closer to the wind

68 *high carged* meaning obscure: perhaps it means that the ship was built up high above the water.
laid the Revenge aboard drew alongside the *Revenge*
Bertendona Ralegh's spelling is *Brittan Dona*. Martin de Bertendona had fought with the Spanish Armada. His ship, the *St. Philip*, was wrecked by Ralegh in revenge for the *Revenge*, in the attack on Cadiz harbour in 1596.
chase forward guns
crossbarshot cannon balls with a bar through the middle, with the purpose of damaging masts and rigging.

69 *a dressing* having his wounds dressed
composition peace terms

70 *fifteen thousand men* Hakluyt corrects to *above ten thousand men*.

71 *swounded* fainted
approved shown
Flyboats frigates
two thousand Haklyut corrects to *one thousand*.
recovered the road reached the off shore anchorage

72 *to keep the weather gauge of* to be to the windward of
runagate renegade

75 *Target* shield

75 *and might have been won . . . persuaded thereunto* Ralegh means that when Christianizing attempts were made, they were almost totally successful.

The Discovery of Guiana:
The *Discovery* was first published in 1596; there were four English editions in the same year, and it was soon translated into Latin and other European languages. I have modernized some of the place names (e.g. *Orinoco* for Ralegh's *Orenoque*) but have kept Ralegh's forms for those which will be familiar to the reader and which might mark a difference in pronunciation (e.g. *Trinidado, Amazones*). Ralegh's Guiana, the Orinoco basin, is part of modern Venezuela. As well as the omissions signalled in the text, I have left out the Preface 'To the Reader', which comes immediately after the Epistle Dedicatory.

76 *Charles Howard* and *Sir Robert Cecil* Howard was Lord High Admiral. Cecil, the son of Lord Burleigh, was at this time of his life, Ralegh's friend. Ralegh grew to mistrust him, and possibly wrote a bitter epigram on his death, which included the lines

> For Oblation to Pan his custom was thus,
> He first gave a Trifle, then offered up us;
> And through his false worship such power he did gain,
> As kept him o'th' Mountain, and us on the plain.

adventures investments in the voyage
factors agents
colour pretext
bodies One early edition of the *Discovery* reads *boies* (i.e. *boys*).
77 *constructions* misinterpretations
journies of picorie robbing and pillaging
79 *I have written a particular treatise* This has not survived.
Cassiqui the caçiques: war lords of Guiana
foreslow neglect
80 *the Burlings, and the rock* the Isles of Berlengas and Cape Roca, on the coast of Portugal.
oysters upon the branches of the trees In the West Indies the mangrove tree grows as far down as the low water mark, and often supports dozens of oysters which have attached themselves to it.
81 *abundance of stone pitch* in the asphalt lake of Trinidad, near Tierra de Brea.
cassavi manioc, the source of cassava bread for the Indians, and our tapioca.
Magazine storehouse
82 *bruit* rumour
arquebus musket
cassado finishing stroke
83 *interessed* actively engaged
Castellani i.e. the Spaniards (from Castile)
84 *pestered* crowded
85 *mare caspium* the Caspian Sea
86 *budgets* sacks
billets bars

89 *brigantines* small vessels, equipped for rowing or sailing
those warlike women Ralegh went deeper into the possible existence of the Amazons in the *History* (IV.ii.15).
90 *spleen stones* Ralegh brought back a number of medicinal items from Guiana which he often prescribed for friends' illnesses.
91 *delivered* expressed his opinion
92 *at adventure* at risk
banks benches
disembogue come out at the mouth of the river
93 *conceit* opinion
94 *yielding for reason* arguing that
presently immediately
so main a cry shouting so loudly
handfasted seized hold of
95 *deliberate* careful and slow
palmitos palm trees
96 *spell* relieve
97 *volumes of herbals* treatises on plants
watchet light blue
case situation
98 *Lagartos* crocodiles
99 *Cavallero* gentleman
100 *prevented* anticipated
opus laboris but not ingenii a work of physical effort, not intelligence
101 *Pina* pineapple
102 *Tortuga* turtle
next way shortest route
digested and purged heated and purified
104 *champaign* level, flat country
105 *vulgar* familiar to all
continent mainland
106 *Renocero* rhinoceros
to wind to blow
110 *Marquesites* fool's gold (iron pyrites)
Bristol Diamond a kind of gem stone
111 *Mandeville* Mandeville's *Travels*, written in French, appeared in the second half of the fourteenth century, and were translated into English at least as early as the beginning of the fifteenth century.
112 *sensibly* perceptibly
113 *want of shift* change of clothes
116 *Gravelin* i.e. Gravelines, between Dunkirk and Calais.
117 *affected* disposed
118 *Gesnerus . . . Decades* Konrad Gesner's descriptions of the flora and fauna, and Peter Martyr d'Anghera's news letters about the New World discoveries.
Salvaios savages
119 *provant* rations
Cama, or Anta the tapir
Callentura an hallucinating fever

120 *painting* cosmetics
lee shore shore towards which the wind blows
turned cultivated
sledges hammers
121 *Orellana . . . taketh name* The river was originally named the Orellana, after its first explorer Francisco de Orellana; but he called it the River of Amazons.
crumsters a kind of galley
122 *Columbus* Henry VIII rejected Columbus's plan of voyage in 1488.
younger brethren i.e. those needing an inheritance
Contractation house On the model of the Casa de Contractacion in Seville, which oversaw all Spanish trade with the Indies.
composition mutual agreement

The History of the World:
The text is based on the first edition of the *History* (1614). As with the *Discovery of Guiana*, I have modernized some of the place names and proper names, but kept Ralegh's forms for those which will be familiar to the reader and which might mark a difference in pronunciation. I have also retained the original punctuation and italicization. My chief omissions are Ralegh's Latin quotations, in cases where he goes on to translate them himself: these omissions are always signalled in the text. Ralegh's running-title for the work is *The First Part of the History of the World*.

The titles for the five books are:

I Intreating of the Beginning, and first ages of the same, from the Creation unto Abraham.
II Intreating of the Times from the Birth of Abraham to the destruction of the Temple of Solomon.
III Intreating of the Times from the destruction of Jerusalem to the time of Philip of Macedon.
IV Intreating of the Times from the reign of Philip of Macedon, to the establishing of that kingdom, in the race of Antigonus.
V Intreating of the Times from the settled rule of Alexander's Successors in the East, until the Romans, prevailing over all, made conquest of Asia and Macedon.

The elaborate frontispiece of the first edition was accompanied by an explanatory poem by Ben Jonson, relating it to the Ciceronian definition of history (in *De Oratore*), that it 'bears witness to the passing of ages' (*vero testis temporum*), is 'the light of truth, the life of memory' (*lux veritatis, vita memoriae*), the 'judge of life' and the 'newsbearer of antiquity' (*magistra vitae, nuntia vetustatis*). This is Jonson's poem:

The Mind of The Front

From Death and dark Oblivion (near the same)
The Mistress of Man's life, grave History,
Raising the World to good, or Evil fame,
Doth vindicate it to Eternity.

High Providence would so: that nor the good
Might be defrauded, nor the Great secur'd,

But both might know their ways are understood,
And the reward, and punishment assur'd.

This makes, that lighted by the beamy hand
Of Truth, which searcheth the most hidden springs,
And guided by Experience, whose straight wand
Doth mete, whose Line doth sound the depth of things.

She cheerfully supporteth what she rears;
Assisted by no strengths, but are her own,
Some note of which each varied Pillar bears,
By which as proper titles she is known,

Time's witness, Herald of Antiquity,
The light of Truth, and life of Memory.

Preface

124 *his Majesty* James I, in *Daemonology*.

125 *Mala . . . delectat* It is a pleasure to have a bad name in a good cause.
sic vos non vobis thus you do, not for yourselves; i.e. others get the benefit of your efforts.

128 *Eo crevit . . . sua* It grew so great that it toppled itself.

130 *spretaeque injuria formae* and the insult of a slighted beauty.

139 *non obstante* The king's licence to do a thing, regardless of laws to the contrary.

140 *Materia prima* The primal matter out of which the universe was made.

142 *quod . . . re stulta* becausę they are wise in a foolish thing.
Esay Isaiah

143 *Divitias . . . quaesitas* riches not fraudulently gained.
Hieremie Jeremiah

144 *O quam . . . descendunt* O how many of you go down with this hope to eternal sorrows and torments.

146 *He shall find nothing remaining . . .* Cp. the poem 'Farewell to the Court', above, p. 30.
Omnia . . . jacent All future things lie in uncertainty.
qui . . . imperatorem who follow their leader weeping.

147 *Magni . . . sensibus* It belongs to great minds to withdraw themselves from the world of the senses.

149 *gracili avena* with a slender pipe.

150 *Unus . . . erat* One man is worth a whole population to me.
Hoc . . . sed tibi I mean this for you and not for the many.
Satis . . . nullus If one is enough, then none is enough.
Prince Henry The Prince of Wales, Ralegh's supporter, who said of his imprisonment in the Tower, that only his father could keep such a bird in that cage. His death, in November 1612, is the great burden of mortality which lies over the later parts of the *History*; see below, pp. 218 and 272.
Eadem . . . datur We approve and condemn the same things. This is the consequence in every case in which many are asked to give judgment.
qui . . . malitia who delight in malice.

Book One

152 *1:15* *hoise* raise aloft

155 *2:5* *the sorrow only abideth* Ralegh's favourite theme; see 'Farewell to the Court', above, p. 30.

161 *9:3* *compassionate* pity
fastidious distasteful

Book Two

163 *13:7* This chapter shows Ralegh's characteristic paralleling of biblical truth and classical myth. Its Miltonic tone is emphasized by the treatment of the Satanic nature of ambition; and then by Ralegh's careful explication of such myths as that of the centaurs.

165 *bottom* a reel, as in Bottom's name in *Midsummer Night's Dream*; and note the coincidence (?) of the word occurring between mention of Theseus and Hippolyta in this chapter.

166 *chirurgeon* surgeon

167 *19:6* [Title] *conjecture* signals that this is Ralegh's own interpretation of events: see *21:6* in this same book (above, p. 169). The interest of this chapter lies in Ralegh's treatment of English history, and the idea of popular response to rebellion against a monarch.

169 *20:6* *contumeliously* contemptuously
hale drag
21:6 This is Ralegh's defence of his historical method, especially his tracing of second rather than first causes.

170 *Sir Philip Sidney* In his *Apologie for Poetry* (c. 1580; pubd. 1595) Sidney repeatedly asserted the primacy of Poetry over Philosophy and History. Ralegh turns the tables on poetry in the next chapter by Englishing Ausonius' epigram in which Dido complains of the travestied way she has been treated by the poets (see above, p. 58).

171 *exorbitant engines* erratic means, with a possible play on Archimedes' engine which would have been able to move the world.

173 *23:4* Ralegh's deliberations on the need historians sometimes have, to trust dubious sources; and the principles they should apply in doing so.

174 *24:5* A fine example of Ralegh's method of explicating legend and myth. Note the pattern which history traces, in Rome's movement from shepherd's crook to shepherd's crook.

Book Three

179 *1:11* *salvage* wild
secundum suum imaginationem according to his own imagination
1:13 Balthasar the grandson of Nebuchadnezzar. Ralegh's reference at the beginning of the extract (*This* may suffice to show . . .) is to his speculation about the Babylonian succession earlier in the chapter.

180 *6:2* *throughly* completely

182 *conceit* thought
his late vision In section one of this chapter Ralegh describes Artabanus' opposition to Xerxes' plan, and writes that through his being either 'terrified by visions' or 'fearing the king's hatred, which he had made known to all

those that opposed his desire to this war', he gave Xerxes all the help he could.

182 *misprised* undervalued

183 *to fear the Greeks* i.e. to frighten them

184 *6:11* Several of the portraits of individual rulers in the *History* bear comparison to James I: the one most commented on at the time was Ralegh's portrait of the effeminate Ninias, the successor of the great Queen Semiramis. But in others, too, one can see, without too much ingenuity, points of sardonic comparison — as in the final sentence of this portrait.

deluded cheated

Book Four

186 *1:1* *rampire* strengthen with ramparts

187 *1:5* *by the drum* by public announcement

1:9 Note the way Ralegh inserts into the account of Philip's immediate descendants the sense of retaliation which his behaviour called upon them.

189 *2:3* *in ill case* in a bad situation

192 *Epaminondas* For Ralegh's eulogy on Epimanondas, see the introduction to this selection, above pp. 15–16.

Targets shields

196 *2:4* *pile* javelin

197 *royals of plate and pistolets* silver and gold coins

198 *cheap* merchandise

199 *retract* retreat

200 *2:7* This section shows Ralegh developing his criticism of Alexander, one of the great 'troublers of the world', for his 'mad ambition'.

207 *2:23* *Sir Francis Bacon* Ralegh's general denigration of Alexander is the more interesting because of its implied contempt for Bacon's high estimation of him. In the first book of the *Advancement* Bacon devotes several pages to Alexander's wisdom and learning, concluding that 'there are the prints and footsteps of learning in those few speeches which are reported of this prince: the admiration of whom . . .. hath carried me too far'.

Book Five

209 *1:1* *conceit* high opinion of one's self

212 *scullions* menials

215 *1:2* *pestered* crowded into

1:6 *during* strength

higher building and charging i.e. they were taller and heavier.

218 *a Lee shore* a shore that the wind blows upon.

Treatise, for the Lord Henry This has not survived. Here Ralegh anticipates the abandonment of the *History* itself, and its closing pages.

Curae . . . stupent Light cares may speak, grief is dumb (Seneca).

2:2i In *2:1* Ralegh tells of how a state of war gradually developed between the Carthaginians and their own mercenaries. This section is a fine example of his deliberations on power and government.

225 *2:2iv* *vegetables* plants

227 *sectators* disciples

229 *Brehon law* The Irish code of law which prevailed up to James' accession.

230 *2:3* *still coasted him* always kept on his flank
letters of advertisement written information
231 *Document* warning
235 *3:4* *it skilled not* it made no difference
242 *3:8* *habit and furniture* dress and weapons
244 *Alman-like* as the Germans do
giving on making an assault
pouldron to pouldron shoulder to shoulder
245 *empaled* fenced in
246 *rendered* surrendered
247 *toward* at hand
present immediate
case condition
249 *contre* opposite
cast up calculated
chargeable burdensome
not sensible not to be felt
250 *3:14* *attending* waiting for
251 *conceits* imaginings
252 *port-sale* public auction
253 *in fine* to conclude
Partisans supporters
256 *3:15* *handicraftsmen* manual workers
261 *6:2* *the Lord Admiral excepted* Lord Charles Howard, Baron of Effingham, one of the dedicatees of the *Discovery of Guiana*.
263 *6:8* *devoir* duty
Targetiers foot soldiers
265 *dehorted* dissuaded
267 *respectively entreated* treated respectably
268 *6:12* *kept watching perforce* forcibly kept awake
270 *embassages* embassies
sume superbiam be proud
272 *Hic jacet* Here lies
that glorious Prince i.e. Prince Henry
Versa . . . flentium 'My harp also is turned to mourning, and my organ into the voice of them that weep'.

Letters

I have taken the text of the letters from Edward Edwards' transcription in *The Life of Sir Walter Ralegh, vol. 2, Letters of Sir Walter Ralegh* (1868). The first three, addressed to Sir Robert Cecil, are in the Cecil Papers in Hatfield House (for Cecil, see the first note to *The Discovery of Guiana*).

To Cecil, July 1592 This letter shows the degree to which Ralegh participated in the unreality of the cult of Elizabeth: she was nearly sixty when it was written.

mean intermediary
the Progress Elizabeth's travelling in state
Clerk of the Check Officer of the royal household, in control of the Yeomen of the Guard. Ralegh held the honorary post of Captain of the Guard.
sithes sighs
Spes et fortuna, valete Farewell hope and good fortune.
list wish

To Cecil, 1594
quo me Fortuna retrudet whither Fortune pushes me
not too credulous i.e. don't believe what others say about me

To Cecil, 1596–7
mind you remind you
participating immortality This makes some sense as it stands, but *anticipating* immortality would make better sense.
repine feel discontent

To Lady Ralegh, 1603
my office of wines From 1583 Ralegh held the patent to grant licences to vintners.
stuff i.e. household stuff
prevented anticipated
Jersey Ralegh was Governor of Jersey for the last three years of Elizabeth's reign.

To Lady Ralegh, 1618 Ralegh wrote this letter on his way back from Guiana, after the failure of the expedition, his son Walter's (Wat) death, and Keymis' suicide.
he left me so weak Ralegh had stayed in Trinidad, too ill to go into the interior of Guiana with the party. Laurence Keymis, Ralegh's captain from as far back as the first voyage to Guiana, had been left in command, and had failed miserably.
the former reasons probably should read *the four reasons*
my being unpardoned Ralegh was still under sentence of death, since the trial of 1603.
Madrill Madrid

Select bibliography

The last collected edition of Ralegh's works was edited by Oldys and Birch in 1829. The most scholarly editions of the poems are the two edited by Agnes Latham, both old-spelling texts, in 1929 and 1951. Miss Latham also edited a modern-spelling selection of Ralegh's poems and prose for the Athlone Press in 1965. An old-spelling selection of the prose, edited by G. E. Hadow, was published by Clarendon Press in 1917; and a selection from the *History of the World*, edited by C. A. Patrides, by Macmillan in 1971. An interesting edition of the *Discovery of Guiana* is the one by a fellow explorer of Guiana, Sir Robert Schomburgk (London, 1848).

As well as the critical essays mentioned in the notes, the following articles and books are recommended:

Anon., 'Ralegh's prose', *Times Literary Supplement*, 31 January 1935.

J. H. Adamson and H. F. Folland, *The Shepherd of the Ocean*, London, 1969.

P. Edwards, *Sir Walter Ralegh*, London, 1953.

C. H. Firth, 'Sir Walter Ralegh's "History of the World" ', in *Essays historical and literary*, London, 1938.

S. J. Greenblatt, *Sir Walter Ralegh: the Renaissance man and his roles*, New Haven, 1973.

W. Oakeshott, *The Queen and the Poet*, London, 1960.

'Sir Walter Ralegh's Library', *The Library* (5th series), XXIII, 1968.

J. Racin, *Sir Walter Ralegh as historian: an analysis of the History of the World*, Salzburg, 1974.

L. Tennenhouse, 'Sir Walter Ralegh and the literature of Clientage', in *Patronage in the Renaissance*, ed. G. F. Lytle and S. Orgel, Princeton, 1981.

Index of first lines

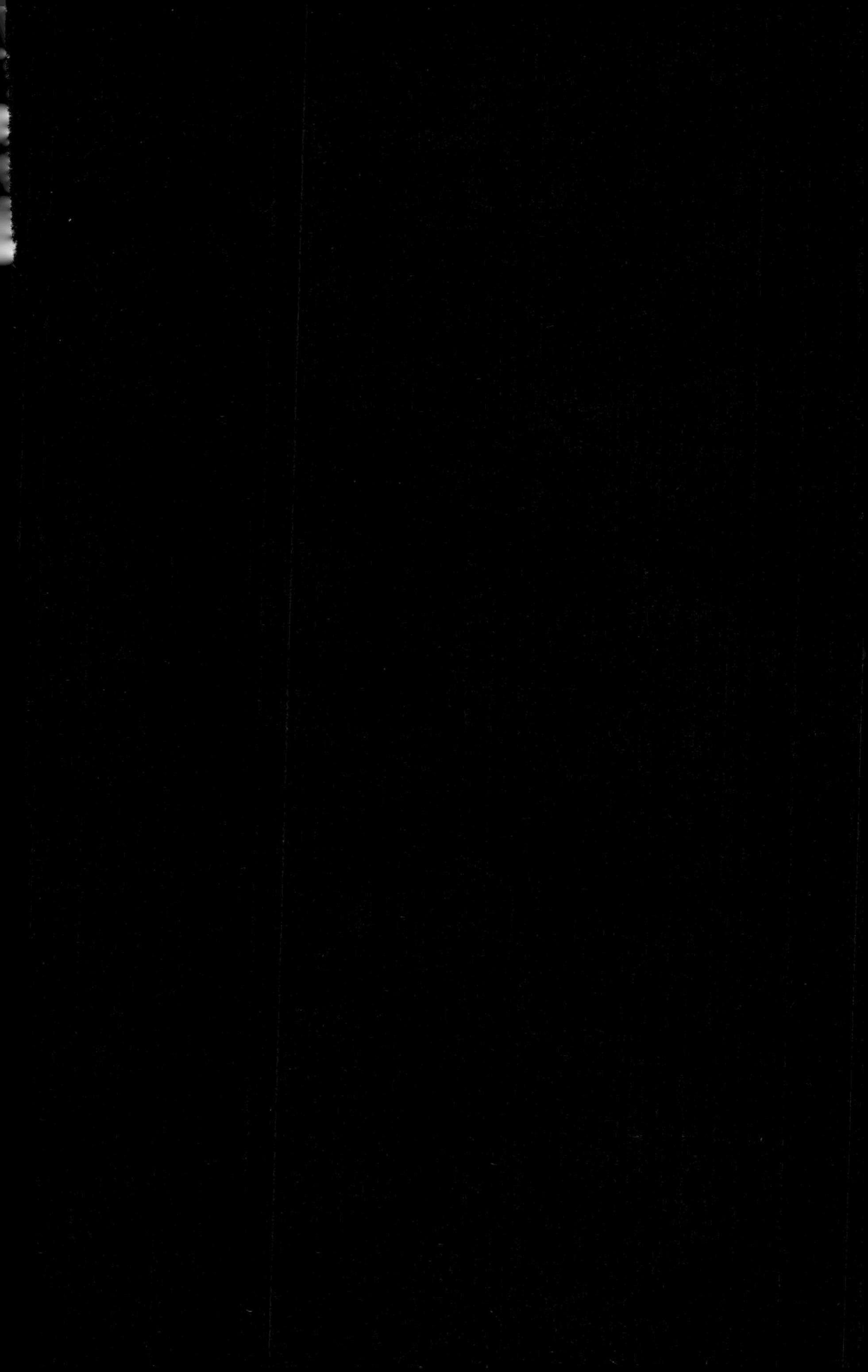